Hands-On RTOS with Microcontrollers

Building real-time embedded systems using FreeRTOS, STM32 MCUs, and SEGGER debug tools

Brian Amos

BIRMINGHAM - MUMBAI

Hands-On RTOS with Microcontrollers

Copyright © 2020 Packt Publishing

Commissioning Editor: Vijin Boricha
Acquisition Editor: Shrilekha Inani
Content Development Editor: Carlton Borges
Senior Editor: Rahul Dsouza
Technical Editor: Dinesh Pawar
Copy Editor: Safis Editing
Project Coordinator: Neil Dmello
Proofreader: Safis Editing
Indexer: Tejal Daruwale Soni
Production Designer: Joshua Misquitta

First published: May 2020

Production reference: 1150520

Published by Packt Publishing Ltd.
Livery Place
35 Livery Street
Birmingham
B3 2PB, UK.

ISBN 978-1-83882-673-4

www.packt.com

Why subscribe?

Contributors

About the author

Brian Amos is an embedded system engineer who has been programming with FreeRTOS since 2012. He is currently a senior firmware engineer in the telecom industry creating embedded systems used in ground stations for satellite communication. In the past, he led a team of engineers creating a flexible architecture to rapidly develop high-precision laboratory test equipment. Prior to this, he worked with early mesh networked energy harvesting sensors used to help predict when industrial machinery needed maintenance.

About the reviewer

Phillip Johnston is a principal at Embedded Artistry, an embedded systems firm focused on improving early-stage hardware product development and educating developers and engineers around the world. Embedded Artistry focuses on building a solid foundation for building systems through systems architecture, modular firmware development, and automated software quality processes. His experience spans consumer electronics, defense, automotive, robotics, cameras, drones, and manufacturing.

Packt is searching for authors like you

If you're interested in becoming an author for Packt, please visit authors.packtpub.com and apply today. We have worked with thousands of developers and tech professionals, just like you, to help them share their insight with the global tech community. You can make a general application, apply for a specific hot topic that we are recruiting an author for, or submit your own idea.

Table of Contents

Preface

This hands-on guide will provide you with the most important functional knowledge for getting a **Real-Time Operating System (RTOS)** up and running on a **microcontroller unit (MCU).** If you're interested in learning how to implement applications using an RTOS with hands-on examples using actual hardware and discussing common performance versus development-time trade-offs, you're in the right place!

We'll be implementing code using the FreeRTOS kernel, working with the popular STM32 ARM MCUs using a low-cost STM Nucleo development board, and debugging/analyzing code with SEGGER debug tools. All of the tools used in this book have been selected because they are easily accessible for the hobbyist or professional just getting started, and also because of their popularity in real-world professional teams. The knowledge and experience you gain through reading this book and working through the examples will be directly applicable to actual development in a professional environment.

Who this book is for

RTOS programming is not a beginner's topic and is definitely not the right starting point for learning about embedded systems. If MCUs or the C language is totally new to you, then you're better off starting by covering the basics and getting some hands-on experience before diving into this more advanced topic.

So, who stands to benefit the most from working through this book?

Professional programmers: You've always programmed on *bare metal* (no OS) and are looking to increase your MCU programming skills by learning how to use an RTOS to meet tight timing requirements, balance concurrent operations, and create modular code.

Students interested in "getting their hands dirty": You've been covering theory, listening to lectures, and coding lab exercises, but now you're looking for a complete guide that helps you to get started with something you can physically touch and interact with.

Makers moving onto more advanced topics: You've written some sketches or scripts, but you're looking for your next challenge. Maybe you'd like to create a full MCU-based system from scratch – the information here will help get you on track for the programming side. You'll even get some tips on what to look for when selecting an MCU for your project.

What this book covers

This book comprises 17 chapters in all, spread across four sections. It isn't necessary to read the book straight through if you're already comfortable with some of the material. For example, if you're already comfortable with basic RTOS concepts and real-time systems, feel free to skip to Chapter 4, *Selecting the Right MCU*. The following are brief descriptions of the chapters that this book is made up of:

Chapter 1, *Introducing Real-Time Systems*, is a simple introduction to what an RTOS is and when and why to use one. Hardware and software alternatives to an MCU-based RTOS are also discussed.

Chapter 2, *Understanding RTOS Tasks*, provides a comparison of super loops with RTOS tasks, including various ways parallel operations can be achieved using both.

Chapter 3, *Task Signaling and Communication Mechanisms*, is a short introduction to more RTOS concepts with lots of diagrams. This chapter, along with Chapter 2, *Understanding RTOS Tasks*, should be useful as a reference and a quick refresher on the concepts and terminology, should you ever need it.

Chapter 4, *Selecting the Right MCU*, helps you understand what considerations should be made when selecting an MCU. After gaining an appreciation of the inter-dependency between hardware and firmware, we look at why it is so important that hardware and firmware engineers both have a hand in system design.

Chapter 5, *Selecting an IDE*, introduces and discusses various types of **Integrated Development Environments (IDEs)**, including reasons why you might decide to choose one over another (or none at all). Instructions on setting up STM32CubeIDE and importing the example code are covered here.

Chapter 6, *Debugging Tools for Real-Time Systems*, covers tools for debugging embedded systems, including the debugging tool we'll be using throughout the remainder of the book – SEGGER Ozone and SEGGER SystemView visualization software. Instructions on how to use Ozone and SystemView are covered here. Hardware-based test equipment and some other useful tools for your embedded system development workflow are also included.

Chapter 7, *The FreeRTOS Scheduler*, teaches you the various ways to create tasks using FreeRTOS and how to troubleshoot startup failures. You will gain an understanding of task states and the different ways performance can be optimized.

Chapter 8, *Protecting Data and Synchronizing Tasks*, covers task synchronization using semaphores and data protection using mutexes, as well as how to avoid race conditions and priority inversion. Software timers are also covered.

Chapter 9, *Intertask Communication*, examines different ways of passing information between tasks, with different examples of using queues for passing information by value and reference, discussing the advantages and considerations of both approaches. We'll also learn about a lightweight intertask communication mechanism, the direct task notification, including a comparison of task notifications and queues.

Chapter 10, *Drivers and ISRs*, dives deep into several detailed examples of how to implement efficient drivers with various FreeRTOS primitives including semaphores, queues, and stream buffers. We'll also look at how FreeRTOS can be used in conjunction with MCU hardware such as DMA to provide extremely CPU-efficient driver implementations. This chapter works both directly with the MCUs peripheral registers and also with STM32 HAL code.

Chapter 11, *Sharing Hardware Peripherals across Tasks*, teaches you how to create drivers that can be safely used across multiple tasks while sharing hardware resources. We'll adapt the STM-supplied USB CDC implementation to be more user-friendly and efficient, wrapping it with a mutex and queues so it is safe to use across multiple tasks.

Chapter 12, *Tips on Creating a Well-Abstracted Architecture*, covers code reusability, flexibility, and hardware portability, with an eye on creating abstractions that make your job easier. Some suggestions for source code organization to help facilitate reuse are also covered.

Chapter 13, *Creating Loose Coupling with Queues*, is a culmination of all of the concepts covered in the book. It includes a fully fleshed-out example of a loosely coupled architecture used to create a properly abstracted, end-to-end application. We'll use the USB CDC virtual comm port developed earlier, as well as an LED abstraction, to create a loosely coupled, fully reusable LED sequencer using a command queue. This embedded application can be controlled from a PC with a cross-platform UI written in Python.

Chapter 14, *Choosing an RTOS API*, continues our high-level architecture discussion with a look at three different APIs available to use for accessing FreeRTOS functionality: the native FreeRTOS API, ARM's CMSIS-RTOS, and POSIX. Discussion topics include a comparison of the available features and why you might choose one of the others for different projects.

Chapter 15, *FreeRTOS Memory Management*, takes a close look at a few different options for memory management in FreeRTOS. We'll look at static versus dynamic allocation, as well as using a **Memory Protection Unit (MPU)**.

Chapter 16, *Multi-Processor and Multi-Core Systems*, teaches you how multi-processor and multi-core systems are used for a variety of reasons – learn what they are and how to get the different parts of a system to communicate.

Chapter 17, *Troubleshooting Tips and Next Steps*, covers tips for troubleshooting systems, including tips on how to avoid stack overflows and how to troubleshoot a hung system. Some recommendations for the next steps are also covered.

To get the most out of this book

Every effort has been made to make working through the examples in this book as easy as possible for a very wide range of people. To get the most out of the book (by working through the examples), you'll need the following hardware:

- A Windows, macOS, or Linux PC with internet access
- An STM32 Nucleo-F767ZI development board
- Two Micro-USB cables
- Jumper wires—20 to 22 AWG (~0.65 mm) solid core wire

Detailed setup instructions for the different tools used are included in the chapters.

If you are using the digital version of this book, we advise you to type the code yourself or access the code via the GitHub repository (link available in the next section). Doing so will help you avoid any potential errors related to the copying and pasting of code.

Since this book targets programming low-level embedded systems, we'll be using C as the language of choice. Some knowledge of microcontrollers is assumed, as is the ability to read a datasheet. If you have a good understanding of the C language (or C++), then you should be comfortable reading this book – no previous RTOS knowledge is required. Since we'll be working with MCUs in an embedded system, there will be some occasional discussions on the hardware side as well, primarily dealing with features of MCUs and development boards. These topics will be covered in enough detail that someone with minimal hardware knowledge should be able to follow without too much difficulty. You should be comfortable interacting with and handling development hardware, although there isn't any actual assembly required.

Download the example code files

You can download the example code files for this book from your account at https:// github.com/PacktPublishing/Hands-On-RTOS-with-Microcontrollers. If you purchased this book elsewhere, you can visit www.packtpub.com/support and register to have the files emailed directly to you.

You can download the code files by following these steps:

1. Log in or register at www.packt.com.
2. Select the **Support** tab.
3. Click on **Code Downloads**.
4. Enter the name of the book in the **Search** box and follow the onscreen instructions.

Once the file is downloaded, please make sure that you unzip or extract the folder using the latest version of:

- WinRAR/7-Zip for Windows
- Zipeg/iZip/UnRarX for Mac
- 7-Zip/PeaZip for Linux

The code bundle for the book is also hosted on GitHub at https://github.com/ PacktPublishing/Hands-On-RTOS-with-Microcontrollers. In case there's an update to the code, it will be updated on the existing GitHub repository.

We also have other code bundles from our rich catalog of books and videos available at https://github.com/PacktPublishing/. Check them out!

Download the color images

We also provide a PDF file that has color images of the screenshots/diagrams used in this book. You can download it here: http://www.packtpub.com/sites/default/files/ downloads/9781838826734_ColorImages.pdf.

Conventions used

There are a number of text conventions used throughout this book.

CodeInText: Indicates code words in text, database table names, folder names, filenames, file extensions, pathnames, dummy URLs, user input, and Twitter handles. Here is an example: "func1() is responsible for reading the value of a sensor and storing it in the sensorReadings array"

A block of code is set as follows:

```
void func1 ( int16_t calOffset)
{
int16_t tempValue;
tempValue = readSensor();
tempValue = tempValue + calOffset;
sensorReadings[0] = tempValue;
}
```

When we wish to draw your attention to a particular part of a code block, the relevant lines or items are set in bold:

```
/* ADC Config */
hnucleo_Adc.Instance = NUCLEO_ADCx;
/* (ClockPrescaler must not exceed 36MHz) */
hnucleo_Adc.Init.ClockPrescaler = ADC_CLOCKPRESCALER_PCLK_DIV4;
hnucleo_Adc.Init.Resolution = ADC_RESOLUTION12b;
hnucleo_Adc.Init.DataAlign = ADC_DATAALIGN_RIGHT;
hnucleo_Adc.Init.ContinuousConvMode = DISABLE;
hnucleo_Adc.Init.DiscontinuousConvMode = DISABLE;
```

Bold: Indicates a new term, an important word, or words that you see onscreen. For example, words in menus or dialog boxes appear in the text like this. Here is an example: "Select **System info** from the **Administration** panel."

Warnings or important notes appear like this.

Tips and tricks appear like this.

Get in touch

Feedback from our readers is always welcome.

General feedback: If you have questions about any aspect of this book, mention the book title in the subject of your message and email us at customercare@packtpub.com.

Errata: Although we have taken every care to ensure the accuracy of our content, mistakes do happen. If you have found a mistake in this book, we would be grateful if you would report this to us. Please visit www.packtpub.com/support/errata, selecting your book, clicking on the Errata Submission Form link, and entering the details.

Piracy: If you come across any illegal copies of our works in any form on the Internet, we would be grateful if you would provide us with the location address or website name. Please contact us at copyright@packt.com with a link to the material.

If you are interested in becoming an author: If there is a topic that you have expertise in and you are interested in either writing or contributing to a book, please visit authors.packtpub.com.

Reviews

Please leave a review. Once you have read and used this book, why not leave a review on the site that you purchased it from? Potential readers can then see and use your unbiased opinion to make purchase decisions, we at Packt can understand what you think about our products, and our authors can see your feedback on their book. Thank you!

For more information about Packt, please visit packt.com.

Section 1: Introduction and RTOS Concepts

What is a real-time system and what are the major components that make up a **real-time operating system** (**RTOS**)? These are the questions we'll be answering in the first section of this book. This prerequisite knowledge will serve as a foundation we'll build upon with working examples and hands-on exercises in later chapters. If you're already familiar with another RTOS, you can probably skim or skip this section.

This section comprises the following chapters:

- Chapter 1, *Introducing Real-Time Systems*
- Chapter 2, *Understanding RTOS Tasks*
- Chapter 3, *Task Signaling and Communication Mechanisms*

Introducing Real-Time Systems

Real-time systems come in a wide variety of implementations and use cases. This book focuses on how to use a **real-time OS (RTOS)** to create real-time applications on a **microcontroller unit (MCU)**.

In this chapter, we'll start with an overview of what an RTOS is and get an idea of the wide range of systems that can have real-time requirements. From there, we'll look at some of the different ways of achieving real-time performance, along with an overview of the types of systems (such as hardware, firmware, and software) that may be used. We'll wrap up by discussing when it is advisable to use an RTOS in an MCU application and when it might not be necessary at all.

In a nutshell, we will cover the following topics in this chapter:

- What is "real-time" anyway?
- Defining RTOS
- Deciding when to use an RTOS

Technical requirements

There are no software or hardware requirements for this chapter.

What is real-time anyway?

Any system that has a deterministic response to a given event can be considered "real-time." If a system is considered to *fail* when it doesn't meet a timing requirement, it must be real-time. How failure is defined (and the consequences of a failed system) can vary widely. It is extremely important to realize that real-time requirements can vary widely, both in the speed of the timing requirement and also the severity of consequences if the required real-time deadlines are not met.

The ranges of timing requirements

To illustrate the range of timing requirements that can be encountered, let's consider a few different systems that acquire readings from **analog-to-digital converters (ADCs)**.

The first system we'll look at is a control system that is set up to control the temperature of a soldering iron (as seen in the following diagram). The parts of the system we're concerned with are the MCU, ADC, sensor, and heater.

The MCU is responsible for the following:

- Taking readings from a temperature sensor via the ADC
- Running a closed-loop control algorithm (to maintain a constant temperature at the soldering iron tip)
- Adjusting the output of the heater as needed

These can be seen in the following diagram:

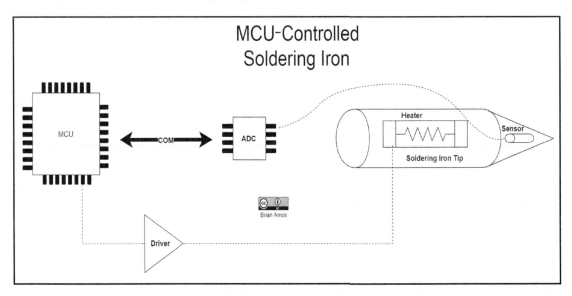

Since the temperature of the tip doesn't change incredibly quickly, the MCU may only need to acquire 50 ADC samples per second (50 Hz). The control algorithm responsible for adjusting the heater (to maintain a constant temperature) runs at an even slower pace, 5 Hz:

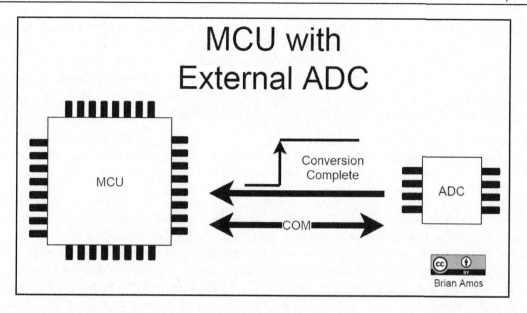

The ADC will assert a hardware line, signaling a conversion has been completed and is ready for the MCU to transfer the reading to its internal memory. The MCU reading the ADC has up to 20 ms to transfer data from the ADC to internal memory before a new reading needs to be taken (as seen in the following diagram). The MCU also needs to be running the control algorithm to calculate the updated values for the heater output at 5 Hz (200 ms). Both of these cases (although not particularly fast) are examples of real-time requirements:

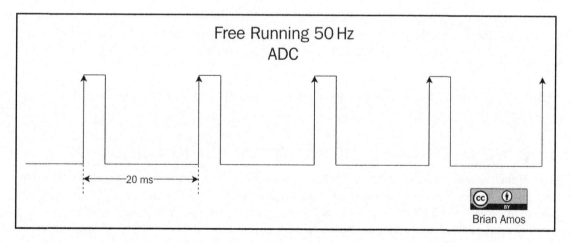

Now, on the other end of the ADC reading spectrum, we could have a high bandwidth network analyzer or oscilloscope that is going to be reading an ADC at a rate of tens of GHz! The raw ADC readings will likely be converted into the frequency domain and graphically displayed on a high-resolution front panel dozens of times a second. A system like this requires huge amounts of processing to be performed and must adhere to extremely tight timing requirements, if it is to function properly.

Somewhere in the middle of the spectrum, you'll find systems such as closed-loop motion controllers, which will typically need to execute their PID control loops between hundreds of Hz to tens of kHz in order to provide stability in a fast-moving system. So, *how fast* is real-time? Well, as you can see from the ADC examples alone, it depends.

In some of the previous cases, such as the oscilloscope or soldering iron, failure to meet a timing requirement results in poor performance or incorrect data being reported. In the case of the soldering iron, this might be poor temperature control (which could cause damage to components). For the test equipment, missing deadlines could cause erroneous readings, which is a failure. This may not seem like a big deal to some people, but for the users of that equipment, who are relying on the accuracy of the data being reported, it is likely to matter a great deal. Some laboratory equipment that is used in standard verification provides checks for product conformance. If there is an undetected malfunction in the equipment that results in an inaccurate measurement, an incorrect value could be reported. It may be possible for a suspect test to be rerun. Eventually, however, if retesting is required too often and reliable readings can't be counted on, then the test equipment will start to become suspect and viewed as unreliable and sales will decline—all because a real-time requirement wasn't being consistently met.

In other systems, such as the flight control of a UAV or motion control in industrial process control, failing to run the control algorithm in a timely manner could result in something more physically catastrophic, such as a crash. In this case, the consequences are potentially life-threatening.

Thankfully, there are steps that can be taken to avoid all of these failure scenarios.

The ways of guaranteeing real-time behavior

One of the easiest ways to ensure a system does what it is meant to do is to make sure it is as simple as possible while still meeting the requirements. This means resisting the urge to over-complicate a simple task. If a toaster is meant to toast a slice of bread, don't put a display on it and make it tell you the weather too; just have it turn on a heating element for the right amount of time. This simple task has been accomplished for years without requiring any code or programmable devices whatsoever.

As programmers, if we come across a problem, we have a tendency to immediately reach for the nearest MCU and start coding. However, some functions of a product (especially true if a product has electro-mechanical components) are best handled without code at all. A car window doesn't really need an MCU with a polling loop to run, turning on motors through drivers and watching sensors for feedback to shut them off. This task can actually be handled by a few mechanical switches and diodes. If a feedback-reporting mechanism is required for a given system—such as an error that needs to be asserted in the case of a stuck window—then there may be no choice but to use a more complex solution. However, our goal as engineers should always be the same—solve the problem as simply as possible, without adding additional complexity.

If a problem can be solved by hardware alone, then explore that possibility with the team first, before breaking out the MCU. If a problem can be handled by using a simple *while* loop to perform some polling of the sensor status, then simply poll the sensor for the status; there may be no need to start coding **interrupt service routines** (ISRs). If the functionality of the device is single-purposed, there are many cases where a full-blown RTOS can simply get in the way—so don't use one!

Types of real-time systems

There are many different ways of achieving real-time behavior. The following section is a discussion on the various types of real-time systems you might encounter. Also note that it is possible to have combinations of the following systems working together as subsystems. These different subsystems can occur at a product, board, or even chip level (this approach is discussed in `Chapter 16`, *Multi-Processor and Multi-Core Systems*).

Hardware

The original real-time system, hardware, is still the go-to for extremely tight tolerance and/or fast timing requirements. It can be implemented with discrete digital logic, analog components, programmable logic, or an **application-specific integrated component (ASIC)**. **Programmable logic devices (PLDs)**, **complex programmable logic devices (CPLDs)**, and **field-programmable gate arrays (FPGAs)** are the various members of the programmable logic device portion of this solution. Hardware-based real-time systems can cover anything from analog filters, closed loop control, and simple state machines to complex video codecs. When implemented with power saving in mind, ASICs can be made to consume less power than an MCU-based solution. In general, hardware has the advantage of performing operations in parallel and *instantly* (this is, of course, an over-simplification), as opposed to a single-core MCU, which only gives the illusion of parallel processing.

The downsides for real-time hardware development generally include the following:

- The inflexibility of non-programmable devices.
- The expertise required is generally less commonly available than software/firmware developers.
- The cost of full-featured programmable devices (for example, large FPGAs).
- The high cost of developing a custom ASIC.

Bare-metal firmware

Bare-metal firmware is considered (for our purposes) to be any firmware that isn't built *on top of* a preexisting kernel/scheduler of some type. Some engineers take this a step further, arguing that true bare-metal firmware can't use any preexisting libraries (such as vendor supply hardware abstraction libraries)—there is some merit to this view as well. A bare-metal implementation has the advantage that the user's code has *total* control of *all* aspects of the hardware. The only way for the main loop code execution to be interrupted is if an interrupt fires. In this case, the only way for anything else to take control of the CPU is for the existing ISR to finish or for another higher-priority interrupt to fire.

Bare-metal firmware solutions excel when there is a small number of relatively simple tasks to perform—or one monolithic task. If the firmware is kept focused and best practices are followed, deterministic performance is generally easy to measure and guarantee due to the relatively small number of interactions between ISRs (or in some cases, a lack of ISRs). In some extreme cases for heavily loaded MCUs (or MCUs that are highly constrained in ROM/RAM), bare-metal is the only option.

As bare-metal implementations get to be more elaborate when dealing with events asynchronously, they start to overlap with functionality provided by an RTOS. An important consideration to keep in mind is that by using an RTOS—rather than attempting to roll your own thread-safe system—you automatically benefit from all of the testing the RTOS provider has put in. You'll also have the opportunity to use code that has the power of hindsight behind it—all of the RTOSes available today have been around for several years. The authors have been adapting and adding functionality the entire time to make them robust and flexible for different applications.

RTOS-based firmware

Firmware that runs a scheduling kernel on an MCU is RTOS-based firmware. The introduction of the scheduler and some RTOS-primitives allows tasks to operate under the illusion they have the processor to themselves (discussed in detail in `Chapter 2`, *Understanding RTOS Tasks*). Using an RTOS enables the system to remain responsive to the most important events while performing other complex tasks *in the background*.

There are a few downsides to all of these tasks running. Inter-dependencies can arise between tasks sharing data—if not handled properly, the dependency will cause a task to block unexpectedly. Although there are provisions for handling this, it does add complexity to the code. Interrupts will generally use task signaling to take care of the interrupt as quickly as possible and defer as much processing to a task as possible. If handled properly, this solution is excellent for keeping complex systems responsive, despite many complex interactions. However, if handled improperly, this design paradigm can lead to more timing jitter and less determinism.

RTOS-based software

Software running on a *full* OS that contains a **memory management unit** (**MMU**) and **central processing unit** (**CPU**) is considered RTOS-based software. Applications that are implemented with this approach can be highly complex, requiring many different interactions between various internal and external systems. The advantage of using a full OS is all of the capability that comes along with it—both hardware and software.

On the hardware side, there are generally more CPU cores available running at higher clock rates. There can be gigabytes of RAM and persistent memory available. Adding peripheral hardware can be as simple as the addition of a card (provided there are pre-existing drivers).

On the software side, there is a plethora of open source and vendor proprietary solutions for networking stacks, UI development, file handling, and so on. Underneath all of this capability and options, the kernel is still implemented in such a way that the critical tasks won't be blocked for an indefinite period of time, which is possible with a traditional OS. Because of this, getting deterministic performance is still within reach, just like with RTOS firmware.

Carefully crafted OS software

Similar to RTOS-based software, a standard OS has all of the libraries and features a developer could ask for. What's missing, however, is a strict focus on meeting timing requirements. Generally speaking, systems implemented with a traditional OS are going to have much less deterministic behavior (and none that can be truly counted on in a safety-critical situation). If there is a lax real-time requirement without catastrophic consequences, if a wishy-washy deadline isn't met on time, a standard OS can be made to work, as long as care is taken in choosing what software stacks are running and their resource use is kept in check. The Linux kernel with PREEMPT_RT patches is a good example of this type of real-time system.

So, now that all of the options for achieving a real-time system have been laid out, it's time to define exactly what we mean when we say RTOS, specifically an MCU-based RTOS.

Defining RTOS

OSes (such as Windows, Linux, and macOS) were created as a way to provide a consistent programming environment that abstracted away the underlying hardware to make it easier to write and maintain computer programs. They provide the application programmer with many different *primitives* (such as threads and mutexes) that can be used to create more complex behavior. For example, it is possible to create a multi-threaded program that provides protected access to shared data:

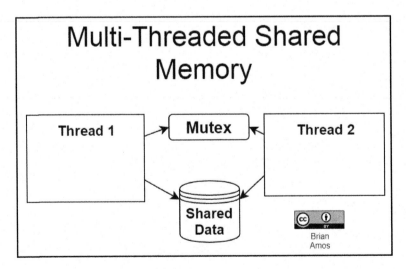

The preceding application doesn't *implement* thread and mutex primitives, it only makes use of them. The actual implementations of threads and mutexes are handled by the OS. This has a few advantages:

- The application code is less complex.
- It is easier to understand—the same primitives are used regardless of the programmer, making it easier to understand code created by different people.
- The is better hardware portability—with the proper precautions, the code can be run on any hardware supported by the OS without modification.

In the preceding example, a *mutex* is used to ensure that only one thread can access the *shared data* at a time. In the case of a general-purpose OS, each thread will happily wait for the mutex to become available indefinitely before moving on to access the shared data. This is where RTOSes diverge from general-purpose OSes. In an RTOS, all blocking system calls are time-bound. Instead of waiting for the mutex indefinitely, an RTOS allows a maximum delay to be specified. For example, if **Thread 1** attempts to acquire **Mutex** and still doesn't have it after 100 ms, or 1 second, it will continue waiting for the mutex to become available.

In an RTOS implementation, the maximum amount of time to wait for **Mutex** to become available is specified. If **Thread 1** specifies that it must acquire the mutex within 100 ms and still hasn't received the mutex after 101 ms, **Thread 1** will receive a notification that the mutex hasn't been acquired in time. This timeout is specified to help create a deterministic system.

Any OS that provides a deterministic way of executing a given piece of code can be considered a real-time OS. This definition of RTOS covers a fairly large number of systems.

There are a couple of characteristics that tend to differentiate one RTOS application from another: how often *not* meeting a real-time deadline is acceptable and the severity of not meeting a real-time deadline. The different ranges of RTOS applications are usually lumped into three categories—hard, firm, and soft real-time systems.

Don't get too hung up on the differences between firm and soft real-time systems. The definitions for these terms don't even have unanimous agreement from within our industry. What *does* matter is that you know your system's requirements and design a solution to meet them!

The severity of a failure is generally deemed *safety-critical* if a failure will cause the loss of life or significant property. There are hard real-time systems that have nothing to do with safety.

Hard real-time systems

A hard real-time system must meet its deadline 100% of the time. If the system does not meet a deadline, then it is considered to have failed. This doesn't necessarily mean a failure will hurt someone if it occurs in a hard real-time system—only that the system *has* failed if it misses a single deadline.

Some examples of hard real-time systems can be found in medical devices, such as pacemakers and control systems with extremely tightly controlled parameters. In the case of a pacemaker, if the pacemaker misses a deadline to administer an electrical pulse at the right moment in time, it might kill the patient (this is why pacemakers are defined as safety-critical systems).

In contrast, if a motion control system on a **computer numerical control** (**CNC**) milling machine doesn't react to a command in time, it might plunge a tool into the wrong part of the part being machined, ruining it. In these cases that we have mentioned, one failure caused a loss of life, while the other turned some metal into scrap—but both were failures caused by a single missed deadline.

Firm real-time systems

As opposed to hard real-time systems, firm real-time systems need to hit their deadlines *nearly* all of the time. If video and audio lose synchronization momentarily, it probably won't be considered a system failure, but will likely upset the consumer of the video.

In most control systems (similar to the soldering iron in a previous example), a few samples that are read slightly outside of their specified time are unlikely to completely destroy system control. If a control system has an ADC that automatically takes a new sample, if the MCU doesn't read the new sample in time, it will be overwritten by a new one. This can occur occasionally, but if it happens too often or too frequently, the temperature stability will be ruined. In a particularly demanding system, it may only take a few missed samples before the entire control system is *out of spec*.

Soft real-time systems

Soft real-time systems are the most lax when it comes to how often the system must meet its deadlines. These systems often offer only a *best-effort* promise for keeping deadlines.

Cruise control in a car is a good example of a soft real-time system because there are no hard specifications or expectations of it. Drivers typically don't expect their speed to converge to within +/- *x* mph/kph of the set speed. They expect that given *reasonable* circumstances, such as no large hills, the control system will eventually get them *close* to their desired speed *most of the time*.

The range of RTOSes

RTOSes range in their functionality, as well as the architecture and size of the processor they're best suited to. On the smaller side, we have smaller 8–32-bit MCU-focused RTOSes, such as FreeRTOS, Keil RTX, Micrium µC, ThreadX, and many more. This class of RTOS is suitable for use on microcontrollers and provides a compact real-time kernel as the most basic offering. When moving from MCUs to 32- and 64-bit application processors, you'll tend to find RTOSes such as Wind River VxWorks and Wind River Linux, Green Hills' Integrity OS, and even Linux with PREEMPT_RT kernel extensions. These full-blown OSes offer a large selection of software, providing solutions for both real-time scheduling requirements as well as general computing tasks. Even with the OSes we've just rattled off, we've only scratched the surface of what's available. There are free and paid solutions (some costing well over USD$10,000) at all levels of RTOSes, big and small.

So, why would you choose to pay for a solution when there is something available for free? The main differentiating factors between freely available RTOS solutions and paid solutions are safety approvals, middleware, and customer support. Because RTOSes provide a highly deterministic execution environment, they are often used in complex safety-critical applications. By *safety critical*, we generally mean a system whose failure could harm people or cause significant damage. These systems require deterministic operation because they must behave in a predictable way all the time. Guaranteeing the code responds to events within a fixed amount of time is a significant step toward ensuring they behave consistently. Most of these safety-critical applications are regulated and have their own sets of governing bodies and standards, such as DO-178B and DO-178C for aircraft or IEC 61508 SIL 3 and ISO 26262 ASILD for industrial applications. To make safety-critical certifications more affordable, designers will typically either keep code for these systems extremely simple (so it is possible to prove mathematically that the system will function consistently and nothing can go wrong) or turn to a commercial RTOS solution, which has been through certification already, as a starting point. WITTENSTEIN SafeRTOS is a derivative of FreeRTOS that carries approvals for industrial, medical, and automotive use.

Middleware can also be an extremely important component in complex systems. Middleware is code that runs between the *user code* (code that *you*, the application programmer, write) and lower layers, such as the RTOS or bare metal (no RTOS). Another value proposition of paid solutions is that the ecosystem offers a suite of pre-integrated high-quality middleware (such as filesystems, networking stacks, GUI frameworks, industrial protocols, and so on) that minimizes development and reduces overall project risk. The reason for using middleware, rather than *rolling your own*, is to reduce the amount of original code being written by an in-house development team. This reduces both the risk and the total time spent by the team—so it can be a worth-while investment, depending on factors such as project complexity and schedule requirements.

Paid solutions will also typically come with some level of customer support directly from the firmware vendor. Engineers are expensive to hire and keep on staff. There's nothing a manger dreads more than walking into a room full of engineers who are puzzling over their tools, rather than working on the *real* problems that need to be solved. Having expert help that is an email or phone call away can increase a team's productivity dramatically, which leads to a shorter turnaround and a happier workplace for everyone.

FreeRTOS has both paid support and training options, as well as paid middleware solutions, that can be integrated. However, there are also open source and/or freely available middleware components available, some of which will be discussed in this book.

The RTOS used in this book

With all of the options available, you might be wondering: why is it that this book is only covering one RTOS on a single model of MCU? There are a few reasons, one being that most of the concepts we'll cover are applicable to nearly any RTOS available, in the same way that good coding habits transcend the language you happen to be coding. By focusing on a single implementation of an RTOS with a single MCU, we'll be able to dive into topics in more depth than would have been possible if all of the alternatives were also attempted to be discussed.

FreeRTOS is one of the most popular RTOS implementations for MCUs and is very widely available. It has been around for over 15 years and has been ported to dozens of platforms . If you've ever spoken to a true low-level embedded systems engineer who is familiar with RTOS programming, they've certainly heard of FreeRTOS and have likely used it at least once. By focusing our attention on FreeRTOS, you'll be well-positioned to quickly migrate your knowledge of FreeRTOS to other hardware or to transition to another RTOS, if the situation calls for it.

The other reason we're using FreeRTOS? Well, it's FREE! FreeRTOS is distributed under the MIT license. See `https://www.freertos.org/a00114.html` for more details on licensing and other FreeRTOS derivatives, such as SAFERTOS and OpenRTOS.

The following is a diagram showing where FreeRTOS sits in a typical ARM firmware stack. *Stack* refers to all of the different *layers* of firmware components that make up the system and how they are *stacked* on top of one another. A *user* in this context refers to the programmer using FreeRTOS (rather than the end user of the embedded system):

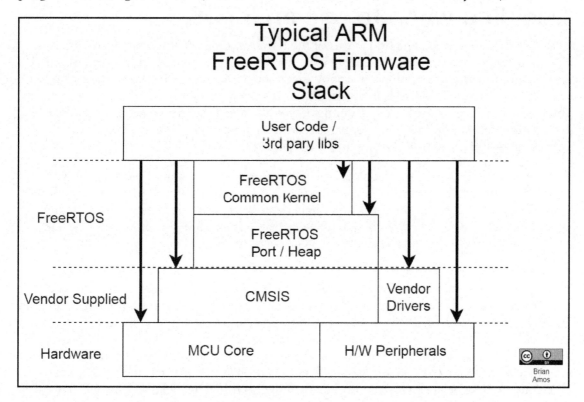

Some noteworthy items are as follows:

- **User code** is able to access the same FreeRTOS API, regardless of the underlying hardware port implementation.
- **FreeRTOS** does not prevent **User code** from using vendor-supplied drivers, CMSIS, or raw hardware registers.

Having a standardized API that is consistent across hardware means code can be easily migrated between hardware targets, without being constantly rewritten. The ability to have code talk directly to hardware also provides the means to write *extremely* efficient code when necessary (at the expense of portability).

Now that we know what an RTOS is, let's have a closer look at when it is appropriate to use an RTOS.

Deciding when to use an RTOS

Occasionally, when someone first learns of the term *real-time OS*, they mistakenly believe that an RTOS is the only way to achieve real-time behavior in an embedded system. While this is certainly understandable (especially given the name) it couldn't be further from the truth. Sometimes, it is best to think of an RTOS as a *potential* solution, rather than *the* solution to be used for everything. Generally speaking, for an MCU-based RTOS to be the ideal solution for a given problem, it needs to have a *Goldilocks*-level of complexity—not too simple, but not too complicated.

If there is an *extremely* simple problem, such as monitoring two states and triggering an alert when they are both present, the solution could be a straightforward hardware solution (such as an AND gate). In this case, there may be no reason to complicate things further, since the AND gate solution is going to be very fast, with high determinism and extreme reliability. It will also require very little development time.

Now, consider a case where there are only one or two tasks to be performed, such as controlling the speed of a motor and watching an encoder to ensure the correct distance is traversed. This could certainly be implemented in discrete analog and digital hardware, but having a configurable distance would add some complexity. Additionally, tuning the control loop coefficients would likely require twiddling the potentiometer settings (possibly for each individual board), which is undesirable in some or most cases, by today's manufacturing standards. So, on the hardware solution side, we're left with a CPLD or FPGA to implement the motion control algorithm and track the distance traveled. This happens to be a very good fit for either, since it is potentially small enough to fit into a CPLD, but in some cases, the cost of an FPGA might be unacceptable. This problem is also handled by MCUs regularly. If existing in-house resources don't have the expertise required with hardware languages or toolchains, then a bare-metal MCU firmware solution is probably a good fit.

Let's say the problem is more complicated, such as a device that controls several different actuators, reads data from a range of sensors, and stores those values in local storage. Perhaps the device also needs to sit on some sort of network, such as Ethernet, Wi-Fi, **controller area network (CAN)**, and so on. An RTOS can solve this type of problem quite well. The fact that there are many different tasks that need to be completed, more or less asynchronously to one another, makes it very easy to argue that the additional complexity the RTOS brings will pay off. The RTOS helps us to ensure the lower priority, more complex tasks, such as networking and the filesystem stacks, won't interfere with the more time-critical tasks (such as controlling actuators and reading sensors). In many cases, there may be some form of control system that generally benefits from being run at well-defined intervals in time—a strength of the RTOS.

Now, consider a similar system to the previous one, but now there are multiple networking requirements, such as serving a web page, dealing with user authentication in a complex enterprise environment, and pushing files to various shared directories that require different network-based file protocols. This level of complexity *can* be achieved with an RTOS, but again, depending on the available team resources, this might be better left to a full-blown OS to handle (either RTOS or general-purpose), since many of the complex software stacks required already exist. Sometimes, a multi-core approach might be taken, with one of the cores running an RTOS and the other running a general-purpose OS.

By now, it is probably obvious that there is no definitive way to determine exactly which real-time solution is correct for *all* cases. Each project and team will have their own unique requirements, backgrounds, skill-sets, and contexts that set the stage for this decision. There are many factors that go into selecting a solution to a problem; it is important to keep an open mind and to choose the solution that is best for your team and project at that point in time.

Summary

In this chapter, we've covered how to identify real-time requirements, as well as the different platforms available for implementing real-time systems. At this point, you should have an appreciation for both the wide range of systems that can have real-time requirements, as well as the variety of ways there are to meet those real-time requirements.

In the next chapter, we'll start digging into MCU-based real-time firmware by taking a closer look at two different programming models—super loops and RTOS tasks.

Questions

As we conclude, here is a list of questions for you to test your knowledge with on this chapter's material. You will find the answers in the *Assessments* section of the appendix:

1. Does a system with real-time requirements always need to be extremely fast?
2. Is an RTOS always required for real-time systems?
3. Is firmware the only way to satisfy real-time requirements?
4. What is a real-time system?
5. Name 3–4 types of real-time systems.
6. When is it appropriate to use an RTOS to meet real-time requirements?

2
Understanding RTOS Tasks

The super loop programming paradigm is typically one of the first programming methods that an embedded systems engineer will encounter. A program implemented with a super loop has a single top-level loop that cycles through the various functions the system needs to perform. These simple `while` loops are easy to create and understand (when they are small). In FreeRTOS, tasks are very similar to super loops – the main difference is that the system can have more than one task, but only one super loop.

In this chapter, we will take a closer look at super loops and different ways of achieving a degree of parallelism with them. After that, a comparison between super loops and tasks will be made and a theoretical way of thinking about task execution will be introduced. Finally, we'll take a look at how tasks are *actually* executed with an RTOS kernel and compare two basic scheduling algorithms.

The following topics will be covered in this chapter:

- Introducing super loop programming
- Achieving parallel operations with super loops
- Comparing RTOS tasks to super loops
- Achieving parallel operations with RTOS tasks
- RTOS tasks versus super loops – pros and cons

Technical requirements

There are no software or hardware requirements for this chapter.

Introducing super loop programming

There is one common property that all embedded systems share – they don't have an exit point. Because of its nature, embedded code is generally expected to always be available – silently running in the background, taking care of housekeeping tasks, and ready for user input at any time. Unlike desktop environments that are meant to start and stop programs, there isn't anything for a micro-controller to do if it exits the main() function. If this happens, it is likely that the entire device has stopped functioning. For this reason the main() function in an embedded system never returns. Unlike application programs, which are started and stopped by their host OS, most embedded MCU-based applications start at power on and end abruptly when the system is powered off. Because of this abrupt shutdown, embedded applications typically don't have any of the shutdown tasks normally associated with applications, such as freeing memory and resources.

The following code represents the basic idea of a super loop. Take a look at this before moving on to the more detailed explanations:

```
void main ( void )
{
    while(1)
    {
        func1();
        func2();
        func3();
        //do useful stuff, but don't return
        //(otherwise, where would we go. . what would we do. . .?!)
    }
}
```

While extremely simple, the preceding code has a number of features worth pointing out. The while loop never returns – it goes on forever executing the same three functions (this is intended). The three innocent-looking function calls can hide some nasty surprises in a real-time system.

The basic super loop

This main loop that never returns is generally referred to as a *super loop*. It's always fun to think *super* because it has control over most things in the system – nothing gets done in the following diagram unless the super loop makes it happen. This type of setup is perfect for very simple systems that need to perform just a few tasks that don't take a considerable amount of time. Basic super loop structures are extremely easy to write and understand; if the problem you're trying to solve can be done with a simple super loop, then use a simple super loop. Here is the execution flow of the code presented previously – each function is called sequentially and the loop never exits:

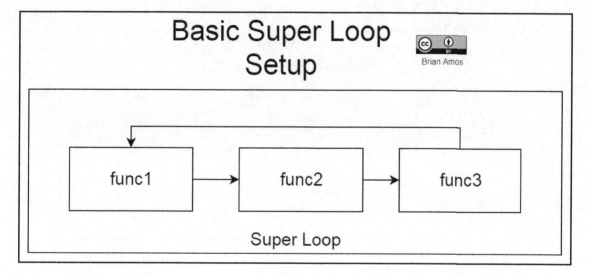

Now, let's have a look at what this execution looks like in a real-time system and some of the drawbacks associated with this approach.

Super loops in real-time systems

When simple super loops are operating quickly (usually because they have limited functionality/responsibility), they are quite responsive. However, the simplicity of the super loop can be a blessing and a curse. Since each function always follows the preceding function, they are always called in the same sequence and fully dependent on one another. Any delay introduced by one function propagates to the next function, which causes the total amount of time it takes to execute that iteration of the loop to increase (as seen in the following diagram). If func1 takes 10 us to execute one time through the loop, and then 100 ms the next, func2 isn't going to be called nearly as quickly the second time through the loop as it was the first time through:

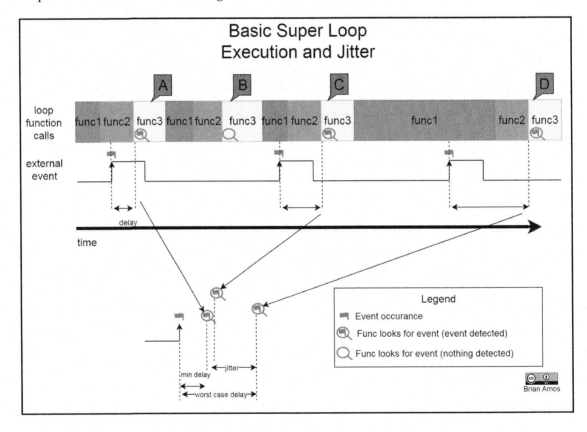

Let's take a look at this in a little bit more depth. In the preceding diagram, `func3` is responsible for checking the state of a flag representing an external event (this event signals a rising edge of a signal). The frequency of how often `func3` checks the flag is dependent on how long `func1` and `func2` take to execute. A well designed and responsive super loop will typically execute very rapidly, checking for events more often than they occur (callout B). When an external event does occur, the loop doesn't detect the event until the next time `func3` executes (callouts A, C, and D). Notice that there is a delay between when the event is generated and when it is detected by `func3`. Also note that the delay isn't always consistent: this difference in time is referred to as jitter.

 In many super loop-based systems, the execution speed of the super loop is extremely high compared to slowly occurring events being polled. We don't have enough room on the page to show a loop executing hundreds (or thousands) of iterations between detecting an event!

If a system has a known maximum amount of jitter when responding to an event, it is considered to be deterministic. That is, it will reliably respond to an event within the specified amount of time after that event occurs. A high level of determinism is crucial for time-critical components in a real-time system because, without it, the system could fail to respond to important events in a timely manner.

Consider the case of a loop checking a hardware flag repeatedly for an event (this is referred to as polling). The tighter the loop, the faster the flag is checked – when the flag is checked often, the code will be more responsive to the event of interest. If we have an event that needs to be acted upon in a timely manner, we could just write a really tight loop and wait for the important event to occur. This approach works – but *only* if that event is the only thing of interest for the system. If the *only* responsibility the entire system has is watching for that event (no background I/O, communication, and so on), then this is a valid approach. This type of situation rarely occurs in today's complex real-world systems. Poor responsiveness is the limitation of solely polled-based systems. Next up, we'll take a look at how to get a bit more parallelism in our super loop.

Achieving parallel operations with super loops

Even though a basic super loop can only step through functions sequentially, there are still ways to achieve parallelism. MCUs have a few different types of specialized hardware designed to take some of the burden away from the CPU, while still enabling a highly responsive system. This section will introduce those systems and how they can be used within the context of a super loop style program.

Introducing interrupts

Polling for a single event is not only wasteful in terms of CPU cycles and power – it also results in a system that isn't responsive to anything else, which should generally be avoided. So then, how can we get a single core processor to do things in parallel? Well, we can't – there's only one processor after all. . . but since our processor is likely to be running millions of instructions per second, it is possible to get it to perform things that are close enough to parallel. MCUs also include dedicated hardware for generating interrupts. Interrupts provide signals to the MCU that allow it to jump directly to an **interrupt service routine** (**ISR**) when the event occurs. This is such a critical piece of functionality that ARM Cortex-M cores provide a standardized peripheral for it, called the **nested vector interrupt controller** (**NVIC**). The NVIC provides a common way of dealing with interrupts. The *nested* portion of this term signifies that even interrupts can be interrupted by other interrupts with a higher priority. This is quite convenient since it allows us to minimize the amount of latency and jitter for the most time-critical pieces of the system.

So, how do interrupts fit into a super loop in a way that better achieves the illusion of parallel activity? The code inside an ISR is generally kept as short as possible, in order to minimize the amount of time spent in the interrupt. This is important for a few reasons. If the interrupt occurs very often and the ISR contains a *lot* of instructions, there is a chance that the ISR won't return before being called again. For communication peripherals such as UART or SPI, this will mean dropped data (which obviously isn't desirable). Another reason to keep the code short is because other interrupts also need to be serviced, which is why it's a good idea to push off any responsibility to the code that isn't running inside an ISR context.

To quickly get an idea of how ISRs contribute to jitter, let's take a look at a simple example of an external **analog to digital converter** (**ADC**) signaling to an MCU that a reading has been taken and the conversion is ready to be transferred to the MCU (refer to the hardware diagram shown here):

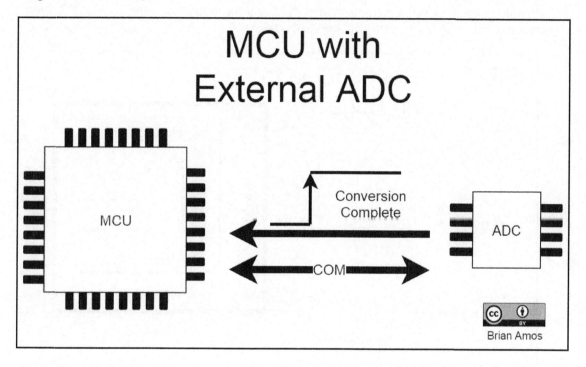

In the ADC hardware, a pin is dedicated to signaling that a reading of an analog value has been converted to a digital representation and is ready for transfer to the MCU. The MCU would then initiate a transfer over the communication medium (COM in the diagram).

Next, let's have a look at how the ISR calls might stack up against one another over time, relative to the rising edge on the conversion ready line. The following diagram shows six different instances of ISR being called in response to a rising edge of a signal. The small amount of time between when the rising edge occurs in the hardware versus when the ISR in firmware is invoked is the minimum latency. The jitter in the response of the ISR is the difference in the latency over many different cycles:

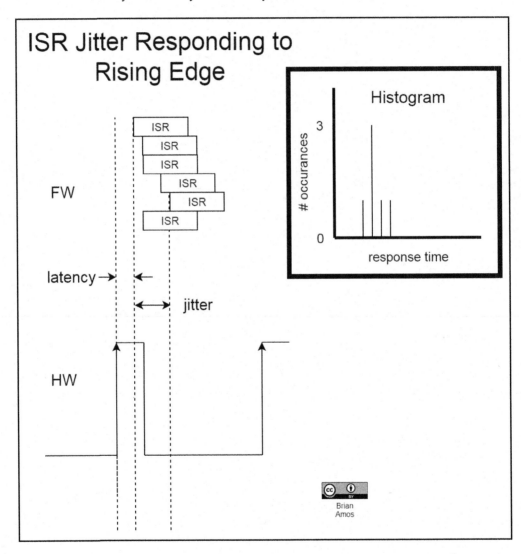

There are different ways to minimize latency and jitter for critical ISRs. In ARM Cortex-M-based MCUs, interrupt priorities are flexible – a single interrupt source can be assigned different priorities at runtime. The ability to reprioritize interrupts is one way of making sure the most important parts of a system get the CPU when they need it.

As mentioned before, it is important to keep the amount of code executing in interrupts as short as possible, since code that is inside an ISR will take precedence over any code that is not in an ISR (for example `main()`). Additionally, lower priority ISRs won't be executed until all of the code in a higher priority ISR has been executed and the ISR exits – which is why it is important to keep ISRs short. It is always a good idea to try and limit how much *responsibility* (and therefore code) an ISR has.

 When multiple interrupts are nested, they don't fully return – there's actually a really useful feature of ARM Cortex M processors called interrupt-tail chaining. If the processor detects that an interrupt is about to exit, but another one is pending, the next ISR will be executed without the processor totally restoring the pre-interrupt state, which further reduces latency.

Interrupts and super loops

One way of achieving minimal instructions and responsibility in the ISR is to do the smallest amount of work possible inside the ISR and then set a flag that is checked by code running in the super loop. This way, the interrupt can be serviced as soon as possible, without the entire system being dedicated to waiting on the event. In the following diagram, notice how the interrupt is being generated multiple times before finally being dealt with by `func3`.

Depending on what exactly that interrupt is trying to achieve, it will typically take a value from the associated peripheral and push it into an array (or take a value from an array and feed it to the peripheral registers). In the case of our external ADC, the ISR (triggered each time the ADC performs a conversion) would go out to the ADC, transfer the digitized reading, and store it in RAM, setting a flag indicating that one or more values are ready for processing. This allows for the interrupt to be serviced multiple times without involving the higher-level code:

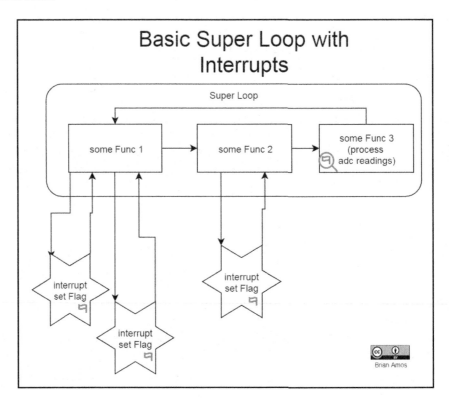

In the case of a communication peripheral that is transmitting large blocks of data, an array can be used as a queue for storing items to be transmitted. At the end of the entire transmission, a flag can be set to notify the main loop of the completion. There are many examples of situations where queuing values are appropriate. For instance, if some processing is required to be performed on a block of data, it is often advantageous to collect the data first and then process the entire block together outside of the interrupt. An interrupt-driven approach isn't the only way to achieve this blocked-data approach. In the next section, we'll take a look at a piece of hardware that can make moving large blocks of data both easier for the programmer, and more efficient for the processor.

Introducing DMA

Remember the assertion that the processor couldn't *really* do things truly in parallel? This is still true. *However* . . . modern MCUs contain more than just a processing core. While our processing core is chugging along dealing with instructions, there are many other hardware subsystems hard at work inside the MCU. One of these hard working subsystems is called a **Direct Memory Access Controller (DMA)**:

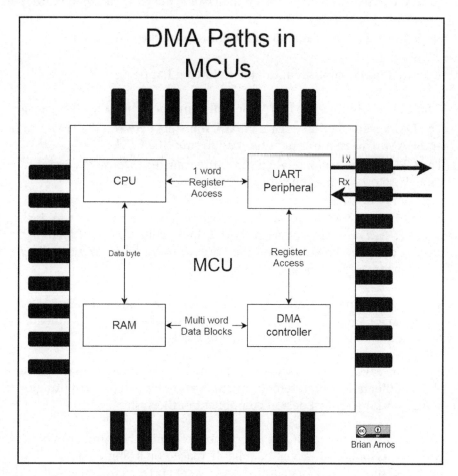

The preceding diagram presents a very simplified hardware block diagram that shows a view of two different data paths available from RAM to a UART peripheral.

In the case of receiving a stream of bytes from a UART without DMA, information from the UART will move into the UART registers, be read by the CPU, and then pushed out to RAM for storage:

1. The CPU must detect when an individual byte (or word) has been received, either by polling the UART register flags, or by setting up an interrupt service routine that will be fired when a byte is ready.
2. After the byte is transferred from the UART, the CPU can then place it into RAM for further processing.
3. Steps 1 and 2 are repeated until the entire message is received.

When DMA is used in the same scenario, the following happens:

1. The CPU configures the DMA controller and peripheral for the transfer.
2. The DMA controller takes care of ALL transfers between the UART peripheral and RAM. This requires no intervention from the CPU.
3. The CPU will be notified when the entire transfer is complete and it can go directly to processing the entire byte stream.

Most programmers find DMA to be nearly magical if they're accustomed to dealing with super loops and ISRs. The controller is configured to transfer a block of memory to the peripheral, as the peripheral needs it, and then provide a notification (typically via an interrupt) when the transfer is complete – that's it!

This convenience does come at a price, of course. It does take some time to set up the DMA transfer initially, so for small transfers, it might actually take more CPU time to set up the transfer than if an interrupt or polled method was used.

There are also some caveats to be aware of: each MCU has specific limitations, so be sure to read the details of the datasheet, reference manual, and errata before counting on the availability of DMA for a critical design component of the system:

*   The bandwidth of the MCU's internal buses limits the number of bandwidth-hungry peripherals that can be reliably placed on a single bus.
*   Occasionally, limited availability of mapped DMA channels to peripherals also complicates the design process.

These types of reasons are why it is important to get all team members involved with the early-stage design of embedded systems, rather than just *throwing it over the wall*.

DMA is great for accessing a large number of peripherals efficiently, giving us the ability to add more and more functionality to the system. However, as we start adding more and more modules of code to the super loop, inter-dependencies between subsystems become more complex as well. In the next section, we'll discuss the challenges of scaling a super loop for complex systems.

Scaling a super loop

So, we've now got a responsive system that is able to reliably process interrupts. Perhaps we've configured a DMA controller to take care of the heavy lifting for the communication peripherals as well. Why do we even need an RTOS? Well, it is entirely possible you don't! If the system is dealing with a limited number of responsibilities and none of them are especially complicated or time-consuming, then there may be no need for anything more sophisticated than a super loop.

However, if the system is also responsible for generating a **User Interface (UI)**, running complex time-consuming algorithms, or dealing with complex communication stacks, it is very likely that these tasks will take a non-trivial amount of time. If a glitzy eye-catching UI with lots of animation starts to stutter a little bit because the MCU is dealing with collecting data from a critical sensor, that is no big deal. Either the animation can be dialed back or eliminated and the important part of the real-time system is left intact. But what happens if that animation still looks perfectly good, even though there was some missed data from the sensor?

There are all sorts of different ways in which this problem plays out every day in our industry. Sometimes, if the system was designed well enough, the missing data will be detected and flagged (but it can't be recovered: it is gone forever). If the design team is really lucky, it may even have failed in this way during in-house testing. However, in many cases, the missed sensor data will go completely unnoticed until somebody notices one of the readings seems to be a little bit off ... sometimes. If everyone is lucky, the bug report for the sketchy reading might include a hint that it only seems to happen when someone is at the front panel (playing with those fancy animations). This would at least give the poor firmware engineer assigned to debug the issue a hint – but we're often not even that lucky.

These are the types of systems where an RTOS is needed. Guaranteeing that the most time-critical tasks are always running when necessary and scheduling lower priority tasks to run whenever spare time is available is a strong point of preemptive schedulers. In this type of setup, the critical sensor readings could be pushed into their own task and assigned a high priority – effectively interrupting anything else in the system (except ISRs) when it was time to deal with the sensor. That complex communication stack could be assigned a lower priority than the critical sensor. Finally, the glitzy UI with the fancy animations gets the left-over processor cycles. It is free to perform as many sliding alpha-blending animations as it wants, but only when the processor doesn't have anything else better to do.

Comparing RTOS tasks to super loops

So far, we've only mentioned tasks very casually, but what is a task, really? An easy way to think about a task is that it is *just another main loop*. In a preemptive RTOS, there are two main differences between tasks and super loops:

- Each task receives its own private stack. Unlike a super loop in main, which was sharing the system stack, tasks receive their own stack that no other task in the system will use. This allows each task to have its own call stack without interfering with other tasks.
- Each task has a priority assigned to it. This priority allows the scheduler to make decisions on which task should be running (the goal is to make sure the highest priority task in the system is always doing useful work).

Given these two features, each task may be programmed as if it is the only thing the processor has to do. Do you have a single flag you'd like to watch AND some calculations for flashy animations to churn through? No problem: simply program the task and assign it a reasonable priority, relative to the rest of the system's functionality. The preemptive scheduler will always ensure that the most important task is executing when it has work to do. When a higher priority task no longer has useful work to perform and it is waiting on something else in the system, a lower priority task will be switched into context and allowed to run.

The FreeRTOS scheduler will be discussed in more detail in `Chapter 7`, *The FreeRTOS Scheduler*.

Achieving parallel operations with RTOS tasks

Earlier, we had looked at a super loop that was looping through three functions. Now, for a very simple example, let's move each one of the three functions into its own task. We'll use these three simple tasks to examine the following:

- **Theoretical task programming model**: How the three tasks can be described theoretically
- **Actual round-robin scheduling**: What the tasks look like when executed using a round-robin scheduling algorithm
- **Actual preemptive scheduling**: What the tasks look like when executed using preemptive scheduling

 In real-world programs, there is almost never a single function per task; we're only using this as an analog to the overly simplistic super loop from earlier.

Theoretical task programming model

Here's some pseudo-code that uses a super loop to execute three functions. The same three functions are also included in a task-based system – each RTOS task (on the right) contains the same functionality as the functions from the super loop on the left. This will be used moving forward as we discuss the differences in how the code is executed when using a super loop versus using a task-driven approach with a scheduler:

Super Loop	RTOS Tasks
| ```
func1()
{
    //functionality 1
}

func2()
{
    //functionality 2
}

func3()
{
    //functionality 3
}

main( )
{
    while(1)
    {
        func1();
        func2();
        func3();
    }
}
``` | ```
Task1( )
{
    while(1)
    {
        //functionality of task 1
    }
}

Task2( )
{
    while(1)
    {
        //functionality of task 2
    }
}

Task3( )
{
    while(1)
    {
        //functionality of task 3
    }
}

main( )
{
    createTask1(&Task1);
    createTask2(&Task2);
    createTask3(&Task3);
    StartScheduler();   //never returns
}
``` |

One of the immediate differences you might notice between the super loop implementation and the RTOS implementation is the number of infinite while loops. There is only a single infinite while loop (in main()) for the super loop implementation, but each task has its own infinite while loop.

In the super loop, the three functions being executed by a super loop are each run to completion before the next function is called, and then the cycle continues onto the next iteration (illustrated by the following diagram):

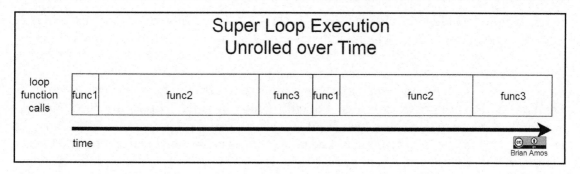

In the RTOS implementation, each task is essentially its own little infinite `while` loop. Whereas functions in the super loop were always sequentially called one after the other (orchestrated by the logic in the super loop), tasks can simply be thought of as all executing in parallel after the scheduler has been started. Here's a diagram of an RTOS executing three tasks:

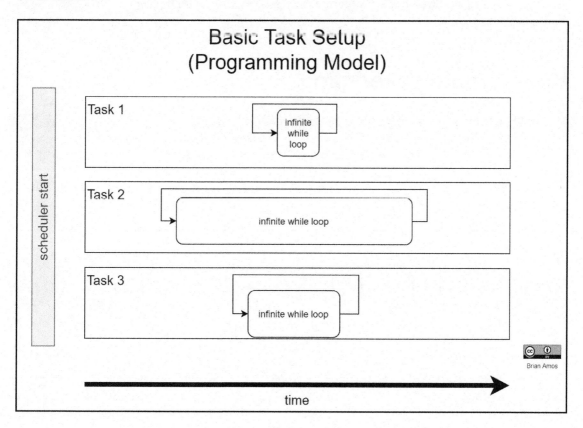

In the diagram, you'll notice that the size of each `while` loop is not the same. This is one of the many benefits of using a scheduler that is executing the tasks in *parallel* versus a super loop – the programmer doesn't need to be immediately concerned with the length of the longest executing loop slowing down the other tighter loops. The diagram depicts `Task 2` having a much longer loop than `Task 1`. In a super loop system, this would cause the functionality in `func1` to execute less frequently (since the super loop would need to execute `func1`, then `func2`, and then `func3`). In a task-based programming model, this isn't the case – the loop of each task can be thought of as being isolated from the other tasks in the system – and they all run in parallel.

This isolation and perceived parallel execution are some of the benefits of using an RTOS; it alleviates some of the complexity for the programmer. So – that's the easiest way of conceptualizing tasks – they're simply independent infinite `while` loops that all execute in parallel . . . in theory. In reality, things aren't quite this simple. In the next two sections, we'll take a glimpse into what goes on behind the scenes to make it *seem* like tasks are executing in parallel.

Round-robin scheduling

One of the easiest ways to conceptualize actual task execution is with round-robin scheduling. In round-robin scheduling, each task gets a small slice of time to use the processor, which is controlled by the scheduler. As long as the task has work to perform, it will execute. As far as the task is concerned, it has the processor entirely to itself. The scheduler takes care of all of the complexity of switching in the appropriate context for the next task:

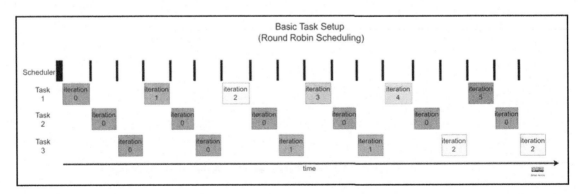

This is the same three tasks that were shown previously, except that instead of a theoretical conceptualization, each iteration through the tasks' loops are enumerated over time. Because the round-robin scheduler assigns equal time slices to each task, the shortest task (Task 1) has executed nearly six iterations of its loop, whereas the task with the slowest loop (Task 2) has only made it through the first iteration. Task 3 has executed three iterations of its loop.

An extremely important distinction between a super loop executing the same functions versus a round-robin scheduling routine executing them is this: Task 3 completed its moderately tight loop before Task 2. When the super loop was running functions in a serial fashion, Function 3 wouldn't even have started until Function 2 had run to completion. So, while the scheduler isn't providing us with true parallelism, each task is getting it's *fair share* of CPU cycles. So, with this scheduling scheme, if a task has a shorter loop, it will execute more often than a task with a longer loop.

All of this switching does come at a (slight) cost – the scheduler needs to be invoked any time there is a context switch. In this example, the tasks are not explicitly calling the scheduler to run. In the case of FreeRTOS running on an ARM Cortex-M, the scheduler will be called from the SysTick interrupt (more details can be found in Chapter 7, *The FreeRTOS Scheduler*). A considerable amount of effort is put into making sure the scheduler kernel is extremely efficient and takes as little time to run as possible. However, the fact remains that it will run at some point and consume CPU cycles. On most systems, the small amount of overhead is generally not noticed (or significant), but it can become an issue in some systems. For example, if a design is on the extreme edge of feasibility because it has extremely tight timing requirements and very few spare CPU cycles, the added overhead may not be desirable (or completely necessary) if the super loop/interrupt approach has been carefully characterized and optimized. However, it is best to avoid this type of situation wherever possible, since the likelihood of overlooking a combination of interrupt stack-up (or nested conditionals taking longer *every once in a while*) and causing the system to miss a deadline is extremely high on even moderately complex systems.

Preemptive-based scheduling

Preemptive scheduling provides a mechanism for ensuring that the system is always performing its most important task. A preemptive scheduling algorithm will give priority to the most important task, regardless of what else in the system is happening – except for interrupts, since they occur *underneath* the scheduler and always have a higher priority. This sounds very straightforward – and it is – except that there are some details that need to be taken into consideration.

Let's take a look at the same three tasks. These three tasks all have the same functionality: a simple `while` loop that endlessly increments a volatile variable.

Now, consider the following three scenarios to figure out which of the three tasks will get context. The following diagram has the same tasks as previously presented with round-robin scheduling. Each of the three tasks has more than enough work to do, which will prevent the task from going out of context:

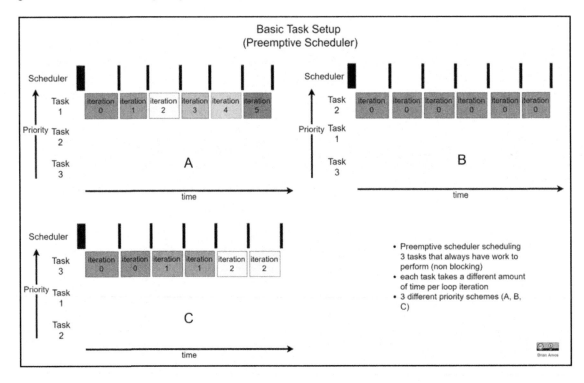

So, what happens when three different tasks are set up with three different sets of priorities (A, B, and C)?

- **A (top left)**: `Task 1` has the highest priority in the system – it gets *all* of the processor time! Regardless of how many iterations `Task 1` performs, if it is the highest priority task in the system and it has work to do (without waiting on anything else in the system), it will be given context and run.

- **B (top right)**: `Task 2` is the highest priority task in the system. Since it has more than enough work to do, not needing to wait on anything else in the system, `Task 2` will be given context. Since `Task 2` is configured as the highest priority in the system, it will execute until it needs to wait on something else in the system.
- **C (bottom left)**: `Task 3` is configured as the highest priority task in the system. No other tasks run because they are lower priority.

Now, obviously, if you were actually designing a system that required multiple tasks to run in parallel, a preemptive scheduler wouldn't be much use if all of the tasks in the system required 100% CPU time and didn't need to wait on anything. This setup also wouldn't be a great design for a real-time system since it was completely overloaded (and ignoring two of the three primary functions the system was meant to perform)! The situation presented is referred to as **task starvation**, since only the highest priority task in the system is getting CPU time and the other tasks are being *starved* of processor time.

Another detail worth pointing out is that the scheduler is still running at predetermined intervals. No matter what is going on in the system, the scheduler will diligently run at its predetermined tick rate.

There is an exception to this. FreeRTOS has a *tick-less* scheduler mode designed for use in extremely low power devices, which prevents the scheduler from running on the same predetermined intervals.

A more realistic use case where a preemptive scheduler is used is shown here:

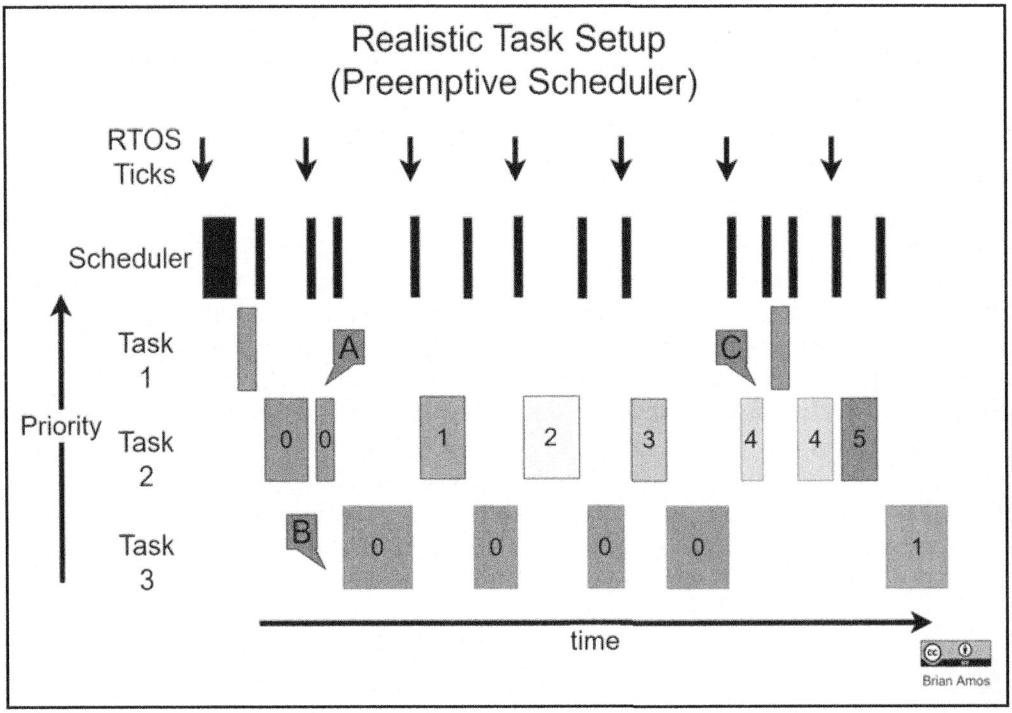

In this case, Task 1 is the highest priority task in the system (it also happens to finish executing very quickly) – the only time Task 1 has context taken from it is when the scheduler needs to run; otherwise, it will keep context until it doesn't have any additional work to perform.

Task 2 is the next highest priority – you'll also notice that this task is set up to execute once per RTOS scheduler tick (indicated by the downward arrows). Task 3 is the lowest priority task in the system: it only gets context when there is nothing else worth doing in the system. There are three main points worth looking at in this diagram:

- **A**: Task 2 has context. Even though it is interrupted by the scheduler, it immediately gets context again after the scheduler has run (because it still has work to perform).
- **B**: Task 2 has finished its work for iteration 0. The scheduler has run and determined that (since no other tasks in the system are required to run) Task 3 could have processor time.

- **C:** Task 2 has started running iteration 4, but Task 1 now has some work to do – even though Task 2 hasn't finished the work for that iteration. Task 1 is immediately switched in by the scheduler to perform its higher priority work. After Task 1 is finished with what it needs to do, Task 2 is switched back in to finish iteration 4. This time, the iteration runs until the next tick and Task 2 runs again (iteration 5). After Task 2 iteration 5 has completed, there is no higher priority work to perform, so the lowest priority task in the system (Task 3) runs again. It looks as if Task 3 has finally completed iteration 0, so it moves on to iteration 1 and chugs along . . .

Hopefully you're still with me! If not, that's OK, given that this is a very abstract example. The key takeaway is that the highest priority task in the system takes precedence.

 This is only a brief introduction to the relevant scheduling concepts covered in detail in Chapter 7, *The FreeRTOS Scheduler*, to put the concept of tasks into context, showing the different ways in which they can be run and scheduled. Many more details and strategies for achieving desired system performance are discussed there, along with real-world examples.

RTOS tasks versus super loops – pros and cons

Super loops are great for simple systems with limited responsibilities. If a system is simple enough, they can provide very low jitter in response to an event, but only if the loop is tight enough. As a system grows more complex and acquires more responsibility, polling rates decrease. This decreased polling rate causes much larger jitter in response to events. Interrupts can be introduced into the system to combat the increased jitter. As a super loop-based system becomes more complex, it becomes harder to track and guarantee responsiveness to events.

An RTOS becomes very valuable with more complex systems that have not only time-consuming tasks, but also require good responsiveness to external events. With an RTOS, an increase in system complexity, ROM, RAM, and initial setup time is the trade-off for a more easily understood system, which can more easily guarantee responsiveness to external events in a timely manner.

Summary

We've covered quite a few concepts in this chapter in relation to super loops and tasks. At this point, you should have a good understanding of how super loops can be combined with interrupts and DMA to provide parallel processing to keep a system responsive, without the use of an RTOS. We introduced task-based architectures at a theoretical level and the two main types of scheduling you'll encounter when using FreeRTOS (round-robin and preemptive). You also had a very brief glimpse at how a preemptive scheduler schedules tasks of different priorities. All of these concepts are important to grasp, so feel free to refer back to these simplistic examples as we move forward and discuss more advanced topics.

In the next chapter, you'll be introduced to the various inter-task communication mechanisms that will cause context switches like the ones covered in this chapter. As we progress through the book and move onto interrupt and task communication mechanisms, many real-world examples will be discussed and we'll take a deep dive into the code that you'll need to write in order to create reliable real-time systems.

Questions

As we conclude, here is a list of questions for you to test your knowledge regarding this chapter's material. You will find the answers in the *Assessments* section of the Appendix:

1. What is a super loop?
    - An infinite `while` loop
    - A loop that oversees all function calls in an embedded system
    - Both of the preceding options
2. RTOS tasks should *always* be preferred over super loops.
    - True
    - False
3. Name a drawback to complex super loops.
4. How can the responsiveness of a super loop-based application be improved?
5. List two ways in which super loops differ from RTOS tasks.

6. What features do RTOS tasks possess to help ensure that the most time-critical task gets CPU time before less time-critical tasks?
   - Time slicing
   - Prioritization
   - Round-robin scheduling
7. What type of scheduler attempts to execute the most critical tasks before less critical tasks?

Further reading

If interrupts and DMA are new to you, here are two resources that describe their use (relative to MCUs) fairly well:

- **For interrupts:** https://www.renesas.com/eu/en/support/technical-resources/engineer-school/mcu-programming-peripherals-04-interrupts.html
- STM application note AN4031 – Using DMA on the STM32F7: https://www.st.com/content/ccc/resource/technical/document/application_note/27/46/7c/ea/2d/91/40/a9/DM00046011.pdf/files/DM00046011.pdf/jcr:content/translations/en.DM00046011.pdf

3
Task Signaling and Communication Mechanisms

In the previous chapter, the task was introduced. Toward the end, we looked at examples of preemptive scheduling for multiple tasks in the system and the fact that a task will run whenever it isn't waiting on something (in the blocked state) and can do something useful. In this chapter, the core mechanisms for task signaling and inter-task communication will be briefly introduced. These primitives are fundamental to event-driven parallel programming, which is the foundation of a well implemented RTOS-based application.

Rather than dive right into the FreeRTOS API, each primitive will be presented along with a few graphical examples and some suggestions on when each of the mechanisms can be used. Don't worry: in later chapters, we'll get into the nitty-gritty of working with the API. For now, let's concentrate on the fundamentals.

In this chapter, we'll be introducing the following topics:

- RTOS queues
- RTOS semaphores
- RTOS mutexes

Technical requirements

There are no software or hardware requirements for this chapter.

RTOS queues

Queues are quite simple in concept, but they are also extremely powerful and flexible, especially if you've traditionally programmed on bare metal with C. At its heart, a queue is simply a circular buffer. However, this buffer contains some very special properties, such as native multi-thread safety, the flexibility for each queue to hold any type of data, and waking up other tasks that are waiting on an item to appear in the queue. By default, data is stored in queues using **First In First Out (FIFO)** ordering – the first item to be put into the queue is the first item to be removed from the queue.

We'll start by taking a look at some simple behavior of queues when they are in different states and used in different ways (sending versus receiving) and then move on to how queues can be used to pass information between tasks.

Simple queue send

The first queue example is simply adding (also referred to as *sending)* an item to a queue that has empty space:

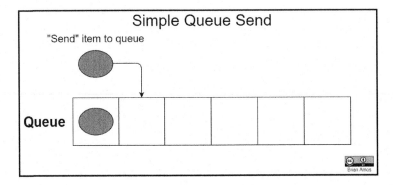

When an item is added to a queue with available space, the addition happens immediately. Because space was available in the queue, the task *sending* the item to the queue continues running, unless there is another higher priority task waiting on an item to appear in the queue.

Although interaction with queues typically happens from within tasks, this isn't *always* the case. There are some special cases where queues can also be accessed from within ISRs (but that behavior has different rules). For the examples in this chapter, we'll assume that tasks are sending and receiving items from the queues.

Simple queue receive

In the following diagram, a task is shown *receiving* an item from a queue:

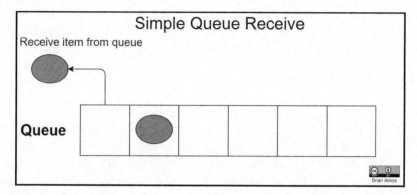

When a task is ready to receive an item from a queue, by default, it will get the oldest item. In this example, since there is at least one item in the queue, the *receive* is processed immediately and the task continues to run.

Full queue send

When a queue is full, no information is thrown away. Instead, the task attempting to *send* the item to the queue will wait for up to a predetermined amount of time for available space in the queue:

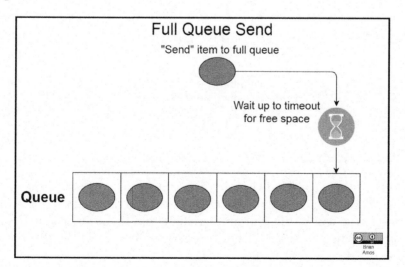

When a queue is full, the task that is attempting to send an item to the queue will wait until a space in the queue becomes available, but only up to the timeout value specified.

In this example, if a task was attempting to send to a full queue and it has a timeout of 10 ms – it would only wait 10 ms for space to become available in the queue. After the timeout expires, the call will return and notify the calling code that the send has failed. What to do regarding this failure is at the discretion of the programmer setting up the calling code and will vary depending on the use case. Extremely large timeout values can be used for truly non-critical functions. Just be aware that this will cause the sending task to effectively wait forever for a slot in the queue to become available (this is obviously no longer real time)!

Your code will typically be structured so that attempts to send to a queue won't timeout. It is up to you, as the programmer, to determine what an acceptable amount of time is on a case-by-case basis. It is also your responsibility to determine the severity and corrective actions if a timeout does occur. Potential corrective actions could range from nothing (think of a dropped frame in a video call) to an emergency shutdown.

Empty queue receive

Another case where accessing a queue can cause a task to block is attempting to *receive* from an empty queue:

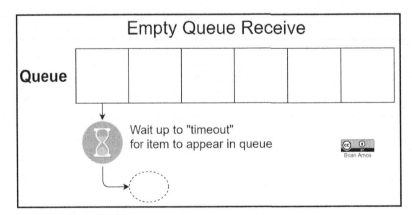

Similar to a *Send* waiting on space to become available, a task *receiving* from a queue also has the potential to be delayed. In the case of an empty queue, the task that is attempting to receive from the queue will be blocked until an item appears in the queue. If no item is available before the timeout expires, the calling code will be notified of the failure. Again, the exact course of action to take varies.

Sometimes, infinite waits are used. You'll often encounter very long wait periods for queues that are receiving input from external interfaces, such as serial ports, which may not be sending data constantly. There is no issue at all if a human user on the other end of a serial port hasn't sent data for an extended period of time.

On the other hand, receive timeouts can also be used to ensure that you have a minimum acceptable amount of data to process. Let's use a sensor that is meant to provide a new reading at 10 Hz (10 readings per second). If you were implementing an algorithm that relies on *fresh* readings from this sensor, a timeout of slightly greater than 100 ms could be used to trigger an error. This timeout would guarantee that the algorithm is always acting on *fresh* sensor readings. In this case, hitting a timeout could be used to trigger some type of corrective action or notification that the sensor wasn't performing as expected.

Queues for inter-task communication

Now that the simple behaviors of queues have been covered, we'll take a look at how they can be used to move data between tasks. A very common use case for queues is to have one task populate the queue while another is reading from the same queue. This is generally straightforward but may have some nuances, depending on how the system is set up:

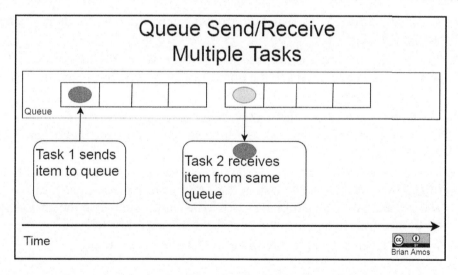

In the preceding example, Task 1 and Task 2 are both interacting with the same Queue. Task 1 will *send* an item to the Queue. As long as Task 2 has a higher priority than Task 1, it will immediately *receive* the item.

Let's consider another instance that often occurs in practice when multiple tasks are interacting with queues. Since a preemptive scheduler always runs the task with the highest priority, if that task always has data to write to the queue, the queue will fill before another task is given a chance to read from the queue. Here is an example of how this may play out:

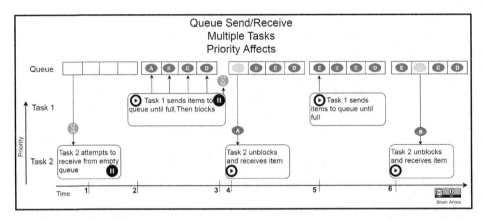

The following numbers correspond to indexes along the time axis:

1. `Task2` attempts to receive an item from the empty queue. No items are available, so `Task2` blocks.
2. `Task1` adds items to queue. Since it is the highest priority task in the system, `Task1` adds items to the queue until it doesn't have any more items to add, or until the queue is full.
3. The queue is filled, so `Task1` is blocked.
4. `Task2` is given context by the scheduler since it is now the highest priority task that may run.
5. As soon as an item is removed from the Queue, `Task1` is given context again (this is the highest priority task in the system and it is now able to run because it was blocking while waiting for space to become available in the queue). After adding a single item, the queue is full and `Task1` is blocked.
6. `Task2` is given context and receives an item from the queue:

 A real-world example of the preceding situation is covered in `Chapter 9`, *Intertask Communication*, in the section *Passing data through queues*. `Chapter_9/src/mainQueueCompositePassByValue.c` illustrates the exact setup and a thorough empirical execution analysis is performed using `SystemView`.

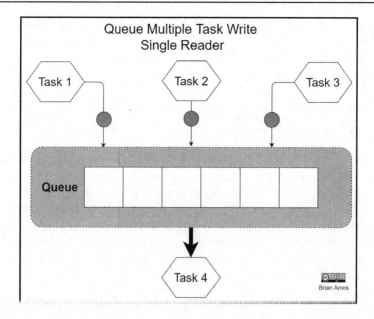

Another extremely common use case for queues is to have a single queue accept input from many different sources. This is especially useful for something like a debug serial port or a log file. Many different tasks can be writing to the queue, with a single task responsible for receiving data from the queue and pushing it out to the shared resource.

While queues are generally used for passing data between tasks, semaphores can be used for signaling and synchronizing tasks. Let's learn more about this next.

RTOS semaphores

Semaphores are another very straightforward, but powerful, construct. The word *semaphore* has a Greek origin – the approximate English translation is *sign-bearer*, which is a wonderfully intuitive way to think about them. Semaphores are used to indicate that something has happened; they signal events. Some example use cases of semaphores include the following:

- An ISR is finished servicing a peripheral. It may *give* a semaphore to provide tasks with a signal indicating that data is ready for further processing.
- A task has reached a juncture where it needs to wait for other tasks in the system to *catch up* before moving on. In this case, a semaphore could be used to synchronize the tasks.
- Restricting the number of simultaneous users of a restricted resource.

One of the convenient aspects of using an RTOS is the pre-existence of semaphores. They are included in every implementation of an RTOS because of how basic (and crucial) their functionality is. There are two different types of semaphores to cover – counting semaphores and binary semaphores.

Counting semaphores

Counting semaphores are most often used to manage a shared resource that has limitations on the number of simultaneous users. Upon creation, they can be configured to hold a maximum value, called a *ceiling*. The example normally given for counting semaphores is readers in a database ... Well, we're talking about an MCU-based embedded system here, so let's keep our examples relevant. If you're interested in databases, you're probably better off with a general-purpose OS! For our example, let's say you're implementing a socket-based communication driver and your system only has enough memory for a limited number of simultaneous socket connections.

In the following diagram, we have a shared network resource that can accommodate two simultaneous socket connections. However, there are three tasks that need access. A counting semaphore is used to limit the number of simultaneous socket connections. Each time a task is finished with the shared resource (that is, its socket closes), it must give back its semaphore so another task can gain access to the network. If a task happens to *give* a semaphore that is already at its maximum count, the count will remain unchanged:

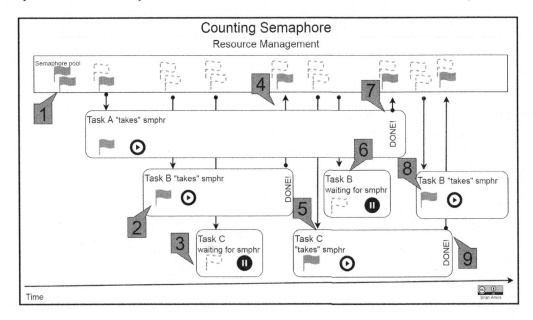

The preceding diagram plays out the example of a shared resource only capable of servicing two simultaneous tasks (although three tasks in the system need to use the resource). If a task is going to use a socket, which is protected by the counting semaphore, it must first *take* a semaphore from the pool. If no semaphore is available, then the task must wait until a semaphore becomes available:

1. Initially, a semaphore is created with a maximum (ceiling) of 2 and an initial count of 0.
2. When `TaskA` and `TaskB` attempt to *take* a `semphr`, they're immediately successful. At this point, they can each open up a socket and communicate over the network.
3. `TaskC` was a bit later, so it will need to wait until the count of `semphr` is less than 2, which is when a network socket will be free to use.
4. After `TaskB` is finished communicating over its socket, it returns the semaphore.
5. Now that a semaphore is available, `TaskC` completes its *take* and is allowed network access.
6. Shortly after `TaskC` gets access, `TaskB` has another message to send, so it attempts to take a semaphore, but needs to wait for one to become available, so it is put to sleep.
7. While `TaskC` is communicating over the network, `TaskA` finishes and returns its semaphore.
8. `TaskB` is woken up and its take completes, which enables it to start communicating over the network.
9. After `TaskB` is given its semaphore, `TaskC` completes its transaction and gives back the semaphore it had.

Waiting for semaphores is where an RTOS differs from most other semaphore implementations – a task can *timeout* during a semaphore wait. If a task fails to acquire the semaphore in time, it must not access the shared resource. Instead, it must take an alternative course of action. This alternative could be any number of actions that can range from a failure so severe that it triggers an emergency shutdown sequence, to something so benign that it is merely mentioned in a log file or pushed to a debug serial port for analysis later on. As a programmer, it is up to you to determine what the appropriate course of action is, which can sometimes prompt some difficult discussions with other disciplines.

Binary semaphores

Binary semaphores are really just counting semaphores with a maximum count of 1. They are most often used for synchronization. When a task needs to synchronize on an event, it will attempt to *take* a semaphore, blocking until the semaphore becomes available or until the specified timeout has elapsed. Another asynchronous part of the system (either a task or an ISR) will *give* a semaphore. Binary semaphores can be *given* more than once; there is no need for that piece of code to *return* them. In the following example, TaskA only *gives* a semaphore, while TaskB only *takes* a semaphore:

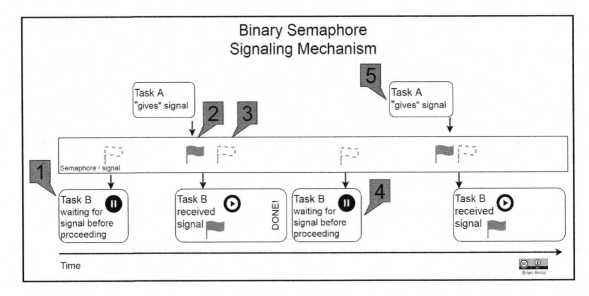

`TaskB` is set up to wait for a signal (semaphore) before proceeding with its duties:

1. Initially, `TaskB` attempts to *take* the semaphore, but it wasn't available, so `TaskB` went to sleep.
2. Sometime later, `TaskA` *gives* the signal.
3. `TaskB` is woken up (by the scheduler; this happens in the background) and now has the semaphore. It will go about the duties required of it until it is finished. Notice, however, that `TaskB` doesn't need to give back the binary semaphore. Instead, it simply waits for it again.
4. `TaskB` is blocked again because the semaphore isn't available (just like the first time), so it goes to sleep until a semaphore is available.
5. The cycle repeats.

 If `TaskB` were to "give back" the binary semaphore, it would immediately run again, without receiving the go-ahead from `TaskA`. The result would just be a loop running full speed, rather than being signaled on a condition signaled from `TaskA`.

Next, we'll discuss a special type of semaphore with some additional properties that make it especially well suited for protecting items that can be accessed from different tasks – the mutex.

RTOS mutexes

The term **mutex** is shorthand for **mutual exclusion.** In the context of shared resources and tasks, mutual exclusion means that, if a task is using a shared resource, then that task is the *only task* that is permitted to use the resource – all others will need to wait.

If all this sounds a lot like a binary semaphore, that's because it is. However, it has an additional feature that we'll cover soon. First, let's take a look at the problem with using a binary semaphore to provide mutual exclusion.

Priority inversion

Let's look at a common problem that occurs when attempting to use a binary semaphore to provide mutual exclusion functionality.

Consider three tasks, A, B, and C, where A has the highest priority, B the middle priority, and C the lowest priority. Tasks A and C rely on a semaphore to give access to a resource that is shared between them. Since Task A is the highest priority task in the system, it should always be running before other tasks. However, since Task A and Task C both rely on a resource shared between them (guarded by the binary semaphore), there is an unexpected dependency here:

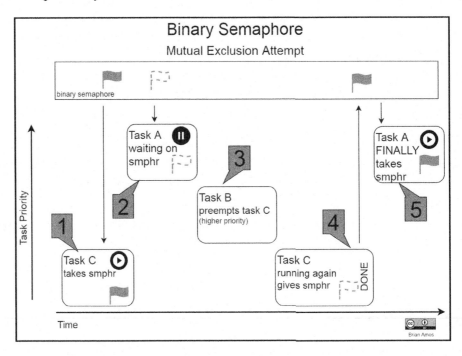

Let's walk step by step through the example to see how this scenario plays out:

1. `Task C` (the lowest priority task in the system) acquires a binary semaphore and starts to do some work.
2. Before `Task C` completes its work, `Task A` (the highest priority task) interrupts and attempts to acquire the same semaphore, but is forced to wait because `Task C` has already acquired the semaphore.
3. `Task B` preempts `Task C` as well, because `Task B` has a higher priority than `Task C`. `Task B` performs whatever work it has and then goes to sleep.
4. `Task C` runs through the remainder of its work with the shared resource, at which point it gives the semaphore back.
5. `Task A` is *finally* able to run.

`Task A` was able to run, eventually, but not until TWO lower priority tasks had run. `Task C` finishing its work with the shared resource was unavoidable (unless a design change could have been made to prevent it from accessing the same shared resource as `Task A`). However, `Task B` also had an opportunity to run to completion, even though `Task A` was waiting around and had a higher priority! This is priority inversion – a higher priority task in the system is waiting to run, but it is forced to wait while a lower priority task is running instead – the priorities of the two tasks are effectively *inverted* in this case.

Mutexes minimize priority inversion

Earlier, we had said that, in FreeRTOS, mutexes were binary semaphores with one important additional feature. That important feature is priority inheritance – mutexes have the ability to temporarily change the priority of a task to avoid causing major delays in the system. This plays out when the scheduler finds that a high priority task is attempting to acquire a mutex already held by a lower priority task. In this specific case, the scheduler will temporarily increase the priority of the lower task until it releases the mutex. At this point, the priority of the lower task will be set back to what it was prior to the priority inheritance. Let's take a look at the exact same example from the preceding diagram implemented using a mutex (instead of a binary semaphore):

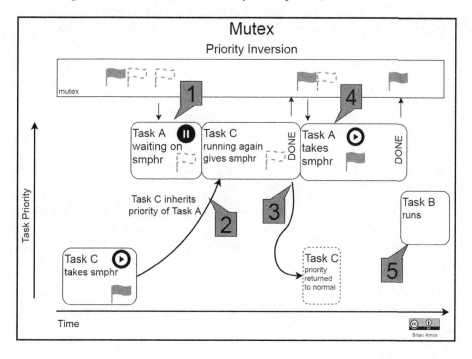

Let's walk step by step through the example to see how this scenario plays out:

1. `Task A` is still waiting for `Task C` to return the mutex.
2. The priority of `Task C` is brought up to be the same as that of the higher priority `Task A`. `Task C` runs to completion since it holds the mutex and is a high priority task.
3. `Task C` returns the mutex and its priority is demoted to whatever it was before it was holding a mutex that was delaying the high priority task.
4. `Task A` takes the mutex and completes its work.
5. `Task B` is allowed to run.

Depending on how long `Task C` is taking with the shared resource and how time sensitive `Task A` is, this could either be a major source of concern or no big deal. Timing analysis can be performed to ensure that `Task A` is still meeting deadlines, but tracking all possible causes of priority inversion and other high priority asynchronous events could prove to be challenging. At a minimum, the user should make use of the built-in timeouts provided for taking mutexes and perform a suitable alternative action if a mutex has failed to be taken in a timely manner. More details on exactly how to accomplish this can be found in `Chapter 9`, *Intertask Communication*.

Mutexes and semaphores are fairly standard mechanisms for signaling between tasks. They are very standard between different RTOSes and provide excellent flexibility.

Summary

This chapter introduced queues, semaphores, and mutexes. A few common use cases of each of these core building blocks for RTOS applications were also discussed at a high level and some of the more subtle behaviors of each were highlighted. The diagrams presented in this chapter should serve as a reference point to return to as we move on to more complex real-world examples in later chapters.

We've now covered some of the core RTOS concepts. In the next chapter, we'll turn our attention to another very important step of developing a solid real-time system. This step affects how efficiently firmware can be run and has a major impact on system performance – MCU selection.

Questions

As we conclude, here is a list of questions for you to test your knowledge regarding this chapter's material. You will find the answers in the *Assessments* section of the Appendix:

1. Which RTOS primitive is most commonly used for sending and receiving data between tasks?
2. Is it possible for a queue to interact with more than two tasks?
3. Which RTOS primitive is commonly used for signaling and synchronizing tasks?
4. What is an example of when a counting semaphore could be used?
5. Name one major difference between binary semaphores and mutexes.
6. When protecting a resource shared between tasks, should a binary semaphore or a mutex be used?
7. What is priority inversion and why is it dangerous for a real-time system?

Section 2: Toolchain Setup

If you've ever felt overwhelmed when trying to decide which microcontroller or IDE to use, this section is for you. In this section, you'll learn what differentiates one MCU from another, how to select an IDE or toolchain that fits your workflow, and how to go about debugging and troubleshooting a real-time system. Instructions for setting up STMCubeIDE are in Chapter 5, *Selecting an IDE*, and the SEGGER debugging tools setup is covered in Chapter 6, *Debugging Tools for Real-Time Systems*. Both of these will be required for working through the examples.

This section comprises the following chapters:

- Chapter 4, *Selecting the Right MCU*
- Chapter 5, *Selecting an IDE*
- Chapter 6, *Debugging Tools for Real-Time Systems*

4
Selecting the Right MCU

This chapter is a crash course on **microcontroller unit** (**MCU**) selection, targeted at engineers who don't have a deep hardware background. It doesn't try to be an exhaustive list of absolutely everything you need to know and consider when selecting hardware for your new project. It does provide an introduction to many of the contributing factors for differentiating between and selecting MCU devices. By the end, you'll be aware of enough key considerations to efficiently research MCUs and discuss potential candidates with the hardware engineers on the team. By increasing hardware/firmware collaboration and selecting the right MCU for the project the first time around, you'll avoid both hardware redesigns and schedule delays.

We'll start by introducing a wide range of considerations that go into selecting a suitable MCU for your project. After that, trade-offs between different development hardware will be discussed. A short introduction to the STM32 line is provided to show how vendors tend to group their product families. At the end of this chapter, we'll compare a few different **development boards** (**dev boards**) with STM32 MCUs at their heart to show why we're using the dev board we are!

This chapter will cover the following topics:

- The importance of MCU selection
- MCU considerations
- Dev board considerations
- Introducing the STM32 MCU product line
- How our dev board was selected

Technical requirements

All you need for this chapter is access to the internet in order to browse a few websites.

The importance of MCU selection

After reading the title of this section, you might be asking yourself:

> *"Hey! I thought this was a book about how to program a microcontroller using an RTOS—what's all this about MCU selection? I'm a software developer!"*

FreeRTOS is almost exclusively targeted at MCUs. It is primarily a scheduling kernel with a stable API, which makes it very well-suited to extremely low-level design. Unlike a full-blown CPU system with practically unlimited virtual addressing space and more clock cycles than you know what to do with, you're going to be working with a resource-constrained system. If you're developing firmware on this type of system, it means you're going to be much closer to the hardware than if you were writing software—which, in turn, means you're very likely going to be getting your hands very dirty, compared to your software counterparts. By dirty, we're talking *logic analyzer probing pins* dirty. . . *DMM permanently sitting on your desk* dirty. . . *learn how to solder so you can tack a lead onto the MCU in the quad flat pack* dirty. . . you get the idea! If you're from an exclusively software background, you've got some learning to do because we're about to dive into the gray area that resides between software and hardware—firmware—and it should be a lot of fun!

Firmware and hardware are very closely linked, which is why it is so important that firmware engineers are brought into the fray early on in the development process. In some organizations, there is still only one person performing the electrical design work and writing the firmware. However, there is a growing trend that drives disciplines to be more and more specialized in their domains of expertise. Even in this case, it is important that multiple team members are brought in to make important design decisions up front, so everyone is aware of the trade-offs being made.

If you're not the person immediately responsible for selecting an MCU, then there's a chance a design might be *thrown over the wall* to you. This is almost always a bad thing because it encourages sub-optimal system designs to avoid schedule delays caused by hardware being significantly redesigned after some core piece of functionality of the system is discovered. Instead of committing to a significant board revision to address a major design shortcoming, many teams are pressured to *just fix it with some code*.

So, assuming you have some input in selecting an MCU—even if your involvement is just a case of "*Hey, Ted, what do you think of this micro for that new project?*", it's on you to arm yourself with enough background knowledge to form an intelligent opinion (or at least ask intelligent questions). This chapter isn't meant to be an exhaustive list with absolutely everything you need to know and consider when selecting hardware for your new project, but it does aim to provide an introduction to many of the contributing factors for differentiating and selecting between MCU devices. The other thing to keep in mind when reading this chapter is that it only applies to deciding between MCUs. As we saw from Chapter 1, *Introducing Real-Time Systems*, there's more than one way to skin a real-time system cat—MCUs aren't *always* the best choice.

In order to limit the scope of this chapter to what is immediately relevant, for the examples presented in the remainder of the book, we'll be limiting our discussion to features found in ARM Cortex-M-based devices. We're focusing on ARM Cortex-M MCUs because the devices based on the Cortex-M core bring a really useful blend of features that enable engineers to create medium to highly complex real-time embedded systems using a **real-time operating system** (**RTOS**), while still being able to architect the solution in such a way that modules are reusable for other projects. STM32 MCUs have been selected because of their popularity, the wide range of MCUs available, their approachable **integrated circuit** (**IC**) packaging, and the included hardware peripherals. While we're focusing on STM32 parts in this chapter, keep in mind that there are plenty of other manufacturers out there with tons of great products and the vast majority of what's covered will apply to non-STM32 (and non-ARM) parts as well.

MCU considerations

There are a few considerations that need to be made into selecting a microcontroller itself, rather than the dev board. Assuming the project contains fully custom electronics, there is no limitation on the exact MCU chosen as there would be if you were only selecting between dev boards. Students and hobbyists sometimes artificially limit themselves even further, sometimes staying loyal to certain ecosystems and only selecting from dev boards within those ecosystems (such as Arduino or mBed). While there is certainly nothing inherently *wrong* with any of the ecosystems, you'll fail to grow as a professional engineer if you're incapable of considering other solutions or appreciating the unique strengths each piece of hardware brings to a particular project.

Core considerations

First, we'll discuss how to address some key questions that will immediately narrow down the field of potential MCU candidates for a project:

- Will it fit?
- Can it run all of my code?
- How much does it cost?
- Is it readily available?

Let's answer these questions one by one.

Physical size

Depending on the design, the MCU's size can be an important factor. If you're developing a wearable or portable device, size is likely to be at the top of your list. Sometimes, pre-packaged MCUs are too large and the designers are required to resort to *chip on board* (where the MCU silicon die is directly bonded to the **printed circuit board** (**PCB**), instead of being placed in a separate plastic package). On the other hand, large pieces of rack-mounted equipment tend to have more than enough space for any size MCU that is suitable to do the job.

A note to those of you who are interested in designing your own hardware—the packaging type will play a role in the PCB complexity as well as the ease of assembly (especially at the prototyping stage). If your prototypes will be hand-assembled, any of the gull-wing packages, such as **quad flat pack** (**QFP**), are the most approachable. After QFPs, **quad flat pack no-lead** (**QFN**) packages are still easily hand soldered. **Ball grid arrays** (**BGAs**) are generally best avoided for hand assembly, unless you're a soldering wizard!

ROM

Read-only memory (ROM) is a fairly large differentiating factor for MCUs in the same family, with ROM size being strongly correlated to price. Depending on the number of different models available in a product family, there could be multiple MCUs with very similar peripheral sets. These MCUs will likely share the same physical footprint but have significantly different amounts of memory. If your application is cost-sensitive but the required ROM is unknown, consider the following approach:

1. Select an MCU family that provides multiple flash sizes in a compatible footprint.
2. Start development with the MCU that has the most ROM in the family. This provides the most flexibility for adding features.
3. After the final image size is known, the exact MCU (with a smaller flash size) can be selected before beginning mass production.

 When taking this approach, you'll need to be sure to leave enough room for future features, assuming your product will be capable of receiving field-updates to its firmware. Also, be sure to double-check peripheral assignments between models—*pin compatible* doesn't always mean *firmware compatible*!

The amount of ROM required varies greatly and is dependent on how much code needs to be loaded onto the device. If you've been working with 8-bit MCUs, then you might be in for a nasty surprise when moving to a 32-bit architecture such as ARM. A similar program will require more flash space to implement on a 32-bit architecture versus an 8-bit architecture. The good news here is that flash sizes have kept up, so it's nearly always possible to find an MCU with enough onboard flash to accommodate your application. Pulling third-party libraries into your code base is generally fairly costly in terms of flash, so be mindful if you choose to go down this route.

RAM

The amount of on-chip **random access memory (RAM)** is another factor to consider—it will generally follow the amount of flash a given device has. Parts with larger ROM will usually have more RAM. A few examples where large amounts of RAM will be required are data processing that requires large buffers for data, complex network stacks, deep buffers for communication, GUIs (especially those that require frame buffers), and any interpreted languages that run a virtual machine (that is, MicroPython and Lua).

For example, let's say your application calls for a high-resolution display. If the display doesn't have an on-board controller with its own frame buffer, you're likely already in external RAM territory. The size buffer required to drive that type of display will likely exceed the RAM available on board the MCU. On the other hand, if you're building a simple control system with limited connectivity and UI capability, then a small amount of RAM may be all that is required.

Also, note that each task in FreeRTOS requires its own stack (generally with a bare minimum of 512 bytes on the Cortex-M port), so if a large number of tasks is required, it will be easy to quickly utilize several KB of RAM.

From a firmware engineer's perspective, external RAM seems like a get-out-of-jail-free card (who wouldn't want to increase the available RAM by nearly an order of magnitude)—but all of that functionality does come at a cost. Unless your system absolutely requires it, external RAM on the MCU's address/data bus is best avoided. It will require additional PCB real estate, consume more power, and ultimately, drive up PCB and bill of materials (**BOM**) costs. The PCB layout can be considerably more complicated when adding an external high-speed parallel bus used for accessing an external RAM because of length-tuning requirements and the number of signals involved. The design will also be more likely to emit EMI because of all the high-speed signals. Although it offers plenty of space, external RAM is often marginally slower than on-board RAM, which can lead to a more complex linker file (if certain functions have very tight timing constraints). Other factors worthy of consideration include properly setting up RAM timing parameters and caching coherency issues if you attempt to speed up access to external RAM by using data caching (refer to *Further reading* section for details).

With all of its downsides, having external RAM enables a lot of functionality, such as the ability to cache entire firmware images in RAM for upgrades, feature-rich GUI frameworks, complex networking stacks, and sophisticated signal processing techniques. As with any other requirement, there are trade-offs to be made.

The CPU clock rate

Since we're limiting our discussion to MCUs with the same underlying architecture, an MCU with a faster core clock rate will execute the same set of pure software functions faster than one with a slower clock rate. Notice the keyword *pure* in the previous statement—sometimes, there are on-board hardware peripherals that can make a huge difference to execution speed that have nothing to do with the CPU clock rate (such as the hardware floating point and DSP functionality available on the Cortex-M4 core).

Another thing to be mindful of is the absolute maximum clock rate of the device versus the practical clock rate for an application. For example, some MCUs' maximum clock frequency is incompatible with generating an internal 48 MHz clock required for a USB peripheral, so it can't be used at maximum speed if the USB peripheral is also used.

Interrupt processing

Within the ARM Cortex-M family, interrupt processing is all very similar. All of the devices include a **nested vector interrupt controller** (**NVIC**) with a relocatable vector table and an **external interrupt controller** (**EXTI**). Device-specific considerations include the exact peripheral interrupts that are available and how they are mapped to the NVIC, as well as how external interrupts are multiplexed into the EXTI.

Price

Depending on the application, the BOM's cost may be a significant driver or hardly a consideration. Generally, BOM costs come under increasing scrutiny in high-volume applications. However, with lower volume products, it is often wise to focus more on minimizing the development time and effort of a product, rather than achieving the lowest BOM cost possible. By focusing on minimizing the amount of engineering effort and development time for a low-volume product, the product will get to market sooner. Not only does the product start generating revenue faster, but it also accrues less **non-recurring engineering** (**NRE**) costs. Less NRE leads to a faster **return on investment** (**ROI**) for the product being developed. Faster ROI ultimately makes managers and CEOs really happy! In these situations, worrying about spending a few dollars on a BOM for a product selling dozens per year—at the expense of weeks or months of development effort—is rarely a wise trade-off.

Availability

An often-overlooked aspect of an MCU by junior engineers is its expected and guaranteed availability. Just because a part is available for purchase at the beginning of the project does not mean it will be available for the entire time that the end product will be sold. In the case of consumer devices, this probably isn't a huge issue. This is because these devices can have extremely high volumes, but any single revision is only in production for a limited amount of time (from months to a year or two).

Contrast the consumer electronics mindset of planned obsolescence with something on the industrial, telecom, or aerospace side. In these industries, development timelines can be measured in years and required support periods are often a decade or more. This is why part availability is a very real consideration. Be sure to investigate the manufacture guarantees on availability and weigh these against their history, reputation, and the risk to the project—it's not a pleasant experience to get 80% of a design complete only to find out that the MCU can't be sourced during a pre-production run!

Now that we've covered some of the initial considerations to be aware of, we'll move on to some of the more unique considerations for embedded processors—hardware peripherals.

Hardware peripherals

Compared to the desktop world of CPUs, where the processor itself is generally the center of attention, selecting the *right* MCU is more complex due to the increase in scope. Many different pieces of hardware are included on the same chip, which enables us to optimize the solution for speed, power, CPU utilization, or BOM cost. In a highly constrained design, all of these factors can come into play and trade-offs will need to be made.

This section will cover some of the hardware peripherals commonly available on Cortex-M-based MCUs and aims to provide an extremely brief introduction to them, with the goal of informing you why each type of peripheral may be helpful to have in a design.

Connectivity

In today's ever-increasingly connected ecosystem of the **Internet of Things (IoT)**, having on-board networking capability on the MCU can be a boon to a project. . . as long as the right firmware exists to drive it. It is important to realize that having a peripheral is not the same as having full functionality. For example, just because an MCU supports a **reduced media independent interface (RMII)** and a **physical layer in networking (PHY)** does not mean you can immediately get a full TCP/IP stack—all of that firmware functionality needs to come from somewhere. Potential connectivity baked into devices can include Ethernet, RMII, 802.11 (WiFi), 802.15.1 (Bluetooth), and 802.15.4 (Zigbee, HART, and so on).

When it comes to wireless communications, things get a bit more complex, since the product will need to be pushed through an approval process from the appropriate agency, depending on geographic location. Pre-certified **radio frequency (RF)** modules can be used to minimize the amount of effort and cost to develop a properly certified end product.

Due to a specialized PCB layout, regulatory requirements, and complex network stacks, on-board MCU peripherals that facilitate wireless communications aren't quite as useful as they first appear for a low-volume product. Again, don't be lulled into a false sense of accomplishment by simply specifying a part that has hardware available, since wireless communication stacks can be extremely complex and wireless certification testing is expensive.

Memory protection units

Memory protection units (**MPUs**) are used to ensure that code only accesses the range of RAM it is permitted to. When used correctly, MPUs ensure greater system stability and increased security, since the application is less likely to cause unintended consequences by accessing memory it shouldn't.

 FreeRTOS includes support for MPU-protected tasks, which we'll cover in Chapter 15, *FreeRTOS Memory Management*.

Hardware floating-point units

If your application is going to be crunching lots of floating point numbers, a **hardware floating-point unit** (**FPU**) can be extremely helpful. Until the past decade or so, floating point numbers were generally best avoided in most MCU-based embedded systems. The availability of faster processors started to change this. Now, FPUs are often implemented in hardware. Thanks to FPUs, many different applications can benefit from using floating point math, without incurring the CPU performance penalty commonly associated with software-based library implementations.

Single-precision (32-bit) FPUs are optional on Cortex-M4 processors, while Cortex-M7-based processors add optional hardware support for double-precision (64-bit) floating point arithmetic.

Digital signal processing functions

Along with increased performance from hardware-based, floating point support, the Cortex-M4- and Cortex-M7-based MCUs also have optional **digital signal processing** (**DSP**) functionality baked into the hardware, which can greatly accelerate some complex algorithms and potentially help reduce the coding burden for firmware engineers.

Direct memory access channels

Direct memory access (DMA) can be extremely useful in a variety of situations where high bandwidth or highly event-driven code is desired. DMA controllers are typically able to interact with MCU peripherals, as well as different parts of RAM. They take care of populating peripheral registers and RAM without involving the CPU at all. These autonomous transfers can free up significant CPU time by greatly reducing the interrupt load and context switching.

One thing to keep in mind regarding DMA peripherals is that all channels aren't always mapped to all peripherals. Certain channels can be of a higher bandwidth than others. This is most significant in systems that require multiple high-bandwidth devices. For challenging systems such as these, it is important for firmware and hardware engineers to work together to ensure that a hardware design doesn't cause a handicap for firmware down the road.

Communication interfaces

We've already introduced external network connectivity relative to Ethernet and wireless technologies. There are many different communication interfaces that are more traditionally associated with embedded devices and are commonly available as hardware peripherals on an MCU. The interfaces that are used for communicating with on- and off-board sensors and actuators are as follows:

- **Inter-IC Communication (I2C)**
- **Serial peripheral interface (SPI)**
- **Universal Synchronous/Asynchronous Receiver Transmitter (USART)**

The following peripherals are regularly used in automotive and industrial environments for inter-module communication:

- **USARTs**
- **Controller area network (CAN)**
- **Local interconnect network (LIN)**

Hardware crypto engines

If your application calls for external connectivity, then your mind should also be focused on security. In the same way that FPUs make floating point operations more CPU efficient, hardware-based cryptography engines are available on some MCUs, which will greatly reduce the CPU burden required to securely transfer data over public networks.

Timing hardware

There are often several different timing peripherals included on an MCU. The peripherals themselves will often include input capture, output compare, and **pulse width modulation (PWM)** functionality as a minimum. Some devices will also include timing hardware for interfacing with quadrature encoders.

Input capture deals with *capturing* the time a digital input to the MCU changes state. MCU peripherals do this with a much higher resolution than firmware because they use high-frequency counters and hardware gates to capture the signal transition (rather than relying on multiple CPU instructions). There are often several channels of input capture available, which can be used in parallel. Output compare is effectively the reverse of input capture (a signal is output with precise timing characteristics)—*compare* refers to the hardware comparator used to determine when to perform the transition.

PWM and input capture are both very commonly used in control systems to interact with sensors and actuators. Some actuators will take PWM as inputs. PWM can also be used to provide proportional control of a binary driver (such as a transistor), which can be used to precisely change the amount of power delivered to a load. Many different encoders will often supply information in PWM format as well, which can be read by the MCU using a timer peripheral's input capture mode.

Quadrature encoder inputs (QEIs) are extremely useful in motion feedback systems. Although similar functionality can be achieved using multiple channels of input capture (or slowly, without any dedicated hardware), having dedicated QEI hardware allows for very minimal CPU intervention, even at high input rates.

Integrated analog

Digital to Analog Converters (DACs) and **Analog to Digital Converters** (ADCs) are used when converting between continuously varying analog values and associated digital representations of that value. Most often, these types of on-board peripherals will be lower resolution and lower frequency than what you'll find with external chips. However, depending on the requirements of your system, they can be extremely useful. Another useful peripheral is on-board comparators, which will signal the processor when an analog value is above or below a given threshold.

Some more specialized devices (for example, Cypress PSoC) include fully reconfigurable analog peripherals (including op-amps, DACs, and ADCs) as well as flexible digital peripherals, flexibly integrating a very large feature set into a signal chip. Analog Devices and Maxim offer some of the more exotic mixed-signal MCUs, which tend to integrate application-specific components onto the same chip as the MCU, making development for a specific end product easier. You can find a very wide range of application-specific MCUs aimed at everything from industrial process control, automotive distance sensing, and IoT sensors to TV remote control applications.

If there is a popular use case for a mixed-signal problem, chances are, there is also a fully integrated piece of silicone that integrates an MCU with most of the required analog frontend available to solve most of the problem. The question then becomes one of balancing the BOM cost, detailed specifications, the size, development time, and long-term sourcing risk mitigation.

Dedicated touch interfaces

Thanks to the increased prevalence of touch interfaces, full implementations of touch controllers are now included on some MCUs. This can greatly reduce the amount of expertise and effort required to have a fully functional and robust touch interface implementation.

Display interfaces

Generally found in higher performance devices with larger pin counts, sophisticated display interfaces and even graphics acceleration are becoming fairly common. Expect to find parallel LCD/TFT interfaces (for example, 6800 and 8080) on a large number of parts, with interfaces such as MIPI DSI capable of driving inexpensive, high-resolution displays to displays with only a few lines. Hardware protocol conversion ICs can be used to adapt to a number of different display standards, such as LVDS and HDMI. MCUs are now capable of delivering a rich user experience, with added hardware acceleration and efficiently written middleware and drivers. The CPU load is perfectly tolerable as well.

External memory support

In higher pin count packages, expect to find support for **static random access memory (SRAM)**. **Synchronous dynamic random access memory (SDRAM)** support, with an on-board controller taking care of the tight timing requirements and refresh cycles, can be found in higher performance devices. Devices aimed at performance will generally bring in support for quad-SPI. Often, external RAM—and even quad-SPI devices—can be memory-mapped and used similar to internal storage, albeit with a performance hit. Many devices have **MultiMediaCard (MMC)** and **secure digital card (SD card)** controllers as well, so commodity consumer-grade removable storage is easily added.

Real-time clock

Hardware calendars are available on some devices as well; all that is needed is a 32 kHz crystal and a back-up power source, such as a CR2032 primary lithium battery. Something that is also generally offered with this capability is a limited amount of battery backed-up RAM.

Audio support

High-fidelity audio support through **Inter-IC Sound** (I^2S) is commonly available. Expect to find DMA channels attached to the I^2S peripheral to minimize the amount of CPU intervention required for feeding data-hungry DACs and collecting data from ADCs on these buses.

This concludes our long list of hardware peripherals to look out for when evaluating MCUs. Next up is a topic that will be of specific interest to anyone interested in designing battery-or energy-harvesting devices: power consumption.

Power consumption

Lower-power MCUs have been the trend for well over a decade. However, what was historically a specialized use case with limited options (such as the 16-bit MSP430) has now become mainstream, thanks to the plethora of battery-powered, IoT-based devices coming onto the market. Now, full 32-bit MCUs are available, which can quickly cycle between low deep sleep and high-clockrate, data-crunching run modes.

Power efficiency

It may sound simple, but a fairly good way of making sure something draws less power is to turn it off (don't laugh—this can be surprisingly complicated depending on the parts involved, thanks to various leakage currents!). If complex MCUs with dozens of peripherals have any hope of being power efficient, there needs to be a way to turn off whatever functionality isn't required to minimize wasted power. This is typically accomplished by shutting off clocks to peripherals that aren't in use and ensuring that CMOS-based I/O pins are not floating (remember, it's the transitions in CMOS devices that draw the most power).

Another spec that is commonly found in datasheets is how much power is consumed per MHz of CPU clock—generally specified in µA/MHz. If the amount of processing per wake-up period is fairly constant, this provides another metric to compare different MCU models.

Low-power modes

Devices that are aimed at lower-power applications will typically have a few different levels of shutdown states to choose from. These states will allow the programmer to trade off between current consumption, available features (such as keeping RAM content intact and some peripherals on), the number of interrupts available to trigger a wake-up event, and the wake-up time. Thankfully, many lower-power IoT applications are fairly limited in their scope of operations, so sometimes a combination of novel features in a particular MCU will prove to be a very good fit for a specific application.

Wake-up time

If a device has an amazingly low shutdown current, but takes an abnormally long time to *wakeup* and get itself into a usable running state, it might not be the best choice for an application that requires fairly frequent wake-ups, since significant time will be spent getting the system up and running instead of getting it to perform the necessary processing and then going back to sleep.

Power supply voltage

Lower power supply voltages will typically lead to lower current consumption. Depending on the design, trade-offs can be made between eliminating power conditioning circuitry (which consumes current due to less than 100% efficiency) and extending the usable operating voltage range of a given battery cell. The MCU's voltage requirement (as well as any ancillary circuitry) will be a driving factor for how much flexibility there is on the regulation side. Also, be aware that the maximum clock typically scales with supply voltage as well, so don't expect to be able to drive the CPU at the maximum specified frequency and lowest possible supply voltage.

Migrating MCUs mid-project

Occasionally, 100% of the project requirements won't be known up front, or everyone might not be 100% confident about how exactly to solve every detailed problem on day 1. If you happen to be fortunate enough to know that there is a high level of uncertainty, then it is always better to plan for it, rather than be caught by surprise. Here are a few areas where selecting an MCU that's part of a larger family or ecosystem can help to mitigate some of the risks associated with project uncertainty.

Importance of pin compatibility

When planning for a potential MCU shift, if possible, identify alternative MCUs that are pin-compatible ahead of time. For example, the NXP LPC1850's parts are pin-compatible with LPC 4350 MCUs. STM32 devices are all pin-compatible within a family (and package) but will occasionally be *almost* pin-compatible with other families as well (STM32M4 and STM32M7, for example). ST regularly publishes migration guides for engineers that have *outgrown* one MCU family and need something a bit more capable. If a few likely candidates and alternatives are selected up front, some simple jumper populations on the PCB may facilitate migration between different MCUs with significantly different performance (and cost), helping to eliminate the time required for PCB reworking mid-project.

Peripheral similarity

Most MCUs, within a given family, will inherit the same peripheral IP. Silicon vendors don't necessarily redesign peripherals from scratch every time they create a new MCU family, so there is often a significant amount of overlap in the register maps and behavior for peripherals belonging to a given vendor. Often, if your applications only use a subset of the most basic peripheral functions, to begin with, you might be lucky enough to use largely the same driver, even if the vendor decides to drastically change their API between MCU families. Ironically, sometimes, the raw hardware proves to be more consistent over time than the abstraction layers above it.

The concept of an MCU family

Many silicon vendors have concepts of device families, and **STMicroelectronics** (**STM**) is no exception—datasheets are typically written for entire families of devices. The most notable differences between devices in an STM family are typically RAM/ROM and the package size. However, additional peripherals are added to more capable devices as well—for example, larger packages will start to include parallel RAM controllers. Devices with more RAM/ROM will include more capable timer peripherals, more comm peripherals, or domain-specific peripherals, such as cryptographic modules.

Moving between devices in a given device family should be easy to do, so it is advisable to start on one end of the family (high is usually advisable) and see where the project goes. If scope creep was kept to a minimum, it may be possible to painlessly downgrade the MCU after all of the major features have been developed, saving some BOM cost.

That wraps up our list of considerations for the raw MCU. However, going out and buying a single chip and letting it sit on a desk won't do us much good for writing firmware. We need a way of powering the device, and communicating with it—we need a dev board!

Development board considerations

A dev board is any piece of hardware that engineers use during the early development phase of a project. Dev boards aren't just for MCUs; they are useful for many different types of hardware—anything from op-amps to **field-programmable gat arrays** (**FPGAs**).

MCU dev boards should provide a few key functions:

- Ancillary circuitry, required to power and run the MCU
- A way to program and communicate with the MCU
- Connectors for easy connection to external circuitry
- Possibly, some useful on-board ICs to exercise some of the peripherals

There are many different routes that can be taken when it comes to evaluating MCUs. We're currently enjoying a period of time where hardware is inexpensive and commonly available. Because of this, there are a plethora of options to choose from for evaluating hardware. There are three major groupings that a piece of prototyping hardware tends to fall into, each of which has strengths and weaknesses. Of course, you can also roll your own dev board or prototype, if you have specific requirements.

What a development platform is and why it matters

For our purposes, a development platform is an ecosystem of products that allows for a high degree of abstraction across multiple vendors. The primary focus of a platform is delivering large amounts of functionality with the smallest amount of effort possible, which is excellent when the main purpose is to create a prototype as quickly as possible.

In order to deliver large amounts of functionality across multiple vendors, standardized interfaces, ease of use, and flexibility tends to be emphasized. With these values, the platform itself is what the focal point is (as it should be) and individual differentiating features of particular devices tend to go largely unnoticed, that is, unless you're interested in coding them specifically, which takes additional time and ends up requiring you to put more focus into developing *for* the platform instead of *with* the platform.

Ecosystems develop around platforms, gently guiding platform users into tooling, workflows, least-common denominator feature sets, and available hardware. This is all well and good if the goal is to produce a proof-of-concept in the least amount of time possible. However, if a long-term development and production-worthy solution is to be found using the platform approach, the platform will likely need to be high quality, extremely well established, and stable. This generally means using platforms based on industrial standards available from multiple vendors (such as SMARC, QSeven, and COM Express), rather than the current "flavor of the year" in the maker space:

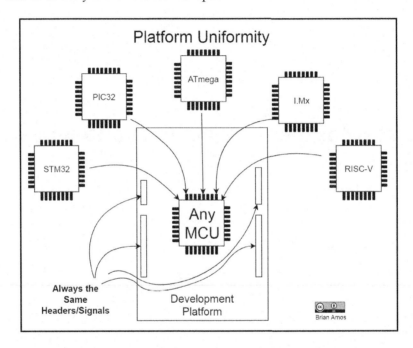

The bottom line is that a platform's interest is generally making the platform easy to use so that it gains further adoption. This accessibility can lead to common interfaces (as seen in the preceding diagram), which can be a boon to productivity during fast prototyping efforts but abstract away considerable differences in the underlying hardware. Often, platform-specific functionality is so important that the platform code will simply virtualize interfaces to make them more accessible, often at very significant costs (that is, bit-banging PWM or SPI so they can be assigned to specific predetermined pins). So, if you choose to use a platform to evaluate hardware (or specifically, an MCU), you should realize that you're likely evaluating the platform and its implementation on a given piece of hardware, rather than the hardware itself.

Evaluation kits

An **evaluation kit** (**eval kit**) is at the other end of the spectrum when it comes to standardized footprints versus focus on the hardware itself. Eval kits are generally outfitted with the biggest, most feature-filled model of MCU available and are made with the sole intent of *showing off* that piece of hardware. This means they will generally not share a common footprint or connectors between different target MCUs (refer to the following diagram) because each MCU has different primary features and is targeted at a different market. Eval boards will have as many peripherals broken out to actual connectors as possible (such as serial, Ethernet, SD cards, a CAN bus, and multiple USBs). They also typically include a slew of peripheral hardware, such as RAM, eMMC, buttons, sliders, potentiometers, displays, and audio codecs to drive speakers. They will almost always break out all the interesting MCU pins to easily accessible headers, so developers are able to quickly try out any specific hardware configuration they can dream up. Manufacturers typically showcase their other non-MCU silicons on eval kit boards as well, in an effort to drive more sales in relation to their own products:

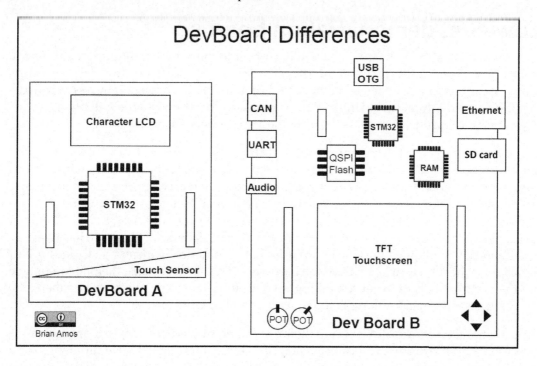

To best demonstrate a device's capabilities, eval kits will also ship with a plethora of working example code that allows an engineer to interact with all of the peripherals included. Unlike the generalized implementations you'd generally find with a platform-based implementation, these examples are tailored to demonstrate the unique differentiating features of the target device to be evaluated. In the first part of this chapter, we discussed choosing hardware based on specific use cases. If you're seeking a specific solution to a challenging aspect of a design, the importance of having a guided example to working code that exemplifies the key differentiating aspects of an MCU can be a serious timesaver (and eye opener) compared to having to implement all of those features from scratch yourself.

All of this functionality comes at a cost—full-blown eval kits typically cost a few hundred dollars. However, if your goal is to quickly evaluate a potential MCU with a specific purpose in mind, they can quickly pay for themselves by saving engineering time and mitigating risk.

Low-cost demonstration boards

Low-cost demonstration boards have really come into their own in recent years. Prices have come down significantly; manufacturers will occasionally sell demonstration boards for the same cost as the bare IC that sits on them (occasionally, they were actually *less* expensive than buying individual ICs!). Unlike hardware platforms, these boards will often have *similar* footprints, but not necessarily the same connectors or pinouts.

Recently, more low-cost demonstration boards that blur the line between platforms and demonstration boards (also called demo boards) have come to the market. Thanks to the ubiquity of Arduino®, most low-cost boards will have at least a set of Arduino headers that are pin-compatible. However, the availability of compatible headers and having a development board that fully embraces an ecosystem are very different things. The demo board may not have any software to accompany those headers; just because hardware exists and can be plugged into the board does not automatically mean you'll get compatible libraries for the target MCU to drive the hardware. This doesn't make them incompatible, but the amount of effort to get something up and running will be much greater than simply plugging a board in and following along with a "hello world" demo.

Some manufacturers are also creating their own standardized headers that are common between demo boards, which is at least helpful when migrating between different product families (but is obviously limited to that manufacturer). The ST Nucleo and NXP Freedom standardized headers are some examples. In an attempt to become more user-friendly, these boards will also typically feature mBed compatibility.

Now that you've been introduced to the different types of development boards, we'll take a more detailed look at a single manufacturer's microcontroller line—the STM32 line.

Introducing the STM32 product line

Over the past several years, STM has developed a fairly wide range of MCUs. Here, we'll discuss how a few of the major swaths of that portfolio fall into place relative to the considerations discussed in the *MCU considerations* section of this chapter . Most other vendors also arrange their products into major segments as well, which tends to make the selection process a bit easier.

Mainstream

The STM32 line started with the STM32F1, a Cortex-M3-based MCU, back in 2007. This portion of the product line is meant to serve the majority of high volume applications, where cost and performance must be balanced, with minimally complex applications. The STM32F0 and the STM32G0 portions of the line are Cortex-M0- and Cortex-M0+-based devices that are aimed at low-cost applications. The original STM32F1 is Cortex-M3-based and has a very wide range of feature sets, but is starting to show its age when its performance is compared to other devices.

The STM32F3 was STM's first attempt at providing integrated, higher precision analog peripherals (other vendors offer higher precision analog components than STM); however, the line falls short of offering truly high-performance analog. It includes a 16-bit sigma delta ADC, but the **effective number of bits (ENOB)** is only stated to be 14 bits, which is slightly better than STM's 12-bit **successive approximation (SAR)** ADC peripherals, which are included most often. The newer Cortex-M4+-based STM32G4 family has the most analog peripherals available, including many instances of **programmable gain op-amps (PGA)**, DACs, ADCs, and several comparators, but there are no integrated high-precision ADCs available at the time of writing.

Look out for the STM32G0 and STM32G4 families increasing the breadth of their offerings through 2020—they are both newer lines and STM will likely start filling these out with many more devices.

High performance

High-performance MCUs from STM started with the Cortex-M4-based STM32F4. The Cortex-M4 is very similar to the Cortex-M3, but it includes (optional) hardware 32-bit FPU and DSP instructions, which are both present on all STM3F4 devices. All of the devices in the high-performance line are capable of comfortably driving very attractive GUIs on controllerless displays, as long as the required RAM is available (usually external to the MCU). Acceleration provided by various hardware peripherals (such as MIPI **Display Serial Interface (DSI)**, memory transfers via FMC and DMA, and some basic graphics acceleration using the **Chrom-Adaptive Real-Time (Chrom-ART)** accelerator) make it possible to off-load a fair amount of the effort involved with communicating with the display to various peripherals so that the CPU can spend time performing other tasks.

Here's a quick breakdown of the two major members of the family and some notable features:

MCU line	CPU	Features
STM32H7	Cortex-M7 (480 MHz) Cortex-M4 (240 MHz) (opt)	Highest performance MCU from STM 64-bit FPU and extended DSP instructions
STM32F7	Cortex-M7 (216 MHz)	64-bit FPU and extended DSP instructions
STM32F2	Cortex-M3	Offers trade-off for performance versus cost High level of integration (camera interface and USB OTG)

This class of MCU can be thought of as *crossover* MCUs. They are powerful enough that they can be used for some application tasks that were traditionally reserved for full-blown CPUs, but they still have the ease of use of an MCU.

The heterogeneous multi-core approach

In 2019, STM launched the STM32MP line, which was the company's first entry into the application processor space. This family offers a single or dual-core Cortex-A7 at 650 MHz, along with a single Cortex-M4 running at 209 MHz. STM appears to be targeting the high-volume, low-cost portion of the market with these solutions by focusing on a lower core count and packages that require fewer PCB layers using less expensive fabrication techniques.

From a software perspective, the main difference between STM's MCU offerings and the new **micro-processor unit** (**MPU**) is that since the MPUs have **memory management units** (**MMUs**), they are capable of running a *full OS* via mainline Linux kernels, which opens up an entirely different ecosystem of open source software (that you don't personally need to write).

The heterogeneous multi-core approach allows designers to split up portions of a design and solve them in the domain that they are best suited to. For example, a dedicated process controller with a GUI and networking capability could use the Cortex-A7 to leverage Linux and gain access to the Qt framework and complex networking stacks, while using the Cortex-M4 for all of the real-time control aspects.

 Implementations of µClinux have been available for the STM32F4 and STM32F7 MCUs for years, but because of the lack of MMU on these devices, there is typically a pretty hefty performance penalty.

Of course, with additional capability comes additional complexity. Unlike MCUs, there's no way to get around integrating external RAM with the STM32MP line, so be prepared for some fairly involved PCB layout (compared to a stand-alone MCU solution).

Low power

STM's low power line is squarely aimed at battery-powered devices. Here's a quick comparison between all of the different family members:

MCU version	CPU	Description
STM32L	Cortex-M0	Lowest performance and RAM and ROM space of the family, but offers fairly good efficiency.
STM32L1	Cortex-M3	Higher ROM capacity and offers faster performance with the trade-off of increased power consumption.
STM32L4 and STM32L4+	Cortex-M4	Have increased number-crunching capability (the STM32L4+ also offers faster clock speeds and larger internal flash storage).
STM32L5	Cortex-M33	Blends performance and power and incorporates the latest ARM v8 architecture. Cortex-M33 offers additional security features, such as Trust.Zone, and executes instructions more efficiently than Cortex-M4, which allows for some additional performance while still keeping power consumption in check.

Depending on the exact workload of a given IoT application, it may make sense to use a low-power 32-bit MCU, such as the ones in the preceding table. However, for very simple applications, low-power 8- and 16-bit MCUs should also be considered.

Wireless

The STM32WB implements a Cortex-M4 with a dedicated Cortex-M0+ to run a Bluetooth BLE stack. This line provides a lot of integration, from large flash memory and RAM to mixed-signal analog peripherals, including touch sensors and small segment LCDs. Various security features, such as crypto algorithms and a random number generator, are also present. Since FCC certification is required for products using this family of devices, they will make the most sense for high volume applications.

With a wide range of MCUs to choose from, STM *probably* has something we can use to experiment with an RTOS! It's time to move on to selecting a development board to use.

How our development board was selected

Now that we've covered the important considerations for MCU selection and the general types of development hardware, let's see how the development board that will be used in this book was selected. STM is the only manufacturer that we are evaluating in order to limit the examples to something easily digestible. In an actual product engineering effort, it behooves the designer to take a fresh look at all possible vendors. While everybody has their own preferred way of accomplishing cross-vendor searches, an easy way is to use distributor websites.

Thanks to well-curated prototyping-oriented distributor websites (such as Digikey and Mouser), an engineer is able to perform parametric searches and comparisons across many different vendors. One downside to this approach is the searches are limited to whatever product lines that specific distributor carries. Another potential downside is that the parametric search results are at the mercy of the distributor's data entry accuracy and categorization. The upsides to using a distributor website directly are that many different vendors are all in one spot, product availability can be checked immediately, and semi-real-world pricing is easily seen and filtered.

 Pricing from prototyping-oriented distributors is considered *semi-real-world* because oftentimes, after a product goes into full production it is generally more economical to use a quantity-oriented distributor or go directly to the vendor for high volumes.

Requirements

Up to this point, we've covered all of the considerations that go into selecting an MCU for a project at a theoretical level. Now, it's time to put all of that into action and select the MCU that will be used for all of the actual *hands-on* exercises. A few things to keep in mind are as follows:

- We'll be selecting a dev board *and* MCU—therefore, some of the requirements will be aimed at the dev board, which generally isn't a good idea if you're making a product that needs to go into long-term production.
- Requirements are going to be specific to this book—the requirements that make something a good choice for a book probably don't translate to the project you're working on. Obviously, your selection criteria will be tailored to your project.

The must-haves—that is, the *requirements*— are as follows:

- The target MCU on your dev board will be an STM32 Cortex-M-based CPU.
- The target MCU must have a **memory protection unit** (MPU).
- The dev board must have a visible means of displaying status.
- A relatively low cost (such as < USD 50).

The nice-to-haves—that is, the *desirements* needed—are as follows:

- Versatility: It would be nice if the dev board could be used with other hardware.
- Virtual communication over USB available as a debug port.
- Multiple cores.

Requirements justification

We're going to be limiting our search to STM32 parts since that's the example family we're using throughout this book. In `Chapter 15`, *FreeRTOS Memory Management* we'll be covering how to prevent tasks from accessing memory they shouldn't, which will require us to make use of a part with a memory protection unit. One of the goals of this book is to keep hardware interaction as accessible as possible, which leads to the next two requirements: status display and cost.

Some means of displaying *status* will likely translate into a simple LED (ideally multiple). There should be some form of feedback for the programmer to be able to see what's going on at a glance in order to ensure the code is actually doing something. In a real embedded environment, this would likely take the form of additional instrumentation, such as oscilloscopes, logic analyzers, and DMMs. In the spirit of keeping this accessible for as many people as possible, we'll be explicitly avoiding those tools. So, rather than relying on external tools and the debugger alone, we're going to be on the lookout for on-board indicators.

The nice-to-haves aren't hard requirements, but they are desirable qualities the system would possess in a perfect world. Ideally, the target dev board would also be part of a larger hardware ecosystem, which would enable people to use existing hardware they might already have to further explore the concepts in this book. A USB port attached to the target MCU would also be great to have—that way, we would be able to use a virtual comm port to output debug instead of using only the debugger. Finally, in `Chapter 16`, *Multi-Processor and Multi-Core Systems*, we will look at a brief introduction and a few tips on developing our board with multiple CPUs. Although this topic is deserving of its own book (many have already been written from an architectural perspective), it would be nice to have some code that we could put into action on actual hardware.

Choosing the dev board

Alright—we now know what we're looking for, so let's get started! As mentioned before, distributor websites can be a great place to start because they offer excellent parametric search capabilities. If you're a hardware person, using the same search engine will reduce the amount of time spent hunting for parts. Of course, this approach isn't perfect, so if there's a really specific part you're looking for, you might be better off going directly to your favourite manufacturer's site and searching there instead:

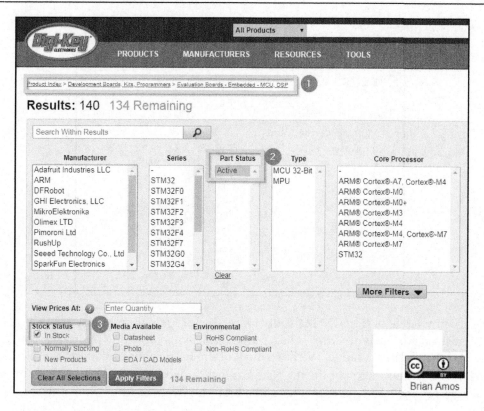

Brian Amos

Here's an example of the steps we've used to narrow down our search using a popular distributor in the United States, DigiKey:

1. From DigiKey's home page, `https://www.digikey.com/`, we've started with a search for STM32 and selected eval boards for the MCUs and DSPs from the selections.
2. We're only interested in parts that are currently available (not obsolete).
3. The dev kit must also be in stock.

Here are the results:

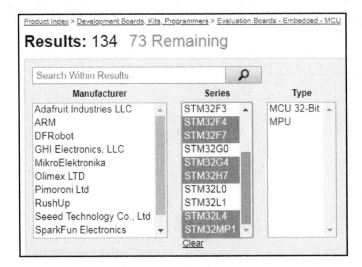

From our knowledge of the STM32 product line, the MCUs with memory protection units have been selected. Currently, this criteria provides 73 available dev platforms, ranging from USD 9-550—quite a range. We have most of the hard requirements covered already—with the exception of the on-board indicator, which isn't likely to show up in a search. Let's see if we can't narrow the field a bit more by including some of the *desirements* as well.

 STM refers to their micro-processors as micro-processor units (MPU), which has created an overloaded term and some ambiguity when also talking about memory protection units (MPU). You'll likely run into both uses of this acronym when browsing websites and documentation.

If we're looking for multiple cores, then the STM32H7 and STM32MP1 lines are valid options. It turns out there are discovery boards with these parts available at a relatively reasonable cost (for what they include) of USD 80, but we're ideally looking for hardware closer to the USD 20 range—let's not let the desirements interfere with the hard requirements!

Narrowing the focus to only the processors that don't violate the pricing requirement of < USD 50 leads us to the STM Nucleo line of dev boards. All of the Nucleo line is mBed-compatible, which will allow the use of that entire ecosystem, should we choose to use it. The other realization that STM had with Nucleo was it was a good idea to support existing popular platforms—so, in addition to breaking out nearly all of the more relevant MCU pins on a proprietary header, Nucleo boards also provide various Arduino-style headers. All Nucleo boards also include an ST-Link on-board programmer, some of which can be re-flashed to appear identical to a SEGGER J-Link , which is a *huge* plus and will eliminate the need to purchase an additional piece of hardware:

Manufacturer part number	Description	Relevant features
NUCLEO-L432KC	Nucl32 platform	Cortex-M4, one user LED, user USB, Arduino Nano v3 compatible, NOT listed as SEGGER J-Link on-board compatible
NUCLEO-F401RE	Nucleo64 platform	Cortex-M4, one user LED, user USB via re-enumeration, Arduino Uno v3 headers, SEGGER J-Link on-board compatible
NUCLEO-L4R5ZI	Nucleo144 platform	Cortex-M4, three user LEDs, a dedicated user USB OTB, ST Morpho, Arduino Uno v3 headers, SEGGER J-Link on-board compatible
NUCLEO-F767ZI	**Nucleo144 platform**	**Cortex-M7, three user LEDs, a dedicated user USB, Ethernet, Arduino Uno v3 headers, SEGGER J-Link on-board compatible**

Our target platform will be the Nucleo-F767ZI, which incorporates the widest range of connectivity and includes the most flexibility for debugging. We'll cover re-flashing the on-board ST-Link to use SEGGER J-Link firmware in Chapter 6, *Debugging Tools for Real-Time Systems*. The three user LEDs will make communicating firmware status feedback very simple since no additional interfaces will need to be configured. Built-in Ethernet allows the development of networked applications. It would have been convenient to have a multi-core MCU for our target platform, but none were available that met our cost requirement:

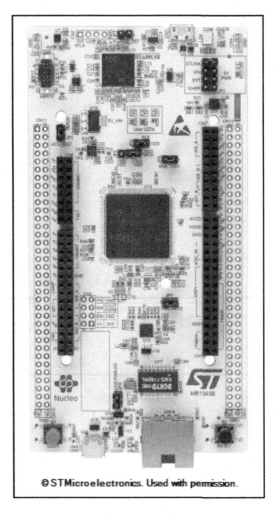

© STMicroelectronics. Used with permission.

Although there are many options when selecting an MCU or development board, it doesn't need to be a daunting process, especially when you know your requirements and the trade-offs to be made.

Summary

This chapter has touched on many considerations for selecting an appropriate MCU and we've explained the selection process by going through the trade-offs made when selecting the dev board used in this book. You should now understand the importance of MCU selection and have enough background to begin researching and selecting MCUs for your projects. If you're part of a multi-disciplinary team, you'll be better positioned to converse with your peers on the trade-offs of using various MCUs for a given application.

In the next chapter, we'll go through a similar exercise, comparing various classes of **Integrated Development Environments (IDEs)** and choose a suitable IDE to code the exercises you'll find in this book, starting with Chapter 7, *The FreeRTOS Scheduler*.

Questions

As we conclude, here is a list of questions for you to test your knowledge regarding this chapter's material. You will find the answers in the *Assessments* section of the Appendix:

1. Why is it important for firmware engineers to be knowledgeable about the MCU they are programming on?
2. When selecting an MCU for performance, clock speed is the only factor at play:
   - True
   - False
3. Today's MCUs contain many different pieces of hardware in addition to the CPU. What is the general name given to these pieces of hardware?
   - Batteries
   - Hardware peripherals
   - Bugs
4. Name one advantage of using a *platform* approach for development.
5. Name one advantage of using a fully featured evaluation board for development.
6. Name two significant device characteristics when designing low-power applications.
7. Why was an inexpensive development board chosen for this book?

Further reading

- AN4839: An STM application note regarding the level 1 cache system on STM32F7 devices: `https://www.st.com/content/ccc/resource/technical/document/application_note/group0/08/dd/25/9c/4d/83/43/12/DM00272913/files/DM0027291 3.pdf/jcr:content/translations/en.DM00272913.pdf`
- More information regarding SEGGER ST-Link on-board: `https://www.segger. com/products/debug-probes/j-link/models/other-j-links/st-link-on- board/`

5
Selecting an IDE

An **integrated development environment** (IDE) has the ability to greatly help or hinder development. Depending on the specific goals of a project, an IDE could prove extremely easy to integrate into a workflow or simply get in the way. IDEs are designed to have a small learning curve and will often offer an easy way to build solutions from existing drivers and middleware.

In this chapter, we'll be discussing how to select an IDE, taking a look at the different types of IDEs, and selecting one to use to create all of the source code you'll find in the code pack used in this book.

Here's a quick list of the main topics we will cover:

- The IDE selection criteria
- Platform-abstracted IDEs
- Open source/free IDEs
- Proprietary IDEs
- Selecting the IDE for this book

Technical requirements

There are no software or hardware requirements for this chapter (software will be installed toward the end).

The IDE selection criteria

The decision to select an IDE can take place at many different levels of an organization. A single engineer may be using the IDE for just one project. In this case, they're likely to simply select whatever they're familiar with or whatever happens to ship with the **microcontroller unit** (**MCU**) for that project. At the other end of the spectrum, an entire department could be integrating the IDE into their development workflow. In this case, the decision could affect dozens of engineers and address multiple target platforms for years down the road.

Some engineers prefer no IDE at all—instead, they'll pull together their favourite text editor and a command-line compiler or linker (such as GCC or Clang), handcraft some makefiles, and set off with coding. This is a perfectly valid approach, too—it will result in a great amount of flexibility and less dependence on proprietary tools and should certainly be considered.

The list of IDEs in the following sections is not meant to be exhaustive. The list is presented in order to provide examples of the wide variety of IDEs available and the different focal points of each. Here are some quick points to consider:

- **Language support**: Not everything on an embedded MCU is written in C99 (or assembly) anymore; there are many language options out there.
- **Debugging support**: Unless you plan on context-switching to a different tool each time, debugging is necessary. Your IDE should have some debugging capability. Many IDEs will rely on the **GNU Debugger** (**GDB**) for the underlying debug protocol, which means they should be compatible with any debug hardware that supports a GDB interface.
- **Thread-aware debugging**: Ideally, the IDE will have thread-aware debug capability. Remember, each task has its own stack. By default, most debug capabilities will only show the stack associated with the current program counter, which becomes problematic when attempting to analyze any task that isn't currently running.
- **Device support**: Pick an IDE that can be made aware of hardware registers in your device (unless you won't be debugging with it).
- **The platform OS**: That is, Windows, Linux, or macOS—you can always run a virtual machine, but it is generally more convenient to run the IDE natively on your preferred OS.

- **Cost**: The initial cost of a tool should take into account both the monetary price and the amount of time it would take to integrate the tool into your team's workflow. This initial cost is tightly coupled with the current state of an organization/individual. For example, the cost (in time) of getting a familiar IDE up and running is generally very low, but this cost is dependent on what is familiar to the team. A high total cost of ownership can be caused by a number of different factors. Some IDEs are freely available but have volatile availability (vendor-supplied IDEs often fall into this category). If an IDE has many bugs, the cost of ownership may be high because of lost productivity. Finally, paid proprietary solutions often require annual maintenance agreements for support, updates for the latest hardware, and new versions.

- **Integration with other tools**: There are many components that make up developing an embedded system. Having an IDE that integrates as much as possible is helpful, but some of the items to consider are the target hardware, test fixtures, debugging hardware, RTOS firmware, user firmware, target middleware, ancillary host software to help configure hardware (that is, STM32Cube), software to help you analyze and debug code (that is, static analysis tools), and testing frameworks.

- **Usability**: Ideally, an IDE will provide a pleasant environment to code in and boost productivity by making code creation easier through automating cross-references (such as IntelliSense).

- **Availability**: In a perfect world, the original IDE would be available, fully supported, and provide updates to make the most of new hardware targets throughout the entire lifetime of a product or project. For long-term projects, it is a good idea to check the history (and licensing model) of the IDE you are planning to use. If the IDE is only available via subscription (with no perpetual licensing option), there could come a day when it is simply no longer available. Ensuring a perpetual license is always on hand enables you to run the IDE indefinitely and gives you the assurance that you'll always be able to reproduce binaries from source code.

- **The eco-system**: Most IDEs come with more than just the IDE itself. They'll have plugins, middleware, forums, and sometimes entire communities of developers with them.

In the next sections, we'll cover a few different conceptual groups of IDEs. Grouping IDEs in this way isn't especially rigid, but it does help to frame expectations of what their motivations and use cases are. Sometimes, an IDE can be placed into more than one group, which is also perfectly acceptable. The groups we'll use to categorize the IDEs are as follows:

- Free MCU vendor IDEs and hardware-centric IDEs
- Platform-abstracted IDEs
- Open source/free IDEs
- Proprietary IDEs

The example IDEs presented in this chapter date to 2019. While embedded system firmware development tools don't change quite as quickly as other software disciplines, expect the landscape to look a bit different over time!

Free MCU vendor IDEs and hardware-centric IDEs

These days, larger MCU manufacturers will generally provide access to a free IDE to help lower the barriers to entry for potential developers. Historically, these IDEs didn't offer much more than a compiler and were generally pretty terrible to work with if you were using them daily. However, in the past few years, there's been a shift to higher quality vendor-supplied IDEs, as chip manufacturers try to differentiate themselves from their competitors. Sometimes, they have extra features integrated that will help configure hardware and/or vendor-supplied drivers, which can be helpful during hardware development, initial board bring-up, and early firmware development, where hardware peripherals are being exercised and integrated with the rest of the system.

Since these tools aren't the core business concern of a hardware manufacturer, they will often be changed on a whim. This makes vendor IDEs a risky choice for long-running projects.

Almost to prove this point, STM changed their IDE offerings while this book was being written. All of the examples needed to be imported into the new software: STM32CubeIDE.

Since we'll be using an STM32 MCU for our target, we'll take a look at the IDE supplied by STM (at the time of writing, this is STM32CubeIDE). For each of the different MCU vendors, you could consider their proprietary IDE—for example, if you were developing on NXP MCUs, you would likely consider MCUXpresso.

STM32CubeIDE

In the case of STM, there are multiple IDEs offered by the same MCU vendor. Sometime after acquiring Atollic, STM rolled in a fully-customized version of Atollic TrueStudio with their STMCubeMX application, resulting in STM32CubeIDE. Although Atollic TrueStudio is still available, it is deprecated and not recommended for new designs.

Here are the quick stats for STM32CubeIDE:

Website	https://www.st.com/en/development-tools/stm32cubeide.html
Host OS	Windows, Linux, or macOS
Debugger support	GDB, STLink, JLink, JTrace, and more
IDE framework	Eclipse
Compiler	GCC, extensible
Cost	Free
License type	Proprietary—freeware

Now that we've looked at the IDEs designed with only one MCU in mind, we'll take a look at the polar opposite to vendor-supplied IDEs: platform-abstracted IDEs.

Platform-abstracted IDEs

The combination of increasingly complex MCUs, ballooning expectations of device functionality, and shrinking development cycles has pushed many software tooling companies to focus on creating abstractions above the hardware, which is meant to make the development of complex devices easier and faster. The most successful platforms and abstractions tend to take on a life of their own after a few years on the market. Mbed and Arduino both have extensive user communities, with many user-created websites and blogs dedicated to each platform.

Because platform consistency is paramount for ease of use, implementations will often include many features that focus on ease of use, sometimes at the expense of performance and good design practice. For example, some hardware targets will expose an API for something such as a PWM output, even though the underlying MCU hardware has no peripheral that supports that functionality. This creates a faster prototyping experience across many different hardware targets, since the API will seamlessly map the functionality to a software routine. However, device performance can be negatively impacted as a result. Sometimes the programmer isn't even aware of the complex trade-offs that are being made underneath the simple API calls they're making.

There are many different contributing factors that determine whether or not it is a good idea to base a project around a platform.

Designing on top of a platform could be good in the following cases:

- **The platform has nearly everything you'll need included with it**: If the platform already has all the major pieces, there is little uncertainty; all that is required is some domain-specific code.
- **Your intended target device has a development board that meets your exact requirements**: This results in less uncertainty than attempting to add many missing subcircuits and properly integrate them with existing platform code.
- **Most engineers on the team already have deep experience with the platform**: *Deep* experience means they have added capability similar to any customizations the project requires.

Designing on top of a platform could be bad in the following cases:

- **Few team members have experience with the desired platform**: Some are more complex than others—not having someone with first-hand experience can be risky.
- **The MCU you intend to use is not already supported by the platform**: There are often many ancillary requirements for adding MCU support to a platform that add no value to your project. Adding support for a new device to an existing complex platform will require more effort for a very simple project than creating the project on top of bare metal or with minimal vendor-supplied libraries.
- **Black box debugging is difficult**: As an embedded engineer moves further away from hardware, it becomes increasingly difficult to understand why the system is behaving the way it is, especially when there are multiple layers of **other people's code** (**OPC**) to dig through.

A young, real-time embedded engineer's professional development can be severely hampered by investing too much time and energy into platforms early on. With all of this additional complexity, there is additional risk and uncertainty around whether deadlines will be met reliably in a real-time system. Digging into a complex code base to try and track down a complex intermittent bug can be a real challenge. This challenge becomes even larger when a solid foundation of low-level knowledge isn't there to draw upon.

In the next couple of sections, we'll cover a few options for platform-abstracted IDEs.

ARM Mbed Studio

ARM Mbed is an IoT-focused platform that provides a very large middleware library and a consistent development environment across many different hardware vendors. Originally, the Mbed platform was only available through a website, but they have now added Mbed Studio—an offline IDE available for Windows and macOS.

Here are the quick stats for ARM Mbed Studio:

Website	https://os.mbed.com/studio/
Host OS	Windows, macOS, or online (Mbed online)
Debugger support	pyOCD for limited graphical debugging or GDB (console only)
IDE framework	Theia
Compiler	ARM Compiler 6, GCC, and IAR
Cost	Free
License type	Apache 2.0

Since Mbed is platform-oriented, projects can be set up with the Mbed IDE, then exported to various offline IDEs, such as ARM Keil uVision, or makefile based projects, which import to Eclipse and Visual Studio Code. If your project requires the functionality provided by the included middleware and it is well implemented, not needing to re-invent the wheel can be a serious timesaver.

Arduino IDE

The Arduino platform is an extremely pervasive platform with a huge ecosystem of hardware and software. Generally used to introduce newcomers to electronics and programming, the Arduino IDE uses strictly structured libraries that expose a dialect of C/C++ for users to write sketches. The goal of Arduino is to make prototyping quick and easy for non-programmers. As such, it hides as many details about the underlying hardware as possible inside libraries.

Here are the quick stats for the Arduino IDE:

Website	https://www.arduino.cc/en/main/software
Host OS	Windows, macOS, Linux, and online
Debugger support	None
IDE framework	Proprietary Java, processing
Compiler	avg-gcc, board-specific
Cost	Free
License type	GNU

There are also many more non-Arudino supplied IDEs that can be used to program the Arduino platform. Some will have additional capabilities and expose more of the underlying C/C++ implementation.

Now that we've covered fully abstracted IDEs, we'll move on to more traditionally oriented IDEs that are open source and/or freely available.

Open source/free IDEs

Since IBM created the Eclipse foundation to promote an open source, highly extensible IDE, many Eclipse-based IDEs have popped up. We'll take a look at two such IDEs in this section. In recent years, Microsoft has started to focus heavily on open source projects, creating the freely available, open source Visual Studio Code text editor, which is also covered in this section.

AC6 System Workbench for STM32 (S4STM32)

AC6 is a consulting firm that has contributed an Eclipse-based IDE that targets STM32 MCUs. System Workbench adds some support for STM-based discovery boards to help get projects set up quickly. AC6 also offers System Workbench for Linux, which can be useful if you are developing an application with one of the multi-core devices (from the STM32MP1 family).

Here are the quick stats for AC6 System Workbench for STM32:

Website	`http://ac6-tools.com/content.php/content_SW4MCU.xphp`
Host OS	Windows, macOS, or Linux
Debugger support	GDB
IDE framework	Eclipse
Compiler	GCC
Cost	Free
License type	Proprietary free

Another alternative to System Workbench is to start with a bare Eclipse CDT install.

Eclipse CDT and GCC

You can also choose to roll your own Eclipse-based IDE from scratch. Eclipse CDT is the de facto standard for C/C++ development. You'll also need to provide a compiler. ARM provides a full GCC site for cross compiling to ARM Cortex M devices from Windows, Linux, and macOS. It can be found
at `https://developer.arm.com/tools-and-software/open-source-software/developer-tools/gnu-toolchain/gnu-rm`.

Here are the quick stats for Eclipse CDT:

Website	`https://www.eclipse.org/cdt/`
Host OS	Windows, macOS, or Linux
Debugger support	GDB
IDE framework	Eclipse
Compiler	GCC
Cost	Free
License type	**Eclipse Public License (EPL)**

For those that don't care for the Eclipse IDE, another alternative exists and is becoming increasingly popular: Visual Studio Code.

Microsoft Visual Studio Code

In 2015, Microsoft released Visual Studio Code, which is a text editor that provides the ability to add extensions. While this sounds fairly straightforward on the surface, there are enough extensions available to give a very respectable IDE experience, including IntelliSense and full debug capability. If you're used to Visual Studio-based IntelliSense and debugging, then this environment will be very familiar.

Here are the quick stats for Visual Studio Code:

Website	https://code.visualstudio.com/
Host OS	Windows, macOS, or Linux
Debugger support	GDB, ST-Link, and others
IDE framework	Visual Studio Code
Compiler	Many
Cost	Free
License type	MIT

Similar to Eclipse CDT, Visual Studio Code will need GCC installed, as well as an extension. In order to get Visual Studio properly set up, follow these steps:

1. To install GCC for Cortex-M, go to `https://developer.arm.com/tools-and-software/open-source-software/developer-tools/gnu-toolchain/gnu-rm`.
2. To install the JLink tools (used to connect to the debug probe), go to `https://www.segger.com/downloads/jlink`.
3. To install the `cortex-debug` extension, go to `https://marketplace.visualstudio.com/items?itemName=marus25.cortex-debug`.

So far, all of the IDEs we have covered have been free of charge (and in some cases, open source). The next section includes IDEs that cost money and are largely closed source. *Why would anyone want such a thing?*, you ask. Read on and find out what these solutions have to offer.

Proprietary IDEs

Once the norm for cross-compiling applications for MCUs, paid proprietary IDEs are starting to be outnumbered by free, open source solutions. However, the mere existence of free options doesn't immediately render paid options obsolete. The selling point of proprietary IDEs is that they provide the widest range of device support and require the least amount of attention from the developer.

Designed to work out of the box, the paid professional-grade solutions' claim to fame is saving developers time. These time savings will typically come in three main forms: unified environments for setting up an MCU, unified debugging environments, and vendor-supplied middleware, common across multiple MCU vendors.

Getting an MCU up and running is easier now than it ever has been, but once a project gets advanced enough that it starts defining specific memory regions in RAM and ROM or adding additional executable space in Quad-SPI-based flash, some additional configuration will be required. The best professional IDEs will provide some help (via GUIs), which makes these configurations a bit easier than needing to dive into scatter files and assembly-based start-up code (although these are *excellent* skills to have!)

Similar to the ability to quickly configure an MCU via a GUI, debugger support in pro-grade IDEs will also typically be very straightforward, generally limited to selecting the debugger from a drop-down list and possibly fine-tuning some settings.

If you read through all of the options that different MCUs could possess, it probably comes as no surprise that the same MCU won't be a great fit for every project you undertake. Being able to quickly move between MCU families (and even vendors) while maintaining a unified interface is an excellent advantage. However, getting locked into a platform-based approach, where hardware interfaces start to become defined (as well as firmware APIs), can be limiting, too (that is, Arduino or MBed hardware definitions).

Using well-written middleware from an established company breaks you free from the tendency of hardware-oriented platforms focusing on only the day-lighted peripherals. It moves the focus from accessing a particular platform's pins to accessing properly abstracted MCU peripherals. This distinction is subtle but quite important when it comes to design flexibility. Well-written middleware will provide consistent abstractions of MCU peripherals, as well as more sophisticated middleware.

The downside to paid tooling is the monetary cost, which needs to be evaluated against the development time, labor, and opportunity costs of a delayed product launch. Do you have an idea of the amount of time you can save by using middleware instead of reinventing that firmware wheel? What about the amount of time gained by having an IDE that works consistently for any processor you choose? Some basic **return-on-investment (ROI)** calculations comparing the cash outlay against *honest and accurate* estimates of the developer's time will typically tip the scales toward bought-in middleware for moderately complex projects. That is, of course, assuming cash is available to purchase software tooling.

ARM/Keil uVision

Keil originally developed one of the first C compilers for the 8-bit 8051 architecture back in the 1980s. The company moved on to support other cores and was eventually acquired by ARM. They currently offer one of the most efficient compilers for ARM Cortex-M devices (Clang/LLVM). A free version of the uVision IDE is available but is limited to 32 KB code space. Various tiers of the IDE are available in several licensing options (such as perpetual, subscription-based, and so on). Modules of code are added through *software packs*, which simplifies rapidly setting up projects. A very fully featured middleware stack is available as a top-tier offering, which comes abstractions for different RTOSes as well as a uniform API on top of all of the supported MCUs.

Here are the quick stats for uVision:

Website	http://www2.keil.com/mdk5/uvision/
Host OS	Windows
Debugger support	Many
IDE framework	Proprietary
Compiler	armcc, armClang, GCC
Cost	free-$$$
License type	Proprietary

FreeRTOS task-aware debugging is not available—Keil uVision has elaborate support for their own freely available CMSIS RTX RTOS instead. The code editor in uVision MDK is also overdue a facelift.

Similar to Keil uVision, IAR Embedded Workbench is another long-standing IDE for embedded work.

IAR Embedded Workbench

In general, IAR Embedded Workbench has a very similar feature set to Keil uVision. One major difference is that IAR doesn't have the advanced capability of incorporating modular software packs. Advanced debugging features are a bit more easily accessible and intuitive in IAR versus uVision. The code editor is equally disappointing.

Here are the quick stats for IAR Embedded Workbench:

Website	https://www.iar.com/iar-embedded-workbench/
Host OS	Windows
Debugger support	Many
IDE framework	Proprietary
Compiler	Proprietary
Cost	$$–$$$
License type	Proprietary

Now that we've covered the old standbys, we'll get into the more recently available offerings, starting with Rowley CrossWorks.

Rowley CrossWorks

Rowley Crossworks is a slightly lower priced entry point than Keil and IAR. Middleware is licensed separately from the IDE. FreeRTOS aware task based debugging is not available from within the IDE; instead, support is available for the **CrossWorks Tasking Library (CTL)** RTOS solution.

Here are the quick stats for CrossWorks:

Website	https://www.rowley.co.uk/
Host OS	Windows, macOS, or Linux
Debugger support	Many
IDE framework	Proprietary
Compiler	GCC, LLVM
Cost	$–$$$
License type	Proprietary

Next up is an IDE created by a company known for its debugging hardware: SEGGER Embedded Studio.

SEGGER Embedded Studio

SEGGER—the manufacturer of the debug probe we'll be using—also offers many software products, including their own IDE (and RTOS). It is available free of charge for non-commercial use, with no limitations. They also have a full middleware stack available, which is licensed separately from the IDE. FreeRTOS-aware debugging is available directly in the IDE, with the appropriate plugin.

Here are the quick stats for Embedded Studio:

Website	https://www.segger.com/products/development-tools/embedded-studio/
Host OS	Windows, macOS, or Linux
Debugger Support	SEGGER
IDE framework	Proprietary
Compiler	GCC, LLVM
Cost	Free for noncommercial use or $$-$$$
License type	Proprietary, JLink as a license dongle

We'll end the list of paid IDEs on a curious note: SysProgs Visual GDB.

SysProgs Visual GDB

Visual GDB isn't actually an IDE. It is a plugin for Microsoft Visual Studio and Visual Studio Code. It has been in existence for quite some time (since 2012). The main purpose of Visual GDB is to provide a consistent UI (Visual Studio) for interacting with GDB-enabled debuggers and GNU make utilities. Its main target user is programmers that are familiar with Visual Studio as a development environment and would like to continue that environment in their embedded work.

Here are the quick stats for Visual GDB:

Website	https://sysprogs.com/
Host OS	Windows, macOS, or Linux
Debugger support	Yes
IDE framework	Visual Studio, Visual Studio Code
Compiler	GCC, ARM
Multi-core debug	Yes
Cost	$
License type	Proprietary

Visual GDB offers integration with a graphical configuration utility—STM Cube—as well as Arduino projects, so migrating from different development frameworks may be a bit easier.

Next, we'll select an IDE specifically for our use case, which is developing the coding exercises.

Selecting the IDE used in this book

Now that we've categorized several different IDEs, it's time to consider which one will be used for the example code covered in the remainder of this book. In keeping with the low-cost theme in order to reduce the barriers to entry, we're going to focus on the IDEs that don't require any monetary investment—anything that is freely available for non-professional use (without time or code limits) can be considered. This immediately eliminates Keil uVision, IAR Embedded Workbench, and SysProgs Visual GDB. Keil has a free version that is code-limited to 32 KB, but we might use that up quickly, depending on how much middleware we elect to include in the examples.

Since a large part of this book also covers debugging with a J-Link probe, we'd like to have an IDE that supports either J-Link or GDB, as well. In a perfect world, the IDE would also support task-aware FreeRTOS debugging, live variable watches, and so on. The FreeRTOS kernel-aware debugging isn't a deal-breaker, as we'll see in the next chapter, because SEGGER Ozone includes this capability.

Finally, the IDE should be multi-platform to promote ease of adoption for anyone brave enough to make the journey. Given this set of criteria, we're left with a limited number of options, as shown:

Potential IDE	Monetarily free version available	No code size limits	SEGGER J-Link supported	FreeRTOS kernel-aware debug	Multi-platform
Keil uVision	✓	X	✓	X	X
IAR	X	N/A	✓	✓	X
Visual GDB	X	N/A	✓	✓	✓
Rowley CrossWorks	X	N/A	✓	✓	✓
VS Code	✓	✓	✓	✓	✓
Eclipse CDT	✓	✓	✓	✓	✓
AC6 S4STM32	✓	✓	✓	✓	✓
Arduino IDE	✓	✓	✓	X	✓
ARM MBed Studio	✓	✓	✓	X	✓
STM32CubeIDE	✓	✓	✓	✓	✓
SEGGER Embedded Studio	✓	✓	✓	✓	✓

So, what are the main points we can derive from this table and the previous observations?

- Eclipse CDT is a potential candidate, but it is slightly less desirable because of the additional setup required compared to some of the other solutions.
- VS Code is an extensible code editor (out of the box), similar to Eclipse. Additional plug-ins will be needed.
- STM32But IDE promises professional-grade debug capability and multi-task RTOS aware debugging.
- SEGGER Embedded Studio promises a very similar feature set to STM32CubeIDE.

We'll be using STM32CubeIDE for the code examples. Since STM32CubeIDE also contains code generators for the STM32 line of MCUs, let's take a look at some of the advantages of using a code generation tool, as well as the tradeoffs to be made.

Considering STM32Cube

STM32CubeIDE is the merger of two components—IDE and the STMCubeMX graphical configuration and code generation utility for STM32 MCUs. The *CubeMX* component can be useful in a few different points in the development cycle. Let's talk about the relevant phases of the development cycle, identify how CubeMX can help, and what the trade-offs are.

Device selection

Most modern MCUs have the option of mapping peripherals to several different pins. However, each pin is usually shared between several different peripherals. So, it is possible, on a pin-constrained device, to have the required peripherals *available* (present on the MCU) but not *accessible* (able to be mapped to a physical pin). Hardware designers can quickly evaluate whether or not individual models of an STM32 MCU break out the necessary combinations of peripherals that are required for a given application. Having the ability to quickly and accurately perform these evaluations across multiple chips can be a major time saver. Usually, designers need to become intimately familiar with datasheets for each chip before making such decisions. CubeMX is by no means a substitute for proper due diligence, but it does help to quickly narrow the field of potential devices.

Each peripheral on STM32 MCUs can be individually turned off, which saves power. With the current proliferation of battery-powered (and energy-harvesting) IoT devices, minimizing power consumption is a hot topic. Another way to reduce power is to clock the chip at a lower frequency. CubeMX allows engineers to quickly calculate how much power the chip will draw under specific configurations. Speed and accuracy are both important when investigating potential MCUs for a project. Getting an accurate power consumption estimate by entering a peripheral/clock configuration into CubeMX is much faster compared to perusing the datasheet and creating a spreadsheet from scratch.

Once a target MCU has been selected and the custom hardware has been manufactured, it is time to *bring up* that new piece of hardware.

Hardware bring-up

Hardware *bring-up* is the act of first powering on a custom-designed piece of hardware and performing some level of verification on it. Custom hardware will often have many differences compared to a development/evaluation board (it is custom, after all!). One area that may differ is clock hardware. STM32 clock trees are fairly complex—a single clock source feeds many different subsystems. The clock frequencies get modified along the way by multipliers and dividers. CubeMX contains a graphical wizard to help properly configure the STM32 clock tree and generate initialization code to get the chip up and running quickly.

Early firmware effort will also be required to verify the hardware is operational. It is always a good idea to double-check whether the MCU can be configured to access all required off-chip circuitry that is present on the board. Often, it is in everyone's best interest to quickly evaluate the viability of the hardware, rather than wait until all aspects of firmware are fully fleshed out.

When it is time to make use of the complex peripherals included on STM32 MCUs, CubeMX can be used to quickly set up pin mapping from the internal peripheral to the external pins of the MCU. It also contains simple, menu-driven interfaces for selecting how the peripheral should be configured. Initialization code is automatically generated, which uses STM's **Hardware Abstraction Layer** (HAL) drivers. The relevant peripheral interrupts are also configured and stubbed out for the user. This enables an embedded engineer to get through verification as quickly as possible.

After all of the hardware is proven, it will be time to add in the additional layers of firmware (middleware) that will live between the low-level drivers and the application firmware.

Middleware setup

STM has partnered with many different middleware providers over the years to make bringing in additional functionality more straightforward for their customers. For example, FreeRTOS primitives can be selected with a few drop-down menus in CubeMX. A FAT file system can be set up, as well as a TCP/IP stack, libraries for JPEG images, and Mbed TLS. Make no mistake, the tool won't perform advanced configuration like a well-versed programmer, but as a bare minimum, it provides a solid start for evaluating unfamiliar libraries. Some engineers may find the initial configurations to fit their requirements directly, which means more time to focus on other portions of their solution.

So, now that we've got a device selected, hardware verified, and some middleware stacks in place, it must be time to move on to coding the final application! Well... not quite. Using all of this code as supplied comes with some gotchas—let's take a look.

Code generation trade-offs

While all of these features sound incredible in theory, developers have had mixed feelings regarding CubeMX and its use in real-world applications. Most of these concerns and trade-offs involve how the tool fits into a workflow; other times, the challenges stem from usability issues.

From a usability standpoint, CubeMX *generally* works well; other times, it generates invalid code that simply won't work as intended. This seems to have been more of an issue when it was first released. Occasionally, versions would ship that would create projects that didn't even compile. However, as a minimum, it has always provided an excellent reference point for the configuration of the advanced peripherals available on the newer STM32 devices.

The challenges engineers face when integrating CubeMX to their workflow are typical of any utility that generates code that tightly couples with user code. Initially, the tool can be used to create a large code base that can be quickly stood up and provide a large portion of the required functionality. However, as the project progresses, tweaks will be almost inevitable; it can become cumbersome keeping the custom user code separate from the auto-generated CubeMX code. You may find yourself in a copy-paste loop, continually copying pieces of working code from one peripheral to another. This is a practice that proliferates in our industry. Embedded firmware engineers desperately need to break out of the copy-paste infinite loop. `Chapter 12`, *Tips for Creating Well-Abstracted Architecture*, covers what tradeoffs are being made when adopting these types of workflows. It also has some suggestions on how to set up your code base for long-term growth, rather than rot.

With all of that being said, portions of code used in our examples will be implemented using STMCubeMX-generated code as a starting point. STM32 HAL is widely used in the industry, so anyone that has programmed STM32 before is likely to be familiar with it. Keep in mind that the example code in this book is meant to be easy to grasp. It is designed to highlight how to implement RTOS concepts, rather than serve as an extensible foundation for future additions. The primary intent of using code that is close to what STM32 CubeMX generates is to make it easier for you to start experimenting on your own.

Setting up our IDE

STM32CubeIDE needs to be installed and the source repository will need to be imported in order to compile and run the example code in the following chapters.

Installing STM32CubeIDE

To install STM32CubeIDE, follow these two simple steps:

1. Download STM32CubeIDE from `https://www.st.com/en/development-tools/stm32cubeide.html`.
2. Install it using the default options.

Now that STM32CubeIDE is installed, we will need to import the source tree. Let's see how to do this.

Importing the source tree into STM32CubeIDE

After installing STM32CubeIDE, you'll need to import the source tree into the Eclipse workspace. A workspace is the Eclipse term for a collection of related projects:

 Since STM32CubeIDE is based on the Eclipse IDE, you'll find the following instructions familiar if you've used Eclipse in the past.

1. Download or clone the GitHub repository from `https://github.com/PacktPublishing/Hands-On-RTOS-with-Microcontrollers`:
    - It is best practice to keep the path to the repo short with no spaces; that is, `c:\projects`.
    - The base git path used in the examples is `c:\projects\packBookRTOS`.

2. Open STM32CubeIDE.

3. Import the entire repo:
    1. Go to **Menu: File | Import**.
    2. Select **General | Existing Projects Into Workspace | Next**.
    3. Browse for and select the folder containing the repo, (`c:\projects\packBookRTOS`), which should look similar to the following after selection:

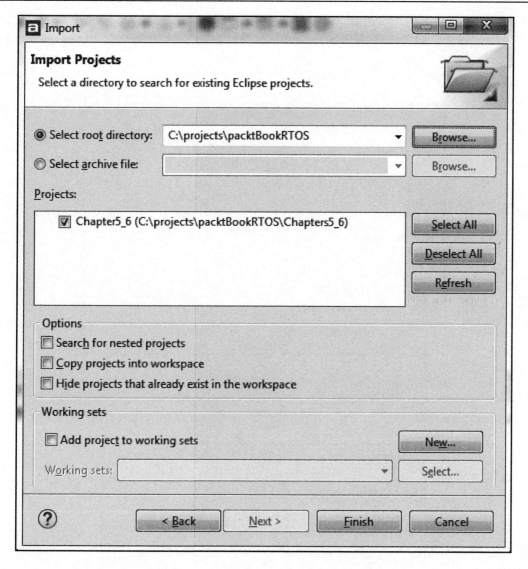

- Click **Finish**. The **Next** button is always gray.

4. At this point, the **Project Explorer** panel will show all of the imported chapters (the following screenshot only shows code for Chapter 5, *Selecting an IDE*, and Chapter 6, *Debugging Tools for Real-Time Systems*, since they are the only examples currently written):

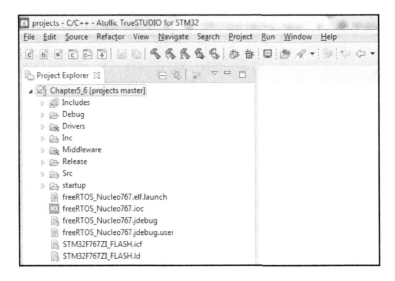

5. To ensure everything is installed correctly, right-click on Chapter5_6 and select **Build**. The output in the **Console** window should look similar to the following:

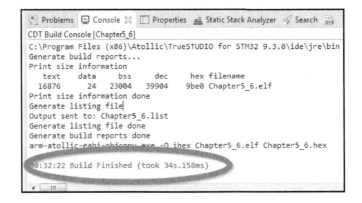

Congratulations! You should now be able to build the FreeRTOS example projects included with this book!

You might have noticed that the Eclipse project doesn't include folders in exactly the same way that they are organized on the disk (that is, Drivers and Middleware aren't subfolders of Chapter5_6 on the filesystem). This is done deliberately to allow reuse of common code across projects/chapters. This concept is covered in more depth in Chapter 12, Tips on Creating Well-Abstracted Architecture.

Summary

In this chapter, we introduced the concept of an IDE and why you might choose to use one. A list of considerations was presented, along with categories of IDEs and suggestions for when it is best to use them. All of this material was put to use as we selected the IDE used in this book. Finally, we took a look at STMCubeMX and discussed how it can be used in different stages of a project.

Having a good understanding of the trade-offs to be made when designing a workflow (which includes choosing software tools) for your embedded system's code development will help you to make informed decisions, which can make a huge impact on productivity.

In the next chapter, we'll continue looking at tools for increasing productivity on FreeRTOS-based embedded firmware projects. The next set of tools allows you to actually *see* how your code is behaving in an extremely convenient way.

Questions

1. There is one IDE that is best for each MCU/language combination:
   * True
   * False

2. Paid IDEs are a must for professional-grade work:
   * True
   * False

3. Vendor-supplied IDEs are always the best IDEs to use for that vendor's hardware:
   * True
   * False

4. Software-generated code is always better than human-crafted code:
    - True
    - False

5. The IDE selected in this book was chosen because it has the best long-term availability and widest device compatibility:
    - True
    - False

6. Name three stages of development where STMCubeMX is helpful.

Further reading

- The STM32CubeIDE user guide can be found
  at `https://www.st.com/resource/en/user_manual/dm00598966-stm32cubeide-quick-start-guide-stmicroelectronics.pdf`.

6
Debugging Tools for Real-Time Systems

Serious debugging tools are incredibly important in serious embedded systems development. Complex RTOS-based systems can have many tasks and dozens of ISRs that need to be completed in a timely manner. Figuring out whether everything is working properly (or *why* it isn't) is way easier with the right tools. If you've been troubleshooting with the occasional print statement or blinking LEDs, you're in for a treat!

We'll be making heavy use of Ozone and SystemView throughout the remainder of this book but first, we'll need to get them set up and look at a quick introduction. Toward the end of this chapter, we'll take a look at other debugging tools, as well as techniques for reducing the number of bugs that get written in the first place.

In a nutshell, we will be covering the following in this chapter:

- The importance of excellent debugging tools
- Using SEGGER J-Link
- Using SEGGER Ozone
- Using SEGGER SystemView
- Other great tools

Technical requirements

Several pieces of software will be installed and configured in this chapter. Here's what you should already have on hand:

- A Nucleo F767 development board
- A micro-USB cable

- A Windows PC (the Windows OS is only required by the ST-Link Reflash utility)
- STM32CubeIDE (ST-Link drivers are required for the ST-Link Reflash utility)

All source code for this chapter can be downloaded from `https://github.com/ PacktPublishing/Hands-On-RTOS-with-Microcontrollers/tree/master/Chapters5_6`.

The importance of excellent debugging tools

When developing any piece of software, it's all too easy to start writing code without thinking about all of the details. Thanks to code generation tools and third-party libraries, we can very quickly develop a feature-filled application and have it running on actual hardware in fairly short order. However, when it comes to getting *every* part of a system working 100% of the time, things are a bit more difficult. If a system is stood up too quickly and the components weren't properly tested before integrating them, there would be pieces that work *most* of the time, but not always.

Often with embedded systems, only a few parts of the underlying application are visible. It can be challenging to evaluate the overall system health from a user's viewpoint. Historically, good debug tooling was less common for embedded work than non-embedded. Putting print statements everywhere only gets you so far, causes timing problems, and so on. Blinking LEDs is cumbersome and doesn't provide much insight. Analyzing signals via hardware can help to verify symptoms but doesn't always isolate the root cause of an issue. Trying to figure out what code is actually running (and when) in an event-driven system is really challenging without the tools to help visualize execution.

This is why having a variety of familiar tools at your disposal is extremely helpful. It allows you to focus your efforts on developing small portions of the application confidently. Confidence comes from rigorously verifying each piece of functionality as it is developed and integrated with the rest of the system. However, in order to perform verification, we need to have transparency in different portions of the code (not just the parts that are observable from outside the system). Many times during verification, situations arise when there is a need to observe inter-task execution.

There are two important areas that help us achieve the objectives of system transparency and observable task relationships: RTOS-aware debugging and RTOS visualization.

RTOS-aware debugging

With traditional debugging setups used for bare-metal (for example, no OS) coding, there was only one stack to observe. Since the programming model was a single super loop with some interrupts, this wasn't much of a problem. At any point in time, the state of the system could be discerned by the following:

- Knowing which function the **program counter** (**PC**) was in
- Knowing which interrupts were active
- Looking at the value of key global variables
- Observing/unwinding the stack

With an RTOS-based system, the basic approach is very similar but the programming model is extended to include multiple tasks running in *parallel*. Remember, each task is effectively an isolated infinite loop. Since each task has its own stack and can be in different operating states, some additional information is required to discern the overall system state:

- Knowing the current operational state of each task
- Knowing which task and function the PC was in
- Knowing which interrupts are active
- Looking at the value of key global variables
- Observing/unwinding the stack of each task

Due to the constrained nature of embedded systems, stack usage is often a concern because of the limited RAM of MCUs. In a bare-metal application, there is only one stack. In an RTOS application, each task has its own stack, which means we have more to monitor. Using a debugging system that provides RTOS-aware stack information helps to quickly evaluate the stack usage of each task in the system.

Monitoring the worst-case performance of the event response is also a critical aspect of real-time systems development. We must ensure that the system will respond to critical events in a timely manner.

There are many different ways to approach this problem. Assuming the event originates with a hardware signal outside the MCU (which is true most of the time), a logic analyzer or oscilloscope can be used to monitor the signal. Code can be inserted in the application to toggle a pin on the MCU after that event has been serviced and the difference in time can be monitored. Depending on the system, access to test equipment, and the events in question, this hardware-centric method may be convenient.

Another method is to use software in combination with **instrumentation** in the RTOS. With this method, small hooks are added into the RTOS that notify the monitoring system when events happen. Those events are then transmitted out of the MCU and onto a development PC running a viewing program. This method is what we'll be focusing on in this book—using SEGGER SystemView. This allows a tremendous amount of information and statistics to be collected with very little development effort. The slight downside to this method is that there is a very small amount of uncertainty added since it is a purely software/firmware approach. It relies on the MCU to record when the events happen, which means if an interrupt is significantly delayed in being serviced, it will not be recorded accurately. There is also a strong dependency on the availability of RAM or CPU cycles. This approach can become inconclusive on heavily loaded systems without adequate RAM. However, these downsides have workarounds and aren't encountered on most systems.

RTOS visualization

Having the ability to see which tasks are running and how they are interacting is also important. In a preemptive scheduling environment, complex relationships can develop between tasks. For example, in order for an event to be serviced, there might be a few tasks that need to interact with one another. On top of that, there may be several more tasks all vying for processor time. In this scenario, a poorly designed system that is consistently missing deadlines may only be perceived as being *sluggish* from the user's perspective. With task visualization, a programmer can literally *see* the relationships between all tasks in the system, which helps considerably with analysis.

> We will work through a real-world example of visualizing scenarios such as this one in `Chapter 8`, *Protecting Data and Synchronizing Tasks*, with the `mainSemPriorityInversion.c` demo.

The ability to easily discern what state tasks are in over a period of time is extremely helpful when unraveling complex inter-task relationships. SEGGER SystemView will also be used to visualize inter-task relationships.

In order to perform an in-depth analysis on a running system, we'll need a way to attach to the MCU and get information out of it. On Cortex-M MCUs, this is most efficiently done with an external debug probe.

Using SEGGER J-Link

A debug probe is a device that allows a computer to communicate and program the non-volatile flash of an MCU. It communicates with special hardware on the MCU (called Coresight on ARM Cortex-M processors). The SEGGER J-Link and J-Trace family of debug probes are among the most popular in the industry. SEGGER also offers useful software that integrates with their tools free of charge. The accessibility of these tools and the quality of the accompanying software makes this an excellent fit for use in this book.

 If you plan on using a paid IDE, the IDE vendor likely has their own proprietary debug probes available. Many excellent software features will likely be tied to their hardware. For example, ARM Keil uVision MDK integrates with ARM Ulink probes and IAR offers their I-Jet debug probes. IDEs such as these also integrate with third-party probes but be aware of what trade-offs there may be before making a purchasing decision.

There are many options when selecting debug probes from SEGGER —we'll briefly go through some of the options currently available and look at the hardware requirements for each.

Hardware options

SEGGER has many different hardware options that cover a wide range of pricing and capabilities. For a complete and current list, check out their website at `https://www.segger.com/products/debug-probes/j-link/models/model-overview/`.

The models generally fit into two main categories: debuggers with full Cortex-M Trace support and those without.

Segger J-Trace

The debuggers with full trace support are referred to as J-Trace. The **Cortex Embedded Trace Macrocell (Cortex ETM)** is an extra piece of hardware inside the MCU that allows every instruction that has been executed to be recorded. Transmitting all of this information off the MCU requires a few extra pins for clocking the data out (a clock line and 1-4 data lines). Having the ability to trace every instruction the MCU has executed enables functionality such as code coverage, which provides insight into how much code has been executed (line by line). Knowing exactly which lines of code have been executed and when gives us the opportunity to see where a program is spending most of its time. When we know which individual lines of code are executed most often, it is possible to optimize that small portion of code when improved performance is required.

In order to take full advantage of the advanced trace features, all of the following is required:

- The MCU must have ETM hardware.
- The specific MCU package must bring the ETM signals out to pins.
- The peripheral configuration must not share ETM signals with other functions.
- The system circuit must be designed to incorporate ETM signals and a connector.

The most common connector used for Debug and ETM signals is a 0.05" pitch header with the following pinout (the trace signals are highlighted):

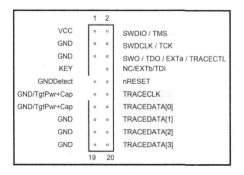

All of this functionality comes at a price, of course. The J-Trace models are at the high end of SEGGER's spectrum, both in terms of functionality and price (typically over USD$1000). Unless you're developing fully custom hardware, also expect to pay for a full evaluation board (over USD$200) rather than the low-cost development hardware used in this book. While these costs are typically completely reasonable for a full-blown engineering budget during new product development, they are too expensive to be widely accessible for individuals.

SEGGER J-Link

SEGGER J-Link has been around in many different forms and has grown to encompass several models. Typically, the higher-end models provide faster clock speeds and a richer experience (faster downloads, responsive debugging, and so on). A few **EDU** models are sold at an extremely large discount for educational purposes (thus the **EDU** designation). These models are fully featured but may not be used for commercial purposes.

 The most common connector used for the Cortex-M is a 0.05" pitch header with the following pinout. Notice, this connector's pinout is the same as the first 10 pins from the Debug+Trace connector (refer to the following diagram).

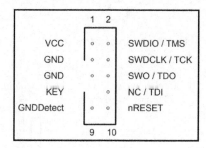

SEGGER has done an excellent job designing software interfaces that aren't tied to the underlying hardware. Because of this, their software tools work across different hardware debugger models without modification. This has also resulted in the hardware option we'll be using in this book—the SEGGER J-Link on-board.

SEGGER J-Link on-board

The specific hardware variant of ST-Link we'll be using in our exercises isn't actually made by SEGGER. It is the ST-Link circuitry already included on the Nucleo development board. Nucleo boards have two separate sub-circuits: programming hardware and target hardware.

The programming hardware sub-circuit is generally referred to as an ST-Link. This **programming hardware** is actually another STM MCU that is responsible for communicating with the PC and programming the **target hardware**—the STM32F767. Since Nucleo hardware is primarily aimed at the ARM Mbed ecosystem, the ST-Link MCU is programmed with firmware that implements both the ST-Link and Mbed functionalities:

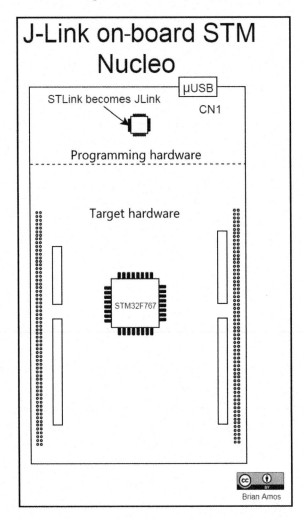

In order to use the programming hardware on the Nucleo board as a SEGGER JLink, we will be replacing its firmware with SEGGER J-Link on-board firmware.

Installing J-Link

Detailed installation instructions are available from SEGGER at https://www.segger.com/products/debug-probes/j-link/models/other-j-links/st-link-on-board/. A few notes are also included here for convenience. In order to convert the on-board ST-Link to a J-Link, we'll be downloading and installing two pieces of software: the J-Link tools and the ST-Link re-flashing utility. You should already have the necessary ST-Link drivers installed from the STM32CubeIDE installation carried out in the previous chapter:

 A Windows PC is only required for the J-Link Reflash utility (it is distributed as *.exe). If you're not using a Windows PC for development and STM32CubeIDE isn't installed, make sure you install USB drivers for the ST-Link (the optional *step 1* in the following list).

1. If you don't have STM32CubeIDE installed already, download and install the ST-Link drivers from http://www.st.com/en/development-tools/stsw-link009.html (this step is optional).
2. Download the appropriate J-Link utilities for your OS from https://www.segger.com/downloads/jlink.
3. Install the J-Link utilities— the default options are fine.
4. Download the SEGGER J-Link Reflash utility (for Windows OS only) from https://www.segger.com/downloads/jlink#STLink_Reflash.
5. Unzip the contents of STLinkReflash_<version>.zip— it will contain two files:
   - JLinkARM.dll
   - STLinkReflash.exe

Now, we will convert ST-Link to J-Link.

Converting ST-Link to J-Link

Follow these steps to upload J-Link firmware to the ST-Link on the Nucleo development board:

1. Plug in a micro USB cable to CN1 on the Nucleo board and attach it to your Windows PC.
2. Open STLinkReflash_<version>.exe.
3. Read through and accept the two license agreements.
4. Select the first option: **Upgrade to J-Link**.

The debugging hardware on the Nucleo board is now effectively a SEGGER J-Link!

Now that a J-Link is present, we will be able to use other SEGGER software tools, such as Ozone and SystemView, to debug and visualize our applications.

Using SEGGER Ozone

SEGGER Ozone is a piece of software that is meant to debug an already-written application. Ozone is independent of the underlying programming environment used to create the application. It can be used in many different modes, but we'll focus on importing an `*.elf` file and crossreferencing it with source code to provide FreeRTOS-aware debugging capability to a project created with any toolchain. Let's take a quick look at the various file types we will be working with in Ozone.

File types used in the examples

There are several file types used when programming and debugging embedded systems. These files are common across many different processors and software products and not exclusive to Cortex-M MCUs or the software used in this book.

Executable and Linkable Format (ELF) files are an executable format that has the ability to store more than the straight `*.bin` or `*.hex` files commonly flashed directly into an MCU's ROM. The `*.elf` files are similar to the `*.hex` files in that they contain all of the binary machine code necessary to load a fully functional project onto a target MCU. The `*.elf` files also contain links to the original source code filenames and line numbers. Software such as Ozone uses these links to display source code while debugging the application:

- `*.bin`: A straight binary file (just 1s and 0s). This file format can be directly "burned" into an MCU's internal flash memory, starting at a given address.
- `*.hex`: Usually a variant of Motorolla S-record format. This ASCII-based file format contains both absolute memory addresses and their contents.
- `*.elf`: Contains both the executable code as well as a header that is used to cross-reference each memory segment to a source file. This means a single ELF file contains enough information to program the target MCU and also cross-reference all of the source code used to create the binary memory segments.

The ELF file does not *contain* the actual source code used, it only contains absolute file paths that crossreference memory segments to the original source code. This is what allows us to open a `*.elf` file in Ozone and step through the C source code while debugging.

- `*.svd`: Contains information that maps registers and descriptions to the memory map of the target device. By providing an accurate `*.svd` file, Ozone will be able to display peripheral views that are very helpful when troubleshooting MCU peripheral code.

A `*.svd` file is a file that is usually included with an IDE that supports your MCU. For example, STM32Cube IDE's location for the `*.svd` files is `C:\ST\STM32CubeIDE_1.2.0\STM32CubeIDE\plugins\com.st.stm32cube.ide.mcu.productdb.debug_1.2.0.201912201802\resources\cmsis\STMicroelectronics_CMSIS_SVD`.

There are other file types used in embedded systems' development as well. This is by no means an exhaustive list—just the ones we'll be using most in the context of the example projects.

Installing SEGGER Ozone

To install SEGGER Ozone, follow these two simple steps:

1. Download SEGGER Ozone: `https://www.segger.com/downloads/jlink/`
2. Install it using the default options.

Now, let's cover the necessary steps to create a FreeRTOS-aware Ozone project and take a quick look at some of the interesting features.

Creating Ozone projects

Since Ozone is completely independent of the programming environment, in order to debug with it, some configuration is required, which is covered in the following steps:

All projects included in the source tree for this book already have Ozone projects created for them. The following steps are for your reference—you'll only need to go through these steps for your own future projects. Ozone project files, the `*.jdebug` files, are already included for all of the projects in this book.

1. When first opened, select the **Create a New Project** prompt.
2. For the **Device** field, select **STM32F767ZI**.
3. For **Peripherals**, input the directory and location of the `STM32F7x7.svd` file:

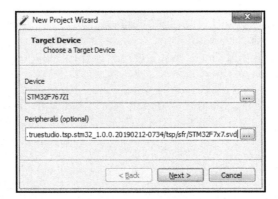

4. On the **Connection Settings** dialog screen, default values are acceptable.
5. On the **Program File** dialog screen, navigate to the `*.elf` file that is generated by TrueStudio. It should be in the **Debug** folder of your project:

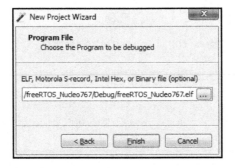

6. Save the `*.jdebug` project file and close Ozone.
7. Open the `*.jdebug` file with a text editor.
8. Add a line to the `*.jdebug` project file to enable the FreeRTOS plugin (only add the last line in bold):

```
void OnProjectLoad (void) {
  //
  // Dialog-generated settings
  //
  Project.SetDevice ("STM32F767ZI");
  Project.SetHostIF ("USB", "");
```

```
Project.SetTargetIF ("JTAG");
Project.SetTIFSpeed ("50 MHz");
Project.AddSvdFile ("C:\Program Files (x86)\Atollic\TrueSTUDIO
for STM32
9.3.0\ide\plugins\com.atollic.truestudio.tsp.stm32_1.0.0.20190212-0
734\tsp\sfr\STM32F7x7.svd");
Project.SetOSPlugin("FreeRTOSPlugin_CM7");
```

> It is a good idea to copy the *.svd file to a location used for storing
> source code or build tools since the installation directory for the IDEs is
> likely to change over time and between machines.

These steps can be adapted to set up Ozone for any other MCU supported by SEGGER
family debuggers.

Attaching Ozone to the MCU

Time to roll up our sleeves and get our hands dirty! The next sections will make more sense
if you've got some hardware up and running, so you can follow along and do some
exploring. Let's get everything set up:

1. Open the STM32Cube IDE and open the Chapter5_6 project.
2. Right-click on Chapter5_6 and select **Build**. This will compile the project into
   an *.elf file (that
   is, C:\projects\packtBookRTOS\Chapters5_6\Debug\Chapter5_6.elf).
3. Open Ozone.
4. Select **Open Existing Project** from the wizard.
5. Select C:\projects\packtBookRTOS\Chapters5_6\Chapters5_6.jdebug.
6. Use Ozone to download the code to the MCU (click the power button):

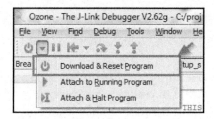

7. Push the play button to start the application (you should see the red, blue, and
   green LEDs flashing).

If your paths are different from what was used when creating the
`*.jdebug` files, you'll need to reopen the `.elf` file (go to **File** | **Open** and
select the file built in *step 2*).

Those same six steps can be repeated for any of the projects included in this book. You can
also create a copy of the `.jdebug` file for other projects by simply opening a
different `*.elf` file.

You may want to bookmark this page. You'll be following these same
steps for the 50+ example programs throughout the rest of the book!

Viewing tasks

A quick view overview of tasks can be seen by enabling the FreeRTOS task view. Using
these tasks can prove to be very beneficial while developing RTOS applications:

1. After the MCU program has been started, pause execution by clicking the *Pause*
   button.
2. Now, navigate to **View** | **FreeRTOS Task View**:

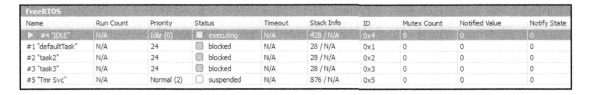

Name	Run Count	Priority	Status	Timeout	Stack Info	ID	Mutex Count	Notified Value	Notify State
#4 "IDLE"	N/A	Idle (0)	executing	N/A	428 / N/A	0x4	0	0	0
#1 "defaultTask"	N/A	24	blocked	N/A	28 / N/A	0x1	0	0	0
#2 "task2"	N/A	24	blocked	N/A	28 / N/A	0x2	0	0	0
#3 "task3"	N/A	24	blocked	N/A	28 / N/A	0x3	0	0	0
#5 "Tmr Svc"	N/A	Normal (2)	suspended	N/A	876 / N/A	0x5	0	0	0

This view shows many useful pieces of information at a glance:

- Task names and priorities.
- **Timeout**: How many *ticks* a blocked task has until it is forced out of the blocked
  state.
- Each task's stack usage (only the current stack usage is shown by default).
  Maximum stack usage is disabled in the preceding screenshot (seen by
  N/A)—(details on configuring FreeRTOS to monitor maximum stack usage will
  be covered in `Chapter 17`, *Troubleshooting Tips and Next Steps*).
- **Mutex Count**: How many mutexes a task currently holds.
- Notifications: Details on each task's notifications.

Having a bird's eye view of all of the tasks in the system can be a huge help when developing an RTOS-based application—especially during the initial phases of development.

Task-based stack analysis

One of the challenges with debugging an RTOS with non-RTOS aware tools is analyzing the call stack of each task. When the system halts, each task has its own call stack. It is quite common to need to analyze the call stack for multiple tasks at a given point in time. Ozone provides this capability by using **FreeRTOS Task View** in conjunction with **Call Stack View**.

After opening both views, each task in **FreeRTOS Task View** can be double-clicked to reveal the current call stack of that task in **Call Stack View**. To reveal local variables for each task on a function-by-function basis, open **Local Data view**. In this view, local variables for the current function highlighted in the call stack will be visible.

An example combining the task-based call stack analysis with a local variable view is shown here:

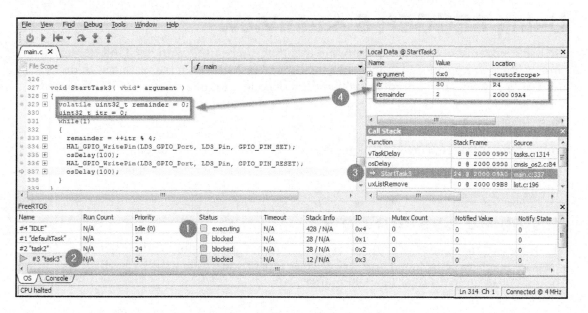

Notice the following from this screenshot:

1. When the MCU was stopped, it was in the "IDLE" task (shown by **executing** in the **Status** column).
2. Double-clicking on **"task 3"** shows the call stack for **"task 3"**. Currently, vTaskDelay is at the top of the stack.
3. Double-clicking on StartTask3 updates the **Local Data** window to show values for all local variables in StartTask3.
4. **Local Variables** for StartTask3 shows the current values for all local variables in StartTask3.

SEGGER Ozone provides both a task-aware call stack view and a heads-up view for all running tasks in the system. This combination gives us a powerful tool to dive into the most minute details of each task running on the system. But what happens when we need a bigger picture view of the system? Instead of looking at each task individually, what if we'd prefer to look at the interaction *between* tasks in the system? This is an area where SEGGER SystemView can help.

Using SEGGER SystemView

SEGGER SystemView is another software tool that can be used with SEGGER debug probes. It provides a means to visualize the flow of tasks and interrupts in a system. SystemView works by adding a small amount of code into the project. FreeRTOS already has Trace Hook Macros, which was specifically designed for adding in this type of third-party functionality.

Unlike Ozone, SystemView doesn't have any programming or debugging capabilities, it is only a **viewer**.

Installing SystemView

There are two main steps required for making your system visible with SystemView. The software needs to be installed and source code must be instrumented so it will communicate its status over the debug interface.

SystemView installation

To install SystemView, follow these steps:

1. Download SystemView for your OS. This is the main binary installer (`https://www.segger.com/downloads/free-utilities`).
2. Install using the default options.

Source code configuration

In order for SystemView to show a visualization of tasks running on a system, it must be provided with information such as task names, priorities, and the current state of tasks. There are hooks present in FreeRTOS for nearly everything SystemView needs. A few configuration files are used to set up a mapping between the trace hooks already present in FreeRTOS and used by SystemView. Information needs to be collected, which is where the specific RTOS configuration and SystemView target sources come into play:

The source code included with this book already has all of these modifications performed, so these steps are *only necessary* if you'd like to add SystemView functionality to *your own FreeRTOS-based projects*.

1. Download SystemView FreeRTOS V10 Configuration (v 2.52d was used) from `https://www.segger.com/downloads/free-utilities` and apply `FreeRTOSV10_Core.patch` to the FreeRTOS source tree using your preferred diff tool.
2. Download and incorporate SystemView Target Sources (v 2.52h was used) from `https://www.segger.com/downloads/free-utilities`:
    1. Copy all the source files into the `.\SEGGER` folder in your source tree and include them for compilation and linking. In our source tree, the `SEGGER` folder is located in `.\Middlewares\Third_Party\SEGGER`.
    2. Copy `SystemView Target Sources\Sample\FreeRTOSV10\SEGGER_SYSVIEW_FreeRTOS.c/h` into the `SEGGER` folder and include it for compilation and linking.
    3. Copy `.\Sample\FreeRTOSV10\Config\SEGGER_SYSVIEW_Config_FreeRTOS.c` into the `SEGGER` folder and include it for compilation and linking.

3. Make the following changes to `FreeRTOSConfig.h`:
    1. At the end of the file, add an include for `SEGGER_SYSVIEW_FreeRTOS.h`: `#include "SEGGER_SYSVIEW_FREERTOS.h"`.
    2. Add `#define INCLUDE_xTaskGetIdleTaskHandle 1`.
    3. Add `#define INCLUDE_pxTaskGetStackStart 1`.

4. In `main.c` make the following changes:
    1. Include `#include <SEGGER_SYSVIEW.h>`.
    2. Add a call to `SEGGER_SYSVIEW_Conf()` after initialization and before the scheduler is started.

Since SystemView is called inside the context of each task, you'll likely find that the minimum task stack size will need to be increased to avoid stack overflows. This is because the SystemView library requires a small amount of code that runs on the target MCU (which increases the call depth and the number of functions that are placed on the stack). For all the gory details on how to troubleshoot stack overflows (and how to avoid them), see `Chapter 17`, *Troubleshooting Tips and Next Steps*.

Using SystemView

After the source-code side of SystemView is straightened out, using the application is very straightforward. To start a capture, make sure you have a running target and your debugger and MCU are connected to the computer:

1. Push the *Play* button.
2. Select the appropriate target device settings (shown here):

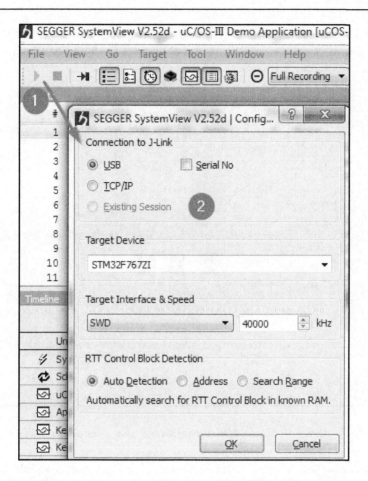

 SystemView requires a *running* target. It will not show any information for a halted MCU (there are no events to display since it is not running). Make sure the LEDs on the board are blinking; follow the steps from the *Attaching Ozone to the MCU* section if they're not.

3. After a second or so, events will be streaming into the log in the top-left **Events** view and you will see a live graphical view of the tasks as they're currently executing in **Timeline**:

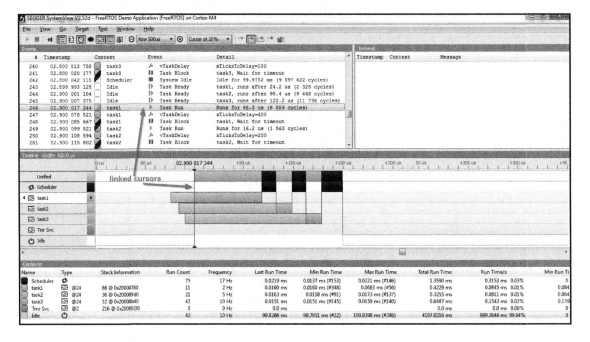

- **Timeline** shows a visual representation of task execution, including different states.
- The **Events** view shows a list of events. Selected events are linked to the timeline.
- The **Context** view shows statistics for all events.
- **Terminal** can be used to show printf-like messages from your code.

There are many more useful features, which will be covered while exploring code.

We're finally done installing the development software! If you've followed along so far, you now have a fully operational IDE, an RTOS visualization solution, and an extremely powerful RTOS-aware debugging system at your disposal. Let's see what other tools can be useful during the course of embedded systems development.

Other great tools

The tools covered in this chapter certainly aren't the only ones available for debugging and troubleshooting embedded systems. There are many other tools and techniques that we simply don't have scope to cover (or that weren't a good fit due to the specific constraints placed on the tools used in this book). These topics are mentioned in the following section, with additional links in the *Further reading* section at the end of the chapter.

Test-driven development

Given the fact that the title of this chapter starts with the word *debugging,* it only seems appropriate to mention the ideal way to *debug* code is to not write buggy code in the first place. Unit testing isn't a single piece of software, but a component of **Test-Driven Development (TDD)**—a development methodology that inverts the way embedded engineers traditionally go about developing their systems.

Instead of writing a bunch of code that doesn't work and then debugging it, test-driven development starts out by writing tests. After tests are written, production code is written until the tests pass. This approach tends to lead to code that is both testable and easily refactored. Since individual functions are tested using this approach, the resulting production code is much less tied to the underlying hardware (since it isn't easy to test code tied to real hardware). Forcing tests to be written at this level tends to lead to loosely coupled architecture, which is discussed in Chapter 13, *Creating Loose Coupling with Queues*. Using the techniques in Chapter 13, *Creating Loose Coupling with Queues*, works very well in conjunction with unit testing and TDD.

Generally, TDD isn't as popular in embedded systems. But if it is something you're interested in learning more about, check out a book written specifically on the topic—*Test Driven Development for Embedded C* by James Grenning.

Static analysis

Static analysis is another way of reducing the number of bugs that creep into a code base. *Static* refers to the fact that the code doesn't need to be executing for this analysis to take place. A static analyzer looks for common programming errors that are syntactically correct (for example, they compile) but are *likely* to create buggy code (that is, out-of-bounds array access, and so on) and provides relevant warnings.

There are many commercially available packages for static analysis, as well as some that are freely available. Cppcheck is included in STM32CubeIDE (simply right-click on a project and select **Run C/C++ Code Analysis**). A link to a **Free Open Source Software (FOSS)** static analyzer from the Clang project is included at the end of this chapter. PVS-Studio Analyzer is an example of a commercial package that can be used freely for non-commercial projects.

Percepio Tracealyzer

Percepio Tracealyzer is a tool similar to SEGGER SystemView in that it helps the developer to visualize system execution. Tracealyzer takes less effort to set up out of the box than SystemView and provides a more aesthetically focused user experience than SystemView. However, since it is supplied by a different company, the cost of the software is not included with the purchase of a SEGGER debug probe. You can find out more about Tracealyzer at `https://percepio.com/tracealyzer/`.

Traditional testing equipment

Before all of the attractive pieces of software for visualizing RTOS behavior on a computer screen existed, this task would fall to more traditional test equipment.

Logic analyzers have been around since MCUs first came into existence and are still among the most versatile tools an embedded system engineer can have in their kit. With a logic analyzer, the timing can be directly measured between when an input enters the system and when an output is provided by the system, as well as the timing between each of the tasks. Looking at the raw low-level signals going in and out of an MCU provides a level of visibility and gut feel for when something isn't right in a way that hexadecimal digits on a screen simply can't. Another advantage of habitually instrumenting at the hardware level - glitches in timing and other erratic behaviors are often noticed without directly looking for them.

Other tools you'll want to acquire if you're just starting out with embedded systems include a handheld **digital multi-meter** (**DMM**) and oscilloscope for measuring analog signals.

Summary

In this chapter, we've covered why having access to excellent debugging tools is important. The exact tools we'll be using to analyze system behavior (SEGGER Ozone and SystemView) have been introduced. You've also been guided through how to get these tools set up for use with future projects. Toward the end, we touched on a few other tools that won't be covered in this book just to raise awareness of them.

Now that we've covered MCU and IDE selection, and we have all of our tooling squared away, we have enough background to get into the real meat of RTOS application development.

Using this toolset will help you gain an in-depth understanding of RTOS behavior and programming as we dive into working examples in the upcoming chapters. You'll also be able to use this same tooling to create high-performing, custom real-time applications in the future.

In the next chapter, we'll get started with writing some code and go into more detail regarding the FreeRTOS scheduler.

Questions

1. J-Link hardware must be purchased to use the tools in this book.
   - True
   - False

2. The only way to evaluate the effectiveness of a real-time system is to wait and see whether something breaks because a deadline was missed.

   - True
   - False

3. Since RTOSes have one stack per task, they are impossible to debug using a debugger since only the main system stack is visible.

   - True
   - False

4. The only way to ensure a system is completely functional is to write all of the code and then debug it all at once at the end of the project.

   - True
   - False

5. What is the style of testing called where each individual module is tested?
   - Unit testing
   - Integration testing
   - System testing
   - Black box testing

6. What is the term given for writing tests before developing production code?

Further reading

- *Test-Driven Development for Embedded C* by *James Grenning*
- SEGGER Ozone manual (UM08025): `https://www.segger.com/downloads/jlink/UM08025`
- SEGGER SystemView manual (UM08027): `https://www.segger.com/downloads/jlink/UM08027`
- Clang Static Analyzer: `https://clang-analyzer.llvm.org`
- PVS-Studio Analyzer: `https://www.viva64.com/en/pvs-studio/`

Section 3: RTOS Application Examples

3

The most commonly used components in RTOSes will be covered in this section. You'll use the knowledge gained from the first section and put it to work through hands-on examples with real hardware. You'll learn how to get the scheduler up and running and how to create tasks, queues, semaphores, mutexes, and more. To get the most out of this section, make sure to have your development board, IDE, and debug toolchains ready to go before digging in!

This section comprises the following chapters:

- Chapter 7, *The FreeRTOS Scheduler*
- Chapter 8, *Protecting Data and Synchronizing Tasks*
- Chapter 9, *Intertask Communication*

The FreeRTOS Scheduler 7

The FreeRTOS scheduler takes care of all task switching decisions. The most basic things you can do with an RTOS include creating a few tasks and then starting the scheduler – which is exactly what we'll be doing in this chapter. Creating tasks and getting the scheduler up and running will become something you'll be well accustomed to after some practice. Even though this is straightforward, it doesn't always go smoothly (especially on your first couple of tries), so we'll also be covering some common problems and how to fix them. By the end, you'll be able to set up your own RTOS application from scratch and know how to troubleshoot common problems.

We'll start by covering two different ways of creating FreeRTOS tasks and the advantages each offer. From there, we'll cover how to start the scheduler and what to look for to make sure it is running. Next, we'll briefly touch on memory management options. After that, we'll take a closer look at task states and cover some tips on optimizing your application so that it uses task states effectively. Finally, some troubleshooting tips will be offered.

Here's what we'll cover in this chapter:

- Creating tasks and starting the scheduler
- Deleting tasks
- Trying out the code
- Task memory allocation
- Understanding FreeRTOS task states
- Troubleshooting startup problems

Technical requirements

To carry out the exercises in this chapter, you will require the following:

- Nucleo F767 development board
- Micro USB cable

- STM32CubeIDE and its source code
- SEGGER JLink, Ozone, and SystemView installed

 For the installation instructions for STM32CubeIDE and its source code, please refer to Chapter 5, *Selecting an IDE*. For SEGGER JLink, Ozone, and SystemView, please refer to Chapter 6, *Debugging Tools for Real-Time Systems*.

You can find the code files for this chapter here: https://github.com/PacktPublishing/ Hands-On-RTOS-with-Microcontrollers/tree/master/Chapter_7. For individual files, whose code snippets can be found throughout the text, please go to the src folder.

You can build live projects that can be run with the STM32F767 Nucleo by downloading the entire tree and importing Chapter_7 as an Eclipse project. To do this, go to https:// github.com/PacktPublishing/Hands-On-RTOS-with-Microcontrollers.

Creating tasks and starting the scheduler

In order to get an RTOS application up and running, a few things need to happen:

1. The MCU hardware needs to be initialized.
2. Task functions need to be defined.
3. RTOS tasks need to be created and mapped to the functions that were defined in *step 2*.
4. The RTOS scheduler must be started.

 It is possible to create additional tasks after starting the scheduler. If you are unsure of what a task is, or why you would want to use one, please review Chapter 2, *Understanding RTOS Tasks*.

Let's break down each of these steps.

Hardware initialization

Before we can do anything with the RTOS, we need to make sure that our hardware is configured properly. This will typically include carrying out activities such as ensuring GPIO lines are in their proper states, configuring external RAM, configuring critical peripherals and external circuitry, performing built-in tests, and so on. In all of our examples, MCU hardware initialization can be performed by calling `HWInit()`, which performs all of the basic hardware initialization required:

```
int main(void)
{
    HWInit();
```

In this chapter, we'll be developing an application that blinks a few LED lights. Let's define the behavior we'll be programming and take a look at what our individual task functions look like.

Defining task functions

Each of the tasks, that is, `RedTask`, `BlueTask`, and `GreenTask`, has a function associated with it. Remember – a task is really just an infinite `while` loop with its own stack and a priority. Let's cover them one by one.

`GreenTask` sleeps for a little while (1.5 seconds) with the Green LED on and then deletes itself. There are a few noteworthy items here, some of which are as follows:

- Normally, a task will contain an infinite `while` loop so that it doesn't return. `GreenTask` still doesn't return since it deletes itself.
- You can easily confirm `vTaskDelete` doesn't allow execution past the function call by looking at the Nucleo board. The green light will only be on for 1.5 seconds before shutting off permanently. Take a look at the following example, which is an excerpt from `main_taskCreation.c`:

```
void GreenTask(void *argument)
{
    SEGGER_SYSVIEW_PrintfHost("Task1 running \
                while Green LED is on\n");
    GreenLed.On();
    vTaskDelay(1500/ portTICK_PERIOD_MS);
    GreenLed.Off();

    //a task can delete itself by passing NULL to vTaskDelete
    vTaskDelete(NULL);
```

```
        //task never get's here
        GreenLed.On();
    }
```

 The full source file for `main_taskCreation.c` is available at `https://github.com/PacktPublishing/Hands-On-RTOS-with-Microcontrollers/blob/master/Chapter_7/Src/main_taskCreation.c`.

`BlueTask` blinks the blue LED rapidly for an indefinite period of time, thanks to the infinite `while` loop. However, the blue LED blinks are cut short because `RedTask` will delete `BlueTask` after 1 second. This can be seen in the following example, which is an excerpt from `Chapter_7/Src/main_taskCreation.c`:

```
void BlueTask( void* argument )
{
    while(1)
    {
        SEGGER_SYSVIEW_PrintfHost("BlueTaskRunning\n");
        BlueLed.On();
        vTaskDelay(200 / portTICK_PERIOD_MS);
        BlueLed.Off();
        vTaskDelay(200 / portTICK_PERIOD_MS);
    }
}
```

`RedTask` deletes `BlueTask` on its first run and then continues to blink the red LED indefinitely. This can be seen in the following excerpt from `Chapter_7/Src/main_taskCreation.c`:

```
void RedTask( void* argument )
{
    uint8_t firstRun = 1;

    while(1)
    {
        lookBusy();

        SEGGER_SYSVIEW_PrintfHost("RedTaskRunning\n");
        RedLed.On();
        vTaskDelay(500/ portTICK_PERIOD_MS);
        RedLed.Off();
        vTaskDelay(500/ portTICK_PERIOD_MS);

        if(firstRun == 1)
        {
            vTaskDelete(blueTaskHandle);
```

```
        firstRun = 0;
      }
    }
  }
```

So, the preceding functions don't look like anything special – and they're not. They are simply standard C functions, two of which have infinite `while` loops in them. How do we go about creating FreeRTOS tasks out of these plain old functions?

Creating tasks

Here's what the prototype for FreeRTOS task creation looks like:

```
BaseType_t xTaskCreate( TaskFunction_t pvTaskCode,
                        const char * const pcName,
                        configSTACK_DEPTH_TYPE  usStackDepth,
                        void *pvParameters,
                        UBaseType_t uxPriority,
                        TaskHandle_t *pxCreatedTask);
```

In our example, the call to the preceding prototype looks like this:

```
retVal = xTaskCreate(Task1, "task1", StackSizeWords, NULL, tskIDLE_PRIORITY
+ 2, tskHandlePtr);
```

This function call might be a little longer than expected – let's break it down:

- `Task1`: The name of the function that implements the infinite `while` loop that makes up the task.
- `"task1"`: This is a human-friendly name used to reference the task during debugging (this is the string that shows up in tools such as Ozone and SystemView).
- `StackSizeWords`: The number of *words* reserved for the task's stack.
- `NULL`: A pointer that can be passed to the underlying function. Make sure the pointer is still valid when the task finally runs after starting the scheduler.
- `tskIDLE_PRIORITY + 2` : This is the priority of the task being created. This particular call is setting the priority to two levels higher than the priority of the IDLE task (which runs when no other tasks are running).

- `TaskHandlePtr`: This is a pointer to a `TaskHandle_t` data type (this is a *handle* that can be passed to other tasks to programmatically reference the task).
- **Return value**: The x prefix of **x**`TaskCreation` signifies that it returns something. In this case, either `pdPASS` or `errCOULD_NOT_ALLOCATE_REQUIRED_MEMORY` is returned, depending on whether or not heap space was successfully allocated. **You must check this return value!**

 At least one task needs to be created before starting the scheduler. Because the call to start the scheduler doesn't return, it won't be possible to start a task from `main` after making a call to start the scheduler. Once the scheduler is started, tasks can create new tasks as necessary.

Now that we've got a good idea of what the input parameters for creating a task are, let's take a look at why it's so important to check the return value.

Checking the return value

When creating a few tasks in `main` before starting the scheduler, it's necessary to check the return values as each task is created. Of course, there are many ways to accomplish this. Let's take a look at two of them:

1. The first is by wrapping the call in an `if` statement with an inlined infinite `while` loop:

   ```
   if( xTaskCreate(GreenTask, "GreenTask", STACK_SIZE, NULL,
                   tskIDLE_PRIORITY + 2, NULL) != pdPASS) { while(1) }
   ```

2. The second is by using ASSERT rather than the infinite `while` loop. If your project has ASSERT support, then it would be better to use ASSERT, rather than the infinite `while` loop. Since our project already has HAL included, we can make use of the `assert_param` macro:

   ```
   retVal = xTaskCreate(BlueTask, "BlueTask", STACK_SIZE, NULL,
   tskIDLE_PRIORITY + 1, &blueTaskHandle);
   assert_param(retVal == pdPASS);
   ```

   `assert_param` is an STM supplied macro that checks whether a condition is true. If the condition evaluates as false, then `assert_failed` is called. In our implementation, `assert_failed` prints out the failing function name and line and enters an infinite `while` loop:

   ```
   void assert_failed(uint8_t *file, uint32_t line)
   {
   ```

```
SEGGER_SYSVIEW_PrintfHost("Assertion Failed:file %s \
                        on line %d\r\n", file, line);
    while(1);
}
```

You will learn more about using assertions and how to configure them in Chapter 17, *Troubleshooting Tips and Next Steps*.

Now that we have created some tasks, let's get the scheduler started and the code running on our hardware, and watch some lights blink!

Starting the scheduler

With all of the options we have for creating tasks, you might be thinking that starting the scheduler would be a complex affair. You'll be pleasantly surprised at how easy it is:

```
//starts the FreeRTOS scheduler - doesn't
//return if successful
vTaskStartScheduler();
```

Yep, just one line of code and no input parameters!

The v in front of the function name indicates it returns void. In reality, this function never returns – unless there is a problem. It is the point where vTaskStartScheduler() is called that the program transitions from a traditional single super loop to a multi-tasking RTOS.

After the scheduler is started, we'll need to think about and understand the different states the tasks are in so we can debug and tune our system properly.

For reference, here's the entirety of main() we've just built up through the various examples. This excerpt has been taken from main_taskCreation.c:

```
int main(void)
{
HWInit();

    if (xTaskCreate(GreenTask, "GreenTask",
    STACK_SIZE, NULL,
    tskIDLE_PRIORITY + 2, NULL) != pdPASS)
    { while(1); }

    assert_param(xTaskCreate(BlueTask, "BlueTask", STACK_SIZE,NULL,
```

```
                   tskIDLE_PRIORITY + 1, &blueTaskHandle) == pdPASS);

    xTaskCreateStatic( RedTask, "RedTask", STACK_SIZE, NULL,
                          tskIDLE_PRIORITY + 1,
                          RedTaskStack, &RedTaskTCB);

    //start the scheduler - shouldn't return unless there's a problem
    vTaskStartScheduler();

    while(1){}
}
```

Now that we've learned how to create tasks and get the scheduler up and running, the last detail to cover in this example is how to go about deleting a task.

Deleting tasks

In some cases, it may be advantageous to have a task run and, eventually, after it has accomplished everything it needs to, remove it from the system. For example, in some systems with fairly involved startup routines, it might be advantageous to run some of the late initialization code inside a task. In this case, the initialization code would run, but there is no need for an infinite loop. If the task is kept around, it will still have its stack and TCB wasting FreeRTOS heap space. Deleting the task will free the task's stack and TCB, making the RAM available for reuse.

All of the critical initialization code should be run long before the scheduler starts.

The task deletes itself

The simplest way to delete a task after it has finished doing useful work is to call vTaskDelete() with a NULL argument from within the task, as shown here:

```
void GreenTask(void *argument)
{
  SEGGER_SYSVIEW_PrintfHost("Task1 running \
                                while Green LED is on\n");
  GreenLed.On();
  vTaskDelay(1500/ portTICK_PERIOD_MS);
  GreenLed.Off();
```

```
    //a task can delete itself by passing NULL to vTaskDelete
    vTaskDelete(NULL);

    //task never get's here
    GreenLed.On();
}
```

This will immediately terminate the task code. The memory on the FreeRTOS heap associated with the TCB and task stack will be freed when the IDLE task runs.

In this example, the green LED will turn on for 1.5 seconds and then shut off. As noted in the code, the instructions after vTaskDelete() will never be reached.

Deleting a task from another task

In order to delete a task from another task, blueTaskHandle needs to be passed to xTaskCreate and its value populated. blueTaskHandle can then be used by other tasks to delete BlueTask, as shown here.

```
TaskHandle_t blueTaskHandle;
int main(void)
{
    HWInit();
    assert_param( xTaskCreate(BlueTask, "BlueTask", STACK_SIZE,
                    NULL, tskIDLE_PRIORITY + 1, &blueTaskHandle) ==
                    pdPASS);
    xTaskCreateStatic( RedTask, "RedTask", STACK_SIZE, NULL,
                    tskIDLE_PRIORITY + 1, RedTaskStack,
                    &RedTaskTCB);
    vTaskStartScheduler();
    while(1);
}

void RedTask( void* argument )
{
    vTaskDelete(blueTaskHandle);
}
```

The actual code in `main.c` results in the blue LED blinking for ~ 1 second before being deleted by `RedTask`. At this point, the blue LED stops blinking (since the task turning the LED on/off isn't running anymore).

There are a few things to keep in mind before deciding that deleting tasks is desirable:

- The heap implementation used must support freeing memory (refer to `Chapter 15`, *FreeRTOS Memory Management*, for details).
- Like any embedded heap implementation, it is possible for a heavily used heap to become fragmented if different sized elements are constantly being added and removed.
- `#define configTaskDelete` must be set to `true` in `FreeRTOSConfig.h`.

That's it! We now have a FreeRTOS application. Let's get everything compiled and program the image onto the Nucleo board.

Trying out the code

Now that you've learned how to set up a few tasks, let's go through how to get it running on our hardware. Running the examples, experimenting with breakpoints to observe execution, and sifting through traces in SystemView will greatly enhance your intuition of how an RTOS behaves.

Let's experiment with the preceding code:

1. Open the `Chapter_7 STM32CubeIDE` project and set `TaskCreationBuild` as the active build:

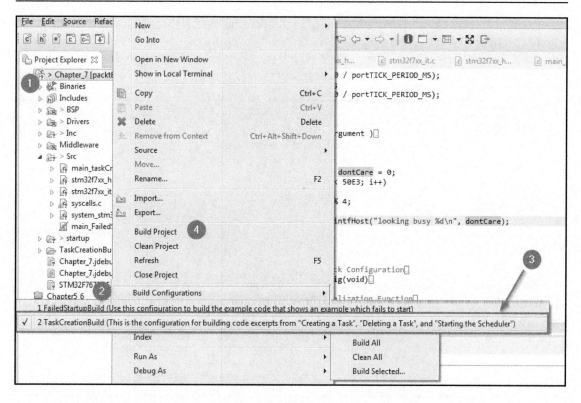

2. Right-click on the project and select **Build Configurations.**
3. Select the desired build configuration (`TaskCreationBuild` contains `main_taskCreation.c`).
4. Select **Build Project** to build the active configuration.

After that, experiment with using Ozone to load and single-step through the program (details on how to do this were covered in `Chapter 6`, *Debugging Tools for Real-Time Systems*). SystemView can also be used to watch the tasks run in real time. Here's a quick example of a bird's-eye view of what's going on:

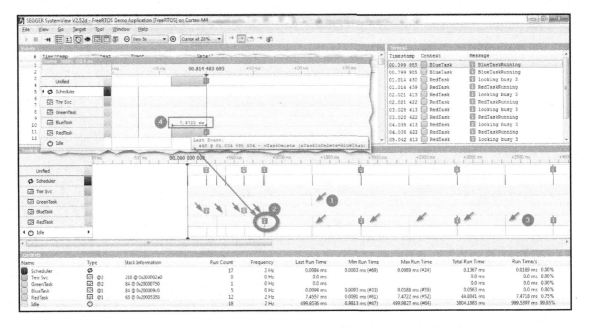

Let's go over this step by step:

1. `GreenTask` sleeps for 1.5 seconds, then deletes itself and never runs again (notice the absence of additional tick lines in the `GreenTask` row).

2. `BlueTask` executes for 1 second before being deleted by `RedTask`.

3. `RedTask` continues to blink the red LED indefinitely.

4. `RedTask` deletes `BlueTask`. Deletions aren't trivial – we can see from the callout it takes 7.4 ms to delete `BlueTask`.

Congratulations, you've just made it through writing, compiling, loading, and analyzing an RTOS application! What?! You haven't gone through and actually *run* the application on hardware yet?! Really? If you're serious about learning, you should *seriously* consider getting a Nucleo board so that you can run the examples on actual hardware. All of the examples in this book are full-blown projects, ready to go!

One of the things we glossed over here was why a call to `xTaskCreate()` can fail. That's an excellent question – let's find out!

Task memory allocation

One of the parameters for xTaskCreate() defines the task's stack size. But where does the RAM being used for this stack come from? There are two options – *dynamically allocated* memory and *statically allocated* memory.

Dynamic memory allocation is implemented with a heap. FreeRTOS ports contain several different options regarding how heaps are implemented. Chapter 15, *FreeRTOS Memory Management,* provides details on how to select an appropriate heap implementation for a given project. For now, it is sufficient to assume a heap is available.

Static allocation permanently reserves RAM for a variable for the life of the program. Let's see what each approach looks like.

Heap allocated tasks

The call from the beginning of this section uses the heap to store the stack:

```
xTaskCreate(Task1, "task1", StackSizeWords, TaskHandlePtr, tskIDLE_PRIORITY
+ 2, NULL);
```

xTaskCreate() is the simpler of the two methods to call. It will use memory from the FreeRTOS heap for Task1's stack and the **Task Control Block (TCB)**.

Statically allocated tasks

Tasks that are created without using the FreeRTOS heap require the programmer to perform allocation for the task's stack and TCB before creating the task. The static version of task creation is xTaskCreateStatic().

The FreeRTOS prototype for xTaskCreateStatic() is as follows:

```
TaskHandle_t xTaskCreateStatic( TaskFunction_t pxTaskCode,
                                const char * const pcName,
                                const uint32_t ulStackDepth,
                                void * const pvParameters,
                                UBaseType_t uxPriority,
                                StackType_t * const puxStackBuffer,
                                StaticTask_t * const pxTaskBuffer );
```

Let's take a look at how this is used in our example, which creates a task with a statically allocated stack:

```
static StackType_t RedTaskStack[STACK_SIZE];
static StaticTask_t RedTaskTCB;
xTaskCreateStatic( RedTask, "RedTask", STACK_SIZE, NULL,
                   tskIDLE_PRIORITY + 1,
                   RedTaskStack, &RedTaskTCB);
```

Unlike xTaskCreate(), xTaskCreateStatic() is guaranteed to always create the task, provided RedTaskStack or RedTaskTCB isn't NULL. As long as your toolchain's linker can find space in RAM to store the variables, the task will be created successfully.

configSUPPORT_STATIC_ALLOCATION must be set to 1 in FreeRTOSConfig.h if you wish to make use of the preceding code.

Memory protected task creation

Tasks can also be created in a memory protected environment, which guarantees a task only accesses memory specifically assigned to it. Implementations of FreeRTOS are available that take advantage of on-board MPU hardware.

Please refer to Chapter 4, *Selecting the Right MCU*, for details on MPUs. You can also find a detailed example on how to use the MPU in Chapter 15, *FreeRTOS Memory Management*.

Task creation roundup

Since there are a few different ways of creating tasks, you might be wondering which one should be used. All implementations have their strengths and weaknesses, and it really does depend on several factors. The following table shows a summary of the three ways of creating tasks, with their relative strengths represented by arrows – ⇑ for better, ⇓ for worse, and ⇔ for neutral:

Characteristic	Heap	MPU Heap	Static
Ease of use	⇑	⇓	⇔
Flexibility	⇑	⇓	⇔
Safety	⇓	⇑	⇔
Regulatory Compliance	⇓	⇑	⇔

As we can see, there is no clear-cut answer as to which system to use. However, if your MCU doesn't have an MPU on-board, there won't be an option to use the MPU variant.

The FreeRTOS heap-based approach is the easiest to code, as well as the most flexible of the three choices. This flexibility comes from the fact that tasks can be deleted, rather than simply forgotten about. Statically created tasks are the next easiest, with only an additional two lines required to specify the TCB and the task stack. They aren't as flexible since there is no way to free memory defined by a static variable. Static creation can also be more desirable in some regulatory environments that forbid the use of the heap altogether, although in most cases, the most FreeRTOS heap-based approach is acceptable – especially heap implementations 1, 2, and 3.

 What is a heap implementation? Don't worry about it yet. We'll learn about heap options for FreeRTOS in detail in `Chapter 15`, *FreeRTOS Memory Management*.

The MPU variant is the most involved of the three, but it is also the safest since the MPU guarantees the task isn't writing outside of its allowed memory.

Using statically defined stacks and TCBs has the advantage that the total program footprint can be analyzed by the linker. This ensures that if a program compiles and fits into the hardware constraints of the MCU, it won't fail to run due to a lack of heap space. With heap-based task creation, it is possible for a program to compile but have a runtime error that causes the entire application not to run. In other cases, the application may run for some time but then fail due to a lack of heap memory.

Understanding FreeRTOS task states

As explained in Chapter 2, *Understanding RTOS Tasks*, all of the context switching between tasks happens *in the background*, which is very convenient for the programmer responsible for implementing tasks. This is because it frees them from adding code into each task that attempts to load balance the system. While the task code isn't *explicitly* performing the task state transitions, it *is* interacting with the kernel. Calls to the FreeRTOS API cause the kernel's scheduler to run, which is responsible for transitioning the tasks between the necessary states.

Understanding different task states

Each transition shown in the following state diagram is caused by either an API call being made by your code or an action being taken by the scheduler. This is a simplified graphical overview of the possible states and transitions, along with a description of each:

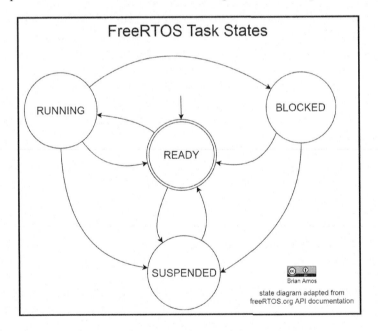

Let's look at them one by one.

Running

A task in the running state is performing work; it is the only task that is in context. It will run until it either makes a call to an API that causes it to move to the `Blocked` state or it gets switched out of context by the scheduler due to a higher priority (or time-sliced task of equal priority). Examples of API calls that would cause a task to move from `Running` to `Blocked` include attempting to read from an empty queue or attempting to take a mutex that isn't available.

Ready

Tasks that are sitting in the ready state are simply waiting for the scheduler to give them processor context so they can run. For example, if *Task A* has gone into the `Blocked` state, waiting on an item to be added to a queue it was waiting on, then *Task A* will move into the `Ready` state. The scheduler will evaluate whether or not *Task A* is the highest priority task ready to run in the system. If *Task A* is the highest priority task that is ready, it will be given processor context and change to the `Running` state. Note that tasks can share the same priority. In this case, the scheduler will switch them between `Ready` and `Running` by using a round-robin scheduling scheme (see `Chapter 2`, *Understanding RTOS Tasks*, for an example of this).

Blocked

A `Blocked` task is a task that is waiting for something. There are two ways for a task to move out of the `Blocked` state: either an event will trigger a transition from `Blocked` to `Ready` for the task, or a timeout will occur, placing the task in the `Ready` state.

This is a very important feature of an RTOS: *each blocking call is time-bound*. That is, a task will only block while waiting for an event for as long as the programmer specifies it can be blocked. This is an important distinction between RTOS firmware programming and general-purpose application programming. For example, *an attempt to take a mutex that will fail if the mutex isn't available within the specified amount of time*. The same is true for API calls that accept and push data onto queues, as well as all the other non-interrupt API calls in FreeRTOS.

While a task is in the `Blocked` state, it doesn't consume any processor time. When a task is transitioned out of the `Blocked` state by the scheduler, it will be moved to the `Ready` state, allowing the calling task to run when it becomes the highest priority task in the system.

Suspended

The `Suspended` state is a bit of a special case since it requires explicit FreeRTOS API calls to enter and exit. Once a task enters the `Suspended` state (via the `vTaskSuspend()` API call), it is effectively ignored by the scheduler until the `vTaskRusme()` API call is made. This state causes the scheduler to effectively ignore the task until it is moved into the `Ready` state by an explicit API call. Just like the `Blocked` state, the `Suspended` state will not consume any processor time.

Now that we understand the various task states and how they interact with different parts of the RTOS, we can learn how to optimize an application so that it makes efficient use of tasks.

Optimizing task states

Thoughtful optimizations can be made to minimize the time tasks stay in the `Running` state. Since a task only consumes significant CPU time when in the `Running` state, it is usually a good idea to minimize time spent there on legitimate work.

As you'll see, polling for events does work but is usually an unnecessary waste of CPU cycles. If properly balanced with task priorities, the system can be designed to be both responsive to important events while also minimizing CPU time. There can be a few different reasons for optimizing an application in this way.

Optimizing to reduce CPU time

Often, an RTOS is used because many different activities need to happen almost simultaneously. When a task needs to take action because an event occurs, there are a few ways of monitoring for the event.

Polling is when a value is continuously read in order to capture a transition. An example of this would be waiting for a new ADC reading. A *polled* read might look something like this:

```
uint_fast8_t freshAdcReading = 0;
while(!freshAdcReading)
{
    freshAdcReading = checkAdc();
}
```

While this code *will* detect when a new ADC reading has occurred, it will also cause the task to continually be in the `Running` state. If this happens to be the highest priority task in the system, this will *starve* the other tasks of CPU time. This is because there is nothing to force the task to move out of the `Running` state – it is continually checking for a new value.

To minimize the time a task spends in the `Running` state (continually polling for a change), we can use the hardware included in the MCU to perform the same check without CPU intervention. For example, **interrupt service routines (ISRs)** and **direct memory access (DMA)** can both be used to offload some of the work from the CPU onto different hardware peripherals included in the MCU. An ISR can be interfaced with RTOS primitives to notify a task when there is valuable work to be done, thereby eliminating the need for CPU-intensive polling. `Chapter 8`, *Protecting Data and Synchronizing Tasks*, will cover polling in more detail, as well as multiple efficient alternatives.

Optimizing to increase performance

Sometimes, there are tight timing requirements that need a low amount of jitter. Other times, a peripheral requiring a large amount of throughput may need to be used. While it may be possible to meet these timing requirements by polling inside a high priority task, it is often more reliable (and more efficient) to implement the necessary functionality inside an ISR. It may also be possible to not involve the processor at all by using DMA. Both of these options prevent tasks from expending worthless CPU cycles on polling loops and allow them to spend more time on useful work.

 Take a look at the *Introducing DMA* section in `Chapter 2`, *Understanding RTOS Tasks*, for a refresher on DMA. Interrupts are also covered.

Because interrupts and DMA can operate completely below the RTOS (not requiring any kernel intervention), they can have a dramatically positive effect on creating a deterministic system. We'll look at how to write these types of drivers in detail in `Chapter 10`, *Drivers and ISRs*.

Optimizing to minimize power consumption

With the prevalence of battery-powered and energy harvesting applications, programmers have another reason to make sure the system is using as few CPU cycles as possible. Similar ideas are present in creating power-conscious solutions, but instead of maximizing determinism, the focus is often on saving CPU cycles and operating with slower clock rates.

There is an additional feature in FreeRTOS that is available for experimentation in this space – the tickless IDLE task. This trades timing accuracy for a reduction in how often the kernel runs. Normally, if the kernel was set up for a 1 ms tick rate (waiting up to every millisecond to check for the next activity), it would wake up and run the code at 1 kHz. In the case of a *tickless* IDLE task, the kernel only wakes up when necessary.

Now that we've covered some starting points on how to improve an already running system, let's turn our attention to something more dire: a system that doesn't start at all!

Troubleshooting startup problems

So, let's say you're working on a project and things haven't gone as planned. Instead of being rewarded with blinky lights, you're left staring at a very non-blinky piece of hardware. At this stage, it's usually best to get the debugger up and running, rather than making random guesses about what might be wrong and sporadically changing sections of code.

None of my tasks are running!

Most often, startup problems in the early stages of development will be caused by not allocating enough space in the FreeRTOS heap. There are typically two symptoms that result from this.

Task creation failed

In the following case, the code will get *stuck* before running the scheduler (no lights will be blinking). Perform the following steps to determine why:

1. Using a debugger, step through task creation until you find the offending task. This is easy to do because all of our attempts to create tasks will only progress if the tasks were successfully created.
2. In this case, you'll see that `xTaskCreate` doesn't return `pdPASS` when creating `BlueTask`. The following code is requesting a 50 KB stack for `BlueTask`:

```
int main(void)
{
  HWInit();

  if (xTaskCreate(GreenTask, "GreenTask",
               STACK_SIZE, NULL,
```

```
                    tskIDLE_PRIORITY + 2, NULL) != pdPASS)
        { while(1); }

    //code won't progress past assert_failed (called by
    //assert_param on failed assertions)
    retval = (xTaskCreate(BlueTask, "BlueTask",
                STACK_SIZE*100, NULL,
                    tskIDLE_PRIORITY + 1, &blueTaskHandle);
    assert_param(retVal == pdPASS);
```

You can find the full source for this example here: https://github.com/
PacktPublishing/Hands-On-RTOS-with-Microcontrollers/blob/master/
Chapter_7/Src/main_FailedStartup.c.

Here's the code for assert_failed. The infinite while loop makes it very easy
to track down the offending line using a debug probe and looks at the call stack:

```
void assert_failed(uint8_t *file, uint32_t line)
{
    SEGGER_SYSVIEW_PrintfHost("Assertion Failed:file %s \
                          on line %d\r\n", file, line);
    while(1);
}
```

3. Using the Ozone call stack, the failed assertion can be tracked back to
   creating BlueTask on line 37 of main_FailedStartup.c:

Call Stack		
Function	Stack Frame	Source
⇨ assert_failed	8 @ 2007 FFE0	Nucleo_F767ZI_Init.c:172
main	24 @ 2007 FFE8	main_FailedStartup.c:37
Reset_Handler	0 @ 2008 0000	startup_stm32f767xx.s:113
Top of stack - no unwinding symbols at 0x0800460E		

4. After determining the cause of failure to be a task that failed to be created, it is
   time to consider increasing the FreeRTOS heap by modifying
   FreeRTOSConfig.h. This is done by modifying configTOTAL_HEAP_SIZE (it's
   currently set to 15 KB). This excerpt has been taken
   from Chapter_7/Inc/FreeRTOSConfig.h:

```
#define configTOTAL_HEAP_SIZE ((size_t)15360)
```

Unlike stack size specifications, which are specified in *words* (for example, `configMINIMAL_STACK_SIZE`) and passed as arguments to `xTaskCreate`, `configTOTAL_HEAP_SIZE` is specified in bytes.

Care needs to be taken when increasing `configTOTAL_HEAP_SIZE`. See the *Important notes* section on considerations to be made.

Scheduler returns unexpectedly

It is also possible to run into issues with `vStartScheduler` returning this:

```
//start the scheduler - shouldn't return unless there's a problem
vTaskStartScheduler();

//if you've wound up here, there is likely
//an issue with overrunning the freeRTOS heap
while(1)
{
}
```

This is simply another symptom of the same underlying issue – inadequate heap space. The scheduler defines an IDLE task that requires `configMINIMAL_STACK_SIZE` words of heap space (plus room for the TCB).

If you're reading this section because you *actually have* a program that isn't starting and you're *not* experiencing either of these symptoms, do not worry! There's an entire chapter in the back of this book, just for you. Check out `Chapter 17`, *Troubleshooting Tips and Next Steps*. It was actually created from real-world problems that were encountered during the creation of the example code in this book.

There are a few more considerations to be made if you have an application that is refusing to start.

Important notes

RAM on MCU-based embedded systems is usually a scarce resource. When increasing the heap space available to FreeRTOS (`configTOTAL_HEAP_SIZE`), you'll be reducing the amount of RAM available to non-RTOS code.

There are several factors to be aware of when considering increasing the heap available to FreeRTOS via `configTOTAL_HEAP_SIZE`:

- If a significantly sized non-RTOS stack has been defined – that is, the stack that is used by any code that isn't running inside a task (typically configured inside the startup file). Initialization code will use this stack, so if there are any deep function calls, this stack won't be able to be made especially small. USB stacks that have been initialized before the scheduler is started can be a culprit here. One possible solution to this on RAM-constrained systems is to move the bloated initialization code into a task with a large enough stack. This may allow for the non-RTOS stack to be minimized further.
- ISRs will be making use of the non-RTOS stack as well, but they'll need it for the entire duration of the program.
- Consider using statically allocated tasks instead – it's guaranteed there will be enough RAM when the program runs.

 A more in-depth discussion on memory allocation can be found in `Chapter 15`, *FreeRTOS Memory Management*.

Summary

In this chapter, we've covered the different ways of defining tasks and how to start the FreeRTOS scheduler. Along the way, we covered some more examples of using Ozone, SystemView, and STM32CubeIDE (or any Eclipse CDT-based IDE). All of this information was used to create a live demo that tied all of the RTOS concepts regarding task creation with the mechanics of actually loading and analyzing code running on embedded hardware. There were also some suggestions on how *not* to monitor for events (polling).

In the next chapter, we'll introduce what you *should* be using for event monitoring. Multiple ways of implementing inter-task signaling and synchronization will be covered – all through examples. There's going to be LOTS of code and a bunch of hands-on analysis using the Nucleo board.

Questions

As we conclude this chapter, here is a list of questions so that you can test your knowledge regarding this chapter's material. You will find the answers in the *Assessments* section of the *Appendix*:

1. How many options are available when starting FreeRTOS tasks?
2. The return value needs to be checked when calling `xTaskCreate()`.
    -   True
    -   False
3. The return value needs to be checked when calling `vTaskStartScheduler()`.
    -   True
    -   False
4. Because RTOSes are bloated middleware, FreeRTOS requires a huge heap for storing all of the task stacks, regardless of what functions the task is performing.
    -   True
    -   False
5. Once a task has been started, it can never be removed.
    -   True
    -   False

Further reading

-   Free RTOS customization (`FreeRTOSConfig.h`): `https://www.freertos.org/a00110.htm`

8
Protecting Data and Synchronizing Tasks

What do race conditions, corrupt data, and missed real-time deadlines all have in common? Well, for one, they are all mistakes that can be easily made when operations are performed in parallel. These are also mistakes that are avoidable (in part) through using the right tools.

This chapter covers many of the mechanisms that are used to synchronize tasks and protect shared data. All the explanations in this chapter will contain example code and analysis that will have been performed using Ozone and SystemView.

First, we will explore the differences between semaphores and mutexes. Then, you will understand how, when, and why to use a semaphore. You'll also learn about race conditions and see how a mutex can avoid such situations. Example code will be provided throughout. The concept of race conditions will be introduced and fixed using a mutex in live code that can be run and analyzed on the Nucleo development board. Finally, FreeRTOS software timers will be introduced and a discussion of common real-world use cases for RTOS-based software timers and MCU hardware peripheral timers will be provided.

We will cover the following topics in this chapter:

- Using semaphores
- Using mutexes
- Avoiding race conditions
- Using software timers

Technical requirements

To complete the hands-on exercises in this chapter, you will require the following:

- Nucleo F767 development board
- Micro USB cable
- ST/Atollic STM32CubeIDE and its source code (the instructions for this can be found in Chapter 5, *Selecting an IDE – Setting Up Our IDE*)
- SEGGER JLink, Ozone, and SystemView (Chapter 6, *Debugging Tools for Real-Time Systems*)

The easiest way to build the examples in this chapter is to build all Eclipse *configurations* at once, and then load and view them using Ozone. To do this, follow these steps:

1. In STM32CubeIDE, right-click on the project.
2. Select **Build.**
3. Select **Build All**. All the examples will be built into their own named subdirectory (this may take a while).
4. In Ozone, you can now quickly load each <exampleName>.elf file. See Chapter 6, *Debugging Tools for Real-Time Systems*, for instructions on how to do this. The correct source files that are linked in the executable will be automatically displayed.

All the source code for this chapter can be found at https://github.com/ PacktPublishing/Hands-On-RTOS-with-Microcontrollers/tree/master/Chapter_8.

Using semaphores

We've mentioned several times now that tasks are meant to be programmed so that they're *running in parallel*. This means that, by default, they have no relation to one another in time. No assumptions can be made as to where tasks are in their execution with respect to one another – unless they are explicitly synchronized. Semaphores are one mechanism that's used to provide synchronization between tasks.

Synchronization via semaphores

The following is a diagram of the abstract example we covered back in Chapter 2, *Task Signaling and Communication Mechanisms*:

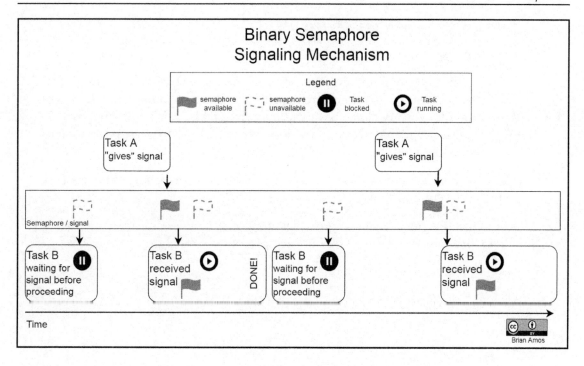

The preceding diagram shows TaskB waiting on a semaphore from TaskA. Each time TaskB acquires the desired semaphore, it will continue its loop. TaskA repeatedly *gives* a semaphore, which effectively synchronizes when TaskB runs. Now that we have a full development environment set up, let's take a look at what this looks like with some actual code. Then, we'll run it on hardware and blink a few LEDs to see exactly what this behavior looks like in the real world.

Setting up the code

First, the semaphore needs to be created, and its handle (or pointer) has to be stored so that it can be used between tasks. The following excerpt has been taken from mainSemExample.c:

```
//create storage for a pointer to a semaphore
SemaphoreHandle_t semPtr = NULL;

int main(void)
{
    //.... init code removed.... //

    //create a semaphore using the FreeRTOS Heap
```

```
semPtr = xSemaphoreCreateBinary();
//ensure pointer is valid (semaphore created successfully)
assert_param(semPtr != NULL);
```

 The semaphore pointer, that is, semPtr, needs to be placed in a location that is accessible to other functions that need access to the semaphore. For example, don't declare semPtr as a local variable inside a function – it won't be available to other functions and it will go out of scope as soon as the function returns.

To see what's going on with the source code *and* see how the system is reacting, we'll associate a few different LEDs with task A and task B.

Task A will toggle the green LED and *give* a semaphore every five times it's run through the blinking loop, as shown in the following excerpt from mainSemExample.c:

```
void GreenTaskA( void* argument )
{
  uint_fast8_t count = 0;
  while(1)
  {
    //every 5 times through the loop, give the semaphore
    if(++count >= 5)
    {
      count = 0;
      SEGGER_SYSVIEW_PrintfHost("Task A (green LED) gives semPtr");
      xSemaphoreGive(semPtr);
    }
    GreenLed.On();
    vTaskDelay(100/portTICK_PERIOD_MS);
    GreenLed.Off();
    vTaskDelay(100/portTICK_PERIOD_MS);
  }
}
```

Task B, on the other hand, will rapidly blink the blue LED three times after successfully *taking* the semaphore, as shown in the following excerpt from mainSemExample.c:

```
/**
 * wait to receive semPtr and triple blink the Blue LED
 */
void BlueTaskB( void* argument )
{
  while(1)
  {
    if(xSemaphoreTake(semPtr, portMAX_DELAY) == pdPASS)
    {
```

```
            //triple blink the Blue LED
            for(uint_fast8_t i = 0; i < 3; i++)
            {
                BlueLed.On();
                vTaskDelay(50/portTICK_PERIOD_MS);
                BlueLed.Off();
                vTaskDelay(50/portTICK_PERIOD_MS);
            }
        }
        else
        {
            // This is the code that will be executed if we time out
            // waiting for the semaphore to be given
        }
    }
}
```

Great! Now that our code is ready, let's see what this behavior looks like.

FreeRTOS allows for indefinite delays in certain circumstances through the use of `portMAX_DELAY`. As long as `#define INCLUDE_vTaskSuspend 1` is present in `FreeRTOSConfig.h`, the calling task will be suspended indefinitely and the return value of `xSemaphoreTake()` can be safely ignored. When `vTaskSuspend()` is not defined as 1, `portMAX_DELAY` will result in a very long delay (0xFFFFFFFF RTOS ticks (~ 49.7 days) on our system), but not an infinite one.

Understanding the behavior

Here's what this example looks like when viewed using SystemView:

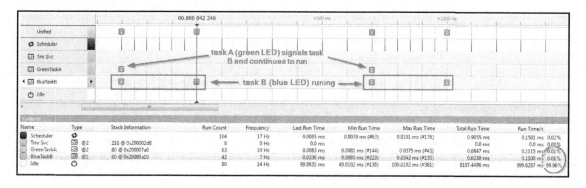

Notice the following:

- Blocking with semaphores is efficient as each task is only using 0.01% of the CPU time.
- A task that is blocked because it is waiting on a semaphore won't run until it is available. This is true even if it is the highest-priority task in the system and no other tasks are currently READY.

Now that you've seen an efficient way of synchronizing tasks with a semaphore, let's have a look at another way of achieving the same behavior using polling.

Wasting cycles – synchronization by polling

The following example has the exact same behavior as when we're looking at LEDs from the outside of the board – the observable pattern of the LEDs is exactly the same as the previous example. The difference is how much CPU time is being used by continuously reading the same variable.

Setting up the code

Here's the updated GreenTaskA() – only a single line has changed. This excerpt has been taken from mainPolledExample.c:

```
void GreenTaskA( void* argument )
{
  uint_fast8_t count = 0;
  while(1)
  {
    //every 5 times through the loop, set the flag
    if(++count >= 5)
    {
      count = 0;
      SEGGER_SYSVIEW_PrintfHost("Task A (green LED) sets flag");
      flag = 1; //set 'flag' to 1 to "signal" BlueTaskB to run
```

Instead of calling xSmeaphoreGive(), we're simply setting the flag variable to 1.

A similar small change has been made to BlueTaskB(), trading out a while loop that polls on flag, instead of using xSemaphoreTake(). This can be seen in the following excerpt from mainPolledExample.c:

```
void BlueTaskB( void* argument )
```

```
{
  while(1)
  {
      SEGGER_SYSVIEW_PrintfHost("Task B (Blue LED) starts "\
                                "polling on flag");

    //repeateadly poll on flag. As soon as it is non-zero,
    //blink the blue LED 3 times
    while(!flag);
    SEGGER_SYSVIEW_PrintfHost("Task B (Blue LED) received flag");
```

These are the only changes that are required. `BlueTaskB()` will wait to move on (indefinitely) until `flag` is set to something other than `0`.

 To run this example, use the `Chapter_8/polledExample` file's build configuration.

Understanding the behavior

Since only a few changes were made, we might not expect there to be *that* much of a difference in terms of how the MCU is behaving, given the new code. However, the output that can be observed with SystemView tells a different story:

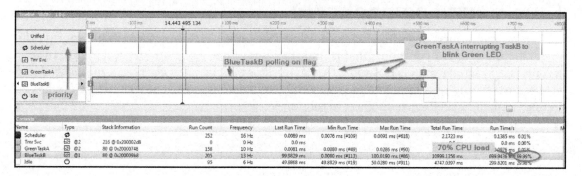

Note the following:

- BlueTaskB is now using 100% of the CPU time while polling the value of flag (the 70% CPU load is lower because the task is sleeping while actually blinking the LED).
- Even though BlueTaskB is hogging the CPU, GreenTaskA still runs consistently since it has a higher priority. GreenTaskA would be starved of CPU if it was a lower priority than BlueTaskB.

So, synchronizing tasks by polling on a variable *does* work as expected, but there are some side effects: increased CPU utilization and a strong dependency on task priorities. Of course, there are ways of reducing the CPU load of BlueTaskB. We could have added a delay between polling, like so:

```
while(!flag)
{
    vTaskDelay(1);
}
```

This will reduce the CPU load of BlueTaskB to around 5%. Beware, though, that this delay also guarantees that BlueTaskB has a worst-case delay of at *least* 1 RTOS tick period (1 ms, in our setup).

Time-bound semaphores

Earlier, we mentioned that one of the critical aspects of RTOSes was their ability to provide a way to time-bound operations; that is, they can guarantee a call doesn't stop a task from executing any longer than is desirable. An RTOS *does not guarantee the successful timeliness of an operation*. It only promises that the call will be returned in an amount of time. Let's have another look at the call for taking a semaphore:

```
BaseType_t xSemaphoreTake( SemaphoreHandle_t xSemaphore,
                           TickType_t xTicksToWait );
```

From the preceding code, we can see the following:

- semPtr is just a pointer to the semaphore.
- maxDelay is the interesting part of this call – it specifies the maximum amount of time to wait for the semaphore (in RTOS *tick* units).

- The return value is `pdPASS` (the semaphore was taken in time) or `pdFALSE` (the semaphore was not taken in time). *It is extremely important to check this return value.*

If a semaphore were to be taken successfully, the return value would be `pdPASS`. This is the only case where the task will continue because a semaphore was given. If the return value is not `pdPASS`, the call to `xSemaphoreTake()` has failed, either because of a timeout or a programming error (such as passing in an invalid `SemaphoreHandle_t`). Let's take a more in-depth look at this with an example.

Setting up the code

In this example, we'll be using all three LEDs on the dev board to indicate different states:

- **Green LED**: `GreenTaskA()` blinks at a steady 5 Hz with a 50% duty cycle.
- **Blue LED**: Rapid blinks three times when `TaskB()` receives the semaphore within 500 ms.
- **Red LED**: Turned on after a timeout from `xSemaphoreTake()`. This is left on until it's reset by `TaskB()`, as long as it receives the semaphore within 500 ms of starting to wait for it.

> In many systems, missing a deadline can be a cause for (major) concern. It all depends on what it is you're implementing. This example is just a simple loop with a red light for when a deadline is missed. However, other systems may require (emergency) procedures to be taken to prevent significant failure/damage if a deadline is missed.

`GreenTaskA()` has two responsibilities:

- Blink the green LED
- *Give* the semaphore at pseudo-random intervals

These responsibilities can be seen in the following code:

```
void GreenTaskA( void* argument )
{
    uint_fast8_t count = 0;
    while(1)
    {
        uint8_t numLoops = StmRand(3,7);
        if(++count >= numLoops)
        {
            count = 0;
```

```
        xSemaphoreGive(semPtr);
    }
        greenBlink();
    }
}
```

`TaskB()` also has two responsibilities:

- Blink the blue LED (as long as the semaphore shows up within 500 ms).
- Turn on the red LED (if the semaphore doesn't show up within 500 ms). The red LED will stay on until the semaphore has successfully been taken within 500 ms of starting to wait for it:

```
void TaskB( void* argument )
{
    while(1)
    {
        //'take' the semaphore with a 500mS timeout
        if(xSemaphoreTake(semPtr, 500/portTICK_PERIOD_MS) ==
pdPASS)
        {
            //received semPtr in time
            RedLed.Off();
            blueTripleBlink();
        }
        else
        {
            //this code is called when the
            //semaphore wasn't taken in time
            RedLed.On();
        }
    }
}
```

This setup guarantees that `TaskB()` will be taking some action *at least* every 500 ms.

Understanding the behavior

When building and loading the firmware included in the `semaphoreTimeBound` build configuration, you'll see something similar to the following when using SystemView:

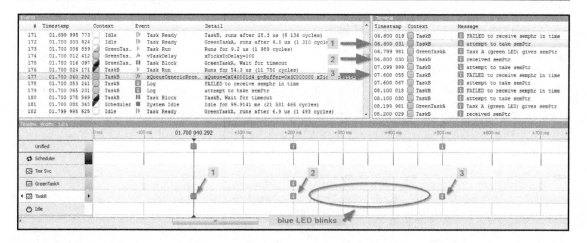

Note the following:

1. **Marker 1** indicates `TaskB` didn't receive the semaphore within 500 ms. Notice there is no followup execution from `TaskB` – it immediately went back to taking the semaphore again.
2. **Marker 2** indicates `TaskB` received the semaphore within 500 ms. Looking at the graph, we can see it was actually around 200 ms. The periodic lines (circled in the preceding image) in the `TaskB` lane are the blue LED turning on and off.
3. After blinking the blue LED, `TaskB` goes back to waiting for the semaphore.

Log messages are indicated by blue *i* icons within the timeline, which helps to associate descriptive comments in code while visualizing behavior. Double-clicking the blue boxes automatically jumps the terminal to the associated log message.

You'll notice that the blue LED doesn't always blink – occasionally, the red LED blinks instead. Each time the red LED blinks, this indicates that `semPtr` was not taken within 500 ms. This shows that the code is attempting to take a semaphore as an upper bound on the amount of time acceptable before *giving up* on the semaphore, possibly triggering an error condition.

As an exercise, see if you can capture a red blink and track where the timeout occurred using the terminal output (on the right) and the timeline output (on the bottom) – how much time elapsed from when `TaskB` attempted to *take the semaphore* and when the red LED blinked? Now, modify the 500 ms timeout in the source code, compile and upload it with Ozone, and watch for the change in SystemView.

Counting semaphores

While binary semaphores can only have values between 0 and 1, counting semaphores can have a wider range of values. Some use cases for counting semaphores include simultaneous connections in a communication stack or static buffers from a memory pool.

For example, let's say we have a TCP/IP stack that supports multiple simultaneous TCP sessions, but the MCU only has enough RAM to support three simultaneous TCP sessions. This would be a perfect use case for a counting semaphore.

The counting semaphore for this application needs to be defined so that it has a maximum count of 3 and an initial value of 3 (three TCP sessions are available):

```
SemaphoreHandle_t semPtr = NULL;
semPtr = xSemaphoreCreateCounting( /*max count*/3, /*init count*/ 3);
if(semPtr != NULL)
```

The code that requests to open a TCP session would *take* semPtr, reducing its count by 1:

```
if(xSemaphoreTake( semPtr, /*timeoutTicks*/100) == pdPASS)
{
    //resources for TCP session are available
}
else
{
    //timed out waiting for session to become available
}
```

Whenever a TCP session is closed, the code closing the session *gives* semPtr, increasing its count by 1:

```
xSemaphoreGive( semPtr );
```

By using a counting semaphore, you can control access to a limited number of available TCP sessions. By doing this, we're accomplishing two things:

- Limiting the number of simultaneous TCP sessions, thus keeping resource usage in check.
- Providing time-bound access for creating a TCP session. This means the code is able to specify how long it will wait for a session to become available.

Counting semaphores are useful for controlling access to a shared resource when more than one instance is available.

Priority inversion (how not to use semaphores)

Since semaphores are used to synchronize multiple tasks and guard shared resources, does this mean we can use them to protect a piece of data that's being shared between two tasks? Since each task needs to know when it is safe to access the data, the tasks need to be synchronized, right? The danger with this approach is that semaphores have no concept of task priority. A higher-priority task waiting on a semaphore being held by a lower-priority task will wait, regardless of what else might be going on in the system. An example of *why* this can become a problem will be shown here.

Here's the conceptual example we covered in `Chapter 3`, *Task Signaling and Communication Mechanisms*:

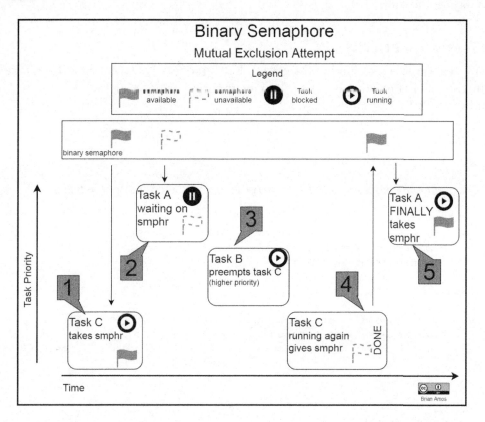

The main problems with this sequence are *steps 3* and *4*. `TaskB` shouldn't be able to preempt `TaskC` if a higher-priority (`TaskA`) task is waiting on the semaphore. Let's look at an example of this *in the wild* with some real code and observe the behavior first-hand!

Setting up the code

For the actual example, we'll maintain the exact same function names as the theoretical example we covered previously. The *shared resource* will be the function that's used to blink the LEDs.

 The *shared LEDs* are only an example. In practice, you'll often find that data that's been shared between tasks needs to be protected. There is also the chance that the multiple tasks may attempt to use the same hardware peripheral, in which case access to that resource may need to be protected.

To provide some visual feedback, we'll also assign some LEDs to the various tasks. Let's have a look at the code.

Task A (highest priority)

Task A is responsible for blinking the green LED, but only *after* semPtr has been taken (within 200 ms of requesting it). The following excerpt has been taken from mainSemPriorityInversion.c:

```
while(1)
{
    //'take' the semaphore with a 200mS timeout
    SEGGER_SYSVIEW_PrintfHost("attempt to take semPtr");
    if(xSemaphoreTake(semPtr, 200/portTICK_PERIOD_MS) == pdPASS)
    {
        RedLed.Off();
        SEGGER_SYSVIEW_PrintfHost("received semPtr");
        blinkTwice(&GreenLed);
        xSemaphoreGive(semPtr);
    }
    else
    {
        //this code is called when the
        //semaphore wasn't taken in time
        SEGGER_SYSVIEW_PrintfHost("FAILED to receive "
                                  "semphr in time");
        RedLed.On();
    }
    //sleep for a bit to let other tasks run
    vTaskDelay(StmRand(10,30));
}
```

This task is the primary focal point of this example, so make sure that you have a solid understanding of the conditional statements around the semaphore being taken within the specified period of time. The semaphore won't always be taken in time.

Task B (medium priority)

Task B periodically utilizes the CPU. The following excerpt has been taken
from `mainSemPriorityInversion.c`:

```
uint32_t counter = 0;
while(1)
{
    SEGGER_SYSVIEW_PrintfHost("starting iteration %ui", counter);
    vTaskDelay(StmRand(75,150));
    lookBusy(StmRand(250000, 750000));
}
```

This task sleeps between 75 and 150 ticks (which doesn't consume CPU cycles) and then
performs a busy loop for a variable number of cycles using the `lookBusy()` function. Note
that `TaskB` is the medium priority task.

Task C (low priority)

Task C is responsible for blinking the blue LED, but only *after* the `semPtr` has been taken
(within 200 ms of requesting it). The following excerpt has been taken
from `mainSemPriorityInversion.c`:

```
while(1)
{
    //'take' the semaphore with a 200mS timeout
    SEGGER_SYSVIEW_PrintfHost("attempt to take semPtr");
    if(xSemaphoreTake(semPtr, 200/portTICK_PERIOD_MS) == pdPASS)
    {
      RedLed.Off();
      SEGGER_SYSVIEW_PrintfHost("received semPtr");
      blinkTwice(&BlueLed);
      xSemaphoreGive(semPtr);
    }
    else
    {
      //this code is called when the semaphore wasn't taken in time
      SEGGER_SYSVIEW_PrintfHost("FAILED to receive "
                                "semphr in time");
      RedLed.On();
    }
}
```

`TaskC()` is relying on the same semaphore as `TaskA()`. The only difference is
that `TaskC()` is blinking the blue LED to indicate the semaphore was taken successfully.

Understanding the behavior

Using Ozone, load `Chapter8_semaphorePriorityInversion.elf` and start the processor. Then, open SystemView and observe the runtime behavior, which will be analyzed here.

There are a few key aspects to keep in mind when looking at this trace:

- `TaskA` is the highest-priority task in the system. Ideally, if `TaskA` is ready to run, it should be running. Because `TaskA` shares a resource with a lower-priority task (`TaskC`), it will be delayed while `TaskC` is running (if `TaskC` is holding the resource).
- `TaskB` should not run when `TaskA` *could* run since `TaskA` has a higher priority.
- We've used the terminal output of SystemView (as well as turned on the red LED) to provide a notification when either `TaskA` or `TaskC` has failed to acquire `semPtr` in time:

```
SEGGER_SYSVIEW_PrintfHost("FAILED to receive "
"semphr in time");
```

Here's how this will look in SystemView:

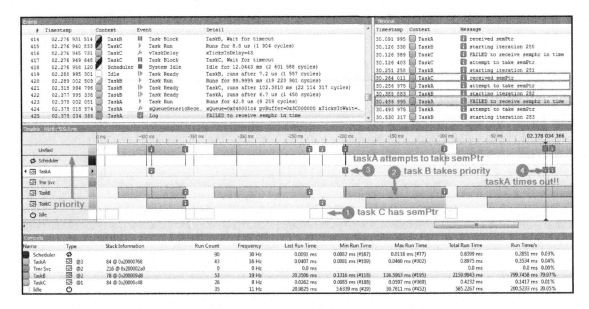

The numbers in this graph line up with the theoretical example, so if you've been following along closely, you may already know what to expect:

1. TaskC (the lowest-priority task in the system) acquires a binary semaphore and starts to do some work (blinking the blue LED).
2. Before TaskC completes its work, TaskB does some work.
3. The highest-priority task (TaskA) interrupts and attempts to acquire the same semaphore, but is forced to wait because TaskC has already acquired the semaphore.
4. TaskA times out after 200 ms because TaskC didn't have a chance to run (the higher-priority task, TaskB, was running instead). It lights up the red LED because of the failure.

The fact that the lower-priority task (TaskB) was running while a higher-priority task was ready to run (TaskA) but waiting on a shared resource is called *priority inversion*. This is a reason to avoid using semaphores to protect shared resources.

 If you look closely at the example code, you'll realize that a semaphore was acquired and then the task holding the semaphore was put to sleep... DON'T EVER DO THIS in a real system. Keep in mind that this is a contrived example *designed to visibly fail*. See the *Using mutexes* section for more information on critical sections.

Luckily, there is an RTOS primitive that has been *specifically designed* for protecting shared resources, all while minimizing the effect of priority inversion – the mutex.

Using mutexes

Mutex stands for **mutual exclusion** – they are explicitly designed to be used in situations where access to a shared resource should be mutually exclusive – meaning the shared resource can only be used by one piece of code at a time. At their heart, mutexes are simply binary semaphores with one (very important) difference: priority inheritance. In the previous example, we saw the highest-priority task waiting on two lower-priority tasks to complete, which caused a priority inversion. Mutexes address this issue with something called *priority inheritance*.

When a higher-priority task attempts to take a mutex and is blocked, the scheduler will elevate the priority of the task that holds the mutex to the same level as the blocked task. This guarantees that the high-priority task will acquire the mutex and run as soon as possible.

Fixing priority inversion

Let's have another try at protecting the shared resource, but this time, we'll use a mutex instead of a semaphore. Using a mutex should help *minimize* priority inversion since it will effectively prevent the mid-priority task from running.

Setting up the code

There are only two significant differences in this example:

- We'll use xSemaphoreCreateMutex() instead of xSemaphoreCreateBinarySemaphore().
- No initial xSemaphoreGive() call is required since the mutex will be initialized with a value of 1. Mutexes are designed to be taken only when needed and then given back.

Here's our updated example with the only significant change. This excerpt can be found in mainMutexExample.c:

```
mutexPtr = xSemaphoreCreateMutex();
assert_param(mutexPtr != NULL);
```

There are some additional name changes related to the semPtr to mutexPtr variable name change, but there is nothing functionally different.

Understanding the behavior

Using Ozone, load Chapter8_mutexExample.elf and run the MCU. Here's what to expect when looking at the board:

- You'll see double blinking green and blue LEDs. The LED blinks of each color will not overlap one another, thanks to the mutex.
- There will only be a few red LED blips every once in a while. This reduction is caused by TaskB not being allowed to take priority over TaskC (and blocking TaskA). This is a lot better than before, but why are we still seeing red occasionally?

By opening SystemView, we'll see something like the following:

Looking through the terminal messages, you'll notice that TaskA – the highest-priority task in the system – has never missed a mutex. This is what we expect since it has priority over everything else in the system. Why does TaskC occasionally miss a mutex (causing a red LED)?

1. TaskC attempts to take the mutex, but it is being held by TaskA.
2. TaskA returns the mutex, but it is immediately taken again. This is caused by a variable amount of delay in TaskA between calls to the mutex. When there is no delay, TaskC isn't allowed to run between when TaskA returns the mutex and attempts to take it again. This is reasonable since TaskA has a higher priority (though this might not be desirable in your system).
3. TaskC times out, waiting for the mutex.

So, we've improved our condition. TaskA, which is the highest-priority task, isn't missing any mutexes any more. But what are some best practices to follow when using mutexes? Read on to find out.

Avoiding mutex acquisition failure

While mutexes *help* to provide protection against some priority inversion, we can take an additional step to make sure the mutex doesn't become an unnecessary crutch. The section of code that's protected by the mutex is referred to as a *critical section*:

```
if(xSemaphoreTake(mutexPtr, 200/portTICK_PERIOD_MS) == pdPASS)
{
    //critical section is here
    //KEEP THIS AS SHORT AS POSSIBLE
    xSemaphoreGive(mutexPtr);
}
```

Taking steps to ensure this critical section is as short as possible will help in a few areas:

- Less time in the critical section makes the shared data more available. The less time a mutex is being held, the more likely it is that another task will gain access in time.
- Minimizing the amount of time low priority tasks hold mutexes also minimizes the amount of time they spend in an elevated priority (if they have a high priority).
- If a low priority task is blocking a higher-priority task from running, the high priority task will have more variability (also known as jitter) in how quickly it is able to react to events.

Avoid the temptation to acquire a mutex at the beginning of a long function. Instead, access data throughout the function and return the mutex before exiting:

```
if(xSemaphoreTake(mutexPtr, 200/portTICK_PERIOD_MS) == pdPASS)
{
    //critical section starts here
    uint32_t aVariable, returnValue;
    aVariable = PerformSomeOperation(someOtherVarNotProtectedbyMutexPtr);
    returnValue = callAnotherFunction(aVariable);

    protectedData = returnValue;
    //critical section ends here
    xSemaphoreGive(mutexPtr);
}
```

The preceding code can be rewritten to minimize the critical section. This still accomplishes the same goals as providing mutual exclusion for `protectedData`, but the amount of time the mutex is held for is reduced:

```
uint32_t aVariable, returnValue;
aVariable = PerformSomeOperation(someOtherVarNotProtectedbyMutexPtr);
returnValue = callAnotherFunction(aVariable);

if(xSemaphoreTake(mutexPtr, 200/portTICK_PERIOD_MS) == pdPASS)
{
    //critical section starts here
    protectedData = returnValue;
    //critical section ends here
    xSemaphoreGive(mutexPtr);
}
```

In the preceding examples, there were no `else` statements listed in case the action didn't complete in time. Remember, it is extremely important that the consequences of a missed deadline are understood and that the appropriate action is taken. If you *don't* have a good understanding of the required timing (and the consequences of missing it), then it is time to get the team together for a discussion.

Now that we have a basic understanding of mutexes, we'll take a look at how they can be used to protect data that's being shared across multiple tasks.

Avoiding race conditions

So, when do we need to use mutexes and semaphores? Any time there is a shared resource between multiple tasks, either a mutex or a semaphore should be used. Standard binary semaphores *can* be used for resource protection, so in some special cases (such as semaphores being accessed from ISRs), semaphores can be desirable. However, you must understand how waiting on the semaphore will affect the system.

We'll see an example of a semaphore being used to protect a shared resource in `Chapter 10`, *Drivers and ISRs.*

We saw a mutex in action in the previous example, but what would it look like if there was no mutex and we only wanted one of the blue or green LEDs to be on at a time?

Failed shared resource example

In our previous mutex example, the LEDs were the shared resource being protected by the mutex. Only one LED was able to blink at a time – either green or blue. It would perform the entire double blink before the next double blink.

Let's take a look at why this is important with a more realistic example. In the real world, you'll often find shared data structures and hardware peripherals among the most common resources that need to be protected.

Accessing a data structure in an atomic fashion is very important when the structure contains multiple pieces of data that must be correlated with one another. An example would be a multi-axis accelerometer providing three readings for the X, Y, and Z axes. In a high-speed environment, it is important for all three readings to be correlated with one another to accurately determine the device's movement over time:

```
struct AccelReadings
{
    uint16_t X;
    uint16_t Y;
    uint16_t Z;
};
struct AccelReadings sharedData;
```

`Task1()` is responsible for updating the data in the structure:

```
void Task1( void* args)
{
    while(1)
    {
        updateValues();
        sharedData.X = newXValue;
        sharedData.Y = newYValue;
        sharedData.Z = newZValue;
    }
}
```

On the other hand, `Task2()` is responsible for reading the data from the structure:

```
void Task2( void* args)
{
    uint16_t myX, myY, myZ;
    while(1)
    {
        myX = sharedData.X;
        myY = sharedData.Y;
        myZ = sharedData.Z;
```

```
        calculation(myX, myY, myZ);
    }
}
```

If one of the readings isn't properly correlated with the others, we'll wind up with an incorrect estimation of the device's movement. `Task1` may be attempting to update all three readings, but in the middle of gaining access, `Task2` comes along and attempts to read the values. As a result, `Task2` receives an incorrect representation of the data because it was in the middle of being updated:

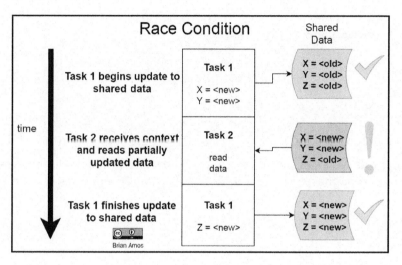

Access to this data structure can be protected by putting all access to the shared data inside a critical section. We can do this by wrapping access in a mutex:

```
void Task1( void* args)
{
    while(1)
    {
        updateValues();
        if(xSemaphoreTake(mutexPtr, timeout) == pdPASS)
        {
            sharedData.X = newXValue;     //critical section start
            sharedData.Y = newYValue;
            sharedData.Z = newZValue;     //critical section end
            xSemaphoreGive(mutexPtr);
        }
        else { /* report failure */}
    }
}
```

It is important to wrap the read accesses as well:

```
void Task2( void* args)
{
    uint16_t myX, myY, myZ;
    while(1)
    {
        if(xSemaphoreTake(mutexPtr, timeout) == pdPASS)
        {
            myX = sharedData.X; //critical section start
            myY = sharedData.Y;
            myZ = sharedData.Z; //critical section end
            xSemaphoreGive(mutexPtr);

            //keep the critical section short
            calculation(myX, myY, myZ);
        }
        else{ /* report failure */ }
    }
}
```

Now that data protection has been covered, we'll take another look at inter-task synchronization. Semaphores were used for this previously, but what if your application calls for actions to occur at a consistent rate? FreeRTOS software timers are one possible solution.

Using software timers

Just like the name states, software timers are timers that are implemented with software. In MCUs, it is extremely common to have many different hardware peripheral timers available. These are often high resolution and have many different modes and features that are used to offload work from the CPU. However, there are two downsides to hardware timers:

- Since they are part of the MCU, you'll need to create an abstraction above them to prevent your code from becoming tightly coupled to the underlying MCU hardware. Different MCUs will have slightly different implementations for timers. Because of this, it is easy for code to become dependent on the underlying hardware.
- They will generally take more development time to set up than using the software-based timer that has already been provided by the RTOS.

Software timers alleviate this coupling by implementing multiple timer channels via software, rather than hardware. So, instead of an application being dependent on specific hardware, it can be used (without modification) on any platform the RTOS supports, which is extremely convenient.

 There are techniques we can use to reduce the firmware's tight coupling to the underlying hardware. Chapter 12, *Tips on Creating Well Abstracted Architecture*, will outline some of the techniques that can be used to eliminate the tight coupling between hardware and firmware.

You may have noticed a task called TmrSvc in the SystemView screenshots. This is the software timer service task. Software timers are implemented as a FreeRTOS task, using many of the same underlying primitives that are available. They have a few configuration options, all of which can be set in FreeRTOSConfig.h:

```
/* Software timer definitions. */
#define configUSE_TIMERS 1
#define configTIMER_TASK_PRIORITY ( 2 )
#define configTIMER_QUEUE_LENGTH 10
#define configTIMER_TASK_STACK_DEPTH 256
```

In order to have access to software timers, configUSE_TIMERS must be defined as 1. As shown in the preceding snippet, the priority of the timer task, as well as the queue length (number of available timers) and stack depth, can all be configured through FreeRTOSConfig.h

But software timers are a FreeRTOS feature – why do I need to worry about stack depth?!

There's one thing to keep in mind with software timers: *the code that's executed when the timer fires is executed inside the context of the Software Timer Task.* This means two things:

- Each callback function executes on the TmrSvc task's stack. Any RAM (that is, local variables) that's used in the callback will come from the TmrSvc task.
- Any long actions that are performed will block other software timers from running, so treat the callback function you pass to the software timer similar to the way you would an ISR – don't deliberately delay the task, and keep everything as short as possible.

The best way to get familiar with software timers is to actually use them in a real system.

Setting up the code

Let's have a look at a few simple examples to see software timers in action. There are two main ways of using software timers: oneshot and repeat. We'll cover each with an example.

Oneshot timers

A *oneshot* is a timer that fires only *one* time. These types of timers are common in both hardware and software and come in very handy when a fixed delay is desired. A oneshot timer can be used when you wish to execute a *short* piece of code after a fixed delay, without blocking the calling code by using `vTaskDelay()`. To set up a oneshot timer, a timer callback must be specified and a timer created.

The following is an excerpt from `mainSoftwareTimers.c`:

1. Declare a `Timer` callback function that can be passed to `xTimerCreate()`. This callback is executed when the timer fires. Keep in mind that the callback is executed within the timer task, so it needs to be non-blocking!

```
void oneShotCallBack( TimerHandle_t xTimer );
```

2. Create a timer. Arguments define whether or not the timer is a oneshot or repeating timer (repeating timers *auto-reload* in FreeRTOS).
3. Perform some due diligence checks to make sure the timer was created successfully by checking that the handle is not `NULL`.
4. Issue a call to `xTimerStart()` and ensure the `uxAutoReload` flag is set to `false` (again, the prototype for `xTimerCreate()` is as follows):

```
TimerHandle_t xTimerCreate (      const char * const pcTimerName,
                                  const TickType_t xTimerPeriod,
                                  const UBaseType_t uxAutoReload,
                                  void * const pvTimerID,
                                  TimerCallbackFunction_t
     pxCallbackFunction );
```

5. So, to create a *one-shot* timer, we need to set `uxAutoReload` to `false`:

```
TimerHandle_t oneShotHandle =
xTimerCreate(    "myOneShotTimer",          //name for timer
                 2200/portTICK_PERIOD_MS, //period of timer in ticks
```

```
                        pdFALSE,                        //auto-reload flag
                        NULL,                           //unique ID for timer
                        oneShotCallBack);               //callback function
        assert_param(oneShotHandle != NULL);            //ensure creation
        xTimerStart(oneShotHandle, 0);                  //start with scheduler
```

6. oneShotCallBack() will simply turn off the blue LED after 1 second has elapsed:

```
void oneShotCallBack( TimerHandle_t xTimer )
{
    BlueLed.Off();
}
```

 Remember that the code that is executing inside the software timer must be kept short. All software timer callbacks are serialized (if one callback performs long operations, it could potentially delay others from executing).

Repeat timers

Repeat timers are similar to oneshot timers, but instead of getting called only *once*, they get called *repeatedly*. After a repeat timer has been started, its callback will be executed repeatedly every xTimerPeriod ticks after being started. Since repeat timers are executed within the TmrSvc task, they can provide a lightweight alternative to tasks for short, non-blocking functions that need to be run periodically. The same considerations regarding stack usage and execution time apply to oneshot timers.

The steps are essentially the same for repeat timers: just set the value of the auto-reload flag to pdTRUE.

Let's take a look at the code in mainSoftwareTimers.c:

```
TimerHandle_t repeatHandle =
xTimerCreate(    "myRepeatTimer",           //name for timer
                 500 /portTICK_PERIOD_MS,   //period of timer in ticks
                 pdTRUE,                    //auto-reload flag
                 NULL,                      //unique ID for timer
                 repeatCallBack);           //callback function
assert_param(repeatHandle != NULL);
xTimerStart(repeatHandle , 0);
```

The repeating timer will toggle the green LED:

```
void repeatCallBack( TimerHandle_t xTimer )
```

```
{
    static uint32_t counter = 0;
    if(counter++ % 2)
    {
        GreenLed.On();
    }
    clsc
    {
        GreenLed.Off();
    }
}
```

> In the preceding code, a static variable is used for the `counter` variable so that its value persists across function calls, while still hiding the variable from all the code outside of the `repeatCallBack()` function.

Understanding the behavior

Upon performing a reset, you'll see the blue LED turn on. To start the FreeRTOS scheduler and the timers, push the blue *USER* button, *B1*, in the lower left of the board. The blue LED will turn off after 2.2 seconds. This only happens once since the blue LED has been set up as a oneshot timer. The green LED toggles every 500 ms since it was set up with a repeat timer.

Let's take a look at the output of the SystemView terminal. In the terminal, all the times are relative to the start of the RTOS scheduler. The blue LED oneshot is only executed once, 2.2 seconds in, while the green LED is toggled every 500 ms:

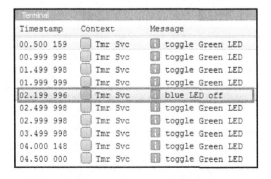

This same information is also available on the timeline. Note that the times are relative to the cursor on the timeline; they are not absolute like they are in the terminal:

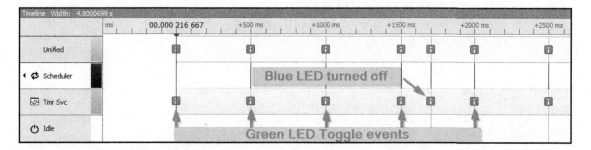

Now that we know how to set up software timers and understand their behavior, let's discuss when they can be used.

Software timer guidelines

Software times can be really useful, especially since they're so easy to set up. They are also fairly lightweight because of the way they have been coded in FreeRTOS – they don't require significant code or CPU resources when used.

Example use cases

Here are some use cases to help you out:

- To periodically perform an action (auto-reload mode). For example, a timer callback function could give a semaphore to a reporting task to provide periodic updates about the system.
- To perform an event only once at some point in the future, without blocking the calling task in the meantime (which would be required if `vTaskDelay()` was used instead).

Considerations

Keep these considerations in mind:

- The priority of the timer service task can be configured in `FreeRTOSConfig.h` by setting `configTIMER_TASK_PRIORITY`.

- Timers can be modified after being created, restarted, and deleted.
- Timers can be created statically (similar to static task creation) to avoid dynamic allocation from the FreeRTOS heap.
- All callbacks are executed in the Software Timer Service Task – they must be kept short and not block!

Limitations

So, what's not to love about software timers? Not too much, as long as the following are kept in mind:

- **Jitter**: Since the callbacks are executed within the context of a task, their exact execution time will depend on all the interrupts in the system, as well as any higher-priority tasks. FreeRTOS allows this to be tuned by adjusting the priority of the timer task being used (which must be balanced with the responsiveness of other tasks in the system).
- **Single Priority**: All software timer callbacks execute inside the same task.
- **Resolution**: A software timer's resolution is only as precise as the FreeRTOS tick rate (defined as 1 ms for most ports).

If lower jitter or higher resolution is required, it probably makes sense to use a hardware timer with ISRs instead of software timers.

Summary

In this chapter, we covered many different aspects of synchronizing tasks and protecting shared data between tasks. We also covered semaphores, mutexes, and software timers. Then, we got our hands dirty by writing some code for each of these types and took a deep dive into analyzing the code's behavior using our Nucleo development board and SystemView.

Now, you have some tools at your disposal for solving synchronization problems, such as one task notifying another that an event has occurred (semaphores). This means you're able to safely share data between tasks by properly wrapping access in a mutex. You also know how to save a bit of RAM when performing simple operations, that is, by using software timers for small periodic operations, instead of dedicated tasks.

In the next chapter, we'll cover more crucial RTOS primitives that are used for inter-task communication and provide the foundations for many RTOS-based applications.

Questions

As we conclude this chapter, here is a list of questions for you to test your knowledge regarding this chapter's material. You will find the answers in the *Assessments* section of the Appendix:

1. What are semaphores most useful for?
2. Why is it dangerous to use semaphores for data protection?
3. What does mutex stand for?
4. Why are mutexes better for protecting shared data?
5. With an RTOS, there is no need for any other type of timer since many instances of software timers are available.
    - True
    - False

Further reading

- A Microsoft paper that provides more detail on problems with semaphores: https://www.microsoft.com/en-us/research/publication/implementing-condition-variables-with-semaphores/
- Phillip Koopman on race conditions: http://course.ece.cmu.edu/~ece642/lectures/26_raceconditions.pdf

Intertask Communication 9

Now that we're able to create tasks, it's time to start passing data between them. After all, you don't often run into systems that have a bunch of parallel tasks operating completely independently of one another; normally, you will need to pass some data between different tasks in the system. This is where intertask communication comes into play.

In FreeRTOS, intertask communication can be achieved using queues and direct task notifications. In this chapter, we'll cover a few different use cases for queues using examples and discuss the pros and cons of each. We will look at all of the details regarding tasks that block while waiting for an item to appear in the queue, as well as timeouts. Once we have looked at queues, we'll move on to task notifications and learn why we should use them and when.

In a nutshell, we will be covering the following topics:

- Passing data through queues by value
- Passing data through queues by reference
- Direct task notifications

Technical requirements

To complete the exercises in this chapter, you will require the following:

- Nucleo F767 development board
- Micro-USB cable
- STM32CubeIDE and source code (see the instructions in Chapter 5, *Selecting an IDE – Setting Up Our IDE*)
- SEGGER JLink, Ozone, and SystemView (see Chapter 6, *Debugging Tools for Real-Time Systems*)

The easiest way to build the examples is to build all Eclipse configurations at once, then load and view them using Ozone:

1. In *STM32CubeIDE*, right-click on the project.
2. Select **Build**.
3. Select **Build All**. All examples will be built into their own named subdirectory (this may take a while).
4. In Ozone, you can now quickly load each `<exampleName>.elf` file—see `Chapter6` for instructions on how to do this. The correct source files that are linked into the executable will automatically be displayed.

 All of the example code in this chapter can be downloaded from `https://` `https://github.com/PacktPublishing/Hands-On-RTOS-with-` `Microcontrollers/tree/master/Chapter_9`. Each `main*.c` has its own Eclipse-based configuration inside the `Chapter_9` project, ready to compile and load onto the Nucleo board.

Passing data through queues by value

Like semaphores and mutexes, queues are among the most widely used (and implemented) structures when operating across multiple asynchronously executing tasks. They can be found in nearly every operating system, so it is very beneficial to understand how to use them. We'll take a look at several different ways of using queues and interacting with them to affect a task's state.

In the following examples, we'll learn how to use queues as a means of sending *commands* to an LED state machine. First, we'll examine a very simple use case, passing a single one-byte value to a queue and operating on it.

Passing one byte by value

In this example, a single `uint8_t` is set up to pass individual enumerations, (`LED_CMDS`), defining the state of one LED at a time or all of the LEDs (on/off). Here's a summary of what is covered in this example:

- `ledCmdQueue`: A queue of one-byte values (`uint8_t`) representing an enumeration defining LED states.
- `recvTask`: This task receives a byte from the queue, executes the desired action, and immediately attempts to receive the next byte from the queue.

- `sendingTask`: This task sends enumerated values to the queue using a simple loop, with a 200 ms delay between each send (so the LEDs turning on/off are visible).

So, let's begin:

1. Set up an `enum` to help us describe the values that are being passed into the queue:

   The following is an excerpt from `mainQueueSimplePassByValue.c`:

   ```
   typedef enum
   {
      ALL_OFF = 0,
      RED_ON = 1,
      RED_OFF = 2,
      BLUE_ON = 3,
      BLUE_OFF= 4,
      GREEN_ON = 5,
      GREEN_OFF = 6,
      ALL_ON = 7

   }LED_CMDS;
   ```

2. Similar to the initialization paradigm of semaphores, queues must first be created and their handles stored so they can be used to access the queue later. Define a handle to be used to point at a queue that is to be used for passing around instances of `uint8_t`:

   ```
   static QueueHandle_t ledCmdQueue = NULL;
   ```

3. Create the queue (verifying its successful creation before continuing) using the `xQueueCreate()` function:

   ```
   QueueHandle_t xQueueCreate( UBaseType_t uxQueueLength,
                               UBaseType_t uxItemSize );
   ```

   Let's quickly outline what we see here:

- `uxQueueLength`: The maximum number of elements the queue can hold
- `uxItemSize`: The size (in bytes) of each element in the queue
- Return value: A handle to the queue that is created (or `NULL` upon error)

Our call to `xQueueCreate` will look like this:

```
ledCmdQueue = xQueueCreate(2, sizeof(uint8_t));
assert_param(ledCmdQueue != NULL);
```

Let's outline what we see here:

- The queue holds up to 2 elements.
- Each element is sized to hold `uint8_t` (a single byte is large enough to store the value of any enumeration we have explicitly defined).
- `xQueueCreate` returns a handle to the queue created, which is stored in `ledCmdQueue`. This "handle" is a global that will be used by various tasks when accessing the queue.

The beginning of our `recvTask()` looks like this:

```
void recvTask( void* NotUsed )
{
  uint8_t nextCmd = 0;

  while(1)
  {
    if(xQueueReceive(ledCmdQueue, &nextCmd, portMAX_DELAY) == pdTRUE)
    {
      switch(nextCmd)
      {
        case ALL_OFF:
          RedLed.Off();
          GreenLed.Off();
          BlueLed.Off();
        break;
        case GREEN_ON:
          GreenLed.On();
        break;
```

Let's have a close look at the actual queue receive line highlighted in the preceding code:

```
if(xQueueReceive(ledCmdQueue, &nextCmd, portMAX_DELAY) == pdTRUE)
```

- The handle `ledCmdQueue` is used to access the queue.
- A local `uint8_t`, `nextCmd`, is defined on the stack. The address of this variable (a pointer) is passed. `xQueueReceive` will copy the next `LED_CMD` enumeration (stored as a byte in the queue) into `nextCmd`.

- An infinite timeout is used for this access—that is, this function will never return if nothing is added to the queue (the same as timeouts for mutex and semaphore API calls).

> The if (<...> == pdTRUE) is redundant since the delay time is infinite; however, it is a good idea to set up error handling ahead of time so that if a noninfinite timeout is later defined, the error state won't be forgotten about down the road. It is also possible for xQueueReceive() to fail for other reasons (such as an invalid queue handle).

The sendingTask is a simple while loop that uses prior knowledge of the enum values to pass different values of LED_CMDS into ledCmdQueue:

```
void sendingTask( void* NotUsed )
{
  while(1)
  {
    for(int i = 0; i < 8; i++)
    {
      uint8_t ledCmd = (LED_CMDS) i;
      xQueueSend(ledCmdQueue, &ledCmd, portMAX_DELAY);
      vTaskDelay(200/portTICK_PERIOD_MS);
    }
  }
}
```

The arguments for the sending side's xQueueSend() are nearly identical to the receiving side's xQueueReceive(), the only difference being that we're sending data *to* the queue this time:

```
xQueueSend(ledCmdQueue, &ledCmd, portMAX_DELAY);
```

- ledCmdQueue: The handle for the queue to send the data to
- &ledCmd: The address of the data to pass to the queue
- portMax_DELAY: The number of RTOS ticks to wait for the queue space to become available (if the queue is full)

Similar to timeouts from `xQueueReceive` when nothing is in the queue before the timeout value is reached, calls to `xQueueSend` can time out if the queue remains full beyond the specified timeout and the item isn't added to the queue. If your application has a noninfinite timeout (which in nearly all cases it should), you'll need to consider what should happen in this case. Courses of action could range from simply dropping the data item (it will be lost forever) to throwing an assert and going into some type of emergency/panic state with an emergency shutdown. A reboot is also popular in some contexts. The exact behavior will generally be dictated by the type of project/product you're working on.

Feel free to build and download `queueSimplePassByValue` to the Nucleo dev board. You'll notice that the LEDs follow the pattern defined by the definition of the `LED_CMDS` enum: `ALL_OFF`, `RED_ON`, `RED_OFF`, `BLUE_ON`, `BLUE_OFF`, `GREEN_ON`, `GREEN_OFF`, `ALL_ON`, with 200 ms between each transition.

But what if we decide we'd like to operate on more than one LED at a time? We *could* add more values to the existing `LED_CMDS` enum, such as `RED_ON_BLUE_ON_GREEN_OFF`, but that would be a lot of very error-prone typing, especially if we had more than 3 LEDs (8 LEDs results in 256 enum values to cover all combinations of each LED being on/off). Instead, let's look at how we can use a struct to describe the LED command and pass that through our queue.

Passing a composite data type by value

FreeRTOS queues (and most other FreeRTOS API functions) take in `void*` as arguments for the individual data types that are being operated on. This is done to provide flexibility for the application writer as efficiently as possible. Since `void*` is simply a pointer to *anything* and the sizes of the elements in the queue is defined when it is created, queues can be used to pass anything between tasks.

The use of `void*` for interacting with queues acts as a double-edged sword. It provides the ultimate amount of flexibility, but also provides the very real possibility for you to pass the *wrong* data type into the queue, potentially without a warning from the compiler. You must keep track of the data type that is being stored in each queue!

We'll use this flexibility to pass in a composite data type created from a struct of instances of uint8_t (each of which is only one bit wide) to describe the state of all three LEDs:

Excerpt from mainQueueCompositePassByValue.c:

```
typedef struct
{
    uint8_t redLEDState : 1; //specify this variable as 1 bit wide
    uint8_t blueLEDState : 1; //specify this variable as 1 bit wide
    uint8_t greenLEDState : 1; //specify this variable as 1 bit wide
    uint32_t msDelayTime; //min number of mS to remain in this state
}LedStates_t;
```

We'll also create a queue that is able to hold eight copies of the entire LedStates_t struct:

```
ledCmdQueue = xQueueCreate(8, sizeof(LedStates_t));
```

Like the last example, recvTask waits until an item is available from the ledCmdQueue queue and then operates on it (turning LEDs on/off as required):

mainQueueCompositePassByValue.c recvTask:

```
if(xQueueReceive(ledCmdQueue, &nextCmd, portMAX_DELAY) == pdTRUE)
{
    if(nextCmd.redLEDState == 1)
        RedLed.On();
    else
        RedLed.Off();
    if(nextCmd.blueLEDState == 1)
        BlueLed.On();
    else
        BlueLed.Off();
    if(nextCmd.greenLEDState == 1)
        GreenLed.On();
    else
        GreenLed.Off();
}
vTaskDelay(nextCmd.msDelayTime/portTICK_PERIOD_MS);
```

Here are the responsibilities of the primary loop of `recvTask`:

- Each time an element is available from the queue, each field of the struct is evaluated and the appropriate action is taken. All three LEDs are updated with a single command, sent to the queue.
- The newly created `msDelayTime` field is also evaluated (it is used to add a delay before the task attempts to receive from the queue again). This is what slows down the system enough so that the LED states are visible.

`mainQueueCompositePassByValue.c sendingTask`:

```
while(1)
  {
    nextStates.redLEDState = 1;
    nextStates.greenLEDState = 1;
    nextStates.blueLEDState = 1;
    nextStates.msDelayTime = 100;

    xQueueSend(ledCmdQueue, &nextStates, portMAX_DELAY);

    nextStates.blueLEDState = 0; //turn off just the blue LED
    nextStates.msDelayTime = 1500;
    xQueueSend(ledCmdQueue, &nextStates, portMAX_DELAY);

    nextStates.greenLEDState = 0;//turn off just the green LED
    nextStates.msDelayTime = 200;
    xQueueSend(ledCmdQueue, &nextStates, portMAX_DELAY);

    nextStates.redLEDState = 0;
    xQueueSend(ledCmdQueue, &nextStates, portMAX_DELAY);
  }
```

The loop of `sendingTask` sends a few commands to `ledCmdQueue` – here are the details:

- `sendingTask` looks a bit different from before. Now, since a struct is being passed, we can access each field, setting multiple fields before sending `nextStates` to the queue.
- Each time `xQueueSend` is called, the contents of `nextStates` is copied into the queue before moving on. As soon as `xQueueSend()` returns successfully, the value of `nextStates` is copied into the queue storage; `nextStates` does not need to be preserved.

To drive home the point that the value of `nextStates` is copied into the queue, this example changes the priorities of tasks so that the queue is filled completely by `sendingTask` before being emptied by `recvTask`. This is accomplished by giving `sendingTask` a higher priority than `revcTask`. Here's what our task definitions look like (`asserts` are present in the code but are not shown here to reduce clutter):

```
xTaskCreate(recvTask, "recvTask", STACK_SIZE, NULL, tskIDLE_PRIORITY + 1,
        NULL);

xTaskCreate(sendingTask, "sendingTask", STACK_SIZE, NULL,
        configMAX_PRIORITIES - 1, NULL);
```

`sendingTask` is configured to have the highest priority in the system. `configMAX_PRIORITIES` is defined in `Chapter9/Inc/FreeRTOSConfig.h` and is the number of priorities available. FreeRTOS task priorities are set up so that 0 is the lowest priority task in the system and the highest priority available in the system is `configMAX_PRIORITIES - 1`.

This prioritization setup allows `sendingTask` to repeatedly send data to the queue until it is full (because `sendingTask` has a higher priority). After the queue has filled, `sendingTask` will block and allow `recvTask` to remove an item from the queue. Let's take a look at how this plays out in more detail.

Understanding how queues affect execution

Task priorities work in conjunction with primitives such as queues to define the system's behavior. This is especially critical in a preemptive RTOS application because context is always given based on priority. Programmed queue interactions need to take into account task priorities in order to achieve the desired operation. Priorities need to be carefully chosen to work in conjunction with the design of individual tasks.

In this example, an infinite wait time was chosen for `sendingTask` so that it could fill the queue.

Here's a diagram depicting the preceding setup in action:

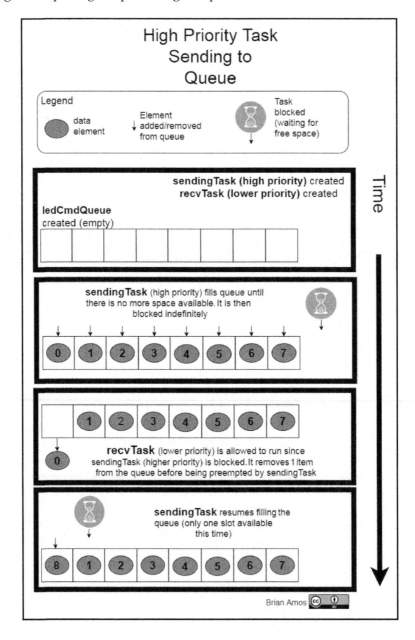

Take a look at this example using Ozone to step through the code and understand its behavior. We can go through a few iterations of the `sendingTask while` loop step by step, watching the `ledCmdQueue` data structure and breakpoint setup in each of these tasks:

1. Make sure you have built the `queueCompositePassByValue` configuration.
2. Open Ozone by double-clicking **Chapter_9\Chapter_9.jdebug**.
3. Go to **File | Open | Chapter_9\queueCompositePassByValue\Chapter9_QueuePassCompositeByValue.elf**.
4. Open the global variables view and observe `ledCmdQueue` as you step through the code.
5. Put a breakpoint in `recvTask` to stop the debugger whenever an item is removed from the queue.
6. When `recvTask` runs the first time, you'll notice that `uxMessagesWaiting` will have a value of 8 (the queue is filled):

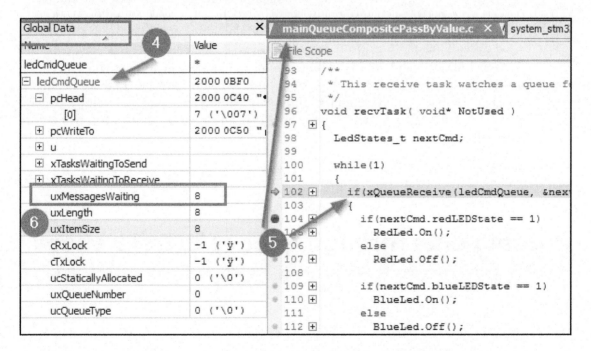

Getting comfortable with whatever debugger you are using *before* you run into serious problems is always a good idea. A second-nature level of familiarity frees your mind to focus on the problem at hand rather than the tools being used.

Important notes on the examples

The previous example's main purpose was to illustrate the following points:

- Queues can be used to hold arbitrary data.
- Queues interact with task priorities in interesting ways.

There were several trade-offs made to simplify behavior and make the example easier to understand:

- **The task receiving from the queue was a low priority**: In practice, you'll need to balance the priority of tasks that are receiving from queues (to keep latency low and prevent queues from filling up) against the priority of other events in the system.
- **A long queue was used for commands**: Deep queues combined with a low-priority task receiving from them will create latency in a system. Because of the combination of low task priority and long queue length, this example contains several seconds worth of queued commands. Elements were added onto the queue that wouldn't be executed until several seconds after they were added because of the depth/priority combination.
- **An infinite timeout was used when sending items to the queue**: This will cause `sendTask()` to wait indefinitely for a slot to become available. In this case, this was the behavior we wanted (for simplicity), but in an actual time-critical system, you'll need to keep in mind exactly how long a task is able to wait before an error occurs.

We're not quite done exploring the flexibility of queues. Next, we'll take a look at a special case of passing data by reference to a queue.

Passing data through queues by reference

Since the data type of a queue is arbitrary, we also have the ability to pass data by reference instead of by value. This works in a similar way to passing arguments to a function by reference.

When to pass by reference

Since a queue will make a copy of whatever it is holding, if the data structure being queued is large, it will be inefficient to pass it around by value:

- Sending and receiving from queues forces a copy of the queue element each time.
- The resulting queue gets very large for large data items if large structures are queued.

So, when there are large items that need to be queued, passing the items by reference is a good idea. Here's an example of a larger structure. After the compiler pads out this struct, it ends up being 264 bytes in size:

mainQueueCompositePassByReference.c:

```
#define MAX_MSG_LEN 256
typedef struct
{
  uint32_t redLEDState : 1;
  uint32_t blueLEDState : 1;
  uint32_t greenLEDState : 1;
  uint32_t msDelayTime; //min number of mS to remain in this state
  //an array for storing strings of up to 256 char
  char message[MAX_MSG_LEN];
}LedStates_t;
```

Rather than copy 264 bytes every time an item is added or removed from `ledCmdQueue`, we can define `ledCmdQueue` to hold a pointer (4 bytes on Cortex-M) to `LedStates_t`:

```
ledCmdQueue = xQueueCreate(8, sizeof(LedStates_t*));
```

Let's look at the difference between passing by value and passing by reference:

Passing by value:

- `ledCmdQueue` **size:** ~ 2 KB (264 bytes * 8 elements).
- 264 bytes copied each time `xQueueSend()` or `xQueueReceive()` is called.
- The original copy of `LedStates_t` that is added to queue can be discarded immediately (a full copy is present inside the queue).

Passing by reference:

- `ledCmdQueue` **size:** 32 bytes (4 bytes * 8 elements).
- 4 bytes copied (the size of a pointer) each time `xQueueSend()` or `xQueueReceive()` is called.
- The original copy of `LedStates_t` that is added to the queue *must be kept* until it is no longer needed (this is the only copy in the system; only a pointer to the original structure was queued).

 When passing by reference, we're making a trade-off between increased efficiency, (potentially) reduced RAM consumption, and more complex code. The extra complexity comes from ensuring that the original value remains valid the entire time it is needed. This approach is very similar to passing references to structures as parameters to functions.

A few instances of `LedStates_t` can be created as well:

```
static LedStates_t ledState1 = {1, 0, 0, 1000,
   "The quick brown fox jumped over the lazy dog.
   The Red LED is on."};
static LedStates_t ledState2 = {0, 1, 0, 1000,
   "Another string. The Blue LED is on"};
```

Using Ozone, we can easily look at what we've created:

1. `uxItemSize` of `ledCmdQeue` is 4 bytes, exactly as we would expect, because the queue is holding pointers to `LedStates_t`.

2. The actual sizes of ledState1 and ledState2 are both 264 bytes, as expected:

Name	Value	Location	Size
led*	*	*	*
⊟ ledCmdQueue	2000 0E00	2000 5118	4
⊞ pcHead	2000 0E50 " ⌐"	2000 0E00	4
⊞ pcWriteTo	2000 0E54 "⌐"	2000 0E04	4
⊞ u		2000 0E08	8
⊞ xTasksWaitingToSend		2000 0E10	20
⊞ xTasksWaitingToReceive		2000 0E24	20
uxMessagesWaiting	8	2000 0E38	4
uxLength	8	2000 0E3C	4
uxItemSize	4	2000 0E40	4
cRxLock	−1 ('ÿ')	2000 0E44	1
cTxLock	−1 ('ÿ')	2000 0E45	1
ucStaticallyAllocated	0 ('\0')	2000 0E46	1
uxQueueNumber	0	2000 0E48	4
ucQueueType	0 ('\0')	2000 0E4C	1
⊟ ledState1		2000 0024	264
redLEDState	1	2000 0024	1
blueLEDState	0	2000 0024	1
greenLEDState	0	2000 0024	1
msDelayTime	1 000	2000 0028	4
⊞ message	"The quick brown	2000 002C	256
⊟ ledState2		2000 012C	264
redLEDState	0	2000 012C	1
blueLEDState	1	2000 012C	1
greenLEDState	0	2000 012C	1
msDelayTime	1 000	2000 0130	4
⊞ message	"Another string.	2000 0134	256

To send an item to the queue, go through the following steps:

1. Create a pointer to the variable and pass in the address to the pointer:

```
void sendingTask( void* NotUsed )
{
    LedStates_t* state1Ptr = &ledState1;
    LedStates_t* state2Ptr = &ledState2;

    while(1)
    {
        xQueueSend(ledCmdQueue, &state1Ptr, portMAX_DELAY);
        xQueueSend(ledCmdQueue, &state2Ptr, portMAX_DELAY);
    }
}
```

2. To receive items from the works, simply define a pointer of the correct data type and pass the address to the pointer:

```
void recvTask( void* NotUsed )
{
    LedStates_t* nextCmd;

    while(1)
    {
        if(xQueueReceive(ledCmdQueue, &nextCmd, portMAX_DELAY) ==
                                                         pdTRUE)
        {
            if(nextCmd->redLEDState == 1)
            RedLed.On();
```

When operating on an item taken out of the queue, remember that you've got a pointer that needs to be dereferenced (that is, `nextCmd->redLEDState`).

Now for the catch(es)...

Important notes

Passing by reference can be more efficient than passing by value for moving large data structures around, but several things need to be kept in mind:

- **Keep the datatypes straight**: Because the argument to a queue is of the `void*` data type, the compiler won't be able to warn you that you're supplying an address to a struct instead of to a pointer.

- **Keep the queued data around**: Unlike passing data by value, when a queue holds pointers to the data, the underlying data passed to the queue needs to stay until it is used. This has the following implications:
    - The data must not live on the stack—no local function variables! Although this *can* be made to work, it is generally a bad idea to define variables on a stack in the *middle* of a call chain and then push a pointer onto a queue. By the time the receiving task pulls the pointer off of the queue, the stack of the sending task is likely to have changed. Even if you do get this to work under some circumstances (such as when the receiving task has a higher priority than the sending task), you'll have created a very brittle system that is likely to break in a very subtle way in the future.
    - A stable storage location for the underlying variable is a must. Global and statically allocated variables are both acceptable. If you'd like to limit access to a variable, use static allocation inside a function. This will keep the variable in memory, just as if it was a global, but limit access to it:

        ```
        void func( void )
        {
            static struct MyBigStruct myVar;
        ```

    - You should dynamically allocate space for the variable (if dynamic allocation is acceptable in your application). See Chapter 15, *FreeRTOS Memory Management*, for details on memory management, including dynamic allocation.

- **Who owns the data?** When a queue has a copy of a struct, the queue owns that copy. As soon as the item is removed from the queue, it disappears. Contrast this with a queue holding a *pointer* to data. When the pointer is removed from the queue, the data is still present in its previous location. Data ownership needs to be made very clear. Will the task receiving the pointer from the queue become the new owner (and be responsible for freeing dynamically allocated memory if it was used)? Will the original task that sent the pointer still maintain ownership? These are all important questions to consider up front.

Now that we've discussed passing around huge amounts of data (avoid it whenever possible!), let's talk about an efficient way of passing around small amounts of data.

Direct task notifications

Queues are an excellent workhorse of an RTOS because of their flexibility. Sometimes, all of this flexibility isn't needed and we'd prefer a more lightweight alternative. Direct task notifications are similar to the other communication mechanisms discussed, except that they do not require the communication object to first be instantiated in RAM. They are also faster than semaphores or queues (between 35% and 45% faster).

They do have some limitations, the largest two being that only one task can be notified at a time and notifications can be sent by ISRs but not received.

Direct task notifications have two main components: the notification itself (which behaves very much like how a semaphore or queue behaves when unblocking a task) and a 32-bit notification value. The notification value is optional and has a few different uses. A notifier has the option of overwriting the entire value or using the notification value as if it were a bitfield and setting a single bit. Setting individual bits can come in handy for signaling different behaviors that you'd like the task to be made aware of without resorting to a more complicated command-driven implementation based on queues.

Take our LEDs, for example. If we wanted to create a simple LED handler that quickly responded to a change request, a multi-element queue wouldn't be necessary; we can make use of the built-in 32-bit wide notification value instead.

 If you're thinking *task notifications sound a bit like semaphores*, you'd be right! Task notifications can also be used as a faster alternative to semaphores.

Let's see how task notifications can be utilized to issue commands and pass information to a task by working through an example.

Passing simple data using task notifications

In this example, our goal is to have recvTask set LED states, which it has been doing this entire chapter. This time, instead of allowing multiple copies of future LED states to pile up and execute some time in the future, recvTask will execute just one state change at a time.

Since the notification value is built into the task, no additional queue needs to be created—we just need to make sure that we store the task handle of recvTask, which will be used when we send it notifications.

Let's look at how we do this by looking at some `mainTaskNotifications.c` excerpts:

1. Outside of `main`, we'll define some bitmasks and a task handle:

```
#define RED_LED_MASK 0x0001
#define BLUE_LED_MASK 0x0002
#define GREEN_LED_MASK 0x0004
static xTaskHandle recvTaskHandle = NULL;
```

2. Inside `main`, we'll create the `recvTask` and pass it the handle to populate:

```
retVal = xTaskCreate(recvTask, "recvTask", STACK_SIZE, NULL,
                        tskIDLE_PRIORITY + 2, &recvTaskHandle);
assert_param( retVal == pdPASS);
assert_param(recvTaskHandle != NULL);
```

3. The task receiving the notification is set up to wait on the next incoming notification and then evaluate each LED's mask, turning LEDs on/off accordingly:

```
void recvTask( void* NotUsed )
{
    while(1)
    {
        uint32_t notificationvalue = ulTaskNotifyTake( pdTRUE,
                                            portMAX_DELAY );
        if((notificationvalue & RED_LED_MASK) != 0)
            RedLed.On();
        else
            RedLed.Off();
```

4. The sending task is set up to send a notification, overwriting any existing notifications that may be present. This results in `xTaskNotify` always returning pdTRUE:

```
void sendingTask( void* NotUsed )
{
    while(1)
    {
        xTaskNotify( recvTaskHandle, RED_LED_MASK,
                    eSetValueWithOverwrite);
        vTaskDelay(200);
```

This example can be built using the `directTaskNotification` configuration and uploaded to the Nucleo. It will sequentially blink each LED as the notifications are sent to `recvTask`.

Other options for task notifications

From the `eNotifyAction` enumeration in `task.h`, we can see that the other options for notifying the task include the following:

eNoAction = 0, /* Notify the task without updating its notify value. */
eSetBits, /* Set bits in the task's notification value. */
eIncrement, /* Increment the task's notification value. */
eSetValueWithOverwrite, /* Set the task's notification value to a specific value even if the previous value has not yet been read by the task. */
eSetValueWithoutOverwrite /* Set the task's notification value if the previous value has been read by the task. */

Using these options creates some additional flexibility, such as using notifications as binary and counting semaphores. Note that some of these options change how `xTaskNotify` returns, so it will be necessary to check the return value in some cases.

Comparing direct task notifications to queues

Compared to queues, task notifications have the following features:

- They always have storage capacity of exactly one 32-bit integer.
- They do not offer a means of waiting to push a notification to a busy task; it will either overwrite an existing notification or return immediately without writing.
- They can only be used with only one receiver (since the notification value is stored inside the receiving task).
- They are faster.

Let's take a look at a real-world example using SystemView to compare the direct notification code we just wrote against the first queue implementation.

The queue implementation from `mainQueueSimplePassByValue.c` looks like this when performing `xQueueSend`:

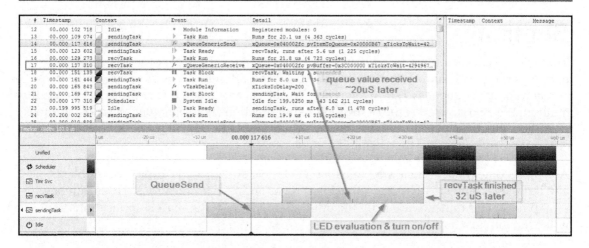

The direct task notification looks like this when calling `xTaskNotify`:

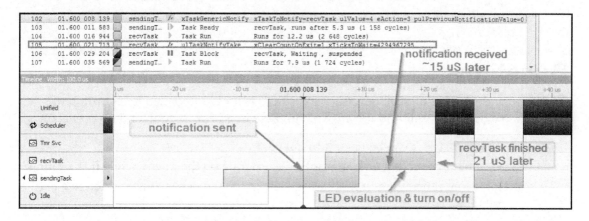

As we can see from the preceding screenshots, the direct task notification is in the range of 25–35% faster than using a queue in this particular use case. There's also no RAM overhead for storing a queue when using direct task notifications.

Summary

You've now learned the basics of how to use queues in a variety of scenarios, such as passing simple and composite elements by value and reference. You're aware of the pros and cons of using queues to store references to objects and when it is appropriate to use this method. We also covered some of the detailed interactions between queues, tasks, and task priorities. We finished with a simple real-world example of how to use task notifications to efficiently drive a small state machine.

As you become more accustomed to using RTOSes to solve a wide variety of problems, you'll find new and creative ways of using queues and task notifications. Tasks, queues, semaphores, and mutexes are truly the building blocks of RTOS-based applications and will help you go a long way.

We're not completely done with any of these elements yet, though—there's still a lot of more advanced material to cover related to using all of these primitives in the context of ISRs, which is up next!

Questions

As we conclude, here is a list of questions for you to test your knowledge regarding this chapter's material. You will find the answers in the *Assessments* section of the *Appendix*:

1. What data types can be passed to queues?
2. What happens to the task attempting to operate on the queue while it is waiting?
3. Name one consideration that needs to be made when passing by reference to a queue?
4. Task notifications can completely replace queues:
   - True
   - False
5. Task notifications can send data of any type:
   - True
   - False
6. What are the advantages of task notifications over queues?

Further reading

- **Explanation of all constants of** `FreeRTOSConfig.h`: `https://www.freertos.org/a00110.html`
- **FreeRTOS direct task notifications:** `https://www.freertos.org/RTOS-task-notifications.html`

Section 4: Advanced RTOS Techniques

4

By building on concepts from the previous section, you'll learn how to get the absolute best real-time performance using both hardware acceleration and firmware techniques. After taking a deep dive into efficient driver implementation, you'll learn how to architect a robust and testable code base that will be a pleasure to work with and transcend multiple hardware designs. Learn what higher-level considerations you should be aware of, such as various options in RTOS APIs and the number of cores or processors you can design into a system. Finally, you'll pick up a few troubleshooting tips and suggested next steps.

This section comprises the following chapters:

10
Drivers and ISRs

Interacting with the peripherals of a **microcontroller unit** (**MCU**) is extremely important in many applications. In this chapter, we'll discuss several different ways of implementing peripheral drivers. Up to this point, we've been using blinking LEDs as a means of interacting with our development board. This is about to change. As we seek to gain a deeper understanding of peripheral drivers, we'll start to focus on different ways of implementing a driver for a common communication peripheral—the **universal asynchronous receiver/transmitter** (**UART**). As we transfer data from one UART to another, we'll uncover the important role that peripheral and **direct memory access** (**DMA**) hardware plays when creating efficient driver implementations.

We'll start by exploring a UART peripheral by implementing an extremely simple polled receive-only driver inside a task. After taking a look at the performance of that driver, we'll take a close look at **interrupt service routines** (**ISRs**) and the different ways they can interact with the RTOS kernel. The driver will be re-implemented using interrupts. After that, we'll add in support for a DMA-based driver. Finally, we'll explore a few different approaches to how the drivers can interact with the rest of the system and take a look at a newer FreeRTOS feature—stream buffers. Throughout this chapter, we'll keep a close eye on overall system performance using SystemView. By the end, you should have a solid understanding of the trade-offs to be made when writing drivers that can take advantage of RTOS features to aid usability.

The following topics will be covered in this chapter:

- Introducing the UART
- Creating a polled UART driver
- Differentiating between tasks and ISRs
- Creating ISR-based drivers
- Creating DMA-based drivers
- FreeRTOS stream buffers
- Choosing a driver model
- Using third-party libraries (STM HAL)

Technical requirements

To complete the exercises in this chapter, you will require the following:

- A Nucleo F767 dev board
- Jumper wires—20 to 22 AWG (~0.65 mm) solid core wire
- A Micro-USB cable
- STM32CubeIDE and source code (instructions in the *Setting up Our IDE* section in Chapter 5, *Selecting an IDE*)
- SEGGER J-Link, Ozone, and SystemView (instructions in Chapter 6, *Debugging Tools for Real-Time Systems*)

All source code used in this chapter is available at https://github.com/PacktPublishing/ Hands-On-RTOS-with-Microcontrollers/tree/master/Chapter_10.

Introducing the UART

As we briefly covered in Chapter 4, *Selecting the Right MCU*, the acronym **UART** stands for **Universal Asynchronous Receiver/Transmitter**. UART hardware takes bytes of data and transmits them over a wire by modulating the voltage of a signal line at a predetermined rate:

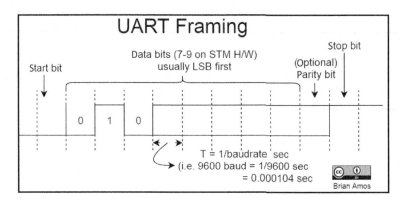

The **asynchronous** nature of a UART means no additional clock line is needed to monitor individual bit transitions. Instead, the hardware is set up to transition each bit at a specific frequency (baud rate). The UART hardware also adds some extra framing to the beginning and end of each packet it transmits. Start and stop bits signal the beginning and end of a packet. These bits (along with an optional parity bit) are used by the hardware to help guarantee the validity of packets (which are typically 8 bits long).

A more general form of UART hardware is the **USART universal synchronous/asynchronous receiver transmitter (USART)**. USARTs are capable of transferring data either synchronously (with the addition of a clock signal) or asynchronously (without a clock signal).

UARTs are often used to communicate between different chips and systems. They form the foundation of many different communication solutions, such as RS232, RS422, RS485, Modbus, and so on. UARTs can also be used for multi-processor communication and to communicate with different chips in the same system—for example, WiFi and Bluetooth transceivers.

In this chapter, we'll be developing a few iterations of a UART driver. In order to be able to observe system behavior, we'll be tying two UARTs on the Nucleo development board together, as in the following diagram. The two connections in the diagram will tie the transmit signal from UART4 to the receive signal of USART2. Likewise, they'll tie USART2 Tx to UART4 Rx. This will allow bidirectional communication between the UARTs. The connections should be made with pre-terminated **jumper wires** or 20-22 AWG (~0.65 mm) solid core wires:

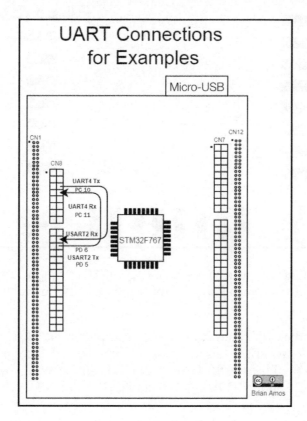

Now that the connections are made, let's take a closer look at what else needs to happen before we can consider transferring data between peripherals on this chip.

Setting up the UART

As we can see from the following simplified block diagram, there are a few components involved when setting up a UART for communication. The UART needs to be properly configured to transmit at the correct baud rate, parity settings, flow control, and stop bits. Other hardware that interacts with the UART will also need to be configured properly:

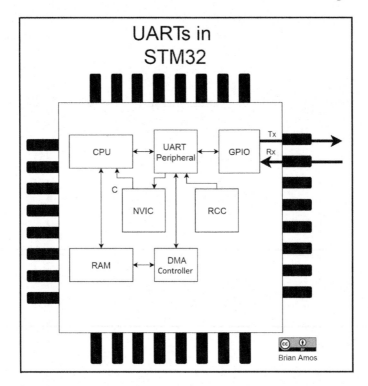

Here's a list of steps that will need to be taken to get UART4 set up. Although we're using UART4 as an example, the same steps will apply to most other peripherals that attach to pins of the MCU:

1. Configure the GPIO lines. Since each GPIO pin on the MCU can be shared with many different peripherals, they must be configured to connect to the desired peripheral (in this case, the UART). In this example, we'll cover the steps to connect PC10 and PC11 to UART4 signals:

You can read more about the pinout of the STM32F7xx series MCUs in *Section 3, Pinouts and Pin Description*, of STM's STM32F767xx datasheet *DoCID 029041*. Datasheets will typically contain information specific to exact models of MCUs, while reference manuals will contain general information about an entire family of MCUs. The following excerpt is of a table is from the datasheet and shows alternate function pin mappings:

Table 13. STM32F765xx, STM32F767xx, STM32F768Ax and STM32F769xx alternate function mapping (continued)													
	AF0	AF1	AF2	AF3	AF4	AF5	AF6	AF7	AF8	AF9	AF10	AF11	AF1
Port	SYS	I2C4/UART5/TIM1/2	TIM3/4/5	TIM8/9/10/11/LPTIM1/DFSDM1/CEC	I2C1/2/3/4/USART1/CEC	SPI1/I2S1/SPI2/I2S2/SPI3/I2S3/SPI4/5/6	SPI2/I2S2/SPI3/I2S3/SAI1/I2C4/UART4/DFSDM1	SPI6/2/S3/16/USART1/2/3/UART5/DFSDM1/SPDIF	SPI6/SAI2/USART6/UART4/5/7/8/OTG_FS/SPDIF	CAN1/2/TIM12/13/14/QUADSPI/FMC/LCD	SAI2/QUADSPI/S/DMMC2/D/FSDM1/O/TG2_HS/OTG1_FS/LCD	I2C4/CAN3/SDMMC2/ETH	UART/FMC/MMC/DIOS/G2_
Port C	PC11	-	-	-	DFSDM1_DATAIN5	-	-	SPI3_MISO	USART3_RX	UART4_RX	QUADSPI_BK2_NCS	-	-	SDM_D
	PC12	TRACED3	-	-	-	-	-	SPI3_MOSI/I2S3_SD	U_	UART5_TX	-	-	-	SDM_C
	PC13	-	-	-	-	-	-	-	-	-	-	-	-	-

2. Reference the desired port and bit. (In this case, we'll be setting up port C bit 11 to map to the UART4_Rx function).

3. Find the desired alternate function for the pin (UART4_Rx).

4. Find the alternate function number (AF8) to use when configuring the GPIO registers.

5. Set up the appropriate GPIO registers to correctly configure the hardware and map the desired UART peripheral to the physical pins.

An STM-supplied HAL function is used here for simplicity. The appropriate GPIO registers will by written when HAL_GPIO_Init is called. All we need to do is fill in a GPIO_InitTypeDef struct and pass a reference to HAL_GPIO_Init; in the following code, the 10 GPIO pin and the 11 GPIO pin on port C are both initialized to alternative push/pull functions. They are also mapped to UART4 by setting the alternate function member to AF8—as determined in step 4:

```
GPIO_InitTypeDef GPIO_InitStruct = {0};
//PC10 is UART4_TX PC11 is UART4_RX
GPIO_InitStruct.Pin = GPIO_PIN_10 | GPIO_PIN_11;
GPIO_InitStruct.Mode = GPIO_MODE_AF_PP;
GPIO_InitStruct.Pull = GPIO_NOPULL;
```

```
GPIO_InitStruct.Alternate = GPIO_AF8_UART4;
HAL_GPIO_Init(GPIOC, &GPIO_InitStruct);
```

6. Enable the necessary peripheral clocks. Since each peripheral clock is turned off by default (for power saving), the UART's peripheral clock must be turned on by writing to the **reset and clock control (RCC)** register. The following line is also from HAL:

```
__UART4_CLK_ENABLE();
```

7. Configure the interrupts (if using them) by configuring settings in the **nested vector interrupt controller (NVIC)**—details will be included in the examples where appropriate.
8. Configure the DMA (if using it)—details will be included in the examples where appropriate.
9. Configure the peripheral with the necessary settings, such as baud rate, parity, flow control, and so on.

   The following code is an excerpt from the STM_UartInit function in BSP/UartQuickDirtyInit.c., where Baudrate and STM_UART_PERIPH are input parameters of STM_UartInit, which makes it very easy to configure multiple UART peripherals with similar settings, without repeating all of the following code every time:

```
HAL_StatusTypeDef retVal;
UART_HandleTypeDef uartInitStruct;
uartInitStruct.Instance = STM_UART_PERIPH;
uartInitStruct.Init.BaudRate = Baudrate;
uartInitStruct.Init.WordLength = UART_WORDLENGTH_8B;
uartInitStruct.Init.StopBits = UART_STOPBITS_1;
uartInitStruct.Init.Parity = UART_PARITY_NONE;
uartInitStruct.Init.Mode = UART_MODE_TX_RX;
uartInitStruct.Init.HwFlowCtl = UART_HWCONTROL_NONE;
uartInitStruct.Init.OverSampling = UART_OVERSAMPLING_16;
uartInitStruct.Init.OneBitSampling = UART_ONE_BIT_SAMPLE_DISABLE;
uartInitStruct.hdmatx = DmaTx;
uartInitStruct.hdmarx = DmaRx;
uartInitStruct.AdvancedInit.AdvFeatureInit =
UART_ADVFEATURE_NO_INIT;
retVal = HAL_UART_Init(&uartInitStruct);
assert_param(retVal == HAL_OK);
```

10. Depending on the desired transmit method (such as polled, interrupt-driven, or DMA), some additional setting up will be required; this setting up is typically performed immediately before beginning a transfer.

Let's see how all of this plays out by creating a simple driver to read data coming into USART2.

Creating a polled UART driver

When writing low-level drivers, it's a must to read through the datasheet in order to understand how the peripheral works. Even if you're not writing a low-level driver from scratch, it is always a good idea to gain some familiarity with the hardware you'll be working with. The more familiarity you have, the easier it will be to diagnose unexpected behavior, as well as to create efficient solutions.

 You can read more about the UART peripheral we're working with in *Chapter 34* of the *STM RM0410 STM32F76xxx* reference manual (*USART*).

Our first **driver** will take an extremely simple approach to getting data from the UART and into a queue that can be easily monitored and consumed by any task in the system. By monitoring the **receive not empty** (RXNE) bit of the UART peripheral's **interrupt status register** (ISR), the driver can determine when a new byte is ready to be transferred from the **receive data register** (RDR) of the UART into the queue. To make this as easy as possible, the while loop is placed in a task (polledUartReceive), which will let other higher-priority tasks run.

The following is an excerpt from Chapter_10/Src/mainUartPolled.c:

```
void polledUartReceive( void* NotUsed )
{
    uint8_t nextByte;
    //setup UART
    STM_UartInit(USART2, 9600, NULL, NULL);
    while(1)
    {
        while(!(USART2->ISR & USART_ISR_RXNE_Msk));
        nextByte = USART2->RDR;
        xQueueSend(uart2_BytesReceived, &nextByte, 0);
    }
}
```

There is another simple task in this example as well; it monitors the queue and prints out whatever has been received:

```
void uartPrintOutTask( void* NotUsed)
{
    char nextByte;
    while(1)
    {
        xQueueReceive(uart2_BytesReceived, &nextByte, portMAX_DELAY);
        SEGGER_SYSVIEW_PrintfHost("%c", nextByte);
    }
}
```

Now that our driver is ready, let's see how it performs.

Analyzing the performance

The preceding code (uartPolled) can be programmed onto the MCU and we can take a look at the performance using SEGGER SystemView:

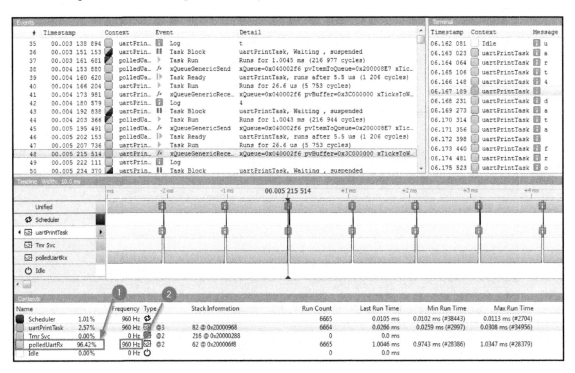

After looking at the execution using SystemView, we quickly realize that—although easy to program—this driver is *horrifically inefficient*:

1. SystemView reports that this driver is utilizing *over 96%* of the CPU's resources.
2. The queue is being called at **960 Hz** (which makes perfect sense given the initial baud rate of 9,600 baud).

We can see that, while easy to implement, this solution comes with significant performance penalties—all while servicing a fairly slow peripheral. Drivers that service peripherals by polling have trade-offs.

Pros and cons of a polled driver

Here are some of the advantages of using a polled driver:

- It is easy to program.
- Any task has immediate access to data in the queue.

At the same time, there are many issues with this approach:

- It must be one of the highest priority tasks in the system.
- There is a high chance of data loss when not executing at high priority.
- It is extremely wasteful of CPU cycles.

In this example, we're only transferring data at 9,600 baud. Granted, most of the time was spent spinning on the RXNE bit, but transferring every byte as it is received in a queue is also fairly expensive (when compared to pushing bytes into a simple array-based buffer). To put this into perspective, USART2 on STM32F767 running at 216 MHz has a maximum baud rate of 27 Mbaud, which would mean we would need to add each character to the shared queue nearly 3 million times a second (it is currently adding < 1,000 characters per second). Transferring this much data through a queue quickly isn't feasible on this hardware since queue additions take 7 µS each (even if the CPU was doing nothing else, we'd be capable of transferring less than 143,000 characters per second into the queue).

More importantly, there are few opportunities to speed up this polled approach, since we may receive a new character once every millisecond. If any other task was executing for more than 2 ms, the peripheral could potentially be overrun (a new byte is received and overwrites the buffer before the previous byte is read). Because of these limitations, there are very specific circumstances where polled drivers are most useful.

Usage of polled drivers

There are a few circumstances where polled drivers are especially helpful:

- **System verification**: This is perfectly acceptable when performing initial system verification, but at that stage of development, it is debatable whether an RTOS should be used at all. If the application happens to be truly single purpose, there is nothing else to be done while waiting for data to be transferred, and there are no power considerations, this would also be an acceptable approach.
- **Special cases**: Occasionally, there may be times when a very special-purpose piece of code is needed for a limited scope. For example, a peripheral may need to be serviced with an extremely low amount of latency. In other cases, the event being polled for could happen extremely quickly. When events are happening in the order of nanoseconds or microseconds ns or µs (instead of ms, as in the previous example), it often makes more sense to simply poll for the event, rather than create a more elaborate synchronization scheme. In event-driven systems, adding in blocking calls must be carefully considered and clearly documented.

Conversely, if a given event is happening very infrequently and there are no specific timing constraints, a polled approach may also be perfectly acceptable.

While the driver in this example focused on the receiving side, where poll-based drivers are rarely acceptable, it is more common to find them used to transmit data. This is because space between the characters is generally acceptable since it doesn't result in loss the of data. This allows the driver to be run at a lower priority so that other tasks in the system have a chance to run. There are a few cases where there is a reasonable argument for using a polled transmit driver that blocks while the transmission is taking place:

- The code using the driver must block until the transmission is complete.
- The transfer is a short amount of data.
- The data rate is reasonably high (so the transfer takes a relatively small amount of time).

If all of these conditions are met, it *may* make sense to simply use a polled approach, rather than a more elaborate interrupt- or DMA-driven approach, which will require the use of callbacks and, potentially, task synchronization mechanisms. However, depending on how you choose to structure your drivers, it is also possible to have the convenience of blocking calls but without the inefficiency of a polled transfer wasting CPU cycles. To take advantage of any of the non-polled approaches, we'll need to develop another skill—programming ISRs.

Differentiating between tasks and ISRs

Before we jump into coding a peripheral driver that utilizes interrupts, let's take a quick look at how interrupts compare to FreeRTOS tasks.

There are many similarities between tasks and ISRs:

- Both provide a way of achieving **parallel** code execution.
- Both only run when required.
- Both can be written with C/C++ (ISRs generally no longer need to be written in assembly code).

But there are also many differences between tasks and ISRs:

- **ISRs are brought into context by hardware; tasks gain context by the RTOS kernel**: Tasks are always brought into context by the FreeRTOS kernel. Interrupts, on the other hand, are generated by hardware in the MCU. There are usually a few different ways of configuring the generation (and masking) of interrupts.
- **ISRs must exit as quickly as possible; tasks are more forgiving**: FreeRTOS tasks are often set up to run in a similar way to an infinite `while` loop—they will be synchronized with the system using primitives (such as queues and semaphores) and switched into context according to their priority. At the complete opposite end of the spectrum are ISRs, which should generally be coded so that they exit quickly. This *quick exit* ensures that the system can respond to other ISRs, which keeps everything responsive and ensures no interrupts are missed because a single routine was hogging the CPU.
- **ISR functions do not take input parameters; tasks can**: Unlike tasks, ISRs can never have input parameters. Since an interrupt is triggered because of a hardware state, the most important job of the ISR is to read the hardware state (through memory-mapped registers) and take the appropriate action(s). For example, an interrupt can be generated when a UART receives a byte of data. In this case, the ISR would read a status register, read (and store) the byte received in a static variable, and clear the interrupt.

 Most (but not all) peripherals on STM32 hardware will automatically clear interrupt flags when certain registers are read. Regardless of how the interrupt is cleared, it is important to ensure the interrupt is no longer pending—otherwise, the interrupt will fire continuously and you will always be executing the associated ISR!

- **ISRs may only access a limited ISR-specific subset of the FreeRTOS API**: FreeRTOS is written in a way that provides flexibility while balancing convenience, safety, and performance. Accessing data structures such as queues from a task is extremely flexible (for example, tasks making API calls to a queue can easily block for any period of time). There is an additional set of functions that are available to ISRs for operating on queues, but these functions have a limited subset of functionality (such as not being able to block—the call always immediately returns). This provides a level of safety since the programmer can't shoot themselves in the foot by calling a function that blocks from inside an ISR. Calling a non-ISR API function from inside an ISR will cause FreeRTOS to trigger `configASSERT`.

- **ISRs may operate completely independently of all RTOS code**: There are many cases where an ISR operates on such a low level that it doesn't *need* access to any of the FreeRTOS API at all. In this case, the ISR simply executes as it normally would without an RTOS present. The kernel never gets involved (and no tasks will interrupt execution). This makes it very convenient for creating flexible solutions that blend high-performing ISRs (operating completely *underneath* the RTOS) with extremely convenient tasks.

- **All ISRs share the same system stack; each task has a dedicated stack**: Each task receives a private stack, but all of the ISRs share the same system stack. This is noteworthy only because, when writing ISRs, you'll need to ensure you reserve enough stack space to allow them to run (possibly simultaneously) if they are nested.

Now that we've covered the differences between tasks and ISRs, let's take a look at how they can be used together to create very powerful event-driven code.

Using the FreeRTOS API from interrupts

Most of the FreeRTOS primitives covered so far have ISR-safe versions of their APIs. For example, `xQueueSend()` has an equivalent ISR-safe version, `xQueueSendFromISR()`. There are a few differences between the ISR-safe version and the standard call:

- The `FromISR` variants won't block. For example, if `xQueueSendFromISR` encounters a full queue, it will immediately return.

- The `FromISR` variants require an extra parameter, `BaseType_t *pxHigherPriorityTaskWoken`, which will indicate whether or not a higher-priority task needs to be switched into context immediately following the interrupt.
- Only interrupts that have a *logically* lower priority than what is defined by `configMAX_API_CALL_INTERRUPT_PRIORITY` in `FreeRTOSConfig.h` are permitted to call FreeRTOS API functions (see the following diagram for an example).

The following is an overview of how the `FreeRTOSConfig.h` and `main_XXX.c` files configure interrupts for the examples in this book. Some noteworthy items are as follows:

- `main_XXX.c` makes a call to `NVIC_SetPriorityGrouping(0)` after all STM HAL initialization is performed (`HAL` sets priority grouping upon initialization). This allows all 4 bits of the **nested interrupt vector controller** (**NVIC**) to be used for priorities and results in 16 priority levels.
- `FreeRTOSConfig.h` is used to set up the relationship between FreeRTOS API calls and NVIC priorities. The Cortex-M7 defines `255` as being the lowest priority level and `0` as being the highest. Since the STM32F7 only implements 4 bits, these 4 bits will be shifted into the 4 MSB bits; the lower 4 bits won't affect operation (see the following diagram):
  - `configKERNEL_INTERRUPT_PRIORITY` defines the lowest priority interrupt in our system (and the ISR priority of the FreeRTOS tasks, since the scheduler is called within a SysTick interrupt). Because 4 bits yields a possible range of `0` (highest priority) to `15` (lowest priority), the lowest NVIC priority used will be `15`. When setting `configKERNEL_INTERRUPT_PRIORITY`, `15` needs to be shifted left into the 8 bit representation (used directly in the CortexM registers) as `(15 << 4) | 0x0F = 0xFF` or `255`. Since the lowest 4 bits are don't cares, `0xF0` (decimal 240) is also acceptable.

- `configMAX_SYSCALL_INTERRUPT_PRIORITY` defines the (logically) highest priority interrupt that is allowed to make calls to the FreeRTOS API. This is set to 5 in our examples. Shifting left to fill out the 8 bits gives us a value of `0x50` or `0x5F` (decimal 80 or 95, respectively):

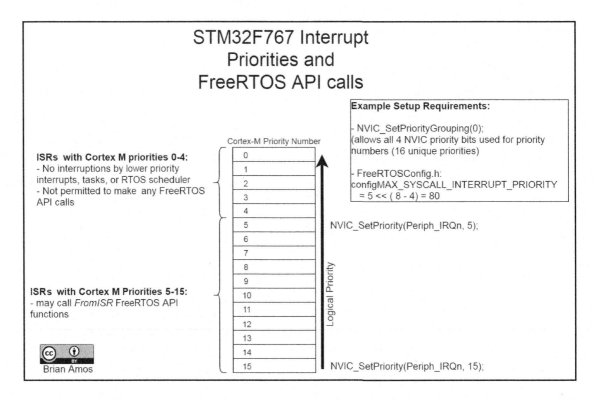

As we can see in the preceding diagram, there are some cases where ISRs can be set up to execute at a priority above anything the RTOS might be doing. When configured as 0 to 4 NVIC priorities, ISRs are identical to traditional "bare-metal" ISRs.

It is *very* important to ensure that the interrupt priority is properly configured *before* enabling the interrupt by calling `NVIC_SetPriority` with a priority of <= 5. If an interrupt with a priority that is logically higher than `configMAX_SYSCALL_INTERRUPT_PRIORITY` calls a FreeRTOS API function, you'll be greeted with a `configASSERT` failure (see `Chapter 17`, *Troubleshooting Tips and Next Steps*, for more details on `configASSERT`).

Now that we have an understanding of the differences between tasks and ISRs, as well as some of the ground rules for using FreeRTOS API functions from within ISRs, let's take another look at the polled driver to see how it can be implemented more efficiently.

Creating ISR-based drivers

In the first iteration of the UART driver, a task polled the UART peripheral registers to determine when a new byte had been received. The constant polling is what caused the task to consume > 95% of CPU cycles. The most meaningful work done by this task-based driver was transferring bytes of data out of the UART peripheral and into the queue.

In this iteration of the driver, instead of using a task to continuously poll the UART registers, we'll set up the UART2 peripheral and NVIC to provide an interrupt when a new byte is received.

Queue-based driver

First, let's look at how to more efficiently implement the polled driver (previously implemented by polling the UART registers within a task). In this implementation, instead of using a task to repeatedly poll the UART registers, a function will be used to set up the peripheral to use interrupts and initiate the transfer. A complete set of ISR function prototypes can be found in the startup file (for the STM32F767 used in our examples, this file is Chapter_10/startup_stm32f767xx.s).

 Each *_IRQHandler instance in startup_stm32f767xx.s is used to map the function name to an address in the interrupt vector table. On ARM Cortex-M0+, -M3, -M4, and -M7 devices, this vector table can be relocated by an offset at runtime. See *Further reading* for some links to more information on these concepts.

This example has four primary components:

- uartPrintOutTask: This function initializes USART2 and associated hardware, starts a reception, and then prints anything placed in the uart2_BytesReceived queue.
- startReceiveInt: Sets up an interrupt-based reception for USART2.

- `USART2_IRQHandler`: An ISR is issued when an interrupt occurs for the USART2 peripheral.
- `startUart4Traffic`: Starts a continuous stream of data transmitted from UART4 to be received by USART2 (provided the jumpers are correctly set).

Let's take a look at each component in detail. All excerpts in this section are from `Chapter_10/Src/mainUartInterruptQueue.c`.

uartPrintOutTask

The only task in this example is `uartPrintOutTask`:

```
void uartPrintOutTask( void* NotUsed)
{
    char nextByte;
    STM_UartInit(USART2, 9600, NULL, NULL);
    startReceiveInt();

    while(1)
    {
        xQueueReceive(uart2_BytesReceived, &nextByte, portMAX_DELAY);
        SEGGER_SYSVIEW_PrintfHost("%c", nextByte);
    }
}
```

`uartPrintOutTask` does the following:

- Performs all peripheral hardware initialization by calling `STM_UartInit`
- Starts an interrupt-based reception by calling `startReceiveInt`
- *Consumes* and prints each character as it is added to the `uart2_BytesReceived` queue by calling `xQueueReceive`

startReceiveInt

The `startReceiveInt` function starts an interrupt-driven reception:

```
static bool rxInProgress = false;

void startReceiveInt( void )
{
    rxInProgress = true;
    USART2->CR3 |= USART_CR3_EIE; //enable error interrupts
    //enable peripheral and Rx not empty interrupts
```

```
        USART2->CR1 |= (USART_CR1_UE | USART_CR1_RXNEIE);
        NVIC_SetPriority(USART2_IRQn, 6);
        NVIC_EnableIRQ(USART2_IRQn);
}
```

startReceiveInt sets up everything required to receive data on USART2:

- rxInProgress is a flag used by the ISR to indicate a reception is in progress. The ISR (USART2_IRQHandler()) will not attempt to write to the queue until rxInProgress is true.
- USART2 is configured to generate receive and error interrupts and is then enabled.
- The NVIC_SetPriority function (defined by CMSIS in Drivers/CMSIS/Include/corex_cm7.h) is used to set the interrupt priority. Since this interrupt will call a FreeRTOS API function, this priority must be set at or *below* the logical priority defined by configLIBRARY_MAX_SYSCALL_INTERRUPT_PRIORITY in FreeRTOSConfig.h. On ARM CortexM processors, smaller numbers signify a higher logical priority—in this example, #define configLIBRARY_MAX_SYSCALL_INTERRUPT_PRIORITY 5, so assigning a priority of 6 to USART2_IRQn will be adequate for allowing the ISR to make calls to the ISR-safe function (xQueueSendFromISR) provided by FreeRTOS.
- Finally, the interrupt requests generated by USART2 will be enabled by making a call to NVIC_EnableIRQ. If NVIC_EnableIRQ is not called, USART2 will still generate requests, but the interrupt controller (the "IC" in NVIC) will not *vector* the program counter to the ISR (USART2_IRQHandler will never be called).

In this example, as with nearly all the code in this chapter, we're writing directly to the hardware peripheral registers and not using considerable amounts of abstraction. This is done to keep the focus on how the RTOS interacts with the MCU. If code reuse is one of your goals, you'll need to provide some level of abstraction above raw registers (or STM HAL code, if you're using it). Some guidelines on this can be found in Chapter 12, *Tips on Creating Well-Abstracted Architecture*.

USART2_IRQHandler

Here is the code for `USART2_IRQHandler`:

```c
void USART2_IRQHandler( void )
{
    portBASE_TYPE xHigherPriorityTaskWoken = pdFALSE;
    SEGGER_SYSVIEW_RecordEnterISR();

    //error flag clearing omitted for brevity

    if( USART2->ISR & USART_ISR_RXNE_Msk)
    {
        uint8_t tempVal = (uint8_t) USART2->RDR;

        if(rxInProgress)
        {
            xQueueSendFromISR(uart2_BytesReceived, &tempVal,
                              &xHigherPriorityTaskWoken);
        }
        SEGGER_SYSVIEW_RecordExitISR();
        portYIELD_FROM_ISR(xHigherPriorityTaskWoken);
    }
}
```

Let's take a closer look at each component of the ISR:

- The USART registers are directly read to determine whether or not the receive not empty (RXNE) is set. If it is, the contents of the receive data register (RDR) are stored to a temporary variable (`tempVal`)—this read clears the interrupt flag. If a receive is in progress, `tempVal` is sent to the queue.

- Calls to `SEGGER_SYSVIEW_RecordEnterISR` and `SEGGER_SYSVIEW_RecordExitISR` are made upon entry and exit, which gives SEGGER SystemView the visibility to display the interrupt with all of the other tasks in the system.

- The `xHigherPriorityTaskWoken` variable is initialized to false. This variable is passed to the `xQueueSendFromISR` function and is used to determine whether a high-priority task (higher than the one currently in the non-ISR context) is blocking because it is waiting on an empty queue. In this case, `xHigherPriorityTaskWoken` will be set to true, indicating a higher-priority task should be woken immediately after the ISR exits. When the call to `portYIELD_FROM_ISR` is made, if `xHigherPriorityTaskWoken` is true, the scheduler will immediately switch to the higher-priority task.

Now that the ISR has been written, we'll need to make sure it will actually be called by the hardware at the appropriate time.

Tips for linking ISRs

When writing ISRs from scratch (as we've done in the previous example), one area that can prove to be a source of unexpected trouble is ensuring your ISR is properly linked in (and executed). That is, even if you've properly set up the peripheral to generate interrupts, your new ISR might never be called because it isn't named properly (instead, the default implementation, defined in a startup file, will likely be called). Here are some tips to make sure that shiny new ISR can be found and properly linked in with the rest of the application:

- STM32 `*_IRQHandler` function names *usually* contain the *exact* peripheral name from the datasheet as a sub-string. For example, USART2 maps to `USART2_IRQHandler` (notice the "S") and UART4 maps to `UART4_IRQHandler` (no "S" in the peripheral or function name).

- When writing a new implementation for an ISR, it is a good idea to copy and paste the exact `_IQRHandler` name from the startup file. This reduces the chance of typos, which can cause debug headaches!

- STM start-up files implement default handlers for every interrupt as an infinite loop. If you notice your application becoming unresponsive, it is possible you've enabled an interrupt and your `*_IRQHandler` definition isn't being linked in properly.

- If you happen to be implementing `*_IRQHandler` inside a C++ file, be sure to use `extern "C"` to prevent *name mangling*. For example, the USART2 definition would be written as `extern "C" void USART2_IRQHandler( void)`. This also means the ISR definition must *not* be inside a class.

When implementing ISRs, take your time and be sure to get the details (such as the *exact* name) right. Don't rush into attempting to debug the rest of your application without first ensuring the ISR is called when expected. Using breakpoints inside the ISR is an excellent way of doing this.

startUart4Traffic

The final component that needs to be explored in this example is how data will be sent to UART2. These examples are meant to simulate external data being received by USART2. To achieve this without additional hardware, we wired together UART4 Tx and USART2 RX pins earlier in the chapter. The call to `startUart4Traffic()` is a `TimerHandler` prototype. A oneshot timer is started and set to fire 5 seconds after the application starts.

The function that does all of the heavy lifting is `SetupUart4ExternalSim()`. It sets up a continuous circular DMA transfer (which executes without CPU intervention) that transmits the string `data from uart4` repeatedly. A full example using DMA will be covered later in this chapter – for now, it is sufficient to realize that data is being sent to USART2 without involvement from the CPU.

`startUart4Traffic()` creates a *continuous* stream of bytes that will be transmitted out of UART4 Tx and into UART2 Rx (with no flow control). Depending on the selected baud rate and the amount of time it takes for the receiving code to execute, we can expect that, eventually, a byte will be missed on the receiving side during some examples. Keep this in mind when running examples on your own. See the *Choosing a driver model* section for more details on selecting the appropriate driver type for your application.

Performance analysis

Now, let's take a look at the performance of this implementation by compiling `mainUartInterruptQueue`, loading it onto the MCU, and using SystemView to analyze the actual execution:

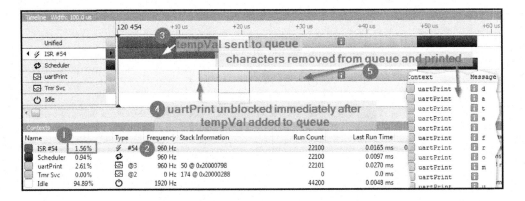

This time around, things look considerably better. Here are some noteworthy items from the preceding screenshot:

1. The ISR responsible for dealing with the incoming data on USART2 Rx is only consuming around 1.6% of the CPU (much better than the 96% we saw when we were using a polled approach).
2. We are still receiving 960 bytes per second—the same as before.
3. The small tick mark shown here is the exact point in time when `tempVal` is added to `uart2_BytesReceived` by the call to the `xQueueSendFromISR` FreeRTOS API function.
4. We can see the effect of `portYIELD_FROM_ISR` here. The light-blue portion of the `uartPrint` task indicates that the task is ready to run. This happens because the `uartPrint` task is ready to run since there is an item in the queue. The call to `portYIELD_FROM_ISR` forces the scheduler to immediately evaluate which task should be brought into context. The green portion (starting at ~21 uS) is SystemView's way of signifying that the task is in a **running** state.
5. After the `uartPrint` task begins running, it removes the next character from the queue and prints it using `SEGGER_SYSVIEW_PrintfHost`.

By switching from a poll-based driver to an interrupt-based driver, we've significantly reduced the CPU load. Additionally, systems that use an interrupt-based driver can run other tasks while still receiving data through USART2. This driver also uses a queue-based approach, which provides a very convenient ring buffer, allowing characters to be continuously received and added to the queue, then read whenever it is convenient for higher-level tasks.

Next, we'll work through an example of a similar driver that doesn't use a queue at all.

A buffer-based driver

Sometimes, the exact size of a transfer is known in advance. In this case, a pre-existing buffer can be passed to the driver and used in place of a queue. Let's take a look at an example of a buffer-based driver, where the exact number of bytes is known in advance. The hardware setup for this example is identical to the previous examples—we'll concentrate on receiving data through USART2.

Instead of using a queue, `uartPrintOutTask` will supply its own buffer to the `startReceiveInt` function. Data received by USART2 will be placed directly in the local buffer until the desired number of bytes have been added, then a semaphore will be given by the ISR to provide notification of the completion. The entire message will be printed as a single string, rather than 1 byte at a time, as it is received (which was done in the last example).

Just like the previous example, there are four main components. However, their responsibilities vary slightly:

- `startReceiveInt`: Sets up an interrupt-based reception for USART2 and configures the necessary variables used by the ISR for the transfer.
- `uartPrintOutTask`: This function initializes USART2 and associated hardware, starts a reception, and waits for completion (with a deadline of 100 ms). The complete message is either printed or a timeout occurs and an error is printed.
- `USART2_IRQHandler`: An ISR is issued when an interrupt occurs for the USART2 peripheral.
- `startUart4Traffic`: Starts a continuous stream of data transmitted from UART4 to be received by USART2 (provided the jumpers are correctly set).

Let's take a look at each component in detail. All excerpts in this section are from `Chapter_10/Src/mainUartInterruptBuffer.c`.

startReceiveInt

The `startReceiveInt` function is very similar to the one used for the queue-based driver:

```
static bool rxInProgress = false;
static uint_fast16_t rxLen = 0;
static uint8_t* rxBuff = NULL;
static uint_fast16_t rxItr = 0;

int32_t startReceiveInt( uint8_t* Buffer, uint_fast16_t Len )
{
    if(!rxInProgress && (Buffer != NULL))
    {
        rxInProgress = true;
        rxLen = Len;
        rxBuff = Buffer;
        rxItr = 0;
        USART2->CR3 |= USART_CR3_EIE; //enable error interrupts
        USART2->CR1 |= (USART_CR1_UE | USART_CR1_RXNEIE);
        NVIC_SetPriority(USART2_IRQn, 6);
```

```
        NVIC_EnableIRQ(USART2_IRQn);
        return 0;
    }
    return -1;
}
```

Here are the notable differences in this setup:

- This variant takes in a pointer to a buffer (Buffer), as well as the desired length of the transfer (Len). A couple of global variables, rxBuff and rxLen (which will be used by the ISR), are initialized using these parameters.
- rxInProgress is used to determine whether a reception is already in progress (returning -1 if it is).
- An iterator (rxItr) that is used to index into the buffer is initialized to 0.

All of the remaining functionality of startReceiveInt is identical to the example covered in the *Queue-based driver* section earlier in the chapter.

uartPrintOutTask

The uartPrintOutTask function that is responsible for printing out data received by USART2 is a bit more complex in this example. This example is also capable of comparing the received data against an expected length, as well as some rudimentary error detection:

1. The buffer and length variables are initialized and the UART peripheral is set up:

```
void uartPrintOutTask( void* NotUsed)
{
    uint8_t rxData[20];
    uint8_t expectedLen = 16;
    memset((void*)rxData, 0, 20);


    STM_UartInit(USART2, 9600, NULL, NULL);
```

2. Then, the body of the while loop starts a reception by calling startReceiveInt and then waits for the rxDone semaphore for up to 100 RTOS ticks for the transfer to complete.
3. If the transfer completes in time, the total number of bytes received is compared against expectedLen.

4. If the correct number of bytes are present, the content of rxData is printed. Otherwise, a message providing an explanation of the discrepancy is printed:

```
while(1)
{
    startReceiveInt(rxData, expectedLen);
    if(xSemaphoreTake(rxDone, 100) == pdPASS)
    {
        if(expectedLen == rxItr)
        {
            SEGGER_SYSVIEW_PrintfHost("received: ");
            SEGGER_SYSVIEW_Print((char*)rxData);
        }
        else
        {
            SEGGER_SYSVIEW_PrintfHost("expected %i bytes received"
                                        "%i", expectedLen, rxItr);
```

The remainder of the while loop and function simply prints timeout if the semaphore is not taken within 100 ticks.

USART2_IRQHandler

This ISR is also slightly more involved since it is required to keep track of the position in a queue:

1. Private globals are used by USART2_IRQHandler because they need to be accessible by both the ISR and used by both USART2_IRQHandler and startReceiveInt:

```
static bool rxInProgress = false;
static uint_fast16_t rxLen = 0;
static uint8_t* rxBuff = NULL;
static uint_fast16_t rxItr = 0;
```

2. The same paradigm for storing xHigherPriorityTaskWoken and SEGGER SystemView tracing is used in this ISR, just like in the last example:

```
void USART2_IRQHandler( void )
{
    portBASE_TYPE xHigherPriorityTaskWoken = pdFALSE;
    SEGGER_SYSVIEW_RecordEnterISR();
```

3. Next, errors are checked by reading the overrun (ORE), noise error (NE), framing error (FE), and parity error (PE) bits in the interrupt state register (USART2->ISR).

If an error is present, it is cleared by a write to the interrupt clear register (USART2->ICR) and the rxDone semaphore is given. It is the responsibility of the caller code to check the number of bits in the buffer by looking at the rxItr variable (shown in the next code block) to ensure the correct number of bits were successfully received:

```
if( USART2->ISR & ( USART_ISR_ORE_Msk |
                    USART_ISR_NE_Msk |
                    USART_ISR_FE_Msk |
                    USART_ISR_PE_Msk ))
{
    USART2->ICR |= (USART_ICR_FECF |
                    USART_ICR_PECF |
                    USART_ICR_NCF |
                    USART_ICR_ORECF);
    if(rxInProgress)
    {
        rxInProgress = false;
        xSemaphoreGiveFromISR(rxDone,
        &xHigherPriorityTaskWoken);
    }
}
```

4. Next, the ISR checks whether a new byte has been received (by reading the RXNE bit of USART2->ISR). If a new byte is available, it is pushed into the rxBuff buffer and the rxItr iterator is incremented.

After the desired number of bytes have been added to the buffer, the rxDone semaphore is given to notify uartPrintOutTask:

```
if( USART2->ISR & USART_ISR_RXNE_Msk)
{
    uint8_t tempVal = (uint8_t) USART2->RDR;
    if(rxInProgress)
    {
        rxBuff[rxItr++] = tempVal;
        if(rxItr >= rxLen)
        {
            rxInProgress = false;
            xSemaphoreGiveFromISR(rxDone,
&xHigherPriorityTaskWoken);
        }
```

```
    }
  }
  SEGGER_SYSVIEW_RecordExitISR();
  portYIELD_FROM_ISR(xHigherPriorityTaskWoken);
```

Don't forget to put a breakpoint in the ISR to make sure it is being called.

startUart4Traffic

Identical to the previous example, this function sets up a DMA transfer to push data out of the UART4 Tx pin into the USART2 Rx pin.

Performance analysis

Now, let's take a look at the performance of this driver implementation. There are several aspects to consider. Unless a transfer is complete, the ISR will normally only transfer a byte into `rxBuff`. In this case, the interrupt is fairly short, taking less than 3 us to complete:

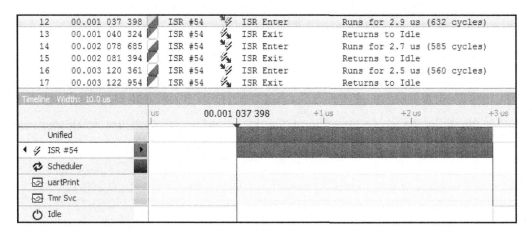

After all 16 bytes have been received, the ISR execution gets a bit more interesting and looks a bit more similar to the previous example:

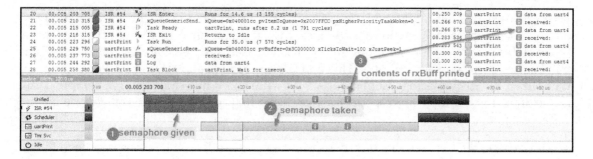

Here are some noteworthy points from the preceding screenshot:

1. After all the bytes have been placed into `rxBuff`, the `rxDone` semaphore is given from the ISR using `xSemaphoreGiveFromISR`.
2. The task is unblocked after the interrupt is executed by taking the available semaphore (`xSemaphoreTake(rxDone, 100)`).
3. The exact contents of `rxBuff` are printed. Note that each line contains the entire string, rather than individual characters. This is because this implementation collects an entire buffer's worth of data before using a semaphore to indicate completion.

Finally, let's have a look at the complete tally of CPU usage:

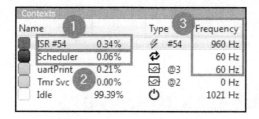

Here are some noteworthy items from the preceding screenshot:

1. The ISR for this implementation is using 0.34% of the CPU (instead of 1.56% when each character was pushed to a queue from inside the ISR).
2. The FreeRTOS scheduler is using only using 0.06% of the CPU instead of 0.94% (each time items are added to queues, the scheduler runs to determine whether or not tasks should be unblocked because of the addition).
3. The frequency of the USART2 ISR remains at **960 Hz**, exactly the same as the previous examples, but now the frequency of the print task has been reduced to only **60 Hz**, since the `uartPrint` task that only runs after 16 bytes has been transferred into `rxBuff`.

As we can see, this ISR implementation of the driver uses even fewer CPU cycles than the queue-based approach. Depending on the use case, it can be an attractive alternative. These types of drivers are commonly found in non-RTOS-based systems, where callback functions will be used instead of semaphores. This approach is flexible enough to be used with or without an RTOS by placing a semaphore in the callback. While slightly more complex, this is one of the most flexible approaches for code bases that see a large amount of reuse in different applications.

To summarize, the two variants of drivers implemented with an ISR so far have been the following:

- **A queue-based driver**: Delivers incoming data to tasks by pushing received data into a queue one character at a time.
- **A buffer-based driver**: Delivers incoming data to a single buffer that is pre-allocated by the calling function.

On the surface, it may seem silly to have two different implementations that both take incoming data from a peripheral and present it to the higher layers of code. It is important to realize these two different variants of a driver for the same hardware vary both in their implementation, efficiency, and ultimately, the interface provided to higher-level code. They may both be moving bytes from the UART peripheral, but they provide higher-level code with drastically different programming models. These different programming models are each suited to solving different types of problems.

Next, we'll look at how another piece of hardware inside the MCU can be used to lighten the burden on the CPU when moving large amounts of data.

Creating DMA-based drivers

We saw that, compared to a polled approach, the interrupt-based driver is considerably better in terms of CPU utilization. But what about applications with a high data rate that require millions of transfers per second? The next step in improved efficiency can be obtained by having the CPU involved as little as possible by pushing most of the work for transferring data around onto specialized peripheral hardware within the MCU.

 A short introduction to DMA was covered in Chapter 2, *Understanding RTOS Tasks*, in case you need a refresher before diving into this example.

In this example, we'll work through creating a driver using the same buffer-based interface as the interrupt-based driver. The only difference will be the use of DMA hardware to transfer bytes out of the peripheral's read data register (RDR) and into our buffer. Since we already have a good handle on configuring the USART2 peripheral from our other drivers, the first order of business for this variant is to figure out how to get data from USART2->RDR to the DMA controller and then into memory.

Configuring DMA peripherals

STM32F767 has two DMA controllers. Each controller has 10 channels and 8 streams to map DMA requests from one location in the MCU to another. On the STM32F767 hardware, streams can do the following:

- Can be thought of as a way to *flow* data from one address to another
- Can transfer data from peripherals to RAM or RAM to peripherals
- Can transfer data from RAM to RAM
- Can only transfer data between two points at any given moment in time

Each stream has up to 10 channels for mapping a peripheral register into a given stream. In order to configure the DMA controller to handle requests from the USART2 receive, we'll reference table 27 from the *STM32F7xx RM0410* reference manual:

Peripheral requests	Stream 0	Stream 1	Stream 2	Stream 3	Stream 4	Stream 5	Stream 6	Stream 7
Channel 0	SPI3_RX	SPDIFRX_DT	SPI3_RX	SPI2_RX	SPI2_TX	SPI3_TX	SPDIFRX_CS	SPI3_TX
Channel 1	I2C1_RX	I2C3_RX	TIM7_UP	-	TIM7_UP	I2C1_RX	I2C1_TX	I2C1_TX
Channel 2	TIM4_CH1	-	I2C4_RX	TIM4_CH2	-	I2C4_RX	TIM4_UP	TIM4_CH3
Channel 3	-	TIM2_UP TIM2_CH3	I2C3_RX	-	I2C3_TX	TIM2_CH1	TIM2_CH2 TIM2_CH4	TIM2_UP TIM2_CH4
Channel 4	UART5_RX	USART3_RX	UART4_RX	USART3_TX	UART4_TX	USART2_RX	USART2_TX	UART5_TX
Channel 5	UART8_TX	UART7_TX	TIM3_CH4 TIM3_UP	UART7_RX	TIM3_CH1 TIM3_TRIG	TIM3_CH2	UART8_RX	TIM3_CH3
Channel 6	TIM5_CH3 TIM5_UP	TIM5_CH4 TIM5_TRIG	TIM5_CH1	TIM5_CH4 TIM5_TRIG	TIM5_CH2	-	TIM5_UP	-
Channel 7	-	TIM6_UP	I2C2_RX	I2C2_RX	USART3_TX	DAC1	DAC2	I2C2_TX
Channel 8	I2C3_TX	I2C4_RX	-	-	I2C2_TX	-	I2C4_TX	-
Channel 9	-	SPI2_RX	-	-	-	-	SPI2_TX	-

Table 27. DMA1 request mapping

In this table, we can see that DMA1 **Channel 4**, **Stream 5** is the appropriate setup to use to handle requests from USART2_RX. If we were also interested in handling requests for the transmit side, **Channel 4**, **Stream 6** would also need to be set up.

Now that we know the channel and stream numbers, we can add some initialization code to set up the DMA1 and USART2 peripherals:

- `DMA1_Stream5` will be used to transfer data from the `receive` data register of USART2 directly into a buffer in RAM.
- `USART2` will not have interrupts enabled (they are not needed since DMA will perform all transfers from the peripheral register to RAM).
- `DMA1_Stream5` will be set up to trigger an interrupt after the entire buffer has been filled.

The next few snippets are from the `setupUSART2DMA` function in `Chapter_10/src/mainUartDMABuff.c`:

1. First, the clock to the DMA peripheral is enabled, interrupt priorities are set up, and the interrupts are enabled in the NVIC:

```
void setupUSART2DMA( void )
{
    __HAL_RCC_DMA1_CLK_ENABLE();
    NVIC_SetPriority(DMA1_Stream5_IRQn, 6);
    NVIC_EnableIRQ(DMA1_Stream5_IRQn);
```

2. Next, the DMA stream is configured by filling out a `DMA_HandleTypeDef` struct (`usart2DmaRx`) and using `HAL_DMA_Init()`:

```
HAL_StatusTypeDef retVal;
memset(&usart2DmaRx, 0, sizeof(usart2DmaRx));
usart2DmaRx.Instance = DMA1_Stream5; //stream 5 is for USART2 Rx

//channel 4 is for USART2 Rx/Tx
usart2DmaRx.Init.Channel = DMA_CHANNEL_4;
//transfering out of memory and into the peripheral register
usart2DmaRx.Init.Direction = DMA_PERIPH_TO_MEMORY;
usart2DmaRx.Init.FIFOMode = DMA_FIFOMODE_DISABLE; //no FIFO

//transfer 1 at a time
usart2DmaRx.Init.MemBurst = DMA_MBURST_SINGLE;
usart2DmaRx.Init.MemDataAlignment = DMA_MDATAALIGN_BYTE;

//increment 1 byte at a time
usart2DmaRx.Init.MemInc = DMA_MINC_ENABLE;

//flow control mode set to normal
usart2DmaRx.Init.Mode = DMA_NORMAL;

//write 1 at a time to the peripheral
```

```
usart2DmaRx.Init.PeriphBurst = DMA_PBURST_SINGLE;

//always keep the peripheral address the same (the RX data
//register is always in the same location)
usart2DmaRx.Init.PeriphInc = DMA_PINC_DISABLE;

usart2DmaRx.Init.PeriphDataAlignment = DMA_PDATAALIGN_BYTE;

usart2DmaRx.Init.Priority = DMA_PRIORITY_HIGH;
retVal = HAL_DMA_Init(&usart2DmaRx);
assert_param( retVal == HAL_OK );

//enable transfer complete interrupts
DMA1_Stream5->CR |= DMA_SxCR_TCIE;

//set the DMA receive mode flag in the USART
USART2->CR3 |= USART_CR3_DMAR_Msk;
```

HAL initialization provides some sanity checking on the values passed to it. Here's a highlight of the most immediately relevant portions:

- DMA1_Stream5 is set as the instance. All calls that use the usart2DmaRx struct will reference stream 5.
- Channel 4 is attached to stream 5.
- Memory incrementing is enabled. The DMA hardware will automatically increment the memory address after a transfer, filling the buffer.
- The peripheral address is not incremented after each transfer—the address of the USART2 receive data register (RDR) doesn't ever change.
- The transfer complete interrupt is enabled for DMA1_Stream5.
- USART2 is set up for DMA receive mode. It is necessary to set this bit in the USART peripheral configuration to signal that the peripheral's receive register will be mapped to the DMA controller.

Additional details about how this struct is used can be found by looking at the DMA_HandleTypeDef struct definition in stm32f7xx_hal_dma.h (line 168) and HAL_DMA_Init() in stm32f7xx_hal_dma.c (line 172). Cross-reference the registers used by the HAL code with section 8 (page 245) in the *STM32F76xxx RM0410* reference manual. This same technique is often most productive for understanding *exactly* what the HAL code is doing with individual function parameters and struct members.

Now that the initial DMA configuration is done, we can explore a few different interrupt implementations using DMA instead of interrupts.

A buffer-based driver with DMA

Here's an implementation of a driver with identical functionality to the one in the *A buffer-based driver* section. The difference is the DMA version of the driver doesn't interrupt the application every time a byte is received. The only `interrupt` generated is when the entire transfer is complete. To realize this driver, we only need to add the following ISR:

```
void DMA1_Stream5_IRQHandler(void)
{
  portBASE_TYPE xHigherPriorityTaskWoken = pdFALSE;
  SEGGER_SYSVIEW_RecordEnterISR();

  if(rxInProgress && (DMA1->HISR & DMA_HISR_TCIF5))
  {
    rxInProgress = false;
    DMA1->HIFCR |= DMA_HIFCR_CTCIF5;
    xSemaphoreGiveFromISR(rxDone, &xHigherPriorityTaskWoken);
  }
  SEGGER_SYSVIEW_RecordExitISR();
  portYIELD_FROM_ISR(xHigherPriorityTaskWoken);
}
```

The significant portions of the driver are in bold. If a reception is in progress (based on the value of `rxInProgress` and the transmit complete flag, `DMA_HISR_TCIF5`, the following takes place:

- The DMA interrupt flag is cleared.
- The `rxDone` semaphore is given.

This is all that is required when using DMA-based transfers since the DMA controller does all of the bookkeeping associated with the buffer. At this point, the rest of the code functions in an identical way to the `interrupt` version (the only difference is that less CPU time is spent servicing interrupts).

Performance analysis

Let's take a look at the performance of the DMA-based implementation compared to the interrupt-driven approach:

Name		Type		Frequency
ISR #32		#32	0.09%	60 Hz
Scheduler			0.06%	60 Hz
uartPrint		@3	0.32%	61 Hz
Tmr Svc		@2	0.00%	0 Hz
Idle			99.53%	120 Hz

This time around, we can make the following observations about the overall system behavior:

1. The (DMA) ISR is now consuming < 0.1% of CPU cycles at 9,600 baud.
2. The **Scheduler** CPU's consumption is still very low.
3. The frequency of the ISR has been reduced to only 60 Hz (from 960 Hz). This is because, rather than creating an interrupt for every byte, there is only an interrupt generated at the end of the transfer of 16 bytes. The **Idle** task is being context-switched significantly less often as well. Although it seems trivial with these simple examples, excessive context-switching can become a very real problem in large applications with many tasks and interrupts.

The overall flow is similar to that of the interrupt buffer-based approach, with the only difference being that there is only a single ISR executed when the entire transfer is complete (instead of one interrupt for each byte transferred):

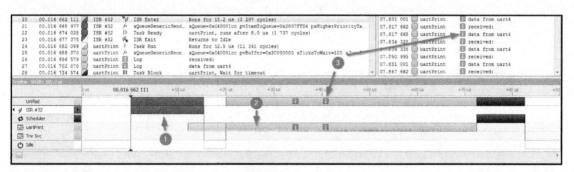

From the preceding screenshot, we can observe the following:

1. The DMA ISR is executed once (after all 16 bytes are transferred into the buffer). A semaphore is shown by the tick mark that arrow 1 is pointing to in the screenshot.

2. The ISR wakes up the blocked `uartPrint` function. Arrow 2 is pointing to where the semaphore is taken.

3. The two **i** infoboxes show where the console print messages are generated (~35 and 40 us after the final byte has been received). The remainder of the time this task spends is on re-initializing the buffer and setting up the next transfer.

Here is a wider view of all of the processor activity. Notice that the only activity occurs approximately once every 16 ms (after all the bytes have been transferred into memory):

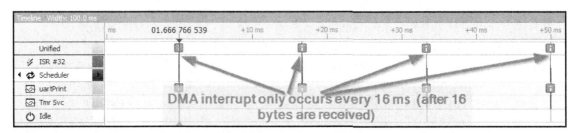

The real capability of a fully DMA-based approach is most valuable when transferring large amounts of data very quickly. The following example shows the same dataset (only 16 bytes) transferred at 256,400 baud (the fastest that could be reliably achieved without error due to poor signal integrity).

The baud rate can be easily changed in the examples by modifying `#define BAUDRATE` in `main<exampleame>.c`. They are configured so that a single change will modify both the USART2 and UART4 baud rates.

The following is an example of transfers being made at 256,000 baud. A new set of 16 bytes is available in the buffer, approximately every 624 µS:

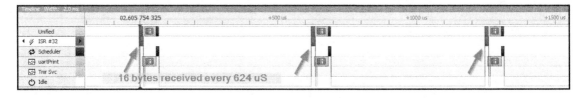

By increasing the baud rate from 9,600 to 256,000, our CPU usage has increased from around 0.5% to around 11%. This is in line with the 26x increase in baud rate—all of the function's calls are proportionate to the baud rate:

Name	Type			Frequency
⬛ ISR #32	⚡ #32	2.29%		1604 Hz
⬛ Scheduler	⟳	1.69%		1604 Hz
⬜ uartPrint	✉ @3	6.24%		1604 Hz
⬜ Tmr Svc	✉ @2	0.00%		0 Hz
⬜ Idle	⏻	89.78%		3208 Hz

Notice the following:

- The DMA interrupt consumes 2.29%.
- Our `uartPrint` task is the highest consumer of CPU cycles (a little over 6%).

Even though we've proved to ourselves that it is possible to efficiently transfer data quickly by using DMA, this current setup doesn't have the same convenience that the interrupt-driven queue solution did. Tasks rely on entire blocks to be transferred, rather than using a queue. This might be fine or might be an inconvenience, depending on what the goals of the higher-level code are.

Character-based protocols will tend to be easier to implement when written on top of a queue-based driver API, rather than a buffer-based driver API (such as the one we've implemented here). However, we saw in the *Queue-based driver* section that queues become computationally expensive very quickly. Each byte took around 30 us to be added to the queue. Transferring data at 256,000 baud would consume most of the available CPU in the UART ISR alone (a new byte is received every 40 us and it takes 30 us to process).

In the past, if you really needed to implement a character-oriented driver, you could roll your own highly efficient ring buffer implementation and feed it directly from low-level ISRs (bypassing most of the FreeRTOS primitives to save time). However, as of FreeROTS 10, there is another alternative—stream buffers.

Stream buffers (FreeRTOS 10+)

Stream buffers combine the convenience of a queue-based system with the speed closer to that of the raw buffer implementations we created previously. They have some flexibility limitations that are similar to the limitations of task notification systems compared to semaphores. *Stream buffers can only be used by one sender and one receiver at a time.* Otherwise, they'll need external protection (such as a mutex), if they are to be used by multiple tasks.

The programming model for stream buffers is very similar to queues, except that instead of functions being limited to queueing one item at a time, they can queue multiple items at a time (which saves considerable CPU time when queuing blocks of data). In this example, we'll explore stream buffers through an efficient DMA-based circular buffer implementation for UART reception.

The goals of this driver example are the following:

- Provide an easy-to-use character-based queue for users of the driver.
- Maintain efficiency at high data rates.
- Always be ready to receive data.

So, let's begin!

Using the stream buffer API

First, let's take a look at an example of how the stream buffer API will be used by uartPrintOutTask in this example. The following excerpts are from mainUartDMAStreamBufferCont.c.

Here's a look at the definition of xSttreamBufferCreate():

```
StreamBufferHandle_t xStreamBufferCreate( size_t xBufferSizeBytes,
                                          size_t xTriggerLevelBytes);
```

Note the following in the preceding code:

- xBufferSizeBytes is the number of bytes the buffer is capable of holding.
- xTriggerLevelBytes is the number of bytes that need to be available in the stream before a call to xStreamBufferReceive() will return (otherwise, a timeout will occur).

The following example code sets up a stream buffer:

```
#define NUM_BYTES 100
#define MIN_NUM_BYTES 2
StreamBufferHandle_t rxStream = NULL;
rxStream = xStreamBufferCreate( NUM_BYTES , MIN_NUM_BYTES);
assert_param(rxStream != NULL);
```

In the preceding snippet, we can observe the following:

- rxStream is capable of holding NUM_BYTES (100 bytes).
- Each time a task blocks data from being added to the stream, it won't be unblocked until at least MIN_NUM_BYTES (2 bytes) are available in the stream. In this example, calls to xStreamBufferReceive will block until a minimum of 2 bytes are available in the stream (or a timeout occurs).
- If using the FreeRTOS heap, be sure to check that there is enough space for the allocation of the stream buffer by checking the returned handle isn't NULL.

The function for receiving data from a stream buffer is xStreamBufferReceive():

```
size_t xStreamBufferReceive( StreamBufferHandle_t xStreamBuffer,
                             void *pvRxData,
                             size_t xBufferLengthBytes,
                             TickType_t xTicksToWait );
```

Here is a straightforward example of receiving data from a stream buffer:

```
void uartPrintOutTask( void* NotUsed)
{
    static const uint8_t maxBytesReceived = 16;
    uint8_t rxBufferedData[maxBytesReceived];

    //initialization code omitted for brevity
    while(1)
    {
        uint8_t numBytes = xStreamBufferReceive(  rxStream,
                                                  rxBufferedData,
                                                  maxBytesReceived,
                                                  100 );

        if(numBytes > 0)
        {
            SEGGER_SYSVIEW_PrintfHost("received: ");
            SEGGER_SYSVIEW_Print((char*)rxBufferedData);
        }
        else
        {
            SEGGER_SYSVIEW_PrintfHost("timeout");
    ...
```

In the preceding snippet, note the following:

- rxStream: The pointer/handle to StreamBuffer.
- rxBufferedData: The local buffer that bytes will be copied into.

- `maxBytesReceived`: The maximum number of bytes that will be copied into `rxBufferedData`.
- The timeout is `100` ticks (`xStreamBufferReceive()` will return after at least `xTriggerLevelBytes` (2 in this example) are available or 100 ticks have elapsed).

Calls to `xStreamBufferReceive()` behave in a similar way to a call to `xQueueReceive()` in that they both block until data is available. However, a call to `xStreamBufferReceive()` will block until the minimum number of bytes (defined when calling `xStreamBufferCreate()`) or the specified number of ticks has elapsed.

In this example, the call to `xStreamBufferReceive()` blocks until one of the following conditions is met:

- The number of bytes in the buffer exceeds `MIN_NUM_BYTES` (2 in this example). If more bytes are available, they will be moved into `rxBufferedData`—but only up to the `maxBytesReceived` bytes (`16` in this example).
- A timeout occurs. All available bytes in the stream are moved into `rxBufferedData`. The exact number of bytes placed into `rxBufferedData` is returned by `xStreamBuffereReceive()` – (`0` or `1` in this example).

Now that we have a good idea of what the receiving side looks like, let's look at some of the details of the driver itself.

Setting up double-buffered DMA

As we saw earlier, using DMA can be very beneficial for reducing CPU usage (versus interrupts). However, one of the features that wasn't covered in the last example was continuously populating a queue (the driver required block-based calls to be made before data could be received). The driver in this example will transfer data into the stream buffer constantly, without requiring any intervention from the code calling it. That is, the driver will always be receiving bytes and pushing them into the stream buffer.

Always receiving data presents two interesting problems for a DMA-based system:

- How to deal with **roll-over**—when a buffer has been completely filled and high-speed data could still be coming in.
- How to terminate transfers before a buffer is completely filled. DMA transfers typically require the number of bytes to be specified before the transfer starts. However, we need a way to stop the transfer when data has stopped being received and copy that data into the stream buffer.

DMA double buffering will be used to ensure our driver will always be able to accept data (even when a single buffer has been filled). In the previous example, a single buffer was filled and an interrupt was generated, then the data was operated on directly before restarting the transfer. With double buffering, a second buffer is added. After the DMA controller fills the first buffer, it automatically starts filling the second buffer:

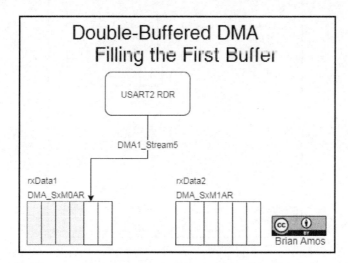

After the first buffer is filled and the interrupt is generated, the ISR can safely operate on data in the first buffer, rxData1, while the second buffer, rxData2, is filled. In our example, we're transferring that data into the FreeRTOS stream buffer from inside the ISR.

It is important to note that `xStreamBufferSendFromISR()` adds a *copy* of the data to the stream buffer, not a reference. So, in this example, as long as the DMA ISR's call to `xStreamBufferSendFromISR()` executes before `rxData2` has been filled, data will be available with no loss. This is unlike traditional **bare-metal** double-buffer implementations since higher-level code making calls to `xStreamBufferReceive()` isn't required to extract data from `rxData1` before `rxData2` is filled. It only needs to call `xStreamBufferReceive()` before the stream buffer has been filled:

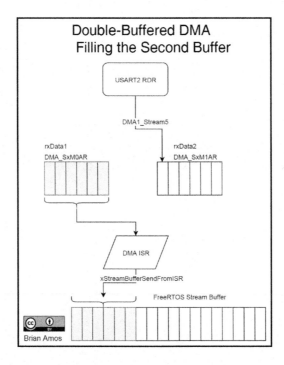

Even if you're programming for an MCU without an explicit **double-buffer mode**, most DMA controllers will have a **circular** mode with **half-transfer** and **full-transfer** interrupts. In this case, the same functionality can be achieved by generating an interrupt after each half of the buffer is filled.

The secondary buffer, `rxData2`, is set up by writing its address to the `DMA_SxM1AR` register (some casting is required to keep the compiler from complaining too loudly that we're writing a pointer to a 32-bit memory address):

```
//setup second address for double buffered mode
DMA1_Stream5->M1AR = (uint32_t) rxData2;
```

Interestingly enough, STM HAL doesn't support double-buffer mode directly. In fact, calls to `HAL_DMA_Start` explicitly disable the mode. So, some manual setup with registers is required (after letting `HAL` take care of most of the leg work):

```
//NOTE: HAL_DMA_Start explicitly disables double buffer mode
// so we'll explicitly enable double buffer mode later when
// the actual transfer is started
if(HAL_DMA_Start(&usart2DmaRx, (uint32_t)&(USART2->RDR), (uint32_t)rxData1,
                RX_BUFF_LEN) != HAL_OK)
{
    return -1;
}

//disable the stream and controller so we can setup dual buffers
__HAL_DMA_DISABLE(&usart2DmaRx);
//set the double buffer mode
DMA1_Stream5->CR |= DMA_SxCR_DBM;
//re-enable the stream and controller
__HAL_DMA_ENABLE(&usart2DmaRx);
DMA1_Stream5->CR |= DMA_SxCR_EN;
```

After the DMA stream is enabled, the UART is enabled, which will start transfers (this is identical to the previous examples).

Populating the stream buffer

The stream buffer will be populated from inside the DMA ISR:

```
void DMA1_Stream5_IRQHandler(void)
{
    uint16_t numWritten = 0;
    uint8_t* currBuffPtr = NULL;
    portBASE_TYPE xHigherPriorityTaskWoken = pdFALSE;
    SEGGER_SYSVIEW_RecordEnterISR();

    if(rxInProgress && (DMA1->HISR & DMA_HISR_TCIF5))
    {
        if(DMA1_Stream5->CR & DMA_SxCR_CT)
            currBuffPtr = rxData1;
        else
            currBuffPtr = rxData2;

        numWritten = xStreamBufferSendFromISR(  rxStream,
                                                currBuffPtr,
                                                RX_BUFF_LEN,
                                                &xHigherPriorityTaskWoken);
```

```
        while(numWritten != RX_BUFF_LEN);

        DMA1->HIFCR |= DMA_HIFCR_CTCIF5;
    }
    SEGGER_SYSVIEW_RecordExitISR();
    portYIELD_FROM_ISR(xHigherPriorityTaskWoken);
}
```

Here are some of the more noteworthy items in this ISR:

- `if(rxInProgress && (DMA1->HISR & DMA_HISR_TCIF5))`: This line guards against the stream buffer being written to before the scheduler is started. Even if the ISR was to execute before the scheduler was started, `rxInProgress` wouldn't be true until after everything was initialized. Checking the transmit complete flag, `DMA_HISR_TCIF5`, guarantees that a transfer has, indeed, completed (rather than entering the ISR because of an error).
- `DMA1_Stream5->CR & DMA_SxCR_CT`: Checks the current target bit. Since this bit indicates which target buffer (`DMA_SxM0AR` or `DMA_SxM1AR`) is currently being **filled** by the DMA controller, we'll take the other and push that data into the stream buffer.
- The call to `xStreamBufferSendFromISR` pushes the entirety of `rxBuff1` or `rxBuff2` (each of an `RX_BUFF_LEN` length) into `rxStream` in one go.

A few things to remember are as follows:

- Data is being transferred to the stream by value (not reference). That is, FreeRTOS is using `memcpy` to make a copy of all of the data moving into the stream buffer (and again when removing data). The larger the buffer, the more time it will take to copy—additional RAM will also be used.
- Instead of performing the copy inside the interrupt, under certain circumstances, it may be preferable to signal a semaphore or task notification and perform the copy in a high-priority task instead—for example, if a large buffer is being filled. However, you'll need to guarantee that other interrupts don't starve the task performing the `xStreamBufferSend` or data will be lost.
- There are trade-offs when using DMA. Larger buffers mean fewer interruptions to transfer data, but they also mean an increase in latency. The larger the buffer, the longer the data will sit in the buffer before being processed.
- This implementation is only well suited to continuous data streams—if the data stream stops, the last DMA transfer will never complete.

This approach to pushing received data from a peripheral into memory works very well when data is continuously streaming. It can also work extremely well for the reception of messages with a known number of bytes. However, there are some ways to improve it.

Improving the stream buffer

In order to deal with an intermittent data stream, there are two possible approaches (for this specific setup):

- The USART peripheral on this MCU is capable of detecting an "idle line" and generating an interrupt by setting the USART_CR1:IDLEE bit when an idle line is detected.
- The USART peripheral also has a receive timeout that can also generate an interrupt after no start bits have been detected for a specified number of bit times (0-16,777,215).
    - This timeout is specified in the USART_RTOR:RTO[23:0] register.
    - The feature can be enabled with USART_CR2:RTOEN and the interrupts can be enabled with USART_CR1:RTOIE.

Either of these features could be used to generate a USART interrupt, cut the DMA transfer short, and transfer the data to the stream buffer.

For extremely high baud rates, care needs to be taken when using the idle line approach because the number of interrupts generated is only capped by the baud rate. If there is inter-character spacing (idle time between each character being sent), you'll wind up with an interrupt-driven approach (with even more overhead than normal).

On the other hand, using the receive timeout feature means additional latency before processing the incoming data. As usual, there is no *one-size-fits-all* solution here.

Analyzing the performance

So, how does this DMA stream buffer implementation compare to the ISR-based queue implementation? Well, on one hand, there is no comparison... *the ISR based implementation doesn't work at 256,400 baud.* At this baud rate, a new character is received every 39 uS. With the ISR taking around 18 us to execute, we simply don't have enough time to also run `printUartTask()` reliably without dropping data:

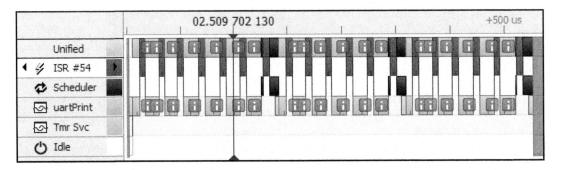

Notice that there is absolutely no time spent on the **Idle** task—the CPU is completely consumed by attempting to keep up with the incoming data from UART2.

As you can see in the following screenshot, data is occasionally dropped when the processor is set up to receive data at 256,400 baud using an ISR that executes once per character:

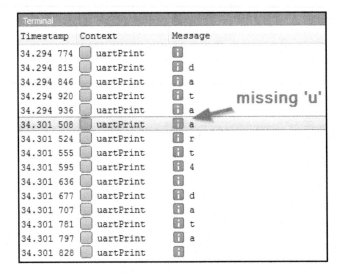

Now, for comparison, here's the (nearly) equivalent implementation using stream buffers and DMA:

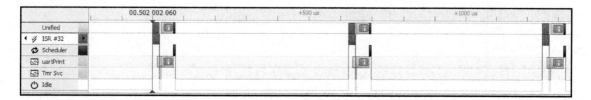

The combination of stream buffers and DMA has freed up quite a bit of the CPU time; the queue-based ISR implementation consumed > 100% of the CPU. As we can see in the following processing breakdown, the total CPU usage for a stream buffer using DMA is around 10%:

Name	Type			Frequency
ISR #32	⚡	#32	3.35%	1430 Hz
Scheduler	⊕		0.95%	1424 Hz
uartPrint	✉	@3	6.09%	1426 Hz
Tmr Svc	✉	@2	0.00%	0 Hz
Idle	⏻		89.61%	2851 Hz

Note the following:

- The DMA-/stream buffer-based solution leaves nearly 90% of the CPU cycles available for other tasks.
- More time is being spent printing debug statements (and pulling bytes off the queue) than servicing the DMA ISR.
- The multi-byte stream buffer transactions also eliminate a large amount of context switching (notice the scheduler is only utilizing around 1% CPU), which will leave more contiguous time for other processing tasks.

So, now that we've worked through a very simple example of each driver type, which one should you implement?

Choosing a driver model

Selecting the *best* driver for a given system depends on several different factors:

- How is the calling code designed?
- How much delay is acceptable?

- How fast is data moving?
- What type of device is it?

Let's answer these questions one by one.

How is the calling code designed?

What is the intended design of higher-level code using the driver? Will it operate on individual characters or bytes as they come in? Or does it make more sense for the higher-level code to batch transfers into blocks/frames of bytes?

Queue-based drivers are very useful when dealing with unknown amounts (or streams) of data that can come in at any point in time. They are also a very natural fit for code that processes individual bytes—uartPrintOutTask was a good example of this:

```
while(1)
{
    xQueueReceive(uart2_BytesReceived, &nextByte, portMAX_DELAY);
    //do something with the byte received
    SEGGER_SYSVIEW_PrintfHost("%c", nextByte);
}
```

While ring-buffer implementations (such as the one in the preceding code) are perfect for streamed data, other code naturally gravitates toward operating on blocks of data. Say, for example, our high-level code is meant to read in one of the structures defined in Chapter 9, *Intertask Communication*, over a serial port.

The following excerpt is from Chapter_9/MainQueueCompositePassByValue.c:

```
typedef struct
{
    uint8_t redLEDState : 1;
    uint8_t blueLEDState : 1;
    uint8_t greenLEDState : 1;
    uint32_t msDelayTime;
}LedStates_t;
```

Rather than operate on individual bytes, it is very convenient for the receiving side to pull in an instance of the entire struct at once. The following code is designed to receive an entire copy of `LedStates_t` from a queue. After the struct is received, it can be operated on by simply referencing members of the struct, such as checking `redLEDState`, in this example:

```
LedStates_t nextCmd;
while(1)
{
    if(xQueueReceive(ledCmdQueue, &nextCmd, portMAX_DELAY) == pdTRUE)
    {
        if(nextCmd.redLEDState == 1)
            RedLed.On();
        else
            . . .
```

This can be accomplished by **serializing** the data structure and passing it over the communication medium. Our `LedStates_t` struct can be serialized as a block of 5 bytes. All three red, green, and blue state values can be packed into 3 bits of a byte and the delay time will take 4 bytes:

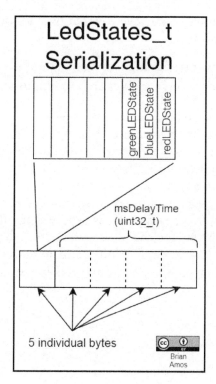

Serialization is a broad topic in itself. There are trade-offs to be made for portability, ease of use, code fragility, and speed. A discussion on all of these points is outside the scope of this chapter. Details of endianness and the *best* way of serializing/deserializing this particular data structure have been purposely ignored in the diagram. The main takeaway is that the struct can be represented by a block of 5 bytes.

In this case, it makes sense for the underlying peripheral driver to operate on a buffer of 5 bytes, so a buffer-based approach that groups a transfer into a block of 5 bytes is more natural than a stream of bytes. The following pseudo-code outlines an approach based on the buffer-based driver we wrote in the previous section:

```
uint8_t ledCmdBuff[5];
startReceiveInt(ledCmdBuff, 5);
//wait for reception to complete
xSemaphoreTake(cmdReceived, portMAX_DELAY);
//populate an led command with data received from the serial port
LedStates_t ledCmd = parseMsg(ledCmdBuff);
//send the command to the queue
xQueueSend(ledCmdQueue, &ledCmd, portMAX_DELAY);
```

In a situation like the previous one, we have covered two different approaches that can provide efficient implementations:

- A buffer-based driver (receiving 5 bytes at a time)
- A stream buffer (the receiving side can be configured to acquire 5 bytes at a time)

FreeRTOS message buffers could also be used instead of a stream buffer to provide a more flexible solution. Message buffers are built on top of stream buffers, but have a more flexible blocking configuration. They allow different message sizes to be configured per receive call, so the same buffer can be used to group receptions into a size of 5 bytes (or any other desired size) each time xMessageBufferReceive is called. With stream buffers, the message size is rigidly defined when creating the stream buffer by setting the xTriggerLevelBytes parameter in xStreamBufferCreate. Unlike stream buffers, message buffers will only return full messages, not individual bytes.

How much delay is acceptable?

Depending on the exact function being implemented, minimal delay may be desired. In this case, buffer-based implementations can sometimes have a slight advantage. They allow the calling code to be set up as an extremely high priority, without causing significant context switching in the rest of the application.

With a buffer-based setup, after the last byte of a message is transferred, the task will be notified and immediately run. This is better than having the high-priority task perform byte-wise parsing of the message since it will be interrupting other tasks continually each time a byte is received. In a byte-wise queue-based approach, the task waiting on the queue would need to be set to a very high priority if the incoming message was extremely important. This combination causes quite a bit of task context switching versus a buffer approach, which only has a single semaphore (or direct task notification) when the transfer is finished.

Sometimes, timing constraints are so tight neither queues nor an entire block transfer may be acceptable (bytes might need to be processed as they come in). This approach will sometimes eliminate the need for intermediate buffers as well. A fully custom ISR can be written in these cases, but it won't be easily reused. Try to avoid lumping **business logic** (application-level logic not immediately required for servicing the peripheral) into ISRs whenever possible. It complicates testing and reduces code reuse. After a few months (or years) of writing code like this, you'll likely notice that you've got dozens of ISRs that look *almost* the same but behave in subtlety different ways, which can make for buggy systems when modifications to higher-level code are required.

How fast is data moving?

While extremely convenient, queues are a fairly expensive way to pass individual bytes around a system. Even an interrupt-based driver has limitations on how long it has to deal with incoming data. Our example used a meager 9,600 baud transfer. Individual characters were transferred into the queue within 40 us of being received, but what happens if the baud rate is 115,200 baud? Now, instead of having around 1 character per millisecond, each character would need to be added to the queue in less than 9 us. A driver that takes 40 us per interrupt isn't going to be acceptable here, so using a simple queue approach isn't a viable option.

We saw that the stream buffer implementation with DMA was a viable solution in place of a queue. Using some type of double-buffering technique for high-speed, continuous streams of data is critical. This becomes an especially convenient technique when coupled with a highly efficient RTOS primitive, such as stream buffers or message buffers.

Interrupts and DMA-based drivers that moved data directly into a **raw** memory buffer are also quite viable when speeds are high, but they don't have the convenience of a queue-like interface.

What type of device are you interfacing?

Some peripherals and external devices will naturally lean toward one implementation or another. When receiving asynchronous data, queues are a fairly natural choice because they provide an easy mechanism for constantly capturing incoming data. UARTs, USB virtual comms, network streams, and timer captures are all very naturally implemented with a byte-wise queue implementation (at least at the lowest level).

Synchronous-based devices, such as a **serial peripheral interface** (SPI) and **Inter-Integrated Circuit** (I2C), are easily implemented with block-based transfers on the master side since the number of bytes is known ahead of time (the master needs to supply the clock signal for both bytes sent and bytes received).

When to use queue-based drivers

Here are some cases where it is an advantage to use a queue as the interface of a driver:

- When the peripheral/application needs to receive data of an unknown length
- When data must be received asynchronously to requests
- When a driver should receive data from multiple sources without blocking the caller
- When data rates are sufficiently slow to allow a minimum of 10's of µS per interrupt (when being implemented on the hardware, in this example)

When to use buffer-based drivers

Some cases where raw buffer-based drivers are extremely useful are as follows:

- When large buffers are required because large amounts of data will be received at once
- During transaction-based communication protocols, especially when the length of the received data is known in advance

When to use stream buffers

Stream buffers provide speed closer to that of raw buffers, but with the added benefit of providing an efficient queue API. They can generally be used anywhere a standard queue would be used (as long as there is only one consumer task). Stream buffers are also efficient enough to be used in place of raw buffers, in many cases. As we saw in the `mainUartDMAStreamBufferCont.c` example, they can be combined with circular DMA transfers to provide true continuous data capture, without using a significant number of CPU cycles.

These are just some of the considerations you'll likely face when creating drivers; they are mainly aimed at communication peripherals (since that's what our examples covered). There are also some considerations to be made when choosing to use third-party libraries and drivers.

Using third-party libraries (STM HAL)

If you've been following along closely, you may have noticed a few things:

- STM HAL (the vendor-supplied hardware abstraction layer) is used for initial peripheral configuration. This is because HAL does a very good job of making peripheral configuration easy. It is also extremely convenient to use tools such as STM Cube to generate some boilerplate code as a point of reference when first interacting with a new chip.
- When it is time to implement details of interrupt-driven transactions, we've been making a lot of calls directly to MCU peripheral registers, rather than letting HAL manage transactions for us. There were a couple of reasons for this:
    - We wanted to be closer to the hardware to get a better understanding of how things were really working in the system.
    - Some of the setups weren't directly supported by HAL, such as DMA double buffering.

In general, you should use as much vendor-supplied code as you (or your project/company) are comfortable with. If the code is well written and works reliably, then there *usually* aren't too many arguments for *not* using it.

That being said, here are some potential issues when using vendor-supplied drivers:

- They may use polling instead of interrupts or DMA.
- Tying into interrupts may be cumbersome or inflexible.
- There is potentially *lots* of extra overhead since many chips/use cases are likely covered by drivers (they need to solve *everyone's* problems, not just yours).
- It might take longer to fully grasp and understand a complex API than working directly with the peripheral hardware (for simple peripherals).

The following are examples of when to write **bare-metal** drivers:

- When a vendors driver is broken/buggy
- When speed matters
- When an exotic configuration is required
- As a learning exercise

Ideally, transitioning between third-party drivers and your own drivers would be perfectly seamless. If it isn't, it means that the higher-level code is tightly coupled to the hardware. This tight coupling is perfectly acceptable for sufficiently small *one-off* and *throw-away* projects, but if you're attempting to develop a code base for the long term, investing in creating a loosely coupled architecture will pay dividends. Having loose coupling (eliminating dependencies between the exact driver implementation and higher-level code) also provides flexibility in the implementation of the individual components. Loose coupling ensures transitioning between custom drivers and third-party drivers doesn't necessitate a major rewrite of high-level code. Loose coupling also makes testing small portions of the code base in isolation possible—see Chapter 12, *Tips on Creating Well-Abstracted Architecture*, for details.

Summary

In this chapter, we introduced three different ways of implementing low-level drivers that interface with hardware peripherals in the MCU. Interrupts and polled- and DMA-based drivers were all covered through examples and their performance was analyzed and compared using SEGGER SystemView. We also covered three different ways that FreeRTOS can interact with ISRs: semaphores, queues, and stream buffers. Considerations for choosing between the implementation options were also discussed, as well as when it is appropriate to use third-party peripheral drivers (STM HAL) and when "rolling your own" is best.

To get the most out of this chapter, you're encouraged to run through it on actual hardware. The development board was chosen (in part) with the hope that you might have access to Arduino shields. After running through the examples, an excellent next step would be to develop a driver for a shield or another piece of real-world hardware.

This chapter was really just the tip of the iceberg when it comes to driver implementation. There are many additional approaches and techniques that can be used when creating efficient implementations, from using different RTOS primitives beyond what is presented in this chapter to configuring MCU-specific functionality. Your designs don't need to be limited by what happens to be provided by a vendor.

You should now have a solid understanding of the many different ways low-level drivers can be implemented. In the next chapter, we'll take a look at how these drivers can be safely presented to higher-level code across multiple tasks. Providing easy access to drivers makes developing the final application fast and flexible.

Questions

As we conclude, here is a list of questions for you to test your knowledge of this chapter's material. You will find the answers in the *Assessments* section of the appendix:

1. What type of driver is more complicated to write and use?
    - Polled
    - Interrupt-driven
2. True or false: In FreeRTOS, it is possible to call any RTOS function from any ISR?
    - True
    - False
3. True or false: When using an RTOS, interrupts are constantly fighting the scheduler for CPU time?
    - True
    - False
4. Which technique for a peripheral driver requires the fewest CPU resources when transferring large amounts of high-speed data?
    - Polling
    - Interrupt
    - DMA
5. What does DMA stand for?
6. Name one case when using a raw buffer-based driver is *not* a good idea.

Further reading

- *Chapter 4* in the *RM0410 STM32F76xxx* reference manual (*USART*)
- B1.5.4, *Exception priorities and preemption* section in the *Arm®v7-M Architecture* reference manual
- FreeRTOS.org's explanation of CortexM priorities, at `https://www.freertos.org/RTOS-Cortex-M3-M4.html`

11
Sharing Hardware Peripherals across Tasks

In the previous chapter, we went through several examples of creating drivers, but they were only used by a single task. Since we're creating a multi-tasking asynchronous system, a few additional considerations need to be made to ensure that the peripherals exposed by our drivers can safely be used by multiple tasks. Preparing a driver for use by multiple tasks requires a number of additional considerations.

Accordingly, this chapter first illustrates the pitfalls of a shared peripheral in a multi-tasking, real-time environment. After understanding the problem we're trying to solve, we'll investigate potential solutions for wrapping a driver in a way that provides an easy-to-use abstraction layer that is safe to use across multiple tasks. We'll be using the STM32 USB stack to implement a **Communication Device Class (CDC)** to provide an interactive **Virtual COM Port (VPC)**. Unlike the previous chapter, which took an extremely low-level approach to driver development, this chapter focuses on writing threadsafe code on top of an existing driver stack.

In a nutshell, we will cover the following topics:

- Understanding shared peripherals
- Introducing the STM USB driver stack
- Developing a StreamBuffer USB virtual COM port
- Using mutexes for access control

Technical requirements

To complete the hands-on experiments in this chapter, you'll require the following:

- Nucleo F767 Dev Board
- Micro-USB cable (x2)
- STM32CubeIDE and source code (instructions in `Chapter 5`, *Selecting an IDE*, under the section entitled *Setting up our IDE*)
- SEGGER JLink, Ozone, and SystemView (instructions in `Chapter 6`, *Debugging Tools for Real-Time Systems*)
- STM USB virtual COM port drivers:
    - Windows: The driver should install automatically from Windows Update (`https://www.st.com/en/development-tools/stsw-stm32102.html`).
    - Linux/ macOS: These use built-in virtual COM port drivers.

- Serial Terminal Client:
    - Tera Term (or similar) (Windows)
    - minicom (or similar) (Linux /macOS)
    - miniterm.py (cross-platform serial client also included with Python modules used in `Chapter 13`, *Creating Loose Coupling with Queues*)

All source code for this chapter is available from `https://github.com/PacktPublishing/Hands-On-RTOS-with-Microcontrollers/tree/master/Chapter_11`.

Understanding shared peripherals

A hardware peripheral is similar to any other shared resource. When there is a single resource with multiple tasks that need access to the resource, some sort of arbitration needs to be created to guarantee orderly access to the resource across tasks. In the previous chapter, we focused on different ways of developing low-level peripheral drivers. Some guidance as to driver selection was provided and it was suggested that the appropriate interface the driver provides should be based on how the driver was to be used in the system (`Chapter 10`, *Drivers and ISR's*, under the section entitled *Choosing a driver model*).

> Shared resources were covered conceptually in `Chapter 3`, *Task Signaling and Communication Mechanisms*.

There are many different examples of sharing peripherals in real-world applications. Communication peripherals such as SPI, I2C, USARTs, and ethernet peripherals can all be used by multiple tasks simultaneously, provided the timing constraints of the application allow for it and the drivers are written in a way that provides safe concurrent access. Since all of the blocking RTOS calls can be time-bound, it is easy to detect when accessing a shared peripheral is causing timing issues.

 It is important to remember that sharing a single peripheral across multiple tasks creates delays and uncertainty in timing.

In some cases where timing is critical, it is best to avoid sharing a peripheral and instead use dedicated hardware. This is part of the reason why there are multiple bus-based peripherals available, including SPI, USART's, and I2C. Even though the hardware for each of these communication buses is perfectly capable of addressing multiple devices, sometimes it is best to use a dedicated peripheral.

In other cases, a driver for a piece of hardware may be so specific that it is best to dedicate an entire peripheral to it for performance reasons. High bandwidth peripherals will typically fall into this category. An example of this would be a medium bandwidth ADC sampling thousands or tens of thousands of data points per second. The most efficient way of interacting with devices such as these is to use DMA as much as possible, transferring data from the communication bus (like SPI) directly into RAM.

Defining the peripheral driver

This chapter provides fully fleshed-out examples of interacting with a driver in a real-world situation. A USB virtual COM port was chosen because it won't require any additional hardware, other than a second micro-USB cable.

Our goal is to make it easy to interact with the Nucleo board using USB CDC in a reasonably efficient way. Desirable features for interaction include the following:

- The ability to easily write to a USB virtual COM port from multiple tasks.
- Efficient event-driven execution (avoiding wasteful polling as much as possible).
- Data should be sent over USB immediately (avoid delayed sending whenever possible).

- Calls should be non-blocking (tasks may add data to be sent without waiting for the actual transaction).
- Tasks may choose how long to wait for space to be available before data is dropped.

These design decisions will have several implications:

- **Transmit timing uncertainty**: While data is queued in a non-blocking manner, the exact timing of the transfer is not guaranteed. This is not an issue for this specific example, but if this were being used for time-sensitive interactions, it could be. USB CDC isn't a great choice for something with extremely sensitive timing requirements to begin with.
- **Trade-offs between buffer size and latency**: In order to provide sufficient space for transmitting large messages, the queue can be made larger. However, it takes longer for data to exit a large queue than a small one. If latency or timing is a consideration, this time needs to be taken into account.
- **RAM usage**: The queue requires additional RAM, on top of what the USB buffers already require.
- **Efficiency**: This driver represents a trade-off between ease of use and efficiency. There are effectively two buffers – the buffer used by USB and the queue. To provide ease of use, data will be copied by value *twice*, once into the queue and once into the USB transmit buffer. Depending on the required bandwidth, this could present a significant performance constraint.

First, let's take a high-level look at the STM USB device driver stack to better understand the options we have when interfacing with the STM-supplied CDC driver.

Introducing the STM USB driver stack

STM32CubeMX was used as a starting point to generate a USB device driver stack with CDC support. Here's an overview of the significant USB source files and where they reside, relative to the root of the repository: https://github.com/PacktPublishing/Hands-On-RTOS-with-Microcontrollers/tree/master/

1. Low-level HAL USB files:

```
DRIVERS\STM32F7XX_HAL_DRIVER\
|--Inc
|     |stm32f7xx_ll_usb.h
|--Src
      |stm32f7xx_ll_usb.c
```

The `stm32f7xx_ll_usb.c/h` files are the lowest level files, which provide access to the USB hardware peripherals. These files are used by the STM-supplied USB driver stack middleware.

2. STM USB device stack:

```
MIDDLEWARE\ST\
|--STM32_USB_Device_Library
    |----Class
    | |----CDC
    |      |----Inc
    |           | usbd_cdc.h
    | ----Src
    | usbd_cdc.c
    |----Core
        |----Inc
        |     usbd_core.h
        |     usbd_ctlreq.h
        |     usbd_def.h
        |     usbd_ioreq.h
        |----Src
              usbd_core.c
              usbd_ctlreq.c
              usbd_ioreq.c
```

The preceding files implement the core USB device and CDC class functionality. These are also supplied by STM. These provide most of the functionality required for dealing with USB transactions and enumeration.

3. Most interaction with the USB library will take place at the CDC interface level, in the BSP folder:

```
BSP\
    Nucleo_F767ZI_Init.c
    Nucleo_F767ZI_Init.h
    usbd_cdc_if.c
    usbd_cdc_if.h
    usbd_conf.c
    usbd_conf.h
    usbd_desc.c
    usbd_desc.h
    usb_device.c
    usb_device.h
```

Here's a brief description of each source file pair and its purpose. These files are the most likely files to be modified during USB development:

- `Nucleo_F767ZI_Init.c/h`: Initialization code for the MCU, which is specific to this hardware. Functions such as clock and individual pin configuration happen here.
- `usbd_cdc_if.c/h`: (STM Cube generated). Contains the USB device CDC interface functions. `CDC_Transmit_FS()` is used to transmit data from the MCU to the USB host (a PC in this case). `CDC_Receive_FS()` is used to receive data from the USB host.
- `usbd_conf.c/h`: (STM Cube generated). Used to map functions and required callbacks of `stm32f7xx_hal_pcd.c` (the USB peripheral control driver) to `stm32f7xx_ll_usb.c` (the low-level USB peripheral interface driver).
- `usbd_desc.c/h`: (STM Cube generated). USB device descriptors that are used during USB enumeration are defined here. This is where product and vendor identification numbers are defined (PID, VID).
- `usb_device.c/h`: (STM Cube generated). Contains the top-level function for initializing the USB stack. This file contains `MX_USB_DEVICE_Init()`, which is used to initialize the entire USB device driver stack. `MX_USB_DEVICE_Init()` should be called *after* all lower-level clock and pin initialization has been performed (`HWInit()` in `Nucleo_F767ZI_Init.c` performs this initialization).

Now that we have a general idea of how the code is structured, let's create a simple example to better understand how to interact with it.

Using the stock CDC drivers

`mainRawCDC.c` contains a minimal amount of code to configure the MCU hardware and USB device stack. It will allow the MCU to enumerate over USB as a virtual COM port when a micro-USB cable is plugged into CN1 (and goes to a USB host such as a PC) and power is applied through CN13. It will attempt to send two messages over USB: *test* and *message:*

1. The USB stack is initialized by using the `MX_USB_Device_Init()` function after the hardware is fully initialized:

```
int main(void)
{
  HWInit();=
  MX_USB_DEVICE_Init();
```

2. There is a single task that outputs two strings over USB, with a forced 100 tick delay after the second transmission using a naive call to usbd_cdc_if.c: CDC_Transmit_FS:

```
void usbPrintOutTask( void* NotUsed)
{
  while(1)
  {
    SEGGER_SYSVIEW_PrintfHost("print test over USB");
    CDC_Transmit_FS((uint8_t*)"test\n", 5);
    SEGGER_SYSVIEW_PrintfHost("print message over USB");
    CDC_Transmit_FS((uint8_t*)"message\n", 8);
    vTaskDelay(100);
  }
}
```

3. After compiling and loading this application to our target board, we can observe the output of the USB port by opening a terminal emulator (**Tera Term** in this case). You'll likely see something similar to the following screenshot:

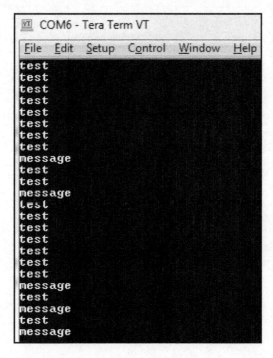

Since we were outputting a single line containing **test** and then a single line containing **message**, we would hope that the virtual serial port would contain that same sequence, but there are multiple *test* lines that aren't always followed by a *message* line.

Watching this same application run from SystemView shows that the code is executing in the order that we would expect:

Timestamp	Context	Message
10.400 061	usbprint	print test
10.400 089	usbprint	print message
10.499 976	usbprint	print test
10.500 005	usbprint	print message
10.600 011	usbprint	print test
10.600 040	usbprint	print message
10.699 976	usbprint	print test
10.699 996	usbprint	print message
10.799 976	usbprint	print test
10.800 005	usbprint	print message

Upon closer inspection of CDC_Transmit_FS, we can see that there is a return value that should have been inspected. CDC_Transmit_FS first checks to ensure that there isn't already a transfer being performed before overwriting the transmit buffer with new data. Here are the contents of CDC_Transmit_FS(automatically generated by STM Cube):

```
uint8_t result = USBD_OK;
/* USER CODE BEGIN 7 */
USBD_CDC_HandleTypeDef *hcdc =
  (USBD_CDC_HandleTypeDef*)hUsbDeviceFS.pClassData

if (hcdc->TxState != 0){
  return USBD_BUSY;
}
USBD_CDC_SetTxBuffer(&hUsbDeviceFS, Buf, Len);
result = USBD_CDC_TransmitPacket(&hUsbDeviceFS);
/* USER CODE END 7 */
return result;
```

Data will only be transmitted if there isn't already a transfer in progress (indicated by `hcdc->TxState`). So, to ensure that all of the messages are transmitted, we have a number of options here.

1. We could simply wrap each and every call to `CDC_Transmit_FS` in a conditional statement to check whether the transfer was successful:

```
int count = 10;
while(count > 0){
    count--;
        if(CDC_Transmit_FS((uint8_t*)"test\n", 5) == USBD_OK)
          break;
        else
          vTaskDelay(2);
}
```

There are several downsides to this approach:

- It is slow when attempting to transmit multiple messages back to back (because of the delay between each attempt).
- If the delay is removed, it will be extremely wasteful of CPU, since the code will essentially poll on transmission completion.
- It is undesirably complex. By forcing the calling code to evaluate whether a low-level USB transaction was valid, we're adding a loop and nested conditional statements to something that could potentially be very simple. This will increase the likelihood that it is coded incorrectly and reduce readability.

2. We could write a new wrapper based on `usbd_cdc_if.c` that uses FreeRTOS stream buffers to efficiently move data to the USB stack. This approach has a few caveats:

- To keep the calling code simple, we'll be tolerant of dropped data (if space in the stream buffer is unavailable).
- To support calls from multiple tasks, we'll need to protect access to the stream buffer with a mutex.
- The stream buffer will effectively create a duplicate buffer, thereby consuming additional RAM.

3. We could use a FreeRTOS queue instead of a stream buffer. As seen in Chapter 10, *Drivers and ISRs*, we would receive a performance hit when using a queue (relative to a stream buffer) since it would be moving only a single byte at a time. However, a queue wouldn't require being wrapped in a mutex when used across tasks.

The *best* solution depends on many factors (there's a list of considerations at the end of `Chapter 10`, *Drivers and ISRs*). For this example, we'll be using a stream buffer implementation. There is plenty of room for the extra space required by the buffer. The code here is only intended to support occasional short messages, rather than a fully reliable data channel. This limitation is mainly being placed to minimize complexity to make the examples easier to read.

Let's now have a look at how options 2 and 3 look, relative to the STM HAL drivers already present:

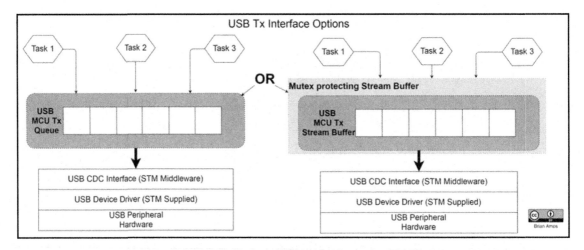

For this driver, we'll be modifying the stubbed out HAL-generated code supplied by ST (`usbd_cdc_if.c`) as a starting point. Its functionality will be replaced by our newly created `VirtualCommDriver.c`. This will be detailed in the next section.

We'll also make a very small modification to the CDC middleware supplied by STM (`usbd_cdc.c/h`) to enable a non-polled method for determining when transfers are finished. The `USBD_CDC_HandleTypeDef` struct in `usbd_cdc.h` already has a variable named `TxState` that can be polled to determine when a transmission has completed. But, to increase efficiency, we'd like to avoid polling. To make this possible, we'll add another member to the struct – a function pointer that will be called when a transfer is complete: `usbd_cdc.h` (additions in **bold**):

```
typedef struct
{
  uint32_t data[CDC_DATA_HS_MAX_PACKET_SIZE / 4U]; /* Force 32bits
                                                      alignment */
  uint8_t CmdOpCode;
```

```
    uint8_t CmdLength;
    uint8_t *RxBuffer;
    uint8_t *TxBuffer;
    uint32_t RxLength;
    uint32_t TxLength;
    //adding a function pointer for an optional call back function
    //when transmission is complete
    void (*TxCallBack)( void );
    __IO uint32_t TxState;
    __IO uint32_t RxState;
}
USBD_CDC_HandleTypeDef;
```

We'll then add the following code to usbd_cdc.c. (additions in bold):

```
    }
    else
    {
        hcdc->TxState = 0U;
        if(hcdc->TxCallBack != NULL)
        {
            hcdc->TxCallBack();
        }
    }
    return USBD_OK;
}
```

This addition executes the function pointed to by TxCallBack if it has been provided (indicated by a non-NULL value). This happens when TxState in the CDC struct is set to 0. TxCallBack was also initialized to NULL in USBD_CDC_Init().

> Modifying drivers supplied by STM will make it harder to migrate between different versions of HAL. These considerations must be weighed against any advantages they provide.
> NOTE: More recent versions of HAL and STMCubeIDE include support for TxCallBack, so this modification won't be necessary if you're starting from scratch with the latest released code from ST.

Developing a StreamBuffer USB virtual COM port

`VirtualComDriver.c` is located in the top-level `Drivers` folder (since we're likely to use it in a future chapter). It is available here: `https://github.com/PacktPublishing/Hands-On-RTOS-with-Microcontrollers/tree/master/Drivers/HandsOnRTOS/`

First, we'll walk through each of the functions that have been created, and their purpose.

Public functions

`VirtualComDriver.c` currently has three publicly available functions:

- `TransmitUsbDataLossy`
- `TransmitUsbData`
- `VirtualCommInit`

`TransmitUsbDataLossy` is simply a wrapper around a stream buffer function call. It uses an ISR-safe variant, which is guaranteed not to block (but may also not copy all data into the buffer). The number of bytes copied into the buffer is returned. In this case, it is up to the calling code to determine whether or not to finish copying data into the buffer:

```
int32_t TransmitUsbDataLossy(uint8_t const* Buff, uint16_t Len)
{
   int32_t numBytesCopied = xStreamBufferSendFromISR( txStream, Buff, Len,
                                                                NULL);
   return numBytesCopied;
}
```

`TransmitUsbData` provides a bit more convenience. It will block up to two ticks waiting for space to become available in the buffer. This is broken into two calls in case the buffer fills part way through the initial transfer. It is likely that enough space will be available 1 tick later when the second call to `xStreamBufferSend` is made. In most cases, there will be very little dropped data using this method:

```
int32_t TransmitUsbData(uint8_t const* Buff, uint16_t Len)
{
   int32_t numBytesCopied = xStreamBufferSend( txStream, Buff, Len, 1);
   if(numBytesCopied != Len)
   {
     numBytesCopied += xStreamBufferSend( txStream, Buff+numBytesCopied,
                                          Len-numBytesCopied, 1);
```

```
    }
    return numBytesCopied;
}
```

VirtualCommInit performs all of the setup required for both the USB stack and the necessary FreeRTOS task. The stream buffer is being initialized with a trigger level of 1 to minimize the latency between when TransmitUsbData is called and when the data is moved into the USB stack. This value can be adjusted in conjunction with the maximum blocking time used in xStreamBufferReceive to achieve better efficiency by ensuring that larger blocks of data are transferred simultaneously:

```
void VirtualCommInit( void )
{
    BaseType_t retVal;
    MX_USB_DEVICE_Init();
    txStream = xStreamBufferCreate( txBuffLen, 1);
    assert_param( txStream != NULL);
    retVal = xTaskCreate(usbTask, "usbTask", 1024, NULL,
                configMAX_PRIORITIES, &usbTaskHandle);
    assert_param(retVal == pdPASS);
}
```

These are all of the publicly available functions. By modifying slightly the interaction with the stream buffer, this driver can be optimized for many different use cases. The remainder of the functionality is provided by functions that aren't publicly accessible.

Private functions

usbTask is a private function that takes care of the initial setup of our CDC overrides. It also monitors the stream buffer and task notifications, making the required calls to the CDC implementation provided by STM.

Before starting its main loop, there are a few items that need to be initialized:

1. The task must wait until all of the underlying peripherals and USB stack initialization are performed. This is because the task will be accessing data structures created by the USB CDC stack:

```
USBD_CDC_HandleTypeDef *hcdc = NULL;

while(hcdc == NULL)
{
    hcdc = (USBD_CDC_HandleTypeDef*)hUsbDeviceFS.pClassData;
    vTaskDelay(10);
}
```

2. A task notification is given, provided a transmission is not already in progress. The notification is also taken, which allows for an efficient way to block in case a transfer is already in progress:

```
if (hcdc->TxState == 0)
{
    xTaskNotify( usbTaskHandle, 1, eSetValueWithOverwrite);
}
ulTaskNotifyTake( pdTRUE, portMAX_DELAY );
```

3. `usbTxComplete` is the callback function that will be executed when a transmission is finished. The USB CDC stack is ready to accept more data to be transmitted. Setting the `TxCallBack` variable to `usbTxComplete` configures the structure used by `usbd_cdc.c`, allowing our function to be called at the right time:

```
hcdc->TxCallBack = usbTxComplete;
```

4. `usbTxComplete` is short, only consisting of a few lines that will provide a task notification and force a context switch to be evaluated (so `usbTask` will be unblocked as quickly as possible):

```
void usbTxComplete( void )
{
    portBASE_TYPE xHigherPriorityTaskWoken = pdFALSE;
    xTaskNotifyFromISR( usbTaskHandle, 1, eSetValueWithOverwrite,
                                    &xHigherPriorityTaskWoken);
    portYIELD_FROM_ISR(xHigherPriorityTaskWoken);
}
```

A function pointed to by `TxCallBack` is executed within the USB ISR, so any code executed by the callback must be kept extremely brief, call only ISR-safe versions of FreeRTOS functions, and have its priority properly configured.

5. The infinite `while` loop portion of `usbTask` follows:

```
while(1)
  {
    SEGGER_SYSVIEW_PrintfHost("waiting for txStream");
    uint8_t numBytes = xStreamBufferReceive( txStream, usbTxBuff,
                                      txBuffLen, portMAX_DELAY);
    if(numBytes > 0)
    {
      SEGGER_SYSVIEW_PrintfHost("pulled %d bytes from txStream",
                                                    numBytes);
      USBD_CDC_SetTxBuffer(&hUsbDeviceFS, usbTxBuff, numBytes);
      USBD_CDC_TransmitPacket(&hUsbDeviceFS);
      ulTaskNotifyTake( pdTRUE, portMAX_DELAY );
      SEGGER_SYSVIEW_PrintfHost("tx complete");
    }
  }
```

The task notification provides an efficient way to gate transmissions without polling:

- Whenever a transmission has finished, the callback (`usbTxComplete`) will be executed from the USB stack. `usbTxComplete` will provide a notification that will unblock the `usbTask`, at which point it will go out to the stream buffer and collect as much data as it can in one call, copying all available data into `usbTxBuff` (up to `numBytes` bytes).
- If a transmission is complete, `usbTask` will block indefinitely until data shows up in the stream buffer (`txStream`). `usbTask` won't be consuming any CPU time while blocking, but it will also automatically unblock whenever data is available.

This method provides a very efficient way of queueing data, while also providing good throughput and low latency. Any tasks adding data to the queue don't need to block or wait until their data is transmitted.

Putting it all together

There's a fair amount going on here, with multiple sources of asynchronous events. Here's a sequence diagram of how all of these functions fit together:

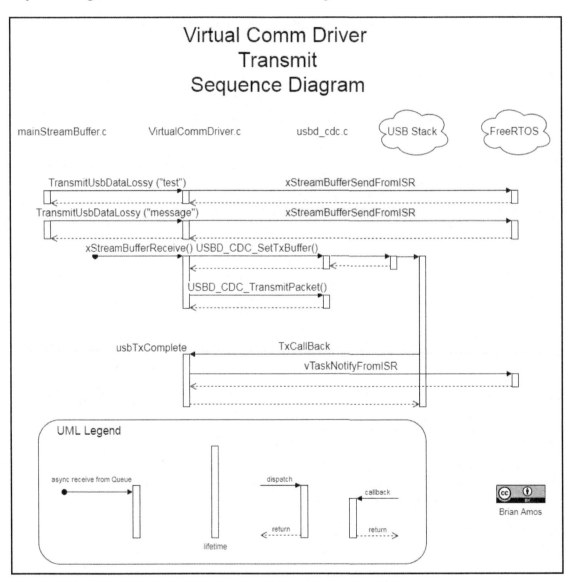

Here are a few noteworthy items from the preceding diagram:

- Calls to `TransmitUsbData` and `TransmitUsbDataLossy` are non-blocking. If space is available, data is transferred into the stream buffer, `txStream`, and the number of bytes copied is returned. Partial messages may be copied into the buffer (which happens under extremely high load when the buffer gets filled).
- Two things need to happen before a packet of data is sent via `USBD_CDC_TransmitPacket`:
  - `usbTask` must receive a task notification, indicating that it is clear to send data.
  - Data must be available in `txStream`.
- Once transmission has started, the USB stack will be called by `OTG_FS_IRQHandler` in `stm32f7xx_it.c` until the transfer is complete, at which point the function pointed to by `TxCallBack` (`usbTxComplete`) will be called. This callback is executed from within the USB ISR, so the ISR-safe version of `vTaskNotify` (`vTaskNotifyFromISR`) must be used.

In `mainStreamBuffer.c`, (available from `https://github.com/PacktPublishing/Hands-On-RTOS-with-Microcontrollers/tree/master/Chapter_11/Src/mainUsbStreamBuffer.c`), the virtual COM port is initialized with a single line, once the hardware initialization has been performed:

```
int main(void)
{
  HWInit();
  VirtualCommInit();
```

A single task has been created in `mainStreamBuffer.c` to push data over to the USB:

```
void usbPrintOutTask( void* NotUsed)
{
  const uint8_t testString[] = "test\n";
  const uint8_t messageString[] = "message\n";

  while(1)
  {
    SEGGER_SYSVIEW_PrintfHost("add \"test\" to txStream");
    TransmitUsbDataLossy(testString, sizeof(testString));
    SEGGER_SYSVIEW_PrintfHost("add \"message\" to txStream");
    TransmitUsbDataLossy(messageString, sizeof(messageString));
    vTaskDelay(2);
  }
}
```

This results in output that alternates as we would expect, thanks to the buffering provided by the stream buffer:

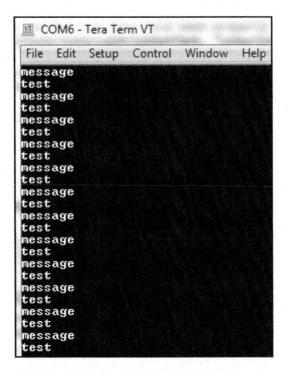

Let's now take a look at a single transfer using SystemView:

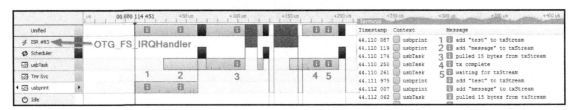

All of the tasks and ISRs are arranged in ascending priority. Numbers in the SystemView terminal on the right have corresponding numbers on the timeline:

1. The first item, *test\n*, was added to the buffer. usbTask is now ready to run (indicated by the blue box).
2. The second item, *message\n*, was added to the buffer. After the usbPrint task blocks, usbTask is brought into context by the scheduler.

3. All 15 bytes are copied from the stream buffer, `txStream`, and placed into the local `usbTxBuff`. This buffer is fed into the USB stack using `USBD_CDC_SetTxBuffer` and a transfer is started with `USBD_CDC_TransmitPacket`. The USB stack takes care of the transfer and issues a callback when it is finished (`usbTxComplete`). This callback sends a task notification to `usbTask`, signaling that the transfer is complete.

4. `usbTask` receives the task notification and continues with the loop.

5. `usbTask` begins waiting on data to become available in `txStream`.

This general sequence repeats every 2 ms, which translates into about 1,000 lines being transmitted each second. Keep in mind that the delay is present to make analysis easier. The non-lossy `TransmitUsbData()` could be utilized instead with no delay, but seeing *exactly* what is occurring is a bit more of a challenge:

Name		Frequency
ISR #83	1.76%	1001 Hz
Scheduler	1.00%	1500 Hz
usbTask	3.89%	1500 Hz
Tmr Svc	0.00%	0 Hz
usbprint	3.06%	500 Hz
Idle	90.29%	1500 Hz

The total CPU time consumed is around 10%, with most of the time spent in `usbTask` and `usbPrint`.

If we wanted to minimize CPU usage, at the expense of introducing a bit more latency between when a message was first printed and when it was transmitted over the line, the following changes could be made:

The following is an excerpt from `VirtualCommDriver.c`:

1. Increase the trigger value used to initialize `txStream` from 1 to 500. This will cause the buffer to attempt to gather 500 bytes before returning data:

```
void VirtualCommInit( void )
{
  MX_USB_DEVICE_Init();
  txStream = xStreamBufferCreate( txBuffLen, 500);
```

2. Decrease the maximum amount of time to wait on data to become available in the stream from an infinite timeout to 100 ticks. This will guarantee that the stream is emptied at least once every 100 ticks (which happens to be 100 ms with the current configuration). This minimizes context switching and how often usbTask will need to run. It also allows for more data to be transferred to the USB stack at a time:

```
uint8_t numBytes = xStreamBufferReceive( txStream, usbTxBuff,
                                         txBuffLen, 100);
```

Increasing the trigger value of the stream buffer from 1 to 500 bytes and increasing the available block time from 1 to 100 ticks *reduces the CPU usage of* usbTask *by a whopping 94%*:

1 byte trigger infinite block Time			500 byte trigger 100 mS block Time		
Name		Frequency	Name		Frequency
ISR #83	1.76%	1001 Hz	ISR #83	0.06%	30 Hz
Scheduler	1.00%	1500 Hz	Scheduler	0.42%	530 Hz
usbTask	3.89%	1500 Hz	usbTask	0.22%	45 Hz
Tmr Svc	0.00%	0 Hz	Tmr Svc	0.00%	0 Hz
usbprint	3.06%	500 Hz	usbprint	2.53%	500 Hz
Idle	90.29%	1500 Hz	Idle	96.77%	530 Hz

Now, this means we also have an increase in latency – the amount of time it takes between when a call to TransmitUsbDataLossy is made and when that message is transmitted across the USB cable. So, there is a trade-off to be made. In this simple example, where the use case is just a simple printout with a human looking at the text, 10 Hz is likely more than fast enough.

Now that we have most of our USB driver written, we can add in some additional safety measures to guarantee that VirtualCommDriver is safe to use across multiple tasks.

Using mutexes for access control

Since we implemented our driver with a stream buffer, if we are interested in having more than one task write to it, access to the stream buffer must be protected by a mutex. Most of the other FreeRTOS primitives, such as queues, don't have this limitation; they are safe to use across multiple tasks without any additional effort. Let's take a look at what would be required to extend VirtualCommDriver to make it usable by more than one task.

Extending VirtualCommDriver

To make usage for the users of VirtuCommPortDriver as easy as possible, we can incorporate all of the mutex handling within the function call itself, rather than requiring users of the function to manage the mutex.

An additional file, `VirtualCommDriverMultiTask.c` has been created to illustrate this:

1. A mutex is defined and created, along with all of the other variables required across multiple functions in this source file:

```
#define txBuffLen 2048
uint8_t vcom_usbTxBuff[txBuffLen];
StreamBufferHandle_t vcom_txStream = NULL;
TaskHandle_t vcom_usbTaskHandle = NULL;
SemaphoreHandle_t vcom_mutexPtr = NULL;
```

To prevent multiple copies of this mutex from being created for each compilation unit `VirtualComDriverMultitTask` is included in, we won't define our *private global* variables as having *static* scope this time. Since we don't have namespaces in C, we'll prepend the names with `vcom_` in an attempt to avoid naming collisions with other globals.

2. The mutex is initialized in `VirtualCommInit()`:

```
vcom_mutexPtr = xSemaphoreCreateMutex();
assert_param(vcom_mutexPtr != NULL);
```

3. A new `TransmitUsbData()` function has been defined. It now includes a maximum delay (specified in milliseconds):

```
int32_t TransmitUsbData(uint8_t const* Buff, uint16_t Len, int32_t
DelayMs)
```

4. Define a few variables to help keep track of elapsed time:

```
const uint32_t delayTicks = DelayMs / portTICK_PERIOD_MS;
const uint32_t startingTime = xTaskGetTickCount();
uint32_t endingTime = startingTime + delayTicks;
```

The previous calls to xStreamBufferSend are wrapped inside the mutex, vcom_mutexPtr. remainingTime is updated after each blocking FreeRTOS API call to accurately limit the maximum amount of time spent in this function:

```
if(xSemaphoreTake(vcom_mutexPtr, delayTicks ) == pdPASS)
{
    uint32_t remainingTime = endingTime - xTaskGetTickCount();
    numBytesCopied = xStreamBufferSend( vcom_txStream, Buff, Len,
                                                      remainingTime);

    if(numBytesCopied != Len)
    {
      remainingTime = endingTime - xTaskGetTickCount();
      numBytesCopied += xStreamBufferSend(   vcom_txStream,
                                             Buff+numBytesCopied,
                                             Len-numBytesCopied,
                                             remainingTime);
    }

    xSemaphoreGive(vcom_mutexPtr);
}
```

A new main file, mainUsbStreamBufferMultiTask, was created to illustrate usage:

1. usbPrintOutTask was created. This takes a number as an argument as a means to easily differentiate which task is writing:

```
void usbPrintOutTask( void* Number)
{
#define TESTSIZE 10
  char testString[TESTSIZE];
  memset(testString, 0, TESTSIZE);
  snprintf(testString, TESTSIZE, "task %i\n", (int) Number);
  while(1)
  {
    TransmitUsbData((uint8_t*)testString, sizeof(testString), 100);
    vTaskDelay(2);
  }
}
```

2. Two instances of `usbPrintOutTask` are created, passing in the numbers *1* and *2*. A cast to `(void*)` prevents complaints from the compiler:

```
retVal = xTaskCreate(   usbPrintOutTask, "usbprint1",
                        STACK_SIZE, (void*)1, tskIDLE_PRIORITY + 2,
                        NULL);
assert_param( retVal == pdPASS);
retVal = xTaskCreate(   usbPrintOutTask, "usbprint2",
                        STACK_SIZE, (void*)2, tskIDLE_PRIORITY +
                        2,
                        NULL);
assert_param( retVal == pdPASS);
```

Now, multiple tasks are able to send data over the USB. The amount of time that each call to `TransmitUsbData` may block is specified with each function call.

Guaranteeing atomic transactions

Sometimes, it is desirable to transmit a message and then be confident that the response is for that message. In these cases, a mutex can be used at a higher level. This allows for groups of messages to be clustered together. An example of when this technique can be especially useful is a single peripheral servicing multiple physical ICs across multiple tasks:

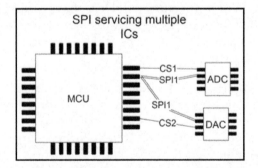

In the preceding diagram, the same peripheral (SPI1) is used to service two different ICs. Although the SPI peripheral is shared, there are separate chip select lines (CS1 and CS2) for each IC. There are also two completely independent drivers for these devices (one is an ADC and one is a DAC). In this situation, a mutex can be used to group multiple messages going to the same device together so they all occur when the correct chip select line is activated; things wouldn't go well if the ADC was meant to receive data when CS2 was asserted (the DAC would receive the data instead).

This approach can work well when all of the the following conditions exist:

- Individual transfers are fast.
- Peripherals have low latency.
- Flexibility (at least several ms, if not 10's of ms) as to exactly when transfers can take place.

Shared hardware isn't much different from any other shared resource. There are many other real-world examples that haven't been discussed here.

Summary

In this chapter, we took a deep dive into creating an efficient interface to a complex driver stack that was very convenient to use. Using stream buffers, we analyzed trade-offs between decreasing latency and minimizing CPU usage. After a basic interface was in place, it was extended to be used across multiple tasks. We also saw an example of how a mutex could be used for ensuring that a multi-stage transaction remained atomic, even while the peripheral was shared between tasks.

Throughout the examples, we focused on performance versus ease of use and coding effort. Now that you have a good understanding of why design decisions are being made, you should be in a good position to make informed decisions regarding your own code base and implementations. When the time comes to implement your design, you'll also have a solid understanding of the steps that need to be taken to guarantee race condition-free access to your shared peripheral.

So far, we've been discussing trade-offs when creating drivers, so that we write something that is as close to perfect for our use case as possible. Wouldn't it be nice if (at the beginning of a new project) we didn't need to re-invent the wheel by copying, pasting, and modifying all of these drivers every time? Instead of continually introducing low-level, hard-to-find bugs, we could simply bring in everything we know that works well and get to work adding new features required for the new project? With a well-architected system, this type of workflow is entirely possible! In the next chapter, we'll cover several tips on creating a firmware architecture that is flexible and doesn't suffer from the copy-paste-modify trap many firmware engineers find themselves stuck in.

Questions

As we conclude, here is a list of questions for you to test your knowledge regarding this chapter's material. You will find the answers in the *Assessments* section of the Appendix:

1. It is *always* best to minimize the number of hardware peripherals being used:
    - True
    - False

2. When sharing a hardware peripheral across multiple tasks, the only concern is creating threadsafe code that ensures that only one task has access to the peripheral at a time:
    - True
    - False

3. What trade-offs do stream buffers allow us to make when creating them?
    - Latency
    - CPU efficiency
    - Required RAM size
    - All of the above

4. Stream buffers can be used directly by multiple tasks:
    - True
    - False

5. What is one of the mechanisms that can be used to create threadsafe atomic access to a peripheral for the entire duration of a multi-stage message?

12
Tips for Creating a Well-Abstracted Architecture

Throughout this book, simple examples of minimal complexity have been provided. Our focus has been to keep the code clear and readable to illustrate the particular **real-time operating system (RTOS)** concepts being addressed and keep the interactions with hardware as easily understood as possible. However, in the real world, the best code bases for long-term development are those that allow developers to move quickly with great flexibility and determination to meet targets. This chapter provides suggestions on how to go about architecting, creating, growing, and maintaining a code base that will be flexible enough for long-term use. We'll be exploring these concepts with real code by cleaning up some of the code developed in earlier chapters through the addition of flexibility and better portability to different hardware.

This chapter is valuable to anyone interested in reusing code across multiple projects. While the concepts presented here are by no means original, they are focused solely on firmware in embedded systems. The concepts covered are applicable to bare-metal systems, as well as highly reusable RTOS task-based systems. By following the guidelines here, you'll be able to create a flexible code base that adapts to many different projects, regardless of what hardware it happens to be running on. Another side effect (or direct intention) of architecting a code base in this manner is extremely testable code.

In this chapter, we'll cover the following topics:

- Understanding abstraction
- Writing reusable code
- Organizing source code

Technical requirements

To run the code introduced in this chapter, you will need the following:

- A Nucleo F767 development board
- A micro-USB cable
- STM32CubeIDE and source code (instructions in `Chapter 5`, *Selecting an IDE*, under the *Setting up our IDE* section)
- SEGGER J-Link, Ozone, and SystemView (instructions in `Chapter 6`, *Debugging Tools for Real-Time Systems*)

All source code for this chapter is available at `https://github.com/PacktPublishing/ Hands-On-RTOS-with-Microcontrollers/tree/master/Chapter_12`.

Understanding abstraction

If our goal is to create a code base that will be usable for a long time, we need flexibility. Source code (just like product feature sets and business tactics) isn't chiseled out of rock—it tends to morph into different forms over time. If our source code is to be flexible, it needs to be able to morph and adapt. Only then will it be able to provide a solid foundation for implementing different feature sets of a product (or entire product lines) as the business landscape driving its development changes. Abstraction is a core tenet of flexibility.

In our context, abstraction means representing a single instance of a complex implementation with a representation that can be applied to many different instances. For example, let's take another look at an earlier example from `Chapter 1`, *Introducing Real-Time Systems*:

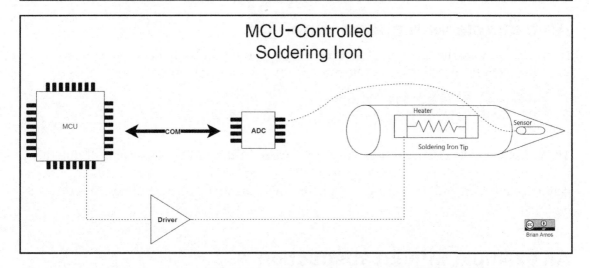

The diagram itself is an abstract representation of the hardware required for a closed-loop control system. The exact part numbers of the ADC, driver circuitry, and **microcontroller unit (MCU)** aren't shown in the diagram; they could be almost anything.

There are at least two primary reasons for using abstractions when creating a flexible code base:

- Grasping an abstraction is fast.
- Abstractions provide flexibility.

Grasping an abstraction is fast

Understanding a well-written abstraction in code is similar to understanding a simple flow chart. Just as you don't need to understand every interconnect and resistor value when observing a flowchart (versus a schematic), reading through a well-commented header file of an abstraction provides nearly all of the information required to use any of the underlying implementations. There is no need to get buried under the details and idiosyncrasies of each implementation.

This limited bird's-eye view means that future developers are more likely to *consume* the code since it is presented in a well-defined, well-documented, and consistent manner. The overall knowledge and time required to grasp an abstraction is much less than that required if implementing the same functionality from scratch.

An example with abstraction

If you saw a call to the following function call, you would probably have a fair chance at guessing what the function did, even without any proper comments:

```
bufferX[i] = adcX->ReadAdcValue();
bufferY[i] = adcY->ReadAdcValue();
bufferZ[i] = adcZ->ReadAdcValue();
```

The preceding code is fairly self-explanatory—we're reading ADC values and storing them in 3 different buffers. If all of our calls to get ADC readings use the same `ReadAdcValue()` calling convention and descriptively name the ADC channel, understanding the code is fast and easy.

An example without abstraction

On the flip side, imagine that instead you were given the following lines of code (they are functionally equivalent to the preceding code):

```
bufferX[i] = adc_avg(0, 1);
bufferY[i] = adc_avg(1, 1);
bufferZ[i] = HAL_ADC_GetValue(adc2_ch0_h);
```

This immediately raises several questions, such as what the arguments being passed into `adc_avg()` and `HAL_ADC_GetValue()` are. At a minimum, we'd likely need to track down the relevant function prototypes and read through them:

```
/**
 * return an average of numSamp samples collected
 * by the ADC who's channel is defined by chNum
 * @param chNum channel number of the ADC
 * @param numSamp number of samples to average
 * @retval avera
**/
uint32_t adc_avg(uint8_t chNum, uint16_t numSamp);
```

OK, so `adc_avg()` takes an ADC channel as the first parameter and the number of samples to average as the second parameter—passing 1 to the second parameter provides a single reading. Now, what about this other call to `HAL_ADC_GetValue(adc2_ch0_h)`? We'd better go find the prototype for it:

```
/**
 * @brief Gets the converted value from
 * data register of regular channel.
 * @param hadc pointer to a ADC_HandleTypeDef
```

```
 *  structure that contains
 *  the configuration information for the
 *  specified ADC.
 *  @retval Converted value
 */
uint32_t HAL_ADC_GetValue(ADC_HandleTypeDef* hadc)
```

It turns out adc2_ch0_h is a handle—probably to channel 0 on the ADC2 STM32 peripheral... now, where's that schematic... is everything wired properly? Should channel 0 really be stored in bufferZ? That seems a little odd...

OK, so this might be a *bit* contrived, but if you've been coding long enough, you've likely seen far worse. The takeaway here is that the consistency provided by a good abstraction makes reading code faster and easier than attempting to track down and understand the details of each specific implementation.

Abstractions provide flexibility

Since a proper abstraction isn't directly tied to an implementation, creating an abstraction for functionality provides flexibility in the way the functionality is implemented, even though the interface to that functionality is consistent. In the following figure, there are five different physical implementations of an ADC value—all represented by the same, simple abstraction, which is int32_t ReadAdcValue(void);:

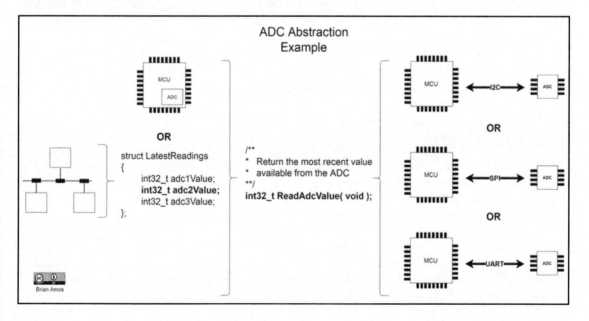

Although the function call remains consistent, there can be drastically different implementations of the ADC. In this diagram alone, there are five different ways for an ADC to provide data through the `ReadAdcValue` function. The ADC could be sitting on a local communication bus, such as I2C, SPI, or UART. It could be an internal ADC that is present on the MCU itself. Alternatively, the ADC reading may be coming from a remote node of an external network. Since there is a consistent, abstract interface, the underlying implementation isn't all that significant. A consumer of the interface doesn't need to be concerned with all of the details required to configure the ADC, collect the reading, and so on; the ADC only needs to make a call to `ReadAdcValue` to access the most up-to-date reading.

There are, of course, many considerations to be made here, such as how recent the reading is, how quickly it must be collected, the resolution and scaling of the underlying reading, and so on. These types of details need to be provided by each provider and consumer that is implementing an abstraction. Naturally, there are cases where this level of abstraction is not appropriate for various reasons, which need to be evaluated on a case-by-case basis. If, for example, an algorithm needs to be run each time a new reading is taken, having it blindly poll `ReadAdValue` asynchronously won't work reliably.

There are many examples of abstraction in the real world. Let's say you're a developer in an organization that makes many different products that all incorporate similar core components. For example, if you're designing a family of process controllers, you'll likely be interfacing with ADCs, DACs, and communication stacks. Each controller may have a slightly different user-facing feature set, but the underlying core components could be shared. Drivers for the ADCs, DACs, and algorithms can all share common code. By sharing common code across multiple products, developers only need to invest their time into writing common code once. As the customer-facing feature sets change over time, individual components may be replaced as needed, as long as they are loosely coupled to one another. Even the underlying MCU doesn't need to be the same, provided its hardware is sufficiently abstracted.

Let's take a closer look at the ADC in a controller as a specific example. The simplest way for a control algorithm to use ADC readings is to take raw readings from the device and use them directly. To reduce the number of source files, the drivers for the ADC, communication peripheral, and algorithm *could* all be combined into a single source file.

Note that for precision applications, there are many issues with using raw readings directly, even without worrying about code elegance and abstraction. Ensuring consistent scaling and offsets and providing a flexible amount of resolution are all easier when code does not interface to the raw units (ADC counts) directly.

When code space and RAM are at a premium, or a quick and dirty one-off, or a proof of concept are all that is desired, this approach might be acceptable. The resulting architecture might look something like the following:

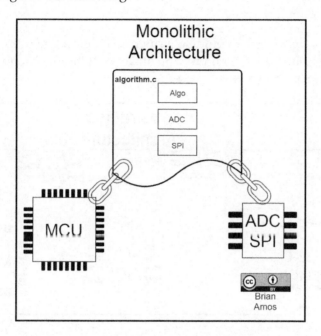

A few things should jump out when looking at this architecture:

- The `algorithm.c` file is coupled with both the MCU and a specific ADC on a specific bus.
- If either the MCU or the ADC changes, a new version of `algorithm.c` will need to be created.
- The visual similarity between the links to the MCU and ADC ICs look very much like chains. This is not an accident. Code like this tightly binds whatever algorithm is inside `algorithm.c` to the underlying hardware in a way that is very inflexible.

There are also a few side effects that might not be as obvious:

- `algorithm.c` will be very difficult (maybe even impossible) to run independently of the hardware. This makes it very hard to test the algorithm in isolation. It also makes it very difficult to test all of the corner cases and error conditions that only occur when something goes wrong in the hardware.

- The immediate, useful life of `algorithm.c` will be limited to this single MCU and specific ADC. To add support for additional MCUs or ADC ICs, `#define` functions will need to be used; otherwise, the entire file will need to be copied and modified.

On the other hand, `algorithm.c` could be written so it doesn't rely directly on the underlying hardware. Instead, it could rely on an abstract interface to the ADC. In this case, our architecture looks more like this:

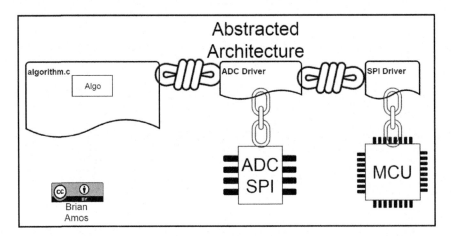

The core points to observe in this variation are as follows:

- `algorithm.c` has no direct reliance on any specific hardware configuration. Different ADCs and MCUs can be used interchangeably, assuming they correctly implement the interface required. This means it could move to an entirely different platform and be used as is, without modification.
- The chains have been replaced by ropes, which *tie* together abstractions with their underlying implementations, rather than tightly bind `algorithm.c` to the underlying hardware.
- Only the implementations are tightly bound to the hardware.

Less obvious points that are also worth mentioning are as follows:

- `ADC Driver` isn't *completely* coupled to the hardware. While this particular driver will probably only support a single ADC, the ADC hardware itself won't be necessary for getting the code to work. The hardware can be imitated by simulating SPI traffic. This allows testing the ADC driver independently of the underlying hardware.
- Both `SPI Driver` and `ADC Driver` can be used in other applications without rewriting them. This is a really big advantage to writing reusable code; it is flexible enough to repurpose with no additional work (or side effects).

Now that we have a few examples of abstraction covered, let's consider why using abstractions may be important for projects.

Why abstraction is important

It is important to ensure your architecture is using abstractions if the following points apply:

- Common components will be reused in other projects.
- Portability to different hardware is desirable.
- Code will be unit tested.
- Teams will be working in parallel

For projects that are part of a larger code base, all four of the preceding points are generally desirable, since they all contribute to decreased time to market in the medium term. They also lead to decreased long-term maintenance costs for the code base:

- It is easier to create quality documentation once for the abstraction, rather than to thoroughly document every intricate piece of spaghetti code that reimplements the same functionality in a slightly different way.
- Abstractions provide ways of cleanly decoupling hardware from many of the other interfaces used in a project.
- Abstracting hardware interfaces makes unit testing code much easier (allowing programmers to run unit tests on their development machine, instead of on the target hardware).

- Unit tests are similar to a type of documentation that's always up to date (if they are run regularly). They provide a source of truth for what the code is intended to do. They also provide a safety net when making changes or providing new implementations, ensuring nothing has been forgotten or inadvertently changed.
- Consistent abstractions lead to code bases that are more quickly understood by new team members. Each project in a code base is slightly more familiar than the last one since there's a large amount of commonality and consistency between them.
- Loosely coupled code is easier to change. The mental burden for understanding a well-encapsulated module is much lower than trying to understand a sprawling implementation spanning multiple portions of a project. Changes to the well-encapsulated module are more likely to be made correctly and without side effects (especially when unit testing is employed).

When abstractions are not used, the following symptoms commonly occur:

- New developers have a hard time making changes since each change has a ripple effect.
- It takes new developers a long time to understand a piece of code well enough to be comfortable changing it.
- Parallel development is very difficult.
- Code is tightly coupled to a specific hardware platform.

For a real-world example where abstraction is required, we don't need to look any further than FreeRTOS itself. FreeRTOS wraps all of the device-specific functionality in two files, `port.c` and `portmacros.h`. To add support to a new hardware platform, only these files need to be created/modified. All of the other files that make up FreeRTOS have only a single copy, shared across dozens of ports for different hardware platforms. Libraries such as FatFs, lwIP, and many others also make use of hardware abstractions; it is the only way they can reasonably provide support for a large range of hardware.

Recognizing opportunities to reuse code

There is no absolute rule to follow when determining whether formalized abstractions should be used (if abstractions are not already present). However, there are some hints, which are as follows:

- **If you're writing code that can be used by more than one project**: Interfacing with the underlying hardware should be done through an abstraction (the ADC driver and algorithm in the preceding section are examples of this). Otherwise, the code will be tied to the specific piece of hardware it was written for.
- **If your code interacts with a vendor-specific API**: Creating a light abstraction layer above it will reduce vendor lock-in. After interfaces are commonly used and set up, you'll start to gravitate toward making vendor-specific APIs conform to your code base, which makes trying out different implementations quick and easy. It also insulates the bulk of your code from changes the vendor might make to the API over time.
- **If the module is in the center of the stack and interacts with other sub-modules**: Using formalized interfaces will reduce the coupling to the other modules, making it easier to replace them in the future.

One common misconception around code reuse is that creating a copy of code is the same as reusing the code. If a copy of the code has been created, it is effectively not being reused—let's look at why.

Avoiding the copy-paste-modify trap

So, we've got a piece of code that has been proven to work well and we have a new project coming up. How should we go about creating the new project—just copy the working project and start making changes? After all, if the code is being copied, it is being reused, right? Creating copies of a code base like this can inadvertently create a mountain of technical debt over time. The problem isn't the act of copying and modifying the code, it is trying to maintain all of the copies over time.

Here's a look at what a monolithic architecture for `algorithm.c` might look like over the course of six projects. Let's assume that that actual algorithm is intended to be identical across all six projects:

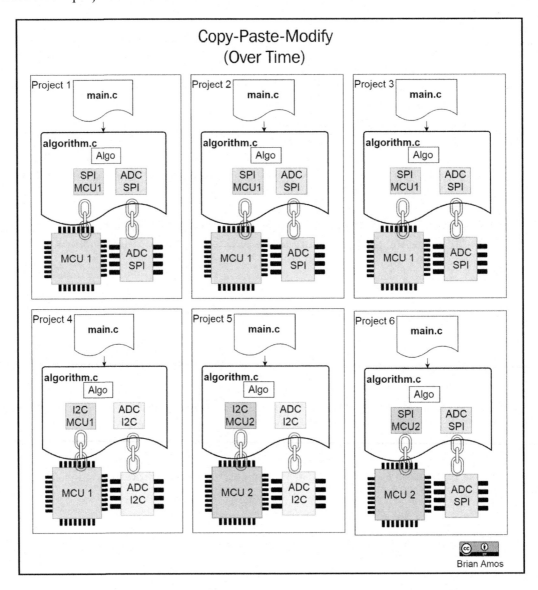

Here are some of the main points in the diagram:

- It is impossible to tell whether the actual algorithm being used is the same since there are six copies of the file.
- In some cases, `algorithm.c` is implemented with different hardware. Since these changes were made in `algorithm.c`, it is isn't easily tell whether or not the algorithm implemented is actually the same without examining each file in detail.

Now, let's take a look at the *drawbacks* to copy-paste-modify in our example:

- If `Algo` has a bug, it will need to be fixed in six different places.
- Testing a potential fix for `Algo` will need to be validated separately for each project. The only way to tell if a fix corrected the bug is probably by testing on actual hardware "in-system"; this is probably a very time-intensive task and it is potentially technically difficult to hit all of the edge cases.
- The forked `Algo` function will likely morph over time (possibly inadvertently); this will further complicate maintenance because examining the differences between implementations will be even more difficult.
- Bugs are harder to find, understand, and fix because of all of the slight differences between the six projects.
- Creating project 7 may come with a high degree of uncertainty (it is hard to tell exactly which features of `Algo` will be brought in, which intricacies/bugs from the `SPI` or `ADC` drivers will follow, and so on).
- If `MCU1` goes obsolete, porting `algorithm.c` will need to happen four separate times.

All of these duplicates can be avoided by creating consistent reusable abstractions for the common components:

- Each common component needs to have a consistent *interface*.
- Any code that is meant to be reused uses the *interface* rather than the *implementation* (`Algo` would use an ADC interface).
- Common drivers, interfaces, and middleware should only have one copy.
- Implementations are provided by the use of **board support packages** (BSPs), which provide an implementation for required interfaces.

If the same algorithm were designed using the preceding guidelines, we might have something that looks more like this:

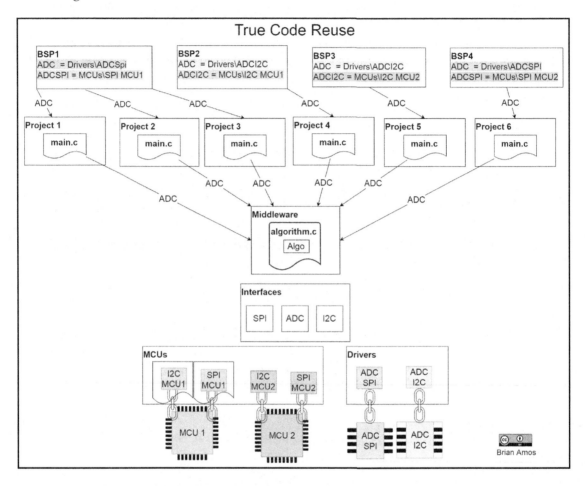

Here are some of the main points in the diagram:

- There is only one copy of `algorithm.c`—it is immediately obvious that the algorithm used is identical across all six projects.
- Even though there are six projects, there are only four BSP folders—`BSP1` has been reused across three projects.

- An ADC interface is specified in a common location (**Interfaces**).
- BSPs define an implementation of ADC, which is tied to specific hardware. These implementations are used by main.c and passed to algorithm.c.
- The ADC interface, which is referenced by Algo, rather than a specific implementation.
- There is only one copy of the I2C and SPI drivers for MCU1 and MCU2.
- There is only one copy of the driver for the SPI-based ADC.
- There is only one copy of the driver for the I2C-based ADC.

Reused code has the following advantages:

- If Algo has a bug, it will only need to be fixed in one place.
- Although final integration testing for Algo will still need to be performed in-system with real hardware (but probably only needs to be performed on the four BSP's, rather than all six projects), the bulk of the testing and development can be done by mocking the ADC interface, which is fast and simple.
- It is impossible for Algo to morph over time since there is only one copy. It will always be trivial to see whether or not the algorithm used is different between projects.
- Bugs are easier to find, understand, and fix due to the decreased interdependencies of the dependencies. A bug in Algo is guaranteed to show up in all six projects (since there is only one copy). However, it is less likely to occur, since testing Algo during development was easier, thanks to the interface.
- Creating project 7 is likely to be fast and efficient with a high degree of certainty due to all of the consistency across the other six projects.
- If MCU1 goes obsolete, porting algorithm.c isn't even necessary since it has no direct dependency on an MCU—only the ADC interface. Instead, a different BSP will need to be selected/developed.

One exception to copy-paste-modify is *extremely* low-level code that needs to be written to support similar but different hardware. This is typically the driver-level code that directly interfaces with MCU peripheral hardware registers. When two MCU families share the same peripherals with only minor differences, it can be tempting to try and develop common code to implement them both, but this is often more confusing for everyone (both the original author and the maintenance developers).

In these cases, it can be quite time-intensive and error-prone to force an existing piece of code to support a different piece of hardware, especially as the code ages and more hardware platforms are added. Eventually, if the code base becomes old enough, a new hardware target will vary significantly enough that it will no longer be remotely viable to incorporate those changes into the existing low-level code. As long as the low-level drivers are conforming to the same interface, they will still hold quite a bit of value in the long term. Keeping this low-level code easily understood and bug-free is the highest priority, followed by conforming to a consistent interface.

Now that we have a good idea of what abstraction is, let's take a closer look at some real-world examples of how to write code that can be easily reused.

Writing reusable code

When you are first getting started with creating abstractions, it can be difficult to know exactly what should be abstracted versus what should be used directly. To make code fully reusable, a module should only perform one function and reference interfaces for the other pieces of functionality. Any hardware-specific calls must go through interfaces, rather than deal with the hardware directly. This is true for accessing actual hardware (such as specific pins) and also MCU-specific APIs (such as STM32 HAL).

Writing reusable drivers

There are a few different levels of drivers that are fairly common in embedded development. MCU peripheral drivers are the drivers used to provide a convenient API to hardware included on the MCU. These types of drivers were developed in Chapter 10, *Drivers and ISRs*. Another commonly used driver is a driver for a specific IC, which is what was alluded to in the preceding ADC example:

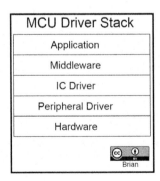

Peripheral drivers sit immediately above the hardware. IC drivers sit above (and often use) peripheral drivers in the stack. If an IC driver is meant to work across multiple MCUs, it must use interfaces that are completely agnostic to the underlying MCU hardware. For example, STM32 HAL can be thought of as a type of peripheral driver, but it does not provide MCU-independent abstractions for the peripherals. In order to create IC drivers that are portable across MCUs, they must only access MCU-independent interfaces.

Developing an LED interface

To illustrate the initial concept in detail, let's take a look at a simple driver that we've been using since the first examples introduced in this book—an LED driver. A simplified version of an interface to drive the LEDs on our Nucleo board has been used since the very first examples in earlier chapters. This interface is located at `BSP\Nucleo_F767ZI_GPIO.c/h`. This code fully abstracted the LEDs from the underlying hardware with a struct named `LED`. The `LED` struct has two function pointers: `On` and `Off`. As expected, the intention of these two functions is to turn an LED on and off. The beauty of this is that the calling code doesn't need to be concerned with the implementation of the LED at all. Each LED could have a completely different hardware interface. It might require positive or negative logic to drive an external transistor or be on a serial bus of some sort. The LED could even be on a remote panel requiring **remote procedure calls (RPCs)** to another board entirely. However, regardless of how the LED is turned on and off, the interface remains the same.

To try and keep things simple, `Nucleo_F767ZI_GPIO.c/h` defined the LED struct in the header file. As we move through this current example, we'll extract the interface definition from the header file, making it completely standalone, requiring no external dependencies. The lack of dependencies will guarantee that we can move the new interface definition to entirely different platforms, without requiring any code specific to a particular MCU at all.

Our new, independent LED interface will be called `iLED`.

> The lowercase "i" is a convention used by some C++ programmers to indicate a class that only contains virtual functions, which is effectively an interface definition. Since we're only dealing with C in this book (not C++), we'll stick to structs and function pointers to provide the necessary decoupling. The methods outlined here are conceptually similar to pure virtual classes in C++.

The interface is defined in the new `Interfaces/iLed.h` file; the core of the contents is as follows:

```
typedef void (*iLedFunc)(void);

typedef struct
{
    //On turns on the LED – regardless of the driver logic
    const iLedFunc On;

    //Off turns off the LED, regardless of the driver logic
    const iLedFunc Off;
}iLed;
```

Let's break down exactly what is going on in the preceding definition:

1. We create a new type:iLedFunc. Now, `typedef void (*iLedFunc)(void);` defines the `iLedFunc` type as a function pointer to a function that takes no arguments and returns nothing.
2. The `iLed` struct is defined as any other struct—we can now create instances of this struct. We're defining a struct so it is convenient to bundle together all of the function pointers and pass a reference to the structs around it.
3. Each `iLedFunc` member is defined as `const` so it can only be set once at the time of definition. This protects us (or other developers) from accidentally overwriting the value of the function pointer (which can be potentially disastrous). The compiler will catch any attempts to write to the `On` or `Off` function pointers and throw an error.

It is extremely important that the header file defining the interface includes as few dependencies as possible to keep it as loosely coupled as possible. The more dependencies this file has, the less future flexibility there will be.

That does it for the interface definition. There is no functionality provided by the preceding code; it only defined an interface. In order to create an implementation of the `iLed` interface, we'll need two more files.

The following is an excerpt from `ledImplementation.h`:

```
#include <iLed.h>
extern iLed BlueLed;
extern iLed GreenLed;
extern iLed RedLed;
```

This header file brings in the `iLed.h` interface definition and declares three instances of `iLed`, which are `BlueLed`, `GreenLed`, and `RedLed`. These implementations of the `iLed` interface can be used by any piece of code that includes `ledImplementation.h`. The `extern` keyword ensures only one copy is ever created, regardless of how many different code modules use `ledImplementation.h`.

Next, we need to provide definitions for the `iLed` instances; this is done in `ledImplementation.c`.

Only the code for `GreenLed` is shown here. The `BlueLed` and `RedLed` implementations only differ in the GPIO pin they set:

```
void GreenOn ( void ) {HAL_GPIO_WritePin(GPIOB, GPIO_PIN_0, GPIO_PIN_SET);}
void GreenOff ( void ) {HAL_GPIO_WritePin(GPIOB, GPIO_PIN_0,
                                          GPIO_PIN_RESET);}
iLed GreenLed = { GreenOn, GreenOff };
```

Breaking it down, we can observe the following:

1. `GreenOn` defines an inline function that turns on the green LED on our Nucleo development board. It takes no parameters and returns nothing, so it can be used as `iLedFunc`, as defined in the previous code.
2. `GreenOff` defines an inline function that turns off the green LED on our Nucleo development board. It is can also be used as `iLedFunc`.
3. An instance of `iLed` is created and named `GreenLed`. The `iLedFunc` function pointers `GreenOn` and `GreenOff` are passed in during initialization. The order of the functions defined in `iLed` is critical. Since `On` is defined in the `iLed` struct first, the first function pointer passed in (`GreenOn`) will be assigned to `On`.

 The only code that relies on specific hardware so far is `ledImplementation.c`.

A pointer to `GreenLed` can now be passed to different pieces of code that only bring in `iLed.h`—they won't be tied to `HAL_GPIO_WritePin` in any way. An example of this is `hardwareAgnosticLedDriver.c/h`.

The following is an excerpt from `hardwareAgnosticLedDriver.h`:

```
#include <iLed.h>
void doLedStuff( iLed* LedPtr );
```

The only `include` function required by this hardware-agnostic driver is `iLed.h`.

> For `hardwareAgnosticLedDriver.h` to be truly hardware agnostic, it must not include any hardware-specific files. It must only access hardware through hardware-independent interfaces, such as `iLed`.

The following is a trivial example that simply turns a single LED on or off. The excerpt is from `hardwareAgnosticLedDriver.c`:

```
void doLedStuff( iLed* LedPtr )
{
    if( LedPtr != NULL )
    {
        if(LedPtr->On != NULL)
        {
            LedPtr->On();
        }

        if( LedPtr->Off != NULL )
        {
            LedPtr->Off();
        }
    }
}
```

Breaking it down, we can observe the following:

1. `doLedStuff` takes in a pointer to a variable of the `iLed` type as a parameter. This allows any implementation of the `iLed` interface to be passed in `doLedStuff`, which provides complete flexibility in how the `On` and `Off` functions are implemented without tying `hardwareAgnosticLedDriver` to any specific hardware.
2. If your interface definition supports leaving out functionality by setting pointers to `NULL`, they will need to be checked to ensure they are not set to `NULL`. Depending on the design, these checks might not be necessary since the values for `On` and `Off` are only able to be set during initialization.
3. The actual implementations of `On` and `Off` are called by using the `LedPtr` pointer and calling them like any other function.

A full example using `doLedStuff` is found in `mainLedAbstraction.c`:

```
#include <ledImplementation.h>
#include <hardwareAgnosticLedDriver.h>
```

```
HWInit();

while(1)
{
    doLedStuff(&GreenLed);
    doLedStuff(&RedLed);
    doLedStuff(&BlueLed);
}
```

Breaking it down, we can observe the following:

1. The implementations for `GreenLed`, `RedLed`, and `BlueLed` are brought in by including `ledImplementation.h`.
2. `doLedStuff` is brought in by including `hardwareAgnosticLedDriver.h`.
3. We provide the implementation for `doLedStuff` by passing in a pointer to the desired instance of `iLed`. In this example, we're toggling each of the green, red, and blue LEDs on the development board by passing the `GreenLed`, `RedLed`, and `BlueLed` implementations to `doLedStuff`.

This example simply toggled the single LEDs, but the complexity is arbitrary. By having well-defined interfaces, tasks can be created that take in pointers to instances of the interface. The tasks can be reused across multiple projects without touching them all—only a new implementation of the interface needs to be created when support for new hardware is required. When there is a considerable amount of code implemented by the hardware-agnostic task, this can dramatically decrease the total amount of time spent on the project.

Let's take a look at a simple example of passing instances of interfaces into tasks.

Reusing code containing tasks

RTOS tasks are among the best suited for reuse because (when well-written) they offer single-purpose functionality that can be easily prioritized against the other functions the system must perform. In order for them to be easily reused in the long term, they need to have as few direct ties to the underlying platform as possible. Using interfaces as described previously works extremely well for this purpose since the interface fully encapsulates the desired functionality while decoupling it from the underlying implementation. To further ease the setup of the FreeRTOS task, the creation of the task can be wrapped inside an initialization function.

`mainLedTask.c` uses `ledTask.c/h` to show an example of this. The following excerpt is from `ledTask.h`:

```
#include <iLed.h>
#include <FreeRTOS.h>
#include <task.h>

TaskHandle_t LedTaskInit( iLed* LedPtr, uint8_t Priority, uint16_t
                                                       StackSize);
```

A few significant notes on this simple header file are as follows:

- The only files included are those required for FreeRTOS and `iLed.h`, none of which are directly dependent on any specific hardware implementation.
- The priority of the task is brought in as an argument of the initialization function. This is important for flexibility because over time, LED tasks are likely to require different priorities relative to the rest of the system.
- `StackSize` is also parameterized—this is required because, depending on the underlying implementation of `LedPtr`, the resulting task may need to use different amounts of stack space.
- `LedTaskInit` returns `TaskHandle_t`, which can be used by the calling code to control or delete the resulting task.

`ledTask.c` contains the definition of `LedTaskInit`:

```
TaskHandle_t LedTaskInit(iLed* LedPtr, uint8_t Priority, uint16_t
StackSize)
{
  TaskHandle_t ledTaskHandle = NULL;
  if(LedPtr == NULL){while(1);}
  if(xTaskCreate(ledTask, "ledTask", StackSize, LedPtr, Priority,
              &ledTaskHandle) != pdPASS){while(1);}

  return ledTaskHandle;
}
```

This initialization function performs the same functions as what we've typically seen in `main`, but now, it is neatly encapsulated into a single file, which can be used across multiple projects. Functions taken care of by `LedTaskInit` include the following:

- Checking that `LedPtr` is not `NULL`.

- Creating a task that runs the `ledTask` function and passing `LedPtr` to it, which provides a specific implementation of the `iLed` interface for that `ledTask` instance. `ledTask` is created with the specified `Priority` task and `StackSize`.
- Verifying whether it has been created successfully before `LedTaskInit` returns the handle to the task that was created.

`ledTask.c` also contains the actual code for `ledTask`:

```
void ledTask( void* LedPtr)
{
    iLed* led = (iLed*) LedPtr;
    while(1)
    {
        led->On();
        vTaskDelay(100);
        led->Off();
        vTaskDelay(100);
    }
}
```

First, `LedPtr` needs to be cast from `void*` into `iLed*`. After this cast, we are able to call the functions of our `iLed` interface. The underlying hardware calls will depend on the implementation of `LedPtr`. This is also the reason for allowing a `StackSize` variable during initialization—`LedPtr` may have a more complex implementation in some cases, which could require a larger stack.

Thanks to `LedTaskInit`, creating tasks that map the `LedPtr` implementations into the task is extremely easy.

The following is an excerpt from `mainLedTask.c`:

```
int main(void)
{
    HWInit();
    SEGGER_SYSVIEW_Conf();
    //ensure proper priority grouping for freeRTOS
    HAL_NVIC_SetPriorityGrouping(NVIC_PRIORITYGROUP_4);
    LedTaskInit(&GreenLed, tskIDLE_PRIORITY+1, 128);
    LedTaskInit(&BlueLed, tskIDLE_PRIORITY+2, 128);
    LedTaskInit(&RedLed, tskIDLE_PRIORITY+3, 128);
    vTaskStartScheduler();
```

GreenLed, BlueLed, and RedLed are passed into LedTaskInit to create three independent tasks with varying priorities and potentially different stack sizes. All of the hardware-specific code has been kept out of ledTask.c/h. When this technique is used for complex tasks, significant time savings and increased confidence can be realized. Along the lines of increasing confidence in the code we write, let's take a quick look at exactly how providing an abstracted interface makes testing tasks easier.

Testing flexible code

Since the iLed interface isn't directly reliant on any hardware, it is extremely easy to push alternative implementations to ledTask. Rather than passing in one of the actual hardware implementations for iLed, we could pass in anything we like to either LedTaskInit (for integration-level tests) or ledTask (for unit tests). The implementations, in these cases, would likely set variables in the testing environment when called. For example, On could set a Boolean to TRUE when called and Off could set the same Boolean to FALSE. These types of tests can be used to verify the logic of the task, without requiring any hardware at all, provided a compiler and an alternative environment is set up on the development machine. FreeRTOS ports exist for desktop OSes that allow testing relative priorities of tasks (without any real-time guarantees). Specific timing dependencies aren't able to be tested this way, but it does allow developers to gain a considerable amount of confidence in the middle layers of code.

See the *Further reading* section for articles that cover unit testing in more detail.

Now that we have an idea of how to write reusable code, we need to make sure it is being stored in a way that allows it to be used across multiple projects without creating unnecessary copies or creating strange inter-project dependencies.

Organizing source code

A well-organized source tree is extremely important if a code base is intended to evolve and grow over time. If projects are meant to live in isolation as atomic entities that never interact with one another, there is little reason to have a strategy when it comes to source control; but if code reuse is a goal, then having a clear idea of how specific projects should fit together with common code is a must.

Choosing locations for source files

Any piece of code that is likely to be used in more than the original project where it is first created should live in a common location (not tied to a specific project). Even if the code started out as being specific to one particular project, it should be moved as soon as it is used by more than one project. Pieces of common code will be different for each team, but will likely include the following:

- **BSPs**: There are often multiple pieces of firmware created for each board. The BSP folder in the code base for this book doesn't have any subfolders (mainly because there, the code only supports a single platform). If this book supported multiple platforms, the BSP folder would likely contain a `Nucleo_F767` subfolder.
- **In-house common code**: This can include custom domain-specific algorithms or drivers for ICs that are commonly used across multiple products or projects. Any code here should be able to be well-abstracted and used across multiple MCUs.
- **Third-party common code**: If multiple projects include source code from a third party, it belongs in a central location. Items such as FreeRTOS and any other middleware can be kept in this central location.
- **MCU-specific code**: Each MCU family should ideally have its own folder. This will likely include things such as STM32 HAL and any custom peripheral drivers developed for that MCU. Ideally, most of the code referenced in these MCU-specific directories will be done so through common interfaces (shown in the ADC example at the beginning of the chapter).
- **Interface definitions**: If interfaces are used extensively, having all of them in one place is extremely convenient.
- **Project folders**: Each project will likely have its own folder (sometimes containing sub-projects). Ideally, projects won't reference code in other projects—only code that is housed in the common areas. If projects start to have inter-dependencies, take a step back and evaluate why, and whether or not it makes sense to move those dependencies to a common location.

The specific folder structure will likely be dependent on your team's version control system and branching strategy.

Dealing with changes

One of the biggest drawbacks to having code that is common to many projects is the implications of a change. Directory structure changes can be some of the most challenging to deal with, especially if there are a large number of projects. Although painful, this type of refactoring is often necessary over time as teams' needs and strategies change. Performing regular check-ins and tagging your repository should be all that is necessary to provide confidence that directory restructuring changes, while painstaking, aren't particularly dangerous.

If you're coming from a high-level language and hear the word *interface,* you might immediately think of something that is set in stone from the first time it is used. Although it is generally good to keep interfaces consistent, there is a bit of latitude to change them (especially when first starting out). Internal interfaces in this specific use case are considerably more forgiving than a public API for a couple of reasons:

- Nearly all of the low-level MCU-based applications are going to have compile-time checks against a given *interface.* There are no dynamically loaded libraries that will mysteriously cease to work properly at runtime if an interface changes over time—(most) errors will be caught at compile time.
- These interfaces are generally internal with full visibility of where they are used, which makes it possible to evaluate the impact of potential changes.

Changes to individual files (such as a shared algorithm) are also a common source of concern. The best advice here is to evaluate whether or not what you are changing is still providing the same functionality or whether it should be an extension or entirely new. Sometimes, working with projects in a vacuum doesn't force us to make these decisions explicitly, but as soon as that piece of code is shared across many projects, the stakes are higher.

Summary

After reading this chapter, you should have a good understanding of why code reuse is important and also how to achieve it. We've looked at the details of using abstraction in an embedded environment and created fully hardware-agnostic interfaces that increase the flexibility of code. We also learned how to use these interfaces in conjunction with tasks to increase code reuse across projects. Finally, we touched on some aspects of storing shared source code.

At this point, you should have enough knowledge to start thinking about how to apply these principles to your own code base and projects. As your code base starts to have more common code that is reused between projects, you'll begin to reap the benefits of a shared code base, such as fewer bugs, more maintainable code, and decreased development time. Remember, it takes practice to become good at creating reusable code with abstract interfaces. Not all implementations need to move to fully reused components at the same time, either—but it is important to start the journey.

Now that we have some background of abstraction, in the next chapter, we'll continue to build flexible architectures by looking more deeply at how queues can be used to provide loosely coupled architectures.

Questions

As we conclude, here is a list of questions for you to use to test your knowledge on this chapter's material. You will find the answers in the *Assessments* section of the appendix:

1. Creating abstractions is only something that can be done using a full desktop OS:
    - True
    - False

2. Only object-oriented code such as C++ can benefit from well-defined interfaces:
    - True
    - False

3. Four examples of why abstraction is important were given. Name one.

4. Copying code into a new project is the best way to reuse it:
    - True
    - False

5. Tasks are extremely specific; they cannot be reused between projects:
    - True
    - False

Further reading

- For an in-depth discussion about multi-layer drivers, see TinyOS TEP101, which uses a layered approach to drivers. The interface approach described in this chapter fits quite well with the TinyOS HPL, HAL, and HIL approach: `https://github.com/tinyos/tinyos-main/blob/master/doc/txt/tep101.txt`

- Here are some more additional resources that should help you out:
  - `https://embeddedartistry.com/blog/2019/08/05/practical-decoupling-techniques-applied-to-a-c-based-radio-driver/`
  - `https://embeddedartistry.com/blog/2020/01/27/leveraging-our-build-systems-to-support-portability/`
  - `https://embeddedartistry.com/blog/2020/01/20/prototyping-for-portability-lightweight-architectural-strategies/`
  - `https://blog.wingman-sw.com/archives/282` – Unit Testing RTOS dependent code- RTOS Test Double

13
Creating Loose Coupling with Queues

Now that we've covered ways of architecting source code for flexibility, we'll take that a step further and explore how queues can be used to provide natural interface definitions for data exchange.

In this chapter, we'll develop a simple command queue that can be accessed from multiple physical interfaces. By the end of this chapter, you'll have an excellent understanding of why using common queue definitions is desirable, as well as how to implement both sides of an extremely flexible command queue. This will help you create flexible architectures with implementations that aren't tied to underlying hardware or physical interfaces.

We will cover the following topics in this chapter:

- Understanding queues as interfaces
- Creating a command queue
- Reusing a queue definition for a new target

Technical requirements

To complete the hands-on experiments included in this chapter, you will require the following:

- A Nucleo F767 development board
- A Micro-USB cable
- STM32CubeIDE and source code (for instructions, visit the *Setting up our IDE* section in Chapter 5, *Selecting an IDE*)

- SEGGER J-Link, Ozone, and SystemView (for instructions, visit `Chapter 6,` *Debugging Tools for Real-Time Systems*)
- Python >= 3.8

All source code for this chapter is available at `https://github.com/PacktPublishing/ Hands-On-RTOS-with-Microcontrollers/tree/master/Chapter_13`.

Understanding queues as interfaces

If you've just finished reading the previous chapter, you've likely picked up on the fact that there are many techniques that can be used to create quality code at one time and then reuse that same code across multiple projects. Just like using layers of abstractions is a technique that increases the likelihood of reusing code across multiple hardware platforms, using queues as interfaces also increases the likelihood that code will be used for more than just one project.

The concepts presented in this chapter aren't limited to queues—they also apply to stream and message buffers. However, since queues have been around since the beginning of FreeRTOS (and are the most commonly available primitive), we'll use them in our examples. Let's take a look at why using queues is a good idea.

Queues make excellent interface definitions

Queues provide a very clear line of abstraction. In order to pass data through a queue and get a desired behavior on the other side, all of the data must be present and both the sender and receiver must have a common understanding of what the data format is. This clean line forces a level of conscientious thought as to what exactly needs to be communicated. Sometimes, this level of active thought isn't present when implementing individual functions. The delineation provided by the queue forces additional thought about what the exact information required is, as well as what its format should be. Responsible developers will be more likely to ensure these types of definitive interfaces are thoroughly documented.

When a queue is viewed as an interface to a subsystem, it pays dividends to document the functionality that will be provided, as well as the exact formatting required to use the subsystem. Often, the fact that an interface is well defined will increase the likelihood of reuse since it will be easily understood.

Queues increase flexibility

Queues are beautiful in their simplicity—a sender places something in the queue and whatever task is monitoring the queue will receive the data and act on it. The only things the sender and the received task need to share are the code required for interacting with the queue and the definition of the data flowing through the queue. Since the list of shared resources is so short, there is a natural decoupling effect when queues are used.

Because of the clean break provided by the queue, the exact implementation of the functionality could change over time. The same functionality can be implemented in many different ways, which won't immediately affect the sender, as long as the queue interface doesn't change.

It also means that data can be sent to the queue from anywhere; there are no explicit requirements for the physical interface—only the data format. This means that a queue can be designed to receive the same data stream from many different interfaces, which can provide system-level flexibility. The functionality doesn't need to be tied to a specific physical interface (such as Ethernet, USB, UART, SPI, CAN, and so on).

Queues make testing easier

Similar to the way hardware abstractions provide easy insertion points for test data, queues also provide excellent places to enter test data. This provides a very convenient entry point for entering test data for code under development. The flexibility of implementation mentioned in the previous section also applies here. If a piece of code is sending data to a queue and expects a response from another queue, the actual implementation doesn't necessarily need to be used—it can be simulated by responding to the command. This approach makes it possible to develop the other side of code in the absence of fully implemented functionality (in case the hardware or subsystem is still under development). This approach is also extremely useful when running unit-level tests; the code-under-test can be easily isolated from the rest of the system.

Now that we've covered some of the reasons to use queues as interfaces, let's take a look at how this plays out through an example.

Creating a command queue

To see how a queue can be used to keep an architecture loosely coupled, we'll take a look at an application that accepts commands over USB and lights LEDs. While the example application itself is very simple, the concepts presented here scale extremely well. So, regardless of whether there are only a few commands or hundreds, the same approach can be used to keep the architecture flexible.

This application also shows another example of how to keep higher-level code loosely coupled to the underlying hardware. It ensures the LED command code only uses a defined interface to access a **Pulse Width Modulation** (**PWM**) implementation, rather than directly interacting with the MCU registers/HAL. The architecture consists of the following major components:

- **A USB driver**: This is the same USB stack that has been used in previous examples. `VirtualCommDriverMultiTask.c/h` has been extended to provide an additional stream buffer to efficiently receive data from a PC (`Drivers/HandsOnRTOS/VirtualCommDriverMultiTask.c/h`).
- **iPWM**: An additional interface definition (`iPWM`) has been created to describe very simple PWM functionality (defined in `Chapter_13/Inc/iPWM.h`).
- **PWM implementation**: The implementation of three `iPWM` interfaces for the Nucleo hardware is found in `Chapter13/Src/pwmImplementation.c` and `Chapter13/Src/pwmImplementation.h`.
- **An LED command executor**: The state machine that drives LED states using pointers to implementations of `iPWM` (`Chapter_13/Src/ledCmdExecutor.c`).
- `main`: The `main` function, which ties all of the queues, drivers, and interfaces together and kicks off the FreeRTOS scheduler (`Chapter_13/Src/mainColorSelector.c`).

We'll get into the details of exactly how all of these parts fit together and the details of their responsibilities; but first, let's discuss what is going to be placed in the command queue.

Deciding on queue contents

When using queues as a way of passing commands to different parts of the system, it is important to think about what the queue should actually hold, instead of what might be coming *across the wire* in a physical sense. Even though a queue might be used to hold payloads from a datastream with header and footer information, the actual contents of the queue will usually only contain the parsed payload, rather than the entire message.

Using this approach allows more flexibility in the future to retarget the queue to work over other physical layers.

Since `LedCmdExecution()` will be operating primarily on the iPWM pointers to interface with the LEDs, it is convenient for the queue to hold a data type that can be used directly by iPWM.

The iPWM definition from `Chapter13/Inc/iPWM.h` is as follows:

```
typedef void (*iPwmDutyCycleFunc)( float DutyCycle );

typedef struct
{
   const iPwmDutyCycleFunc SetDutyCycle;
}iPWM;
```

This struct only (currently) consists of a single function pointer: `iPwmDutyCycleFunc`. `iPwmDutyCycleFunc` is defined as a constant pointer—after the initialization of the iPWM struct, the pointer can never be changed. This helps guarantee the pointer won't be overwritten, so constantly checking to ensure it isn't `NULL` won't be necessary.

Wrapping the function pointer in a struct such as iPWM provides the flexibility of adding additional functions while keeping refactoring to a minimum. We'll be able to pass a single pointer to the iPWM struct to functions, rather than individual function pointers.

If you are creating an *interface* definition that will be shared with other developers, it is important to be very careful to coordinate and communicate changes among your team!

The `DutyCycle` argument is defined as `float`, which makes it easy to keep the interface consistent when interfacing with hardware that has different underlying resolutions. In our implementation, the MCU's timer (`TIM`) peripherals will be configured to have a 16-bit resolution, but the actual code interfacing to iPWM doesn't need to be concerned with the available resolution; it can simply map the desired output from `0.00` (off) to `100.00` (on).

For most applications, `int32_t` would have been preferred over `float` since it has a consistent representation and is easier to serialize. `float` is used here to make it easier to see the differences in the data model versus communication. Also, most people tend to think of PWM as a percentage, which maps naturally to `float`.

There are two main considerations when deciding on what data LedCmd contains:

- ledCmdExecutor will be dealing with iPWM directly, so it makes sense to store floats in LedCmd.
- We'd also like our LED controller to have different modes of operation, so it will also need a way of passing that information. We'll only have a handful of commands here, so a uint8_t 8-bit unsigned integer is a good fit. Each cmdNum case will be represented by enum (shown later).

This results in the following structure for LedCmd:

```
typedef struct
{
    uint8_t cmdNum;
    float red;
    float green;
    float blue;
} LedCmd;
```

The **LED Cmd Executor**'s primary interface will be a queue of LedCmds. State changes will be performed by writing new values in the queue.

Since this structure is only 13 bytes, we'll simply pass it by value. Passing by reference (a pointer to the structure) would be faster, but it also complicates the ownership of the data. These trade-offs are discussed in Chapter 9, *Intertask Communication*.

Now that we have a data model defined, we can look at the remaining components of this application.

Defining the architecture

The command executor architecture is composed of three primary blocks; each block executes asynchronously to the others and communicates via a queue and stream buffer:

- **LED Cmd Executor**: LedCmdExecution in ledCmdExecutor.c receives data from ledCmdQueue and actuates the LEDs via pointers to iPWM (one for each color). LedCmdExecution is a FreeRTOS task that takes CmdExecArgs as an argument upon creation.
- **Frame protocol decoding**: mainColorSelector.c receives raw data from the stream buffer populated by the USB virtual comm driver, ensures valid framing, and populates the LedCmd queue.

- **The USB virtual comm driver**: The USB stack is spread across many files; the primary user-entry point is `VirtualCommDriverMultiTask.c`.

Here's a visual representation of how all of these major components stack up and flow together. Major blocks are listed on the left, while representations of the data they operate on are to the right:

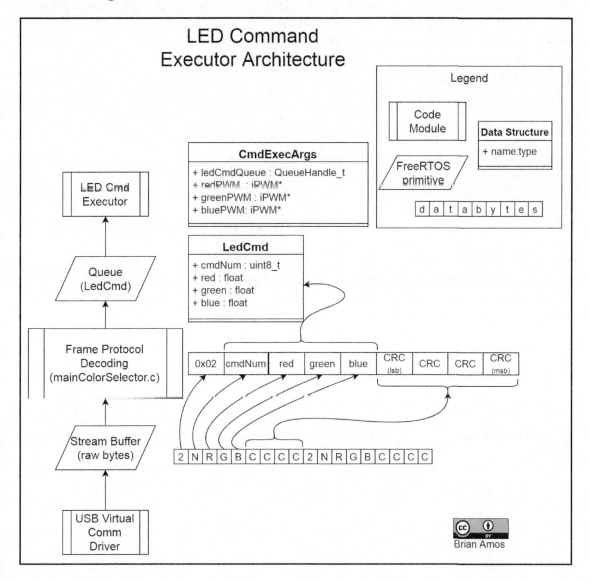

Let's take a closer look at each one of these components.

ledCmdExecutor

`ledCmdExecutor.c` implements a simple state machine, whose state is modified when a command is received from the queue.

The available commands are explicitly enumerated by `LED_CMD_NUM`. Each *command* has been given a human-friendly enumeration, along with an explicit definition. The enums are explicitly defined so they can be properly enumerated on the PC side. We also need to make sure the numbers assigned are <= 255, since we'll only be allocating 1 byte in the frame to the command number:

```
typedef enum
{
  CMD_ALL_OFF = 0,
  CMD_ALL_ON = 1,
  CMD_SET_INTENSITY = 2,
  CMD_BLINK = 3
}LED_CMD_NUM;
```

The only public function is `LedCmdExecution`, which will be used as a FreeRTOS task: `void LedCmdExecution(void* Args)`.

`void* Args` actually has a type of `CmdExecArgs`. However, the function signature for a FreeRTOS task requires a single parameter of `void*`. The actual data type being passed into `LedCmdExecution` is a pointer to this struct:

```
typedef struct
{
  QueueHandle_t ledCmdQueue;
  iPWM * redPWM;
  iPWM * bluePWM;
  iPWM * greenPWM;
}CmdExecArgs;
```

Passing in references to everything allows multiple instances of the task to be created and run simultaneously. It also provides extremely loose coupling to the underlying `iPWM` implementations.

`LedCmdExecution` has a few local variables to track state:

```
LED_CMD_NUM currCmdNum = CMD_ALL_OFF;
bool ledsOn = false;
LedCmd nextLedCmd;
param_assert(Args == NULL);
CmdExecArgs args = *(CmdExecArgs*)Args;
```

Let's take a closer look at these variables:

- `currCmdNum`: Local storage for the current command being executed.
- `ledsOn`: Local storage used by the `blink` command to track state.
- `nextLedCmd`: Storage for the next command coming from the queue.
- `args`: A local variable containing the arguments passed in through the `void*` `Args` parameter of our task (notice the explicit cast and check to ensure `NULL` hasn't been passed in instead).

To ensure none of the pointers change, we're making a local copy. This also could have been accomplished by defining the `CmdExecArgs` struct to contain the `const` variables that could only be set at initialization to save a bit of space.

This main loop has two responsibilities. The first responsibility, seen in the following code, is copying a value from `ledCmdQueue` into the `nextLedCmd` reading, setting the appropriate local variables and the duty cycle of the LEDs.

`ledCmdExecutor.c` is part of the main loop:

```
if(xQueueReceive(args.ledCmdQueue, &nextLedCmd, 250) == pdTRUE)
{
    switch(nextLedCmd.cmdNum)
    {
        case CMD_SET_INTENSITY:
            currCmdNum = CMD_SET_INTENSITY;
            setDutyCycles( &args, nextLedCmd.red,
                        nextLedCmd.green, nextLedCmd.blue);
            break;
        case CMD_BLINK:
            currCmdNum = CMD_BLINK;
            blinkingLedsOn = true;
            setDutyCycles(&args, nextLedCmd.red,
                        nextLedCmd.green, nextLedCmd.blue);
            break;
        //additional cases not shown
```

```
        }
    }
```

The second part of the main loop, seen in the following code, executes if no command has been received from `ledCmdQueue` within 250 ticks (250 ms, since our configuration uses a 1 kHz tick). This code toggles the LEDs between their last commanded duty cycle and `OFF`:

`ledCmdExecutor.c` is the second half of the main loop:

```
else if (currCmdNum == CMD_BLINK)
{
    //if there is no new command and we should be blinking
    if(blinkingLedsOn)
    {
        blinkingLedsOn = false;
        setDutyCycles(&args, 0, 0, 0);
    }
    else
    {
        blinkingLedsOn = true;
        setDutyCycles( &args, nextLedCmd.red,
                        nextLedCmd.green, nextLedCmd.blue);
    }
}
```

Finally, the `setDutyCycles` helper function uses the `iPWM` pointers to actuate the PWM duty cycles for the LEDs. The `iPWM` pointers were verified as not being `NULL` before the main loop, so the check doesn't need to be repeated here:

```
void setDutyCycles( const CmdExecArgs* Args, float RedDuty,
float GreenDuty, float BlueDuty)
{
    Args->redPWM->SetDutyCycle(RedDuty);
    Args->greenPWM->SetDutyCycle(GreenDuty);
    Args->bluePWM->SetDutyCycle(BlueDuty);
}
```

That wraps up the high-level functionality of our LED command executor. The main purpose of creating a task like this was to illustrate a way to create an extremely loosely coupled and scalable system. While it is silly to toggle a few LEDs in this way, this design paradigm is perfectly scalable to complex systems and capable of being used on different hardware without modification.

Now that we have an idea of what the code does at a high level, let's take a look at how the `LedCmd` struct is populated.

Frame decoding

As data comes in from the USB, it is placed in a stream buffer by the USB stack. The `StreamBuffer` function for incoming data can be accessed from `GetUsbRxStreamBuff()` in `Drivers/HandsOnRTOS/VirtualCommDriverMultiTask.c`:

```
StreamBufferHandle_t const * GetUsbRxStreamBuff( void )
{
    return &vcom_rxStream;
}
```

This function returns a constant pointer to `StreamBufferHandle_t`. This is done so the calling code can access the stream buffer directly, but isn't able to change the pointer's value.

The protocol itself is a strictly binary stream that starts with 0x02 and ends with a CRC-32 checksum, transmitted in little endian byte order:

There are many different ways of serializing data. A simple binary stream was chosen here for simplicity. A few points should be considered:

- The `0x02` header is a convenient delimiter that can be used to find the (possible) start of a frame. It is not sufficiently unique since any of the other bytes in the message can also be `0x02` (it is a binary stream, not ASCII). The CRC-32 at the end provides assurance that the frame was correctly received.
- Since the frame has exactly 1 byte per LED value, we can represent the 0-100% duty cycle with 0-255 and we are guaranteed to have valid, in-range parameters, without any additional checking.

- This simple method of framing is extremely rigid and provides no flexibility whatsoever. The moment we need to send something else over the wire, we're back to square one. A more flexible (and complex) serialization method is required if flexibility is desired.

The `frameDecoder` function is defined in `mainColorSelector.c`:

```
void frameDecoder( void* NotUsed)
{
  LedCmd incomingCmd;
  #define FRAME_LEN 9
  uint8_t frame[FRAME_LEN];
  while(1)
  {
    memset(frame, 0, FRAME_LEN);
    while(frame[0] != 0x02)
    {
      xStreamBufferReceive( *GetUsbRxStreamBuff(), frame, 1,
                                          portMAX_DELAY);
    }
    xStreamBufferReceive( *GetUsbRxStreamBuff(),
      &frame[1],
      FRAME_LEN-1,
      portMAX_DELAY);
    if(CheckCRC(frame, FRAME_LEN))
    {
      incomingCmd.cmdNum = frame[1];
      incomingCmd.red = frame[2]/255.0 * 100;
      incomingCmd.green = frame[3]/255.0 * 100;
      incomingCmd.blue = frame[4]/255.0 * 100;
      xQueueSend(ledCmdQueue, &incomingCmd, 100);
    }
  }
}
```

Let's break it down line by line:

- Two local variables, `incomingCmd` and `frame`, are created. `incomingCmd` is used to store the fully parsed command. `frame` is a buffer of bytes that is used to store exactly one frame's worth of data while this function parses/verifies it:

  ```
  LedCmd incomingCmd;
  #define FRAME_LEN 9
  uint8_t frame[FRAME_LEN];
  ```

- At the beginning of the loop, the contents of `frame` are cleared. Only clearing the first byte is strictly necessary so we can accurately detect `0x02` and since the frame is binary and has a well-defined length (only variable-length strings *need* to be null-terminated). However, it is very convenient to see 0 for unpopulated bytes, if you happen to be watching the variable during debugging:

```
memset(frame, 0, FRAME_LEN);
```

- A single byte is copied from the `StreamBuffer` function into the frame until `0x02` is detected. This should indicate the start of a frame (unless we were unlucky enough to start acquiring data in the middle of a frame with a binary value of `0x02` in the payload or CRC):

```
while(frame[0] != 0x02)
{
    xStreamBufferReceive( *GetUsbRxStreamBuff(), frame, 1,
                                        portMAX_DELAY);
}
```

- The remaining bytes of the frame are received from `StreamBuffer`. They are placed in the correct index of the `frame` array:

```
xStreamBufferReceive( *GetUsbRxStreamBuff(), &frame[1],
                FRAME_LEN-1, portMAX_DELAY);
```

- The entire frame's CRC is evaluated. If the CRC is invalid, this data is discarded and we'll begin looking for the start of another frame:

```
if(CheckCRC(frame, FRAME_LEN))
```

- If the frame was intact, `incomingCmd` is filled out with the values in the frame:

```
incomingCmd.cmdNum = frame[1];
incomingCmd.red = frame[2]/255.0 * 100;
incomingCmd.green = frame[3]/255.0 * 100;
incomingCmd.blue = frame[4]/255.0 * 100;
```

- The populated command is sent to the queue, which is being watched by `LedCmdExecutor()`. Up to 100 ticks may elapse, waiting for space in the queue to become available before the command is discarded:

```
xQueueSend(ledCmdQueue, &incomingCmd, 100);
```

It is important to note that none of the framing protocol is being placed in LedCmd, which will be sent through the queue – only the payload is. This allows more flexibility in how data is acquired before being queued, as we will see in the *Reusing a queue definition for a new target* section.

Choosing the number of slots available in the queue can have important effects on the response of the application to incoming commands. The more slots that are available, the higher the likelihood that a command will incur a significant delay before being executed. For a system that requires more determinism on when (and if) a command will be executed, it is a good idea to limit the queue length to only a single slot and perform a protocol-level acknowledgment, based on whether the command was successfully queued.

Now that we've seen how the frame is decoded, the only remaining piece of the puzzle is how data is placed into the USB's receiving stream buffer.

The USB virtual comm driver

The USB's receiving StreamBuffer is populated by CDC_Receive_FS() in Drivers/HandsOnRTOS/usbd_cdc_if.c. This will look similar to the code from Chapter 11, *Sharing Hardware Peripherals across Tasks*, where the transmit side of the driver was developed:

```
static int8_t CDC_Receive_FS(uint8_t* Buf, uint32_t *Len)
{
  /* USER CODE BEGIN 6 */
  portBASE_TYPE xHigherPriorityTaskWoken = pdFALSE;

  USBD_CDC_SetRxBuffer(&hUsbDeviceFS, &Buf[0]);
  xStreamBufferSendFromISR( *GetUsbRxStreamBuff(),
        Buf,
        *Len,
        &xHigherPriorityTaskWoken);

  USBD_CDC_ReceivePacket(&hUsbDeviceFS);
  portYIELD_FROM_ISR(xHigherPriorityTaskWoken);
  return (USBD_OK);
  /* USER CODE END 6 */
}
```

Using a stream buffer instead of a queue allows larger blocks of memory to be copied from the USB stack's internal buffers while providing a queue-like interface that has flexibility in the number of bytes copied out of it. This flexibility is one of the reasons coding the protocol layer was so straightforward.

 Remember that since a stream buffer is being used, only one task can be a designated reader. Otherwise, access to the stream buffer must be synchronized (that is, by a mutex).

That wraps up all of the MCU-side code in this example. Since this example relies on a binary protocol over USB, let's have a look at how the code can be used.

Using the code

One of the goals for choosing this example was to have an approachable, real-world use case that was relevant. Most of the time, the use cases for the embedded systems we develop do not include a person typing away on a terminal emulator. To that end, a very simple GUI was created using Python to make it simple to send commands to the Nucleo board. The script is `Chapter_13/PythonColorSelectorUI/colorSelector.py`.

A Windows binary is also included (`Chapter_13/PythonColorSelectorUI/colorSelector.exe`). `*.exe` doesn't require Python to be installed. For other operating systems, you'll need to install the requisite packages listed in `Chapter_13/PythonColorSelectorUI/requirements.txt` and run a Python 3 interpreter to use the script:

1. You'll first need to select the STM virtual comm port:

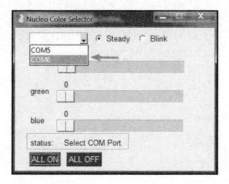

2. After the port has been successfully opened, use the sliders and various buttons to actuate the LEDs on the Nucleo development board. A command frame is constructed on each UI update event and immediately sent over USB to the MCU. The ASCII-encoded hex dump of the last frame sent is displayed:

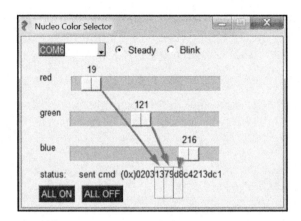

Alternatively, a terminal application capable of sending binary data could also be used (RealTerm is an example for Windows).

So, we have some blinky lights and a (not-so) flashy UI. Let's address the real takeaway of this exercise—the flexibility we've built into our application by using a queue in the way that we did.

Reusing a queue definition for a new target

On the surface, it might be hard to appreciate just how flexible a setup such as this one is. On the command-entry side, we have the ability to acquire commands from anything, not just the binary framed protocol over USB. Since the data being placed into the queue was abstracted to not include any protocol-specific information, the underlying protocol could change without requiring any changes downstream.

Let's take a look at a few examples:

- We could write a different routine for parsing incoming data that uses a comma-separated ASCII string, where duty cycles are represented by percentages between 0 and 100 and a string-based enumeration, terminated by a new line: `BLINK, 20, 30, 100\n`. This would result in the following value being placed in `ledCmdQueue`:

```
LedCmd cmd = {.cmdNum=3, .red=20, .blue=30, .green=100};
xQueueSend(ledCmdQueue, &cmd, 100);
```

- The underlying interface could change completely (from USB to UART, SPI, I2C, Ethernet, an IoT framework, and so on).
- The commands could come in the form of a non-serialized data source (discrete duty cycles or physical pins of the MCU, for example):

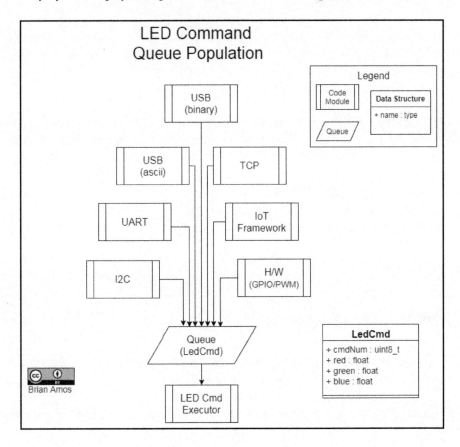

There is also no reason for a queue to be limited to being populated by a single task. If it makes sense from a system design perspective, a command executor's queue could be populated by any number of simultaneous sources. The possibilities of how to get data into the system are truly endless, which is great news—especially if you're developing something considerably more complex that will be used in multiple systems. You're free to invest time in writing quality code once, knowing that the exact code will be used in multiple applications because it is flexible enough to adapt while still maintaining a consistent interface.

There are two components of the ledCmd executor that provide flexibility—the queue interface and the iPWM interface.

The queue interface

After the LedCmdExecution() task is started, the only interaction it has with the higher-level code in the system is through its command queue. Because of this, we are free to change the underlying implementation without directly affecting the higher-level code (as long as the data passed through the queue has the same meaning).

For example, blinking could be implemented differently and none of the code feeding the queue would need to change. Since the only requirements for passing data through the queue are uint8_t and three floating-point numbers, we're also free to completely rewrite the implementation of LedCmdExecution (without the iPWM interface, for example). This change will only affect a single file that starts the task—mainColorSelector.c, in this example. Any other files that deal with the queue directly will be unaffected. If there were multiple sources feeding the queue (such as a USB, I2C, IoT framework, and so on), none of them would need to be modified, even after completely changing the underlying LedCmdExecution implementation.

The iPWM interface

In this implementation, we've taken flexibility one step further by using a flexible interface to actuate the LEDs (iPWM). Since all of the calls (such as setDutyCycles) are defined by a flexible interface (instead of interacting directly with hardware), we're free to substitute any other implementation of iPWM in place of the MCU's TIM peripheral implementation included here.

For example, the LED on the other end of the `iPWM` interface could be an addressable LED driven by a serial interface, which requires a serial data stream rather than PWM. It may even be remotely located and require another protocol to actuate it. As long as it can be represented by a percentage between 0 and 100, it can be controlled by this code.

Now—realistically—in the real world, you're not likely to go to all of this trouble just to blink a few LEDs! Keep in mind that this is an example with fairly trivial functionality, so we're able to keep our focus on the actual architectural elements. In practice, flexible architectures provide a foundation to build long-living, adaptable code bases on.

All of this flexibility does come with a warning—always be careful of the systems you are designing and ensure they meet their primary requirements. There are always tradeoffs to be made, whether they are between performance, initial development time, BOM cost, code elegance, flash space, or maintainability. After all, a beautifully extensible design doesn't do anyone any good if it doesn't fit in the available ROM and RAM!

Summary

In this chapter, you have gained first-hand experience in creating a simple end-to-end command executor architecture. At this point, you should be quite comfortable with creating queues and will have started to gain a deeper understanding of how they can be used to achieve specific design goals, such as flexibility. You can apply variations of these techniques to many real-world projects. If you're feeling particularly adventurous, feel free to implement one of the suggested protocols or add an entry point for another interface (such as a UART).

In the next chapter, we'll change gears a bit and discuss the available APIs for FreeRTOS, investigating when and why you might prefer one over the others.

Questions

As we conclude, here is a list of questions for you to test your knowledge of this chapter's material. You will find the answers in the *Assessments* section of the appendix:

1. Queues decrease design flexibility since they create a rigid definition of data transfer that must be adhered to:
   - True
   - False

2. Queues don't work well with other abstraction techniques; they must only contain simple data types:
   - True
   - False

3. When using queues for commands acquired from a serial port, should the queue contain exactly the same information and formatting as the underlying serialized data stream? Why?

4. Name a reason why passing data by value into queues is *easier* than passing by reference.

5. Name one reason why it is necessary to carefully consider the depth of queues in a real-time embedded system?

Choosing an RTOS API

14

So far, we've only used the native FreeRTOS API in all of our examples. However, this isn't the only API available for using FreeRTOS. Sometimes, there are secondary goals when developing code – it might need to be reused across other projects with other MCU-based embedded operating systems. Other times, code needs to be interoperable with fully featured operating systems. You may also want to utilize code that has been previously developed for a full operating system. In order to support these goals, there are two other APIs for FreeRTOS that are worth considering alongside the native API – CMSIS-RTOS and POSIX.

In this chapter, we'll investigate the features, trade-offs, and limitations of these three APIs when creating applications based on FreeRTOS.

This chapter covers the following topics:

- Understanding generic RTOS APIs
- Comparing FreeRTOS and CMSIS-RTOS
- Comparing FreeRTOS and POSIX
- Deciding which API to use

Technical requirements

To complete the hands-on exercises in this chapter, you will require the following:

- A Nucleo F767 dev board
- A micro-USB cable
- STM32CubeIDE and source code (for instructions, visit `Chapter 5`, *Selecting an IDE,* and read the section *Setting up our IDE*
- SEGGER JLink, Ozone, and SystemView (for instructions, read `Chapter 6`, *Debugging Tools for Real-Time Systems*)

All the source code for this chapter is available from `https://github.com/`
`PacktPublishing/Hands-On-RTOS-with-Microcontrollers/tree/master/Chapter_14`.

Understanding generic RTOS APIs

An RTOS API defines the programming interface that the user interacts with when using
the RTOS. Native APIs expose all of the RTOS's functionality. So far in this book, we've
been using the native FreeRTOS API only. This was done to make it easier to search for
help for a given function and to rule out any possibility of a poorly behaving wrapper layer
between FreeRTOS and a generic API. However, this is not the only API option for
FreeRTOS. There are also generic APIs available that can be used to interface with the
RTOS functionality – but instead of being tied to a specific RTOS, they can be used across
multiple operating systems.

These generic APIs are usually implemented as a wrapper layer above the native RTOS API
(the exception to this is RTX, which has only the CMSIS-RTOS API). Here we can see where
a typical API would live in a generic **Advanced RISC Machines** (**ARM**) firmware stack:

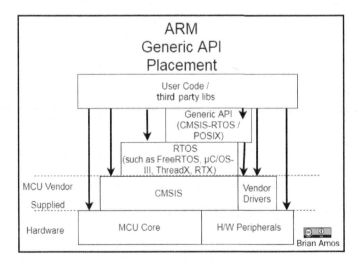

As we can see from the arrows in the preceding diagram, there is no single abstraction that
blocks the user code from accessing the lowest level of functionality. Each layer adds
another potential API to be used, while the lower-level functionality is still available.

There are two generic APIs that can be used to access a subset of FreeRTOS's functionality:

- **CMSIS-RTOS**: ARM has defined a vendor-agnostic API targeting MCUs called the **Cortex Microcontroller Software Interface-RTOS** (CMSIS-RTOS).
- **POSIX**: The **Portable Operating System Interface (POSIX)** is another example of a generic interface that is common across multiple vendors and hardware. This API is more commonly used in full general-purpose operating systems, such as Linux.

We will be discussing these generic APIs in depth throughout this chapter. But first, let's take a look at their advantages and disadvantages.

Advantages of generic APIs

Using a generic RTOS API such as CMSIS-RTOS or POSIX provides several benefits to programmers and middleware vendors. A programmer can write code once and run it on multiple MCUs, changing out the RTOS as desired with few or no changes to their application code. Middleware vendors are also able to write their code to interact with a single API and then support multiple RTOSes and hardware.

As you may have noticed from the previous diagram, CMSIS-RTOS and POSIX APIs do not require exclusive access to FreeRTOS. Since these APIs are implemented as layers on top of the native FreeRTOS API, code can make use of either the more generic API or the native RTOS API at the same time. So, it is perfectly acceptable for some portions of an application to use the CMSIS-RTOS interface while others use the native FreeRTOS API.

For example, if a GUI provider ships their code and it interfaces to CMSIS-RTOS, there is nothing to prevent additional development with the native FreeRTOS API. The GUI vendor's code can be brought in using CMSIS-RTOS, while other code in the system uses the native FreeRTOS API, without the CMSIS-RTOS wrapper.

With these benefits, it seems that a generic API would be the obvious answer to everything. But that's not true.

Disadvantages of generic APIs

What a general-purpose API gains in uniformity, it loses in specificity. A general-purpose, one-size-fits-all implementation needs to be generic enough to be applicable for the majority of RTOSes. This leads to the unique portions being left out of the standardized interface, which can sometimes include some very interesting features.

Since the RTOS vendors themselves aren't always the ones providing support for CMSIS-RTOS, there is the potential that the version of CMSIS-RTOS being shipped is lagging behind the RTOS release cycle. This means that RTOS updates to CMSIS-RTOS *might* not be included as often as for the native API.

There is also the problem of obtaining support if problems are encountered – an RTOS vendor will generally be more willing (and capable) to help with code they actually provided. Often, it will be very difficult to get support for an abstraction that the RTOS vendor hasn't written – both because they are likely to be unfamiliar with it and the abstraction itself can contain bugs/functionality that isn't present in the base RTOS code.

Now that we have a general idea of what a general-purpose RTOS API is, let's take a closer look and compare the FreeRTOS and CMSIS-RTOS APIs.

Comparing FreeRTOS and CMSIS-RTOS

There is a common misconception that there is an RTOS named CMSIS-RTOS. CMSIS-RTOS is actually just an API definition. Its *implementation* is largely a glue layer to the underlying RTOS, but where functional differences exist between the two, some *glue code* will be present to map functionality.

ARM developed CMSIS-RTOS with the same goal in mind as when CMSIS was developed: to add a consistent layer of abstraction that reduces vendor lock-in. The original CMSIS was meant to reduce Silicon vendor lock-in by providing uniform methods for middleware to access common Cortex-M functionality. It accomplished this goal – there are only a few variants of FreeRTOS *ports* for the thousands of Cortex-M-based MCUs it supports. Likewise, ARM is now attempting to reduce RTOS vendor lock-in by making the RTOS itself easier to change out – by providing a consistent API (CMSIS-RTOS) that is vendor-agnostic.

 This chapter refers to CMSIS-RTOS, but this information is specific to the current version of CMSIS-RTOS, which is CMSIS-RTOS v2 (which has a different API from CMSIS-RTOS v1). CMSIS-RTOS v2 is also commonly referred to as CMSIS-RTOS2. The exact version that this chapter references is CMSIS-RTOS 2.1.3.

There are some primary FreeRTOS features that are also exposed by CMSIS-RTOS. Here's a quick overview (more details are included in the *Cross-referencing CMSIS-RTOS and FreeRTOS functions* section):

- **Tasks**: This is the functionality for creating and deleting tasks with both static and dynamically allocated stacks.
- **Semaphores/mutexes**: Binary and counting semaphores as well as mutexes are present in CMSIS-RTOS.
- **Queues**: The Queue APIs are very similar between FreeRTOS's native API and the CMSIS-RTOS API.
- **Software timers**: The Software Timer APIs are very similar between FreeRTOS's native API and the CMSIS-RTOS API.
- **Event groups**: This is used to synchronize multiple tasks.
- **Kernel/scheduler control**: Both APIs have the ability to start/stop tasks and monitor the system.

The feature sets of FreeRTOS and CMSIS-RTOS do not overlap completely. There are some features of FreeRTOS that are not available through CMSIS-RTOS:

- **Stream and message buffers**: The flexible and efficient queue alternative
- **Queue sets**: Used for blocking on multiple queues or semaphores
- **Co-routines**: An explicit time-shared solution for running multiple functions when RAM is too limited to run multiple tasks

Likewise, there are also some features of CMSIS-RTOS that are not available from an off-the-shelf version of FreeRTOS, primarily MemoryPools. For a current list of CMSIS-RTOS2 functions, see https://arm-software.github.io/CMSIS-FreeRTOS/General/html/functionOverview.html#rtos_api2.

A special Note on ST Cube CMSIS-RTOS

It is important to note that when applications are developed using ST Cube, the CMSIS-RTOS version adaptation layer, cmsis_os2.c, is a fork from the original API written by ARM. Many of the changes relate to how the CMSIS-RTOS layer interacts with the system clock. For documentation for the original ARM-supplied CMSIS-FreeRTOS implementation, visit https://arm-software.github.io/CMSIS-FreeRTOS.

Considerations during migration

There are a few noteworthy differences between programming with the CMSIS-RTOS API compared with doing so using the FreeRTOS API.

CMSIS-RTOS task creation functions take the stack size in *bytes*, as opposed to in *words* in FreeRTOS. So, making calls to xTaskCreate in FreeRTOS with a stack size of 128 words equates to calling CMSIS-RTOS osThreadNew with an argument of 512 bytes.

CMSIS-RTOS has fewer functions than FreeRTOS but relies on attribute structs as input to those functions. For example, in FreeRTOS, there are many families of functions that have FromISR equivalents. The FromISR variants typically won't block at all – they *need* to be called if an RTOS API call is made from inside an ISR, but they can also be used selectively in other places. In the CMSIS-RTOS layer, the ISR context is automatically detected. The FromISR API is *automatically* used, depending on whether the caller is being executed within the ISR context or the application context. portYIELD_FROM_ISR is also called automatically. The trade-off for simplicity here is that any blocking delays specified inside an ISR call will be ignored, since the FromISR variants are all non-blocking (since it is never a good idea to block for multiple milliseconds inside an ISR). This is in contrast to the FreeRTOS method of protecting against misuse of the RTOS API from within an ISR context – a configASSERT instance will fail, resulting in an infinite loop that halts the entire application.

With respect to protecting against misuse of RTOS API functionality from an ISR context, CMSIS-RTOS will return error codes when its functions are misused from inside an ISR context. In FreeRTOS, the same misuse will generally result in a failed configASSERT instance with a detailed comment, which halts the entire program. As long as the programmer is being responsible and rigorously checking return values, these errors will be detected. FreeRTOS is a bit more vocal about the errors, by not allowing program execution to continue (verbose comments explaining the reason for the misconfiguration and suggested solutions are almost always present in the FreeRTOS source code when this happens).

Cross-referencing CMIS-RTOS and FreeRTOS functions

Here is a complete comparison of CMSIS-RTOS functions and their associated FreeRTOS functions. Feel free to skim the tables now if you're interested in finding out how various FreeRTOS functions are called from the CMSIS-RTOS API. Otherwise, use the tables as a reference when porting code between the CMSIS-RTOS and FreeRTOS APIs.

Delay functions

Delay functions map cleanly between the two APIs:

CMSIS-RTOS name	FreeRTOS functions called	Notes
osDelay	vTaskDelay	osDelay is in ms or ticks, depending on which documentation and comments you believe. Be sure to check your CMSIS-RTOS implementation of osDelay() if a Systick frequency of something other than 1 kHz is used!
osDelayUntil	vTaskDelayUntil, xTaskGetTickCount	

These basic delay functions work in very similar ways – the biggest difference to keep in mind is that CMSIS-RTOS specifies osDelay in milliseconds instead of *ticks*, as FreeRTOS does.

EventFlags

oseventFlags in CMSIS-RTOS maps to EventGroups in FreeRTOS. The FromISR variant of the FreeRTOS API is automatically used when CMSIS-RTOS functions are called from inside an ISR:

CMSIS-RTOS name	FreeRTOS functions called	Notes
oseventFlagsClear	xEventGroupsClearBits, xEventGroupGetBitsFromISR	
osEventFlagsDelete	vEventGroupDelete	
osEventFlagsGet	xEventGroupGetBits, xEventGroupGetBitsFromISR	
osEventFlagsNew	xEventGroupCreateStatic, xEventGroupCreate	
osEventFlagsSet	xEventGroupSetBits, xEventGroupSetBitsFromISR	
osEventFlagsWait	xEventGroupWaitBits	

EventFlags in CMSIS-RTOS work similarly to EventGroups in FreeRTOS, with nearly 1:1 mapping.

Kernel control and information

The kernel interfaces are similar, although some timer implementations that STM has provided aren't all that intuitive,
specifically `osKernelGetSysTimerCount` and `osKernelGetSysTimerCount`. Also, some functions will return errors if there are issues within the context of an ISR:

- `osKernelInitialize`
- `osKernelRestoreLock`
- `osKernelStart3`
- `osKernelUnlock`

Pay special attention to the notes in this table:

CMSIS-RTOS name	FreeRTOS functions called	Notes
`osKernelGetInfo`	static strings representing FreeRTOS version	
`osKernelGetState`	`xTaskGetSchedulerState`	
`osKernelGetSysTimerCount`	`xTaskGetTickCount`	This returns `xTaskGetTickCount()` * (`SysClockFreq` / `configTICK_RATE_HZ`).
`osKernelGetSysTimerFreq`	ST HAL SystemCoreClock global variable	
`osKernelGetTickCount`	`xTaskGetTickCount`	
`osKernelGetTickFreq`	`configTICK_RATE_HZ`	This is *not* the `SysTick` frequency (that is, 1 kHz) (`SysClockFreq` is being returned (160 MHz)).
`osKernelInitialize`	`vPortDefineHeapRegions` (only if `Heap5` is used)	
`osKernelLock`	`xTaskGetSchedulerState`, `vTaskSuspendAll`	
`osKernelRestoreLock`	`xTaskGetSchedulerState`, `vTaskSuspendAll`	
`osKernelStart`	`vTaskStartScheduler`	

osKernelUnlock	xTaskGetSchedulerState, xTaskResumeAll	

Be aware of the slight differences in time units when moving between kernel-oriented functions using the STM-supplied CMSIS-RTOS port and the native FreeRTOS API.

Message queues

Message queues are quite similar. In CMSIS-RTOS, all queues are registered by name, which can make for a richer debugging experience. Also, CMSIS-RTOS supports static allocation via attributes passed in as function parameters.

Any functions called from inside an ISR will automatically be forced to use the `FromISR` equivalent functions and finish the ISR with a call to `portYIELD_FROM_ISR`. This results in any blocking times being effectively set to 0. So, for example, if a queue doesn't have space available, a call to `osMessageQueuePut` will return immediately from inside an ISR, even if a blocking timeout is specified:

CMSIS-RTOS name	FreeRTOS functions called	Notes
osMessageQueueDelete	vQueueUnregisterQueue, vQueueDelete	
osMessageQueueGet	xQueueReceive	The `FromISR` variant is automatically called and `portYIELD_FROM_ISR` is automatically called if inside an ISR.
osMessageQueueGetCapacity	pxQueue->uxLength	
osMessageQueueGetCount	uxQueueMessagesWaiting, uxQueueMessagesWaitingFromISR	
osMessageQueueGetMsgSize	pxQueue->uxItemSize	
osMessageQueueGetSpace	uxQueueSpacesAvailable	`taskENTER_CRITICAL_FROM_ISR` is automatically called if this function is executed from within an ISR.
osMessageQueueNew	xQueueCreateStatic, xQueueCreate	
osMessageQueuePut	xQueueSendToBack, xQueueSendToBackFromISR	The `msg_prior` parameter is ignored in the STM port.
osMessageQueueReset	xQueueReset	

Queues are very similar between CMSIS-RTOS and FreeRTOS, but it is worth noting that CMSIS-RTOS doesn't have an equivalent of `xQueueSendToFront`, so it will not be possible to place items at the front of a queue using CMSIS-RTOS.

Mutexes and semaphores

Mutexes are also similar between the two APIs, with some considerations to keep in mind:

- In CMSIS-RTOS, the recursive mutex API functions are automatically called, depending on the type of mutex created.
- In CMSIS-RTOS, static allocation is supported via attributes passed in as function parameters.
- osMutexAcquire, osMutexRelease, osMutexDelete, and osMutexRelease will always fail by returning osErrorISR if called within an ISR context.
- osMutexGetOwner and osMutexNew will always return NULL when called from within an ISR.

With those points in mind, here are the relationships between mutexes in CMSIS-RTOS and FreeRTOS APIs:

CMSIS-RTOS name	FreeRTOS functions called	Notes
osMutexAcquire	xSemaphoreTake, xSemaphoreTakeRecursive	The takeRecursive variant is automatically called when the mutex is recursive.
osMutexRelease	xSemaphoreGive, xSemaphoreGiveRecursive	The takeRecursive variant is automatically called when the mutex is recursive.
osMutexDelete	vSemaphoreDelete, vQueueUnregisterQueue	
osMutexGetOwner	xSemaphoreGetMutexHolder	This always returns NULL if called from inside an ISR, which is identical to the expected behavior when the mutex is available.

	xSemaphoreCreateRecursiveMutexStatic,	Different mutex types are created depending on the value of the osMutexAttr_t pointer passed into the function.
osMutexNew	xSemaphoreCreateMutexStatic, xSemaphoreCreateRecursiveMutex, xSemaphoreCreateMutex, vQueueAddToRegistry	
osMutexRelease	xSemaphoreGiveRecursive, xSemaphoreGive	

While the mutex functionality is very similar between the APIs, the way in which it is achieved is quite different. FreeRTOS uses many different functions to create mutexes, while CMSIS-RTOS achieves the same functionality by adding parameters to fewer functions. It also records the mutex type and automatically calls the appropriate FreeRTOS function for recursive mutexes.

Semaphores

The FromISR equivalents of semaphore functions are automatically used when necessary. Static and dynamically allocated semaphores, along with binary and counting semaphores, are all created using osSemaphoreNew.

The fact that semaphores are implemented using queues under the hood in FreeRTOS is evident here, as evidenced by the use of the Queue API to extract information for the semaphores:

CMSIS-RTOS name	FreeRTOS functions called	Notes
osSemaphoreAcquire	xSemaphoreTakeFromISR, xSemaphoreTake, portYIELD_FROM_ISR	The automatic ISR context is accounted for.
osSemaphoreDelete	vSemaphoreDelete, vQueueUnregisterQueue	
osSemaphoreGetCount	osSemaphoreGetCount, uxQueueMessagesWaitingFromISR	

		All semaphore types are created using this function. Semaphores are automatically given unless the initial count is specified as 0.
osSemaphoreNew	xSemaphoreCreateBinaryStatic, xSemaphoreCreateBinary, xSemaphoreCreateCountingStatic, xSemaphoreCreateCounting, xSemaphoreGive, vQueueAddToRegistry	
osSemaphoreRelease	xSemaphoreGive, xSemaphoreGiveFromISR	

In general, semaphore functionality maps very cleanly between CMSIS-RTOS and FreeRTOS, although the function names differ.

Thread flags

CMSIS-RTOS thread flag usage should be reviewed independently (a link to the detailed documentation is provided). As you can see from the FreeRTOS fuctions called, they are built on top of TaskNotifications. Again, ISR-safe equivalents are automatically substituted when the calls are made within an ISR context:

CMSIS-RTOS name	FreeRTOS functions called	Notes
osThreadFlagsClear	xTaskGetCurrentTaskHandle, xTaskNotifyAndQuery, xTaskNotify	https://www.keil.com/pack/doc/CMSIS/RTOS2/html/group__CMSIS__RTOS__ThreadFlagsMgmt.html
osThreadFlagsGet	xTaskGetCurrentTaskHandle, xTaskNotifyAndQuery	
osThreadFlagsSet	xTaskNotifyFromISR, xTaskNotifyAndQueryFromISR, portYIELD_FROM_ISR, xTaskNotify, xTaskNotifyAndQuery	
osThreadFlagsWait	xTaskNotifyWait	

ThreadFlags and TaskNotifications have the largest potential for different behavior between the two APIs. Most of this will depend on how they are used in a specific application, so it is best to review the ThreadFlags documentation in detail before attempting to port TaskNofications to ThreadFlags.

Thread control/information

The basic threading API is very similar between CMSIS-RTOS and FreeRTOS, with the exception of CMSIS-RTOS's `osThreadGetStackSize`, which has no equivalent in FreeRTOS. Other minor differences include the addition of `osThreadEnumerate`, which uses several FreeRTOS functions while it lists the tasks in the system, as well as different names for states (CMSIS-RTOS lacks a `suspend` state). In CMSIS-RTOS, both static and dynamic thread/task stack allocation is supported through the same function, `osThreadNew`.

 If `osThreadTerminate` is called while using the FreeRTOS Heap1 implementation (discussed in the next chapter), an infinite loop with no delay will be entered.

Be aware that CMSIS-RTOS v2 `osThreadAttr_t.osThreadPriority` requires 56 different task priorities! Therefore, `configMAX_PRIORITIES` in `FreeRTOSConfig.h` must have a value of 56, or the implementation of `osThreadNew()` will need to be scaled to fit into the available number of priorities:

CMSIS-RTOS name	FreeRTOS functions called	Notes		
osThreadEnumerate	vTaskSuspendAll, uxTaskGetNumberOfTasks, uxTaskGetSystemState, xTaskResumeAll	This suspends the system and populates an array of task handles.		
osThreadExit	vTaskDelete	This ends the current thread if HEAP1 is being used. This function will cause the caller to go into a tight infinite loop, consuming as many CPU cycles as available given the caller's priority.		
osThreadGetCount	uxTaskGetNumberOfTasks			
osThreadGetId	xTaskGetCurrentTaskHandle			
osThreadGetName	pcTaskGetName			
osThreadGetPriority	uxTaskPriorityGet			
osThreadGetStackSize	always returns 0	https://github.com/ARM-software/CMSISFreeRTOS/issues/14		
osThreadGetStackSpace	uxTaskGetStackHighWaterMark			
osThreadGetState	eTaskGetState	**FreeRTOS Task State**		**CMSIS-RTOS**
		eRunning		osThreadRunning
		eReady		osThreadReady
		eBlocked		osThreadBlocked
		eSuspended		
		eDeleted		osThreadTerminated
		eInvalid		osThreadError

osThreadNew	xTaskCreateStatic, xTaskCreate	
osThreadResume	vTaskResume	
osThreadSetPriority	vTaskPrioritySet	
osThreadSuspend	vTaskSuspend	
osThreadTerminate	vTaskDelete	If Heap1 is used, this function returns osError.
osThreadYield	taskYIELD	

Most of the thread controls are a simple 1:1 mapping, so they are straightforward to substitute between the two APIs.

Timers

Timers are equivalent, with static and dynamic allocation both being defined by the same osTimerNew function:

CMSIS-RTOS name	FreeRTOS functions called	Notes
osTimerDelete	xTimerDelete	If Heap1 is used, this function returns osError. It also frees up TimerCallback_t* used by the timer to be deleted.
osTimerGetName	pcTimerGetName	
osTimerIsRunning	xTimerIsTimerActive	
osTimerNew	xTimerCreateStatic, xTimerCreate	Automatic allocation for TimerCallback_t.
osTimerStart	xTimerChangePeriod	
osTimerStop	xTimerStop	

Timers are very similar between the two APIs, but beware of attempting to use osTimerDelete with Heap1.

Memory pools

Memory pools are a popular dynamic allocation technique commonly found in embedded RTOSes. FreeRTOS does not currently supply a memory pool implementation out of the box. A design decision was made in early development to eliminate it because it added extra user-facing complexity and wasted too much RAM.

ARM and ST have elected to not supply any memory pool implementations on top of FreeRTOS.

That concludes our complete cross-reference of the CMSIS-RTOS and FreeRTOS APIs. It should have been helpful in quickly determining what differences you need to be aware of. While CMSIS-RTOS can be used with RTOSes from different vendors, it does not contain all of the features that FreeRTOS has to offer (such as stream buffers).

Now that we've seen a comparison between the native FreeRTOS API and the CMSIS-RTOS v2 API, let's take a look at an example of an application using CMSSI-RTOS v2.

Creating a simple CMSIS-RTOS v2 application

Armed with an understanding of the differences between the native FreeRTOS API and the CMSIS-RTOS v2 API, we can develop a bare-bones application with two tasks that blink some LEDs. The goal of this application is to develop code that is only dependent on the CMCSIS-RTOS API rather than the FreeRTOS API. All the code found here resides in `main_taskCreation_CMSIS_RTOSV2.c`.

This example is similar to those found in `Chapter` 7, *The FreeRTOS Scheduler*; this one only sets up tasks and blinks LEDs. Follow these steps:

1. Initialize the RTOS using `osStatus_t osKernelInitialize (void)`, checking the return value before continuing:

    ```
    osStatus_t status;
    status = osKernelInitialize();
    assert(status == osOK);
    ```

2. Since CMSIS-RTOS uses structs to pass in thread attributes, populate an `osThreadAttr_t` structure from `cmsis_os2.h`:

    ```
    /// Attributes structure for thread.
    typedef struct {
      const char *name;     ///< name of the thread
      uint32_t attr_bits;   ///< attribute bits
      void *cb_mem;         ///< memory for control block
      ///< size of provided memory for control block
      uint32_t cb_size;
      void *stack_mem;      ///< memory for stack
      uint32_t stack_size;  ///< size of stack
      ///< initial thread priority (default: osPriorityNormal)
    ```

```
    osPriority_t priority;
    TZ_ModuleId_t tz_module; ///< TrustZone module identifier
    uint32_t reserved;       ///< reserved (must be 0)
} osThreadAttr_t;
```

Note: Unlike FreeRTOS stack sizes, which are defined in the number of *words* the stack will consume (4 bytes for Cortex-M7), CMSIS-RTOS sizes are always defined in *bytes*. Previously, when using the FreeRTOS API, we were using 128 words for the stack size. Here, to achieve the same stack size, we'll use 128 * 4 = 512 bytes.

```
#define STACK_SIZE 512
osThreadAttr_t greenThreadAtrribs = {   .name = "GreenTask",
                                        .attr_bits = osThreadDetached,
                                        .cb_mem = NULL,
                                        .cb_size = 0,
                                        .stack_mem = NULL,
                                        .stack_size = STACK_SIZE,
                                        .priority = osPriorityNormal,
                                        .tz_module = 0,
                                        .reserved = 0};
```

In the preceding code, we can see the following:

- Only osThreadDetachted is supported for attr_bits.
- The first task to be created will use dynamic allocation, so the control block and stack-related variables (cb_mem, cb_size, stack_mem, stack_size) will be set to 0 and NULL.
- Normal priority will be used here.
- Cortex-M7 MCUs (STM32F759) do not have a trust zone.

3. Create the thread by calling osThreadNew() and passing in a pointer to the function that implements the desired thread, any task arguments, and a pointer to the osThreadAttr_t structure. The prototype for osThreadNew(is as follows:

```
osThreadId_t osThreadNew (   osThreadFunc_t func,
                             void *argument,
                             const osThreadAttr_t *attr);
```

Here is the actual call to `osThreadNew()`, which creates the `GreenTask` thread. Again, be sure to check that the thread has been successfully created before moving on:

```
greenTaskThreadID = osThreadNew( GreenTask, NULL,
                            &greenThreadAtrribs);
assert(greenTaskThreadID != NULL);
```

4. The `GreenTask` function will blink the green LED (on for 200 ms and off for 200 ms):

```
void GreenTask(void *argument)
{
  while(1)
  {
    GreenLed.On();
    osDelay(200);
    GreenLed.Off();
    osDelay(200);
  }
}
```

It is worth noting that, unlike the case in FreeRTOS's `vTaskDelay()` where the delay is dependent on the underlying tick frequency, CMSIS-RTOS's `osDelay()` is suggested by Keil/ARM documentation to be specified in milliseconds. However, the documentation also refers to the argument as *ticks*. Since a tick isn't necessarily 1 ms long, be sure to check your implementation of `osDelay()` in `cmsis_os2.c`. For example, in the copy of `cmsis_os2.c` obtained from STM, no conversion is performed between ticks and ms.

5. Start the scheduler:

```
status = osKernelStart();
assert(status == osOK);
```

This call should not return when successful.

`main_taskCreation_CMSIS_RTOSV2.c` also contains an example of starting a task with statically allocated memory for the task control block and task stack.

Static allocation requires computing the sizes of RTOS control blocks (such as `StaticTask_t`) that are specific to the underlying RTOS. To reduce the coupling of code to the underlying RTOS, an additional header file should be used to encapsulate all RTOS-specific sizes. In this example, this file is named `RTOS_Dependencies.h`.

Tasks created from statically allocated memory use the same `osThreadCreate()` function call as before. This time, the `cb_mem`, `cb_size`, `stack_mem`, `stack_size` variables will be populated with pointers and sizes.

6. Define an array, which will be used as the task stack:

```
#define STACK_SIZE 512
static uint8_t RedTask_Stack[STACK_SIZE];
```

7. Populate `RTOS_Dependencies.h` with the size of the FreeRTOS task control block used for static tasks:

```
#define TCB_SIZE (sizeof(StaticTask_t))
```

8. Define an array that's large enough to hold the task control block:

```
uint8_t RedTask_TCB[TCB_SIZE];
```

9. Create an `osThreadAttr_t` struct containing all of the name, pointer, and task priorities:

```
osThreadAttr_t redThreadAtrribs = { .name = "RedTask",
        .attr_bits = osThreadDetached,
        .cb_mem = RedTask_TCB,
        .cb_size = TCB_SIZE,
        .stack_mem = RedTask_Stack,
        .stack_size = STACK_SIZE,
        .priority = osPriorityNormal,
        .tz_module = 0,
        .reserved = 0};
```

10. Create the `RedTask` thread, making sure that it has been successfully created before moving on:

```
redTaskThreadID = osThreadNew( RedTask, NULL, &redThreadAtrribs);
assert(redTaskThreadID != NULL);
```

`main_taskCreate_CMSIS_RTOSV2.c` can be compiled and flashed onto the Nucleo board and used as a starting point to experiment with the remainder of the CMSIS-RTOSv2 API. You can use this basic program to jump-start additional CMSIS-RTOSv2 API experimentation.

Now that we have an understanding of a commonly used MCU-centric API for FreeRTOS, let's move on to a standard that has been around since the 1980s and is still going strong.

FreeRTOS and POSIX

The **Portable Operating System Interface (POSIX)** was developed to provide a unified interface for interacting with operating systems, making code more portable between systems.

At the time of writing, FreeRTOS has a beta implementation for a subset of the POSIX API. The POSIX headers that have been (partly) ported are listed here:

- `errno.h`
- `fcntl.h`
- `mqueue.h`
- `mqueue.h`
- `sched.h`
- `semaphore.h`
- `signal.h`
- `sys/types.h`
- `time.h`
- `unistd.h`

Generally speaking, threading, queues, mutexes, semaphores, timers, sleep, and some clock functions are implemented by the port. This feature set sometimes covers enough of a real-world use case to enable porting applications that have been written to be POSIX-compliant to an MCU supporting FreeRTOS. Keep in mind that FreeRTOS does not supply a filesystem on its own without additional middleware, so any application requiring filesystem access will need some additional components before it will be functional.

Let's take a look at what a minimal application using the POSIX API looks like.

Creating a simple FreeRTOS POSIX application

Similarly to the CMSIS API example, the POSIX API example will just blink two LEDs at different intervals.

 Note that after FreeRTOS POSIX moves out of FreeRTOS Labs, the download location (and the corresponding instructions) will likely change.

First, the POSIX wrapper needs to be downloaded and brought into the source tree.
Perform the following steps:

1. Download the FreeRTOS Labs distribution (`https://www.freertos.org/`
   `a00104.html`). Go to `https://www.freertos.org/FreeRTOS-Plus/FreeRTOS_`
   `Plus_POSIX/index.html` for up-to-date download instructions.
2. Import the selected `FreeRTOS_POSIX` files into your source tree. In the example,
   they reside in `Middleware\Third_Party\FreeRTOS\FreeRTOS_POSIX`.
3. Add the necessary `include` paths to the compiler and linker by modifying the
   project properties within STM32CubeIDE:

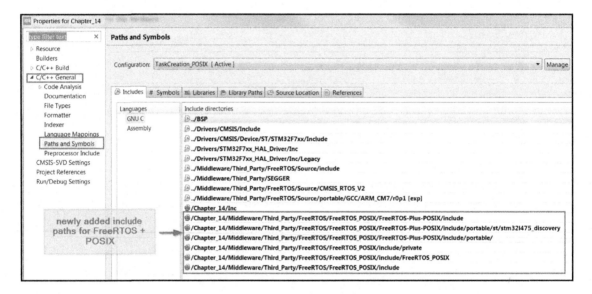

4. Make sure to add the following `#define` lines to `Inc/FreeRTOSConfig.h`:

```
#define configUSE_POSIX_ERRNO 1
#define configUSE_APPLICATION_TASK_TAG 1
```

Now that POSIX APIs are available, we'll use `pthreads` and `sleep` in
`main_task_Creation_POSIX.c`:

1. Bring in the necessary header files:

```
// FreeRTOS POSIX includes
#include <FreeRTOS_POSIX.h>
#include <FreeRTOS_POSIX/pthread.h>
#include <FreeRTOS_POSIX/unistd.h>
```

2. Define the necessary function prototypes:

```
void GreenTask(void *argument);
void RedTask(void *argument);
void lookBusy( void );
```

3. Define global variables to store the thread IDs:

```
pthread_t greenThreadId, redThreadId;
```

4. Use `pthread_create()` to create a thread/task:

```
int pthread_create( pthread_t *thread, const pthread_attr_t *attr,
                    void * (*start_routine) (void *), void *arg);
```

Here's some information about the preceding code:

- thread: A pointer to a pthread_t struct, which will be filled out by pthread_create()
- attr: A pointer to a struct containing the attributes of the thread
- start_routine: A pointer to the function implementing the thread
- arg: The arguments to pass to the thread's function
- Returns 0 in the case of success and errrno in the case of failure (the contents of pthread_t *thread will be undefined in the case of failure)

Here, two threads are started using the functions declared earlier – GreenTask() and RedTask():

```
retVal = pthread_create( &greenThreadId, NULL, GreenTask, NULL);
assert(retVal == 0);

retVal = pthread_create( &redThreadId, NULL, RedTask, NULL);
assert(retVal == 0);
```

5. Start the scheduler:

```
vTaskStartScheduler();
```

When the scheduler is started, both `GreenTask()` and `ReadTask()` will be switched into context as required. Let's have a quick look at each of these functions.

`GreenTask()` is using `sleep()`, brought in from `unistd.h`. Now, `sleep()` will force the task to block for the desired number of seconds (in this case, 1 second after turning the LED on and 1 second after turning the LED off):

```
void GreenTask(void *argument)
{
  while(1)
  {
    GreenLed.On();
    sleep(1);
    GreenLed.Off();
    sleep(1);
  }
}
```

`RedTask()` is similar, sleeping for 2 seconds after the red LED is turned off:

```
void RedTask( void* argument )
{
  while(1)
  {
    lookBusy();
    RedLed.On();
    sleep(1);
    RedLed.Off();
    sleep(2);
  }
}
```

Now `TaskCreation_POSIX` can be compiled and loaded onto the Nucleo board. You're free to use this as a starting point for experimenting with more portions of the POSIX API. Next, let's look at some of the reasons why you might want to use the POSIX API.

Pros and cons to using the POSIX API

There are two primary reasons to consider using the POSIX API for FreeRTOS:

- **Portability to general-purpose operating systems:** By definition, the goal of POSIX is *portability*. There are many general-purpose operating systems meant to be run on CPUs with MMUs that are POSIX-compliant. Increasingly, there are also several lightweight operating systems aimed at MCUs that are also POSIX-compliant. If your goal is to run your code base on these types of systems, the POSIX API is the interface to use. It is the only API for FreeRTOS that will allow code to be portable to a fully fledged operating system (rather than a real-time kernel).
- **Third-party POSIX libraries**: Many open source libraries are written to interface via POSIX. Having the ability to bring in *some* POSIX-compatible third-party code (as long as it only accesses the portions that have been ported by FreeRTOS) has the potential to quickly boost a project's functionality.

Of course, there are some drawbacks to using the POSIX API as well:

- **Still in beta**: At the time of writing (early 2020), the POSIX API is still in FreeRTOS Labs. Here's an explanation from `freertos.org`:

    The POSIX library and documentation are in the FreeRTOS Labs. The libraries in the FreeRTOS Labs download directory are fully functional, but undergoing optimizations or refactoring to improve memory usage, modularity, documentation, demo usability, or test coverage. They are available as part of the FreeRTOS-Labs download: `https://www.freertos.org/a00104.html`.

- **Being limited to the POSIX API may reduce efficiency**: Having code that is portable between many different operating systems running on both MCUs and CPUs will come with a cost. Any code that you'd like to make portable to any platform that supports POSIX will need to contain only POSIX functionality (that is implemented by FreeRTOS). Since only a small subset of the FreeRTOS API is exposed through POSIX, you'll be giving up some of the more efficient implementations. Some of the most time- and CPU-efficient functionality (such as stream buffers and direct task notifications) won't be available if you're aiming to have ultra-portable code that uses only the POSIX API.

Having the POSIX API available to ease the addition of third-party code is an exciting development for embedded developers. It has the potential to bring a large amount of functionality into the embedded space very quickly. But keep this in mind: although today's MCUs are extremely powerful, they're not general-purpose processors. You'll need to be mindful of all of the code's interaction and resource requirements, especially with systems that have real-time requirements.

So, we have three primary options regarding which API to utilize when interacting with FreeRTOS. What kinds of considerations should be made when choosing between them?

Deciding which API to use

Deciding which API to use is largely based on *where* you'd like your code to be portable to and *what* experience various team members have. For example, if you're interested in being able to try out different Cortex-M RTOS vendors, CMSIS-RTOS is a natural choice. It will allow different operating systems to be brought in without changing the application-level code.

Similarly, if your application code needs to be capable of running both in a Linux environment on a fully featured CPU as well as on an MCU, the FreeRTOS POSIX implementation would make a lot of sense.

Since both of these APIs are layered *on top of* the native FreeRTOS API, you'll still be able to use any FreeRTOS-specific functionality that is required. The following sections should provide some points for consideration and help you decide when each API should be chosen. As usual, there is often no right or wrong choice – just a set of trade-offs to be made.

When to use the native FreeRTOS API

There are some cases when using only the native FreeRTOS API is advantageous:

- **Code consistency**: If an existing code base is already using the native FreeRTOS API, there is little benefit to writing new code that adds an additional layer of complexity (and a different API) on top of it. Although the functionality is similar, the actual function signatures and data structures are different. Because of these differences, having inconsistency between which API is used by old and new code might be very confusing for programmers unfamiliar with the code base.

- **Support**: If the API you'd like to use is not written by the same writer as the RTOS, there is a very good chance that the RTOS vendor won't be able/willing to provide support for problems that arise (since the issue could be relevant only to the generic API wrapper layer and not the underlying RTOS). When you're first starting out with an RTOS, you'll likely find it is easier to get support (both by the vendor and forums) if you're referencing their code rather than a third-party wrapper.

- **Simplicity**: When asking an RTOS vendor which API to use, the response will generally be "*the native API we wrote.*" On the surface, this may seem a bit self-serving. After all, if you're using their native API, porting your code to another vendor's operating system won't be as easy. However, there's a bit more to this recommendation than first meets the eye. Each RTOS vendor generally has a strong preference for the style they've chosen when writing their code (and API). Gluing this native API to a different one may be a bit of a paradigm shift. Sometimes this extra layer of glue is so thin as to barely be noticed. Other times, it can turn into a sticky mess, requiring considerable extra code to be written on top of a native API and making it more confusing for developers well versed with the native API.

- **Code space**: Since each of the generic APIs is a wrapper around the native FreeRTOS API, they will require a small amount of additional code space. On larger 32-bit MCUs, this will rarely be a consideration.

When to use the CMSIS-RTOS API

Use CMSIS-RTOS when you'd like your code to be portable to other ARM-based MCUs. Some of the other RTOSes that are aimed at MCUs and support the CMSIS-RTOS API include the following:

- Micrium uCOS
- Express Logic ThreadX
- Keil RTX
- Zephyr Project

By using only functions provided by CMSIS-RTOS API, your code will run on top of any compatible operating system without modification.

When to use the POSIX API

Use the POSIX port when you'd like your code to be portable to these operating systems, or if there is a library that relies on the POSIX API that you'd like to include in your MCU project:

- Linux
- Android
- Zephyr
- Nuttx (POSIX)
- Blackberry QNX

While each of the POSIX-compatible operating systems just listed implements portions of POSIX, not all of the feature sets will necessarily intersect. When writing code that is intended to be run across multiple targets, a *least common denominator* approach will need to be taken – be sure to only use the smallest number of features commonly available across all target platforms.

It is also worth noting that since POSIX-compliant open source applications are designed for fully fledged PCs, they may utilize libraries that are not suitable for an MCU (for example, a filesystem that is not present using the core FreeRTOS kernel).

Summary

In this chapter, we've covered three different APIs that can be used with FreeRTOS – the native FreeRTOS API, CMSIS-RTOS, and POSIX. You should now be familiar with all of the different APIs available for interacting with FreeRTOS and have an understanding of why they exist, as well as an understanding of when it is appropriate to use each one. Moving forward, you will be well positioned to make informed decisions about which API to use, depending on your particular project's requirements.

In the next chapter, we'll switch gears from discussing how to interact with FreeRTOS at a high level and discuss some of the low-level details of memory allocation.

Questions

As we conclude, here is a list of questions for you to test your knowledge regarding this chapter's material. You will find the answers in the *Assessments* section of the *Appendix*:

1. What is CMSIS-RTOS, and which vendor supplies its implementation?
2. Name a common operating system that makes heavy use of POSIX.
3. It is important to choose wisely between the CMSIS-RTOS and FreeRTOS APIs because only one is available at a time:
   - True
   - False
4. By using the POSIX API, any program written for Linux can be easily ported to run on FreeRTOS:
   - True
   - False

Further reading

- The CMSIS-RTOS v2 API documentation: https://www.keil.com/pack/doc/CMSIS/RTOS2/html/
- FreeRTOS POSIX API - https://www.freertos.org/FreeRTOS-Plus/FreeRTOS_Plus_POSIX/index.html
- A detailed list of FreeRTOS POSIX ported functions
- Zephyr POSIX implementation for the STM32 F7 Nucleo-144 dev board: https://docs.zephyrproject.org/latest/boards/arm/nucleo_f767zi/doc/index.html

15
FreeRTOS Memory Management

So far, we've worked through many examples of creating FreeRTOS primitives; however, when these primitives were initially created, there wasn't much of an explanation as to where the memory was coming from. In this chapter, we'll learn exactly where the memory comes from, along with when and how it is allocated. Choosing when and how memory is allocated allows us to make trade-offs between coding convenience, timing determinism, potential regulatory requirements, and code standards. We'll conclude by looking at different measures that can be taken to ensure application robustness.

In a nutshell, this chapter covers the following:

- Understanding memory allocation
- Static and dynamic allocation of FreeRTOS primitives
- Comparing FreeRTOS heap implementations
- Replacing `malloc` and `free`
- Implementing FreeRTOS memory hooks
- Using a **memory protection unit (MPU)**

Technical requirements

To complete the hands-on exercises in this chapter, you will require the following:

- A Nucleo F767 development board
- A Micro-USB cable
- STM32CubeIDE and source code (see the instructions in `Chapter 5`, *Selecting an IDE*, under the section *Setting up our IDE*)

- SEGGER JLink, Ozone, and SystemView (see the instructions in `Chapter 6,` *Debugging Tools for Real-Time Systems*)

All source code for this chapter is available from `https://github.com/PacktPublishing/` `Hands-On-RTOS-with-Microcontrollers/tree/master/Chapter_15`.

Understanding memory allocation

Memory allocation isn't necessarily at the top of a developer's list of favorite topics to consider when developing an application—it just isn't all that glamorous. Dynamic allocation of memory—that is, allocating memory as it is needed rather than at the beginning of the program—is the norm. With desktop-oriented development, memory is generally available whenever it is needed, so it isn't given a second thought; it is simply a `malloc` call away. When it is finished, it will be unallocated with `free`.

Unlike the carefree dynamic memory allocation schemes in a desktop environment, programmers of deeply embedded systems that use MCUs will often need to be more careful about how (and if) memory is dynamically allocated. In an embedded system, regulatory, RAM, and timing constraints can all play a role in whether/how memory can be dynamically allocated.

Many high-reliability and safety-critical coding standards, such as MISRA-C, will not allow the use of dynamic allocation. In this case, it is still perfectly acceptable to use static allocation. Some coding standards disallow dynamic allocation after all tasks are created (*Ten Rules for Safety Critical Coding* by JPL, for example). In this case, static allocation or FreeRTOS's `heap_1.c` implementation would be reasonable.

RAM may be severely limited on a given platform. On the surface, this seems like the perfect use case for dynamic memory allocation; after all, if there is limited memory, it can be given back when it's not in use! In practice, however, things don't always go this smoothly when there is limited heap space available. When small heaps are used to allocate space for arbitrarily sized objects with different lifetimes, fragmentation will often occur eventually (this will be covered in more depth with an example later).

Finally, a need for highly deterministic timing can also limit the options for dynamic allocation. If a portion of code has tight timing constraints, it is sometimes easier to avoid using dynamic allocation, rather than contriving tests that attempt to mimic worst-case timing for a call to `malloc`. It is also worth noting (again) that `malloc` isn't guaranteed to succeed, *especially* on an embedded system with limited memory. Having a large amount of dynamic allocation in a memory-constrained, multithreaded system can create some very complex use cases that have the potential to fail at runtime. Thoroughly testing such a system is a very serious challenge.

With this background information on why memory allocation is so important in constrained embedded systems, let's take a closer look at *where* memory comes from in a few different use cases.

Static memory

Static memory's lifespan is the entire duration of a program. Global variables, as well as any variables declared inside functions using the `static` specifier, will be placed into static memory and they will have a lifetime equal to that of the program.

For example, both `globalVar` and `staticVar` are located in static memory and will persist for the entire lifetime of the program. The initialization of `staticVar` only occurs once during the initial program load:

```
uint8_t globalVar = 12;

void myFunc( void )
{
    static uint8_t staticVar = 0;
    ...
}
```

When variables are declared as static, memory is guaranteed to be available. All of the global and static variables defined by the program are placed into their locations during the linking phase. As long as the amount of memory has been properly configured, the linker guarantees that space is available for these variables.

The downside is that because static variables have such a long lifespan, static variables will *always* be consuming space, even when they are not being used.

Stack memory

A stack is used for function-scoped storage. Each time a function is called, information for that function (like its parameters and local variables) are placed onto a stack. When the function exits, all of the information that was placed onto the stack is removed (this is why passing pointers to local variables is a problem). In FreeRTOS, each task has its own private stack whose size is determined when the task is created.

Since stacks have such an orderly way of being accessed, it isn't possible for them to become fragmented, like a heap. It is possible, however, to overflow the stack by placing more information onto it than its size allows.

On the Cortex-M, there is also one additional stack—the main stack. The main stack is used by ISRs and the FreeRTOS kernel. The kernel and ISRs execute in a privileged mode that modifies the **main stack pointer** (**MSP**). Tasks execute on the process stack and use the **process stack pointer** (**PSP**). All of the stack pointer operations are taken care of by hardware and the kernel depending on whether the kernel, interrupt, or task (process) is currently being executed. It is not something that users of the RTOS API will normally need to worry about.

Initialization of the stack and heap takes place in `Chapter_*\startup\startup_stm32f767xx.s`. The exact size of the main stack is defined in the linker script `STM32F767ZI_FLASH.ld`. If necessary, the size of the stack and heap available to the system before the FreeRTOS scheduler is started can be adjusted by modifying `_Min_Heap_Size` or `_Min_Stack_Size`:

```
_Min_Heap_Size = 0x200; /* required amount of heap */
_Min_Stack_Size = 0x400; /* required amount of stack */
```

It is best to try and keep these both to minimal sizes since any RAM used here will be unavailable to the tasks. These stacks/heaps are only for code that is run before the scheduler is started, as well as the ISRs. This is *not* the same stack that is used by any of the tasks.

Occasionally, you may run into a problem where you'll need to run some memory-intensive initialization code (the USB stack is a good example of this). If the initialization functions are called outside of a task (before the scheduler starts), then they will use the main stack. In order to keep this stack as small as possible and allow more memory to be used for tasks, move memory-intensive initialization inside a task This will allow the RTOS heap to have the additional RAM that would have gone unused after initialization had the main stack size been increased.

The FreeRTOS kernel manipulates the **process stack pointer** (**PSP**) to point to the task stack that has context (is in the running state).

 For the most part, you won't need to be immediately concerned with the various stack pointers—they are taken care of by the kernel and C runtime. If you happen to be developing code that will transition between an RTOS and *bare metal* (that is, a bootloader), then you will need to understand how/when to properly switch the current stack pointer.

The most important thing to keep in mind with stacks is that they must be adequately sized to hold all of the local variables that a task will execute for the deepest call level. We'll discuss ways of getting a handle on this in the *Keeping an eye on stack space* section.

Heap memory

The heap is the portion of memory that is used when a dynamic allocation using `malloc` is called. It is also where a FreeRTOS task stack and **task control block** (**TCB**) are stored when they are created by calling `xTaskCreate()`.

In an MCU FreeRTOS system, there will typically be two heaps created:

- **System heap**: Defined in the startup and linker scripts described previously. This will *not* be available for use by the final application code when allocating space for RTOS primitives.
- **FreeRTOS heap**: Used when creating tasks and other primitives and defined in *Inc\FreeRTOSConfig.h*. It can be resized by adjusting the following line:

  ```
  #define configTOTAL_HEAP_SIZE ((size_t)15360)
  ```

Currently, this line is defining a 15 KB heap. This heap must be adequately sized to accommodate the following:

- Stacks (and **TCBs**) for all tasks that are created using `xTaskCreate`
- Queues, semaphores, mutexes, event groups, and software timers created using `x*Create`

Here's a visual representation of where all of the different variables will come from:

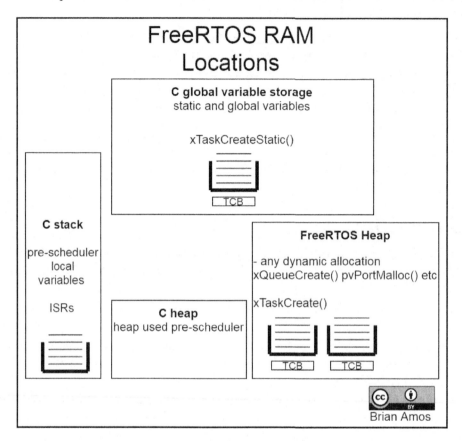

There are two possible locations for FreeRTOS primitives and stacks:

- Statically allocated space for a stack and a **TCB**, passed to a task when calling `xTaskCreateStatic()`
- Dynamically allocated space for a stack/TCB, created when calling `xTaskCreate()`

The C heap is only used for any items that are created without the use of the FreeRTOS heap implementation, while the C stack is only used before the scheduler is started, as well as by ISRs. When using an RTOS, it is best to minimize the size of the C heap as much as possible, or entirely. This will leave more available RAM to allocate to the RTOS heap or static variables.

Heap fragmentation

In an embedded system with limited RAM, heap fragmentation can be a very serious issue. A heap becomes fragmented when items are loaded into the heap and then removed at different points in time. The problem is that if many items that are being removed aren't adjacent to one another, a larger contiguous region of space won't necessarily be available:

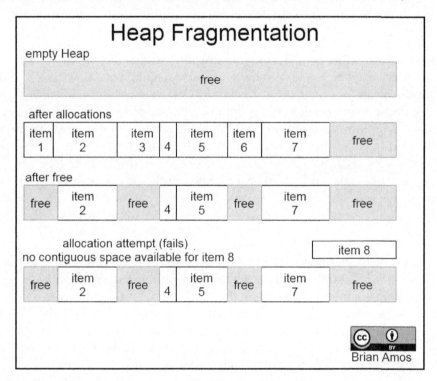

In the preceding example, space won't be successfully allocated for item 8. Even though there is sufficient free space, there isn't enough *contiguous* free space to accommodate the size of item 8. This is especially problematic because it will only occur at runtime, and under certain circumstances that are dependent on the size and timing of when items in the heap are allocated and freed.

Now that we've covered the basics of memory allocation, let's look at some different ways that FreeRTOS primitives can be created to be placed in static or heap memory.

Static and dynamic allocation of FreeRTOS primitives

Details on the mechanics of creating tasks were covered in Chapter 7, *The FreeRTOS Scheduler*. Here, we will only focus on the differences in *where* the memory is coming from and what its *lifetime* is. This will help illuminate the implications of choosing different allocation schemes.

Memory for tasks can either be allocated dynamically or statically. Dynamic allocation allows the memory used by the task to be returned by calling vTaskDelete() if the task no longer needs to run (see Chapter 7, *The FreeRTOS Scheduler*, for details). Dynamic allocation can occur at any point in the program, whereas static allocation occurs before the program starts. The static variants of FreeRTOS API calls follow the same initialization scheme—the standard calls use dynamic allocation (pulling memory from the FreeRTOS heap). All FreeRTOS API functions with CreateStatic in their names (such as xTaskCreateStatic) take additional arguments for referencing preallocated memory. As opposed to the dynamic allocation approach, the memory passed to *CreateStatic variants will typically be statically allocated buffers, which are present for the entire program's lifetime.

While the naming of the *CreateStatic API variants suggests that the memory is static, this isn't actually a requirement. For example, you could allocate a buffer memory on the stack and pass the pointer to a *CreateStatic API function call; however, you'll need to be sure that the lifetime of the primitive created is limited to that function! You may also find it useful to allocate memory using an allocation scheme outside of the FreeRTOS heap, in which case you could also use the *CreateStatic API variants. If you choose to utilize either of these methods, then to avoid memory corruption, you'll need to have detailed knowledge of the lifetime of both the FreeRTOS primitive being created and the allocated memory!

Dynamic allocation examples

Nearly all of the code presented has used dynamic allocation to create FreeRTOS primitives (tasks, queues, mutexes, and so on). Here are two examples to serve as a quick refresher before we look at the differences between creating primitives using static allocation.

Creating a task

When a task is created using dynamically allocated memory, the call will look something like this (see Chapter 7, *The FreeRTOS Scheduler*, for more details on the parameters that are not related to memory allocation):

```
BaseType_t retVal = xTaskCreate( Task1, "task1", StackSizeWords, NULL,
        tskIDLE_PRIORITY + 2, tskHandlePtr);
assert_param(retVal != pdPASS);
```

There are a few relevant pieces of information, relevant to memory allocation, to note about this call:

- The call to xTaskCreate may fail. This is because there is no guarantee that enough space will be available for storing the task's stack and TCB on the FreeRTOS heap. The only way to ensure that it was created successfully is to check the return value, retVal.
- The only parameter to do with a stack is the requested size of the stack.

When created in this manner, if it is appropriate for a task to terminate itself, it may call xTaskDelete(NULL) and the memory associated with the task's stack and TCB will be available to be reused.

The following are a few points to note regarding dynamic allocation:

- Primitive creation may fail at runtime if no heap space is available.
- All memory that FreeRTOS allocates for the primitive will be automatically freed when the task is deleted (as long as Heap_1 is not used and INCLUDE_vTaskDelete is set to 1 in FreeRTOSConfig.h). This doesn't include memory that was dynamically allocated by *user*-supplied code in the actual task; the RTOS is unaware of any dynamic allocation initiated by user-supplied code. It is up to you to free this code when appropriate.

- `configSUPPORT_DYNAMIC_ALLOCATION` must be set to 1 in `FreeRTOSConfig.h` for dynamic allocation to be available:

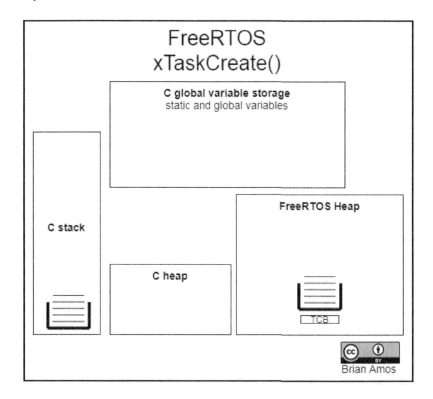

When creating a task using dynamic allocation, all of the memory used for the task, the task's stack, and **TCB** is allocated from the FreeRTOS heap, as shown in the preceding diagram.

Next, let's take a look at the different ways of creating queues.

Creating a queue

For a detailed explanation and working examples regarding how to create queues using dynamically allocated memory, see `Chapter 9`, *Intertask* Communication, in the section on *Passing data through queues by value*. As a quick review, to create a queue of length `LED_CMD_QUEUE_LEN` that holds elements of the `uint8_t` type, we'd go through the following steps:

1. Create the queue:

```
ledCmdQueue = xQueueCreate(LED_CMD_QUEUE_LEN,
                                sizeof(uint8_t));
```

2. Verify that the queue was created successfully by checking the handle, `ledCmdQueue`, is not `NULL`:

```
assert_param(ledCmdQueue != NULL);
```

Now that we've reviewed a few examples of dynamic allocation (which will pull memory during runtime from the FreeRTOS heap), let's move on to static allocation (which reserves memory during compilation/linking, before the application is ever run).

Static allocation examples

FreeRTOS also has a method for creating primitives that don't require us to dynamically allocate memory. This is an example of creating primitives with statically allocated memory.

Creating a task

To create a task using a preallocated stack and TCB (requiring no dynamic allocation), use a call similar to the following:

```
StackType_t GreenTaskStack[STACK_SIZE];
StaticTask_t GreenTaskTCB;
TaskHandle_t greenHandle = NULL;
greenHandle = xTaskCreateStatic(    GreenTask, "GreenTask", STACK_SIZE,
                                    NULL, tskIDLE_PRIORITY + 2,
                                    GreenTaskStack, &GreenTaskTCB);
assert_param( greenHandle != NULL );
```

There are several notable differences between this static allocation and the previous method of dynamic allocation:

- Instead of a return value of `pdPASS`, the `xTaskCreateStatic` function returns a task handle.
- Task creation using `xTaskCreateStatic` will always succeed, provided that the stack pointer and TCB pointers are non-null.
- As an alternative to checking the `TaskHandle_t`, `StackType_t` and `StaticTask_t` could be checked instead; as long as they are not `NULL`, the task will always be successfully created.
- Tasks can also be *deleted*, even if they were created with `xTaskCreateStatic`. FreeRTOS will only take the steps necessary to remove the task from the scheduler; freeing associated memory is the responsibility of the caller.

Here's where the task's stack and TCB are located when we use the previous call:

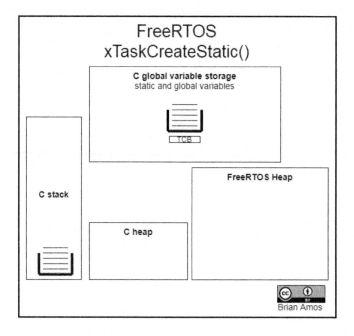

Static creation allows more flexibility in memory allocation than the name implies. Strictly speaking, a call to `vTaskDelete` will only remove a statically created task from the schedule. Since FreeRTOS will no longer access memory from that task's stack or TCB, it is safe to repurpose this memory for other purposes. It is conceivably possible to allocate the stack and TCB from the stack memory rather than static memory. An example of deleting a task created using `xTaskCreateStatic` can be found in `main_staticTask_Delete.c`.

Creating a queue

Now let's take a look at the steps for creating a queue using static memory for both the buffer and queue structure. This code is an excerpt from `mainStaticQueueCreation.c`:

1. Define a variable for holding the queue structure used by FreeRTOS:

   ```
   static StaticQueue_t queueStructure;
   ```

2. Create a raw array, appropriately sized to hold the queue contents:
   - A simple C array of the target datatype can be used; in this case, our queue will hold a datatype of `uint8_t`.
   - Use `#define` to define the array length:

     ```
     #define LED_CMD_QUEUE_LEN 2
     static uint8_t queueStorage[LED_CMD_QUEUE_LEN];
     ```

3. Create the queue within the same length as the array that was previously defined:

   ```
   ledCmdQueue = xQueueCreateStatic(LED_CMD_QUEUE_LEN,
   sizeof(uint8_t), queueStorage, &queueStructure );
   ```

   Here's a breakdown of the parameters:

   - `LED_CMD_QUEUE_LEN`: Number of elements in the queue
   - `sizeof(uint8_t)`: Size of each element (in bytes)
   - `queueStorage`: Raw array used for storing elements in the queue (used only by FreeRTOS)
   - `queueStructure`: Pointer to `StatisQueue_t`, the queue structure used internally by FreeRTOS

4. Check the queue handle `ledCmdQueue`, to ensure that the queue was correctly created by verifying that it is not `NULL`. Unlike dynamically allocated queues, it is unlikely that this call will fail, but leaving the check ensures that if the queue is ever changed to be dynamically allocated, errors will still be caught:

   ```
   assert_param(ledCmdQueue != NULL);
   ```

5. Put it all together:

   ```
   static QueueHandle_t ledCmdQueue = NULL;
   static StaticQueue_t queueStructure;
   #define LED_CMD_QUEUE_LEN 2
   ```

```
static uint8_t queueStorage[LED_CMD_QUEUE_LEN];
ledCmdQueue = xQueueCreateStatic(LED_CMD_QUEUE_LEN,
            sizeof(uint8_t),
            queueStorage, &queueStructure );
assert_param(ledCmdQueue != NULL);
```

The only difference between creating queues with static allocation and creating them with dynamic allocation is how the memory is supplied—both calls return queue handles. Now that we've seen examples of creating queues and tasks without using dynamically allocated memory, what happens if we have a requirement for *no* dynamic allocation to take place?

Eliminating all dynamic allocation

In most of the examples that we've seen, we've focused on working with the dynamic allocation scheme variants when creating FreeRTOS primitives. This has been primarily for ease of use and brevity, enabling us to focus on the core RTOS concepts rather than worrying about exactly where memory was coming from and how we were accessing it.

All FreeRTOS primitives can be created with either dynamically allocated memory or preallocated memory. To avoid all dynamic allocation, simply use the CreateStatic version of a create function, as we've done in the preceding example when we created a task. Some CreateStatic versions exist for queues, mutexes, semaphores, stream buffers, message buffers, event groups, and timers. They share the same arguments as their dynamic counterparts, but also require a pointer to preallocated memory to be passed to them. The CreateStatic equivalents don't require any memory allocation to take place during runtime.

You would consider using the static equivalents for the following reasons:

- They are guaranteed to never fail because of a lack of memory.
- All of the checks that are needed to ensure memory is available happen during linking (before the application binary is created). If memory is not available, it will fail at link time, rather than runtime.
- Many standards targeting safety-critical applications prohibit the use of dynamically allocated memory.
- Internal embedded C coding standards will occasionally prohibit the use of dynamic allocation.

Memory fragmentation could be added to this list as well, but this isn't an issue unless memory is freed (for example, `heap_1` could be used to eliminate heap fragmentation concerns).

Now that we have an understanding of the differences between dynamic and static allocation, let's dive into the differences of FreeRTOS's dynamic allocation schemes—the five heap implementations. Moving ahead, we will see what these different definitions look like in a file (globals, static allocation, and so on). We will also understand the difference between the main stack and task-based stacks where they live in a FreeRTOS heap.

Comparing FreeRTOS heap implementations

Because FreeRTOS targets such a wide range of MCUs and applications, it ships with five different dynamic allocation schemes, all of which are implemented with a heap. The different heap implementations allow different levels of heap functionality. They are included in the `portable/MemMang` directory as `heap_1.c`, `heap_2.c`, `heap_3.c`, `heap_4.c`, and `heap_5.c`.

A note on memory pools:

 Many other RTOSes include memory pools as an implementation for dynamic memory allocation. A memory pool achieves dynamic allocation by only allocating and freeing fixed-size blocks. By fixing the block size, the problem of fragmentation is avoided in memory-constrained environments.

The downside to memory pools is that the blocks need to be sized for each specific application. If they are too large, they will waste precious RAM; too small, and they'll be unable to hold large items. In order to make things easier on users and avoid wasting RAM, Richard Barry elected to exclusively use heaps for dynamic allocation in FreeRTOS.

In order for projects to properly link after compilation, it is important to only have one of the heap implementations visible to the linker. This can either be accomplished by removing the unused files or not including the unused heap files in the list of files available to the linker. For this book, the extra files in `Middleware\Third_Party\FreeRTOS\Source\portable\MemMang` have been removed. For this chapter, however, all of the original implementations are included in `Chapter_15\Src\MemMang`: it is the only place where examples use a heap other than `heap_4.c`.

All of the various heap options exist to enable a project to get exactly the functionality it needs without requiring anything more (in terms of program space or configuration). They also allow for trade-offs between flexibility and deterministic timing. The following is a list of the various heap options:

- `heap_1`: Allocation only—no freeing is allowed. This is best suited for simple applications that don't free anything after initial creation. This implementation, along with `heap_2`, provides the most deterministic timing since neither heap ever performs a search for adjacent free blocks to combine.
- `heap_2`: Allocation and freeing are both allowed, but adjacent free blocks are not combined. This limits appropriate use cases to those applications that can know/guarantee they are reusing a number of items that are the same size each time. This heap implementation is not a great fit for applications that make use of `vPortMalloc` and `vPortFree` explicitly (for example, applications that allocate memory dynamically themselves), unless there is a very large degree of discipline in ensuring that only a small subset of possible sizes are used.
- `heap_3`: Wraps standard `malloc`/`free` implementations to provide thread safety.
- `heap_4`: The same as `heap_2` but combines adjacent free space. Allows locating the entire heap by giving an absolute address. Well suited for applications to use dynamic allocation.
- `heap_5`: The same as `heap_4` but allows for creating a heap that is distributed across different noncontiguous memory regions—for example, a heap could be scattered across internal and external RAM.

Here's a quick comparison between all of the heap implementations:

Heap name	Thread safe	Allocation	Free	Combine adjacent free space	Multiple memory regions	Determinism
heap_1.c	✓	✓				↑
heap_2.c	✓	✓	✓			↑
heap_3.c	✓	✓	✓	✓*		?
heap_4.c	✓	✓	✓	✓		→
heap_5.c	✓	✓	✓	✓	✓	→
std C lib	?	✓	✓	✓*		?

(*) Most, if not all, included heap implementations will combine free space.

Since determinism is dependent on the C library implementation that we happen to be using, it isn't possible to provide general guidance here. Typically, general-purpose heap implementations are created to minimize fragmentation, which requires additional CPU resources (time) and decreases the determinism of the timing, depending on how much memory is moved around.

Each C implementation may approach dynamic allocation differently. Some will make adding thread safety as easy as defining implementations for __mallock_lock and __malloc_unlock, in which case a single mutex is all that is required. In other cases, they will require a few implementations for implementing mutex functionality.

Choosing your RTOS heap implementation

So, how do you go about choosing which heap implementation to use? First, you need to ensure that you're able to use dynamic allocation (many standards for safety-critical applications disallow it). If you don't need to free allocated memory, then heap_1.c is a potential option (as is avoiding a heap entirely).

From a coding perspective, the main difference between using `heap_1` and static allocation is when the checks for memory availability are performed. When using the `*CreateStatic` variants, you'll be notified at link time that you don't have enough memory to support the newly created primitive. This requires a few extra lines of code each time a primitive is created (to allocate buffers used by the primitive). When using `heap_1`, as long as checks are performed (see Chapter 7, *The FreeRTOS Scheduler*) to determine task creation success, then the checking will be performed at runtime. Many applications that are appropriate for the `heap_1` implementation will also create all required tasks before starting the scheduler. Using dynamic memory allocation in this way isn't much different from static allocation; it simply moves the checking from link time to runtime, while reducing the amount of code required to create each RTOS primitive.

If you're working on an application that only requires *one* datatype to be freed, `heap_2` might be an option. If you choose to go down this route, you'll need to be very careful to document this limitation for future maintainers of the code. Failure to understand the limited use case of `heap_2` can easily result in memory fragmentation. In the worst-case scenario, fragmentation might potentially occur after the application has been running for an extended period of time and might not occur until the final code has been released and the hardware is fielded.

When dynamic memory is used, then `heap_3`, `heap_4`, or `heap_5` can be used. As mentioned earlier, `heap_3` simply wraps whatever C runtime implementation of `malloc` and `free` is available, to make it thread safe so it can be used by multiple tasks. This means that its behavior is going to be dependent on the underlying runtime implementation. If your system has RAM in several different, noncontiguous memory locations (for example, internal and external RAM) then `heap_5` can be used to combine all of these locations into one heap; otherwise, `heap_4` provides the same allocation, freeing, and adjacent block collation capabilities as `heap_5`. These are the two general-purpose heap implementations. Since they include code that will collate free blocks, it is possible that they will run for different periods of time when freeing memory. In general, it is best to avoid calls to `vPortMalloc` and `vPortFree` in code that requires a high degree of determinism. In `heap_4` and `heap_5`, calls to `vPortFree` will have the most amount of timing variability, since this is when adjacent block collation occurs.

In general, avoiding dynamic allocation will help to provide more robust code with less effort—memory leaks and fragmentation are impossible if memory is never freed. On the other end of the spectrum, if your application makes use of standard library functions, such as `printf` and string manipulation, you'll likely need to replace the versions of `malloc` and `free` that were included with thread-safe implementations. Let's take a quick look at what's involved in making sure other parts of the application don't end up using a heap implementation that isn't thread safe.

Replacing malloc and free

Many C runtimes will ship with an implementation of `malloc`, but the embedded, oriented versions won't necessarily be thread safe by default. Because each C runtime is different, the steps needed to make `malloc` thread safe will vary. The included STM toolchain used in this book includes `newlib-nano` as the C runtime library. The following are a few notes regarding `newlib-nano`:

- `newlib-nano` uses `malloc` and `realloc` for `stdio.h` functionality (that is, `printf`).
- `realloc` is not directly supported by FreeRTOS heap implementations.
- `FreeRTOSConfig.h` includes the `configUSE_NEWLIB_REENTRANT` setting to make `newlib` thread safe, but it needs to be used in conjunction with the appropriate implementations of all stubs. This will allow you to use newlib-based `printf`, `strtok`, and so on in a thread-safe manner. This option also makes general use case calls to `malloc` and `free` safe to use from anywhere, without you needing to explicitly use `pvPortMalloc` and `vPortFree`.

> See the Dave Nadler link in the *Further reading* section for more information and detailed instructions on how to use `newlib` safely in a FreeRTOS project with the GNU toolchain.

Luckily, there aren't any calls to raw `malloc` in the example code included in this book. Normally, the STM HAL USB CDC implementation would include a call to `malloc`, but this was converted to a statically defined variable instead, which enables us to simply use the heap implementations included with FreeRTOS.

> The `malloc` call in the STM-supplied USB stack was especially sinister because it occurred inside the USB interrupt, which makes it especially difficult to guarantee thread safety during `malloc`. This is because, for every call to `malloc`, interrupts would need to be disabled from within the tasks and also within interrupts that made calls to `malloc` (USB in this case). Rather than go through this trouble, the dynamic allocation was removed altogether.

Now that we've come to terms with different safety options using dynamic allocation, let's take a look at some additional tools that FreeRTOS has for reporting the health of our stacks and heaps.

Implementing FreeRTOS memory hooks

When many people first start programming in an RTOS, one of the immediate challenges is figuring out how to properly size the stack for each task. This can lead to some frustration during development because when a stack is overrun, the symptoms can range from odd behavior to a full system crash.

Keeping an eye on stack space

`vApplicationStackOverflowHook` provides a very simple way of eliminating most of the oddball behavior and halting the application. When enabling `configCHECK_FOR_STACK_OVERFLOW #define` in `FreeRTOSConfig.h`, any time a stack overflow is detected by FreeRTOS, `vApplicationStackOverflowHook` will be called.

There are two potential values for `configCHECK_FOR_STACK_OVERFLOW`:

- `#define configCHECK_FOR_STACK_OVERFLOW 1`: Checks the stack pointer location upon task exit.
- `#define configCHECK_FOR_STACK_OVERFLOW 2`: Fills the stack with a known pattern and checks for the pattern upon exit.

The first method checks the task stack pointer as the task exits the running state. If the stack pointer is pointing to an invalid location (where the stack shouldn't be), then an overflow has occurred:

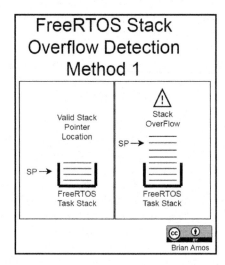

This method is very fast, but it has the potential to miss some stack overflows—for example, if the stack has grown beyond its originally allocated space, but the stack pointer happens to be pointing to a valid spot when checked, then the overflow will be missed. To combat this, a second method is also available.

When setting `configCHECK_FOR_STACK_OVERFLOW` to 2, method 1 will be used, but a second method will also be employed. Instead of simply checking where the stack pointer is located after the task has exited the running state, the top 16 bytes of the stack can be watermarked and analyzed upon exit. This way, if at any point during the task run the stack has overflowed and the data in the top 16 bytes has been modified, an overflow will be detected:

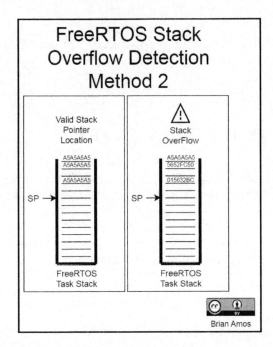

This method helps to ensure that, even if a stack overflow has occurred (or nearly occurred) at any point during the task execution, it will be detected, as long as the overflow passed through the upper 16 words of the stack.

 While these methods are good for catching stack overflows, they are not perfect—for example, if an array is declared on a task stack and extends past the end of the stack with only the end of the array being modified, then a stack overflow won't be detected.

So, to implement a very simple hook that will stop execution when a stack overflow occurs, we'll take the following simple steps:

1. In `FreeRTOSConfig.h`, define the configuration flag:

    ```
    #define configCHECK_FOR_STACK_OVERFLOW 2
    ```

2. In a `*.c` file, add the stack overflow hook:

    ```
    void vApplicationStackOverflowHook( void )
    {
     __disable_irq();
     while(1);
    }
    ```

This very simple method disables all interrupts and executes an infinite loop, leaving no question that something has gone wrong. At this point, a debugger can be used to analyze which stack has overflowed.

Keeping an eye on heap space

If your application makes regular use of the FreeRTOS heap, then you should strongly consider using the `configUSE_MALLOC_FAILED_HOOK` configuration and associated hook, `vApplicationMallocFailedHook`. This hook is called anytime a call to `pvMalloc()` fails.

> Of course, while you're doing this, you're being a responsible programmer and checking the return value of `malloc` and handling these error cases anyway... so this hook may be redundant.

The steps for setting this up are the same as in the previous hook:

1. Add the following in `FreeRTOSConfig.h`:

    ```
    #define configUSE_MALLOC_FAILED_HOOK 1
    ```

2. In a `*.c` file, add the failed `malloc` hook:

    ```
    void vApplicationMallocFailedHook( void )
    {
     __disable_irq();
     while(1);
    }
    ```

There are also two helpful API functions that can be called on a regular basis to help get a general sense of the available space:

- `xPortGetFreeHeapSize()`
- `xPortGetMinimumEverFreeHeapSize()`

These functions return the available heap space and the least amount of free heap space ever recorded. They don't, however, give any clue as to whether or not the free space is fragmented into small blocks.

So, what happens if none of these safeguards provide enough peace of mind that each of your tasks is playing nicely with the rest of the system? Read on!

Using a memory protection unit (MPU)

A **memory protection unit** (MPU) continuously monitors memory access at a hardware level to make absolutely certain that only legal memory accesses are occurring; otherwise, an interrupt is raised and immediate action can be taken. This allows many common errors (which might otherwise go unnoticed for a period of time) to be immediately detected.

Problems like stack overflows that make a stack flow into the memory space reserved for another task are immediately caught when using an MPU, even if they can't be detected by `vApplicationStackOverflowHook`. Buffer overflows and pointer errors are also stopped dead in their tracks when an MPU is utilized, which makes for a more robust application.

The STM32F767 MCU includes an MPU. In order to make use of it, the MPU-enabled port must be used: `GCC\ARM_CM4_MPU`. This way, restricted tasks can be created by using `xTaskCreateRestricted`, which contains the following additional parameters:

```
typedef struct xTASK_PARAMTERS
{
 pdTASK_CODE pvTaskCode;
 const signed char * const pcName;
 unsigned short usStackDepth;
 void *pvParameters;
 unsigned portBASE_TYPE uxPriority;
 portSTACK_TYPE *puxStackBuffer;
 xMemoryRegion xRegions[ portNUM_CONFIGURABLE_REGIONS ];
} xTaskParameters;
```

Restricted tasks have limited execution and memory access rights.

`xTaskCreate` can be used to create tasks that either operate as standard user mode tasks or privileged mode tasks. In privileged mode, a task has access to the entire memory map, whereas in user mode, it only has access to its own flash and RAM that isn't configured for privileged access only.

In order for all of this to come together, the MPU ports of FreeRTOS also require variables to be defined in the linker file:

Variable name	Description
`__FLASH_segment_start__`	The start address of the flash memory
`__FLASH_segment_end__`	The end address of the flash memory
`__privileged_functions_end__`	The end address of the `privileged_functions` named section
`__SRAM_segment_start__`	The start address of the SRAM memory
`__SRAM_segment_end__`	The end address of the SRAM memory
`__privileged_data_start__`	The start address of the `privileged_data` section
`__privileged_data_end__`	The end address of the `privileged_data` section

These variables will be placed into the `*.LD` file.

Congratulations! You're now ready to develop your application using the MPU to protect against invalid data access.

Summary

In this chapter, we've covered static and dynamic memory allocation, all of the available heap implementations in FreeRTOS, and how to implement memory hooks that let us keep an eye on our stacks and heaps. By understanding the trade-offs to be made when using the different allocation schemes, you'll be in a good position to choose the most appropriate method for each of your future projects.

In the next chapter, we'll discuss some of the details of using FreeRTOS in a multicore environment.

Questions

As we conclude, here is a list of questions for you to test your knowledge regarding this chapter's material. You will find the answers in the *Assessments* section of the Appendix:

1. With FreeRTOS, using dynamically allocated memory is extremely safe because it guards against heap fragmentation:
   - True
   - False

2. FreeRTOS requires dynamically allocated memory to function:
   - True
   - False

3. How many different heap implementations ship with FreeRTOS?
4. Name two hook functions that can be used to notify you about problems with the heap or stack.
5. What is an MPU used for?

Further reading

- *The Power of 10: Rules for Developing Safety-Critical Code* by *Gerard J. Holzmann*: http://web.eecs.umich.edu/~imarkov/10rules.pdf
- Dave Nadler – newlib and FreeRTOS re-entry: http://www.nadler.com/embedded/newlibAndFreeRTOS.html
- FreeRTOS stack overflow checking: https://www.freertos.org/Stacks-and-stack-overflow-checking.html

16
Multi-Processor and Multi-Core Systems

So far, we've discussed many different ways of programming a single **microcontroller unit** (**MCU**). But what if the task at hand requires more processing than a single-core MCU can supply? What if the mechanical constraints of the system dictate the use of multiple MCUs physically distributed in the system while working together to complete a task? What about cases where reliability is paramount and a single failed processor results in a catastrophic system failure? All of these cases require the use of more than one processing core and, in some cases, more than one MCU.

This chapter explores multi-core and multi-processor solutions and their different applications. First, we'll take a look at the different design requirements that might drive a multi-core/processor solution. We'll then dive a bit deeper into the different ways FreeRTOS can be used in multi-core/processor systems. Finally, some recommendations on choosing an inter-processor communication scheme will be presented.

In a nutshell, we will cover the following topics:

- Introducing multi-core and multi-processor systems
- Exploring multi-core systems
- Exploring multi-processor systems
- Exploring inter-processor communication
- Choosing between multi-core and multi-processor systems

Technical requirements

There are no technical requirements for this chapter.

Introducing multi-core and multi-processor systems

First, let's get our terminology straight. A **multi-core** design is a single chip with multiple CPUs inside it, with at least some memory shared between the cores:

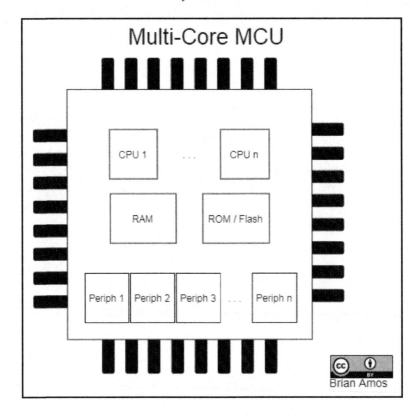

Multi-core parts span a very broad range, from the larger, 64-bit parts that have multiple identical CPU cores to the ARM big.LITTLE architecture, which incorporates both high-bandwidth CPUs and power-conscious MCUs in the same package. Recently, multi-core MCUs have also become more commonly available. **Graphics processing units (GPUs)** can also be grouped into the multi-core category.

A **multi-processor system** is one where there are multiple processor chips in the design. For the purposes of our discussions here, these chips can reside on the same **printed circuit board assembly (PCBA)** or different PCBAs distributed throughout a larger system:

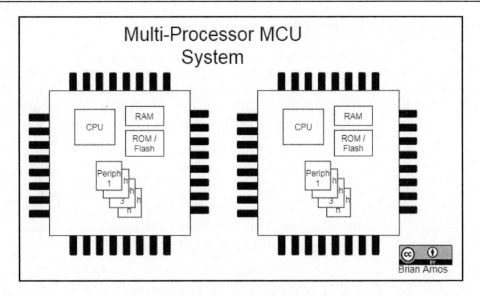

Both multi-core and multi-processor topologies can be found in many different places, such as smartphones, small networked sensing devices, industrial automation equipment, test equipment, medical equipment, appliances, and of course, a range of computing devices, such as desktops, laptops, and so on.

There are many different driving forces for using these two different topologies, beyond a simple need for more or faster processing. Sometimes, a system needs to come online *instantly*, without waiting for a full **general-purpose operating system** (**GPOS**) to boot. Occasionally, there are regulatory requirements that are easier to meet by segregating system functions into multiple cores (and code bases) so that only a portion of the total code (or system) is required to go through a stringent review. There could be electro-mechanical considerations in a system (such as long wire runs to motors/actuators or sensitive analog signals) that are best addressed by having a processor in close physical proximity. In high-reliability systems, redundancy is very common.

Now we have a general idea of the terminology, let's get into some additional details and use cases for these systems, starting with multi-core designs.

Exploring multi-core systems

First, let's cover a few different types of multi-core systems. They have two primary types of configurations/architectures: heterogeneous and homogeneous. A heterogeneous system is one that has multiple cores, but they are different in some way. Contrast this with a homogeneous system, where all CPUs can be treated identically and interchangeably.

Heterogeneous multi-core systems

A heterogeneous multi-core system has at least two processing cores in the same device and includes differences in either the processor architecture of the core or the way the cores access shared resources, such as system memory, peripherals, or I/O. For example, at the lower end of the spectrum, we can have multiple MCU cores on the same chip. The LPC54100 series from NXP incorporates a Cortex-M0+ and a Cortex-M4, both running at 150 Mhz, in the same package.

In this device, the MCU cores are different, but their connection to system peripherals is identical—except for instruction and data buses, which are only available on the Cortex-M4:

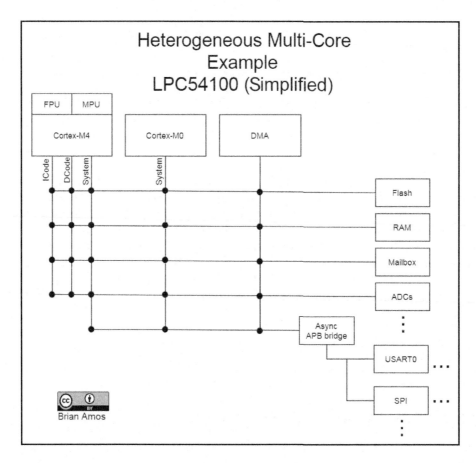

We can use systems like these in different ways:

- **Segmenting hard real-time operations from more general-purpose computing**: The M0+ could handle low-level peripheral or hardware access/control, while the M4 handles the higher-level functionality required, such as GUIs and connectivity.
- **Power conscious design**: Low-level control and interfacing is performed on the lower-power M0+, only activating the M4 when computationally expensive operations are required.

Since the LPC54100 has two MCU cores, we'll focus on bare-metal programming (no operating system) and operating systems that don't require a full-blown **memory management unit** (**MMU**), such as FreeRTOS. Running different (or multiple copies of the same) operating systems on the two cores is called **asymmetric multi-processing**.

The name *asymmetric* comes from the fact that the two cores are treated differently from one another—there is *asymmetry* between them. This is quite a bit different from the *symmetric* multi-core approached used on desktop-based operating systems, where the various cores are all treated equally. Symmetric multi-core systems will be covered in the *Homogeneous multi-core systems* section.

For example, we could run multiple copies of FreeRTOS on each of the two cores:

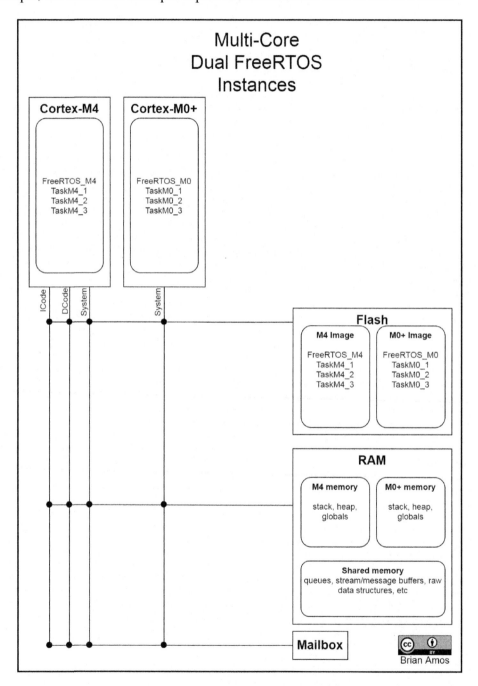

In a configuration like this, the two cores run completely independently from one another. Even though FreeRTOS is being run on both cores, there is no flash program space shared between the cores—each core has a firmware image that is independent from the other. RAM behaves in the same way—the full RAM memory space is available to both cores, but by default, each core will receive its own area for stack, heap, global variables, and so on.

So, each core is running its own program—how do the two programs coordinate activities between each other? We need some way of passing information back and forth—but how?

Inter-core communication

Information sharing between the cores is possible, but is subject to the same concurrent-access considerations that any other multi-threaded environment has, which is why mailbox hardware is typically included onchip. This hardware is dedicated to facilitating communication between the two cores. Mailboxes will generally have the following features:

- **Hardware mutex functionality**: Used to protect RAM shared between the two cores. The idea is identical to mutexes in a pure software environment—they are used to provide mutually exclusive access to a shared resource.
- **Interrupts to/from each core**: These interrupts can be raised by a core after writing data to a shared area of memory, alerting the other core that a message/data is available.

Legacy application extension

We're not limited to running FreeRTOS on both cores—any mixture of RTOSes or bare metal can be mixed or matched between the cores. Let's say a bare-metal legacy application already existed but some new additional functionality was required to take advantage of a new opportunity. For example, to stay competitive, the device might need a *facelift* and have a GUI, web frontend, or IoT stack build added to it. The new functionality could potentially be developed separately from the underlying legacy code, leaving the legacy code largely intact and undisturbed.

For example, the legacy code could be run on the Cortex-M0+, while the new functionality is added to the Cortex-M4:

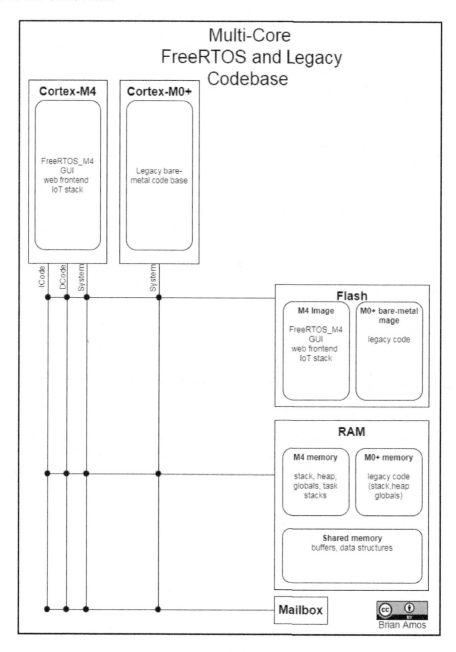

In a setup like this, whether shared RAM is used as a data exchange between the cores will depend greatly on how comfortable a team is in modifying the legacy code base and how the application is structured. For example, rather than modifying an existing code base to use proper mailbox-implemented mutexes before accessing a shared data structure, it might be preferable to use a pre-existing hardware interface as the data transfer mechanism, treating the secondary CPU more like an external client. Since many legacy systems use UARTs as the primary interface to the system, it is possible to use these data streams as an interface between the processors, keeping modifications to the legacy code to a minimum:

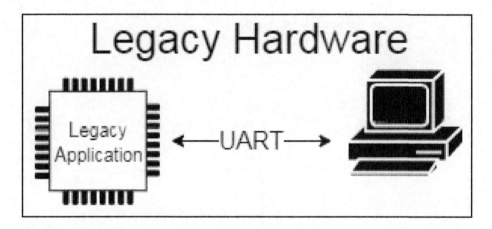

This approach avoids significant modifications to the legacy code base at the expense of using a slower interface (physical peripherals are slower and more CPU-intensive than simple memory transfers) and routing signals outside the processor. Although far from ideal, this approach can be used to test the viability of a new opportunity before investing significant engineering effort in a more elegant solution:

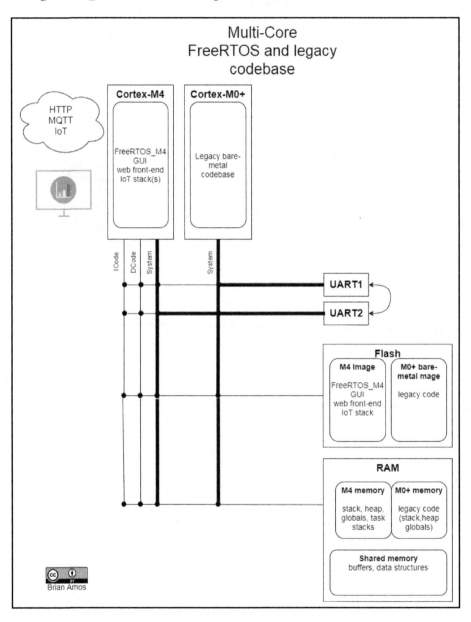

This type of approach allows the team to focus on developing new interfaces for an existing system—whose core functionality doesn't need to change—with minimal impact on the original system.

Depending on the circumstances, it may also make more sense to leave the legacy code on the original MCU, rather than porting it to a core inside a new MCU. Each project will likely have its own the constraints required to guide this decision. Although all of this this might look like a simple task from a very high level, each project usually has some hidden complexities that need to be considered.

High-demand hard real-time systems

At the other end of the heterogenous multi-core spectrum from an NXP LPC54100 would be a device such as the NXP i.Mx8, which contains two Cortex-A72s, four Cortex-A53s, two Cortex-M4Fs, one DSP, and two GPUs. A system such as this one will generally be used where extremely computationally intensive operations are required, in addition to low-latency or hard real-time interactions with hardware. Computer vision, AI, on-target adaptive machine learning, and advanced closed-loop control systems are all reasonable applications for the i.Mx8. So, instead of incorporating an i.Mx8 (or similar CPU) into a product, why not use a more general purpose computing solution for a system that requires this much computing power? After all, general-purpose computers have had GPUs and multi-core CPUs for a decade or more, right?

In some systems, it might be perfectly acceptable to run a more general-purpose computing hardware and operating system. However, when there are *hard real-time requirements* (the system is considered to have failed if a real-time deadline was missed), a GPOS won't be sufficient. A compelling reason for using a device such as the i.Mx8, rather than simply a GPOS on top of a CPU/GPU combination, is that hard real-time capable low-latency cores such as the Cortex-M4 are used to handle hard real-time tasks, where extremely reliable low latency is paramount. The higher-throughput hardware is used for doing the computationally *heavy lifting* operations, where throughput is important, but higher latency and less determinism can be tolerated:

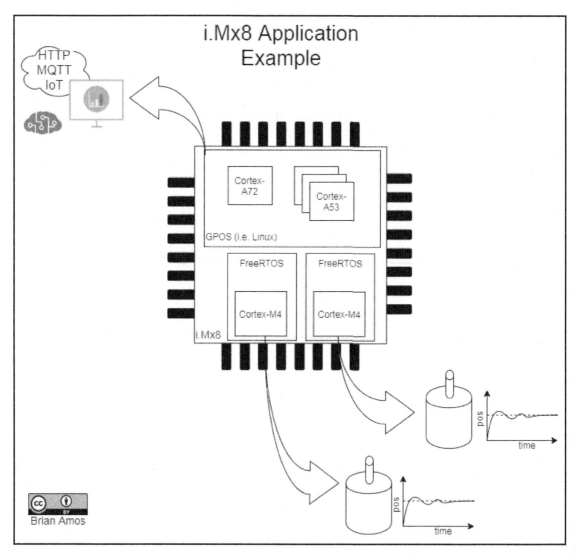

The smaller MCU-based cores are extremely good at performing low-level exchanges with hardware such as sensors and actuators. Timing-sensitive operations requiring the use of specialized timing peripherals are best left to the MCU hardware. For example, a motor control system might require directly controlling an H bridge and reading data from an encoder that uses an obscure/proprietary timing format. This is fairly straightforward to implement using an MCU that has dedicated timing hardware. Differential PWM signals with dead-time insertion used for motor control and high-resolution timing capture are both fairly common features. All of this tightly controlled, low-latency control structure can be implemented using the MCU and its specialized peripherals (either on bare metal or on an RTOS), then higher-level commands can be exposed to a GPOS. Specifically on the i.Mx8, we can now perform very low-level, timing-sensitive operations using MCUs, while simultaneously performing the high-level, massively parallel operations required for computer vision, machine learning, and AI using the higher-performance Cortex-A processors, DSP, and GPUs.

 Heterogeneous systems aren't limited to embedded systems! Heterogeneous topologies have existed for very large computing clusters for decades, but we're keeping our focus on examples most relevant to the embedded space.

So, now that we've covered some examples of heterogenous multi-core systems, what about homogeneous multi-core systems?

Homogeneous multi-core systems

As you might expect from the name, a homogeneous multi-core system is one where all of the cores are the same. These types of multi-core systems have been traditionally found in desktop computing. Rather than having individual cores tailored to perform a few types of tasks very well (as with heterogenous systems), there are multiple cores that are all identical. Rather than programming individual cores with specific tasks that are tied to the cores, all of the cores are treated identically. This type of approach is referred to as symmetric multi-processing (there is symmetry between all of the cores in the system); they are all treated identically. In a symmetric system, cores will be exposed to a single kernel, rather than divided up into multiple kernels/schedulers.

Even in asymmetric multi-processing setups, there can be components that are symmetric. For example, the i.Mx8 mentioned earlier will usually have the Cortex-A53 cores set up in a symmetric multi-processing arrangement, where all four cores are available for scheduling by a single kernel (and all treated identically).

But what about when there is a need for processors in different physical locations? Or what if a single processor is limited in its functionality by the number of pins it has available?

Exploring multi-processor systems

Similar to the way multi-core systems are excellent for segmenting firmware functionality and providing parallel execution, multi-processor systems are useful in many situations for a variety of reasons. Let's take a look at a few examples.

Distributed systems

Embedded systems often have a very large amount of interaction with the physical world. Unlike the digital realm, where 1s and 0s can literally be sent around the world without a second thought, the physical world is a harsh place for sensitive analog signals—minimizing the distanced traversed can be critical. It is a good idea to keep analog processing as close to its source as possible. For a mixed signal system with analog components, this means keeping the signal paths as short as possible and getting the sensitive analog signals processed and converted into their digital representations as close to the source as possible:

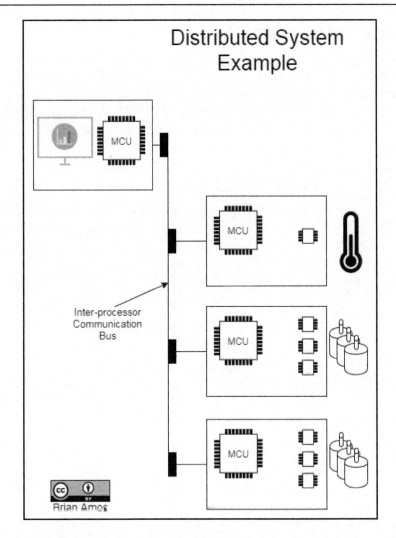

In medium-to-high power systems, reducing the distance traversed by wires carrying current to control motors, solenoids, and other actuators will reduce the radiated electromagnetic emissions of the system (always a good idea). If the I/O in question is physically removed from the rest of the system, including an MCU in close proximity is an excellent way of localizing the digitization of the sensitive signals, which makes the system more immune to **electromagnetic interference** (EMI) while simultaneously minimizing the amount of wiring. In high vibration and motion environments, fewer wires means fewer potential points of mechanical failure, which results in higher reliability, less downtime, and fewer service calls.

Parallel development

Using multiple processors also makes it very easy to provide a level of parallelism in the actual development of the system. Since teams will often find it easiest to focus on a well-defined subsystem, creating multiple subsystems makes running true parallel development (and reducing the overall schedule) a possibility. Each subsystem can be demarcated by its own processor and communication interface, along with a clear list of the responsibilities of the subsystem:

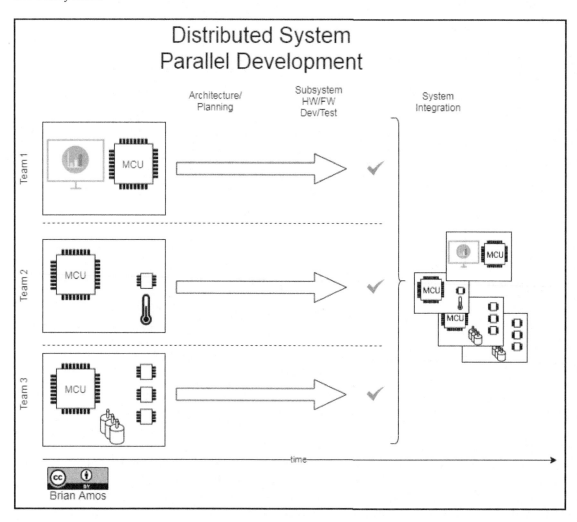

This approach also has the advantage of encouraging each team to fully test their system in isolation, documenting the interfaces and functionality as they move through development. Finally, it tends to keep any surprises during integration to a minimum, since the team is forced to put more thought into the entire architecture before starting development.

Design reuse

As processors begin to have a plethora of I/O connected to them, they may still have plenty of processing resources available but run out of available pins. At this point, there is a decision to make. ICs meant to provide port expansion are available, but should they be used? If you're designing a system with reuse in mind, it is important to see whether a subsystem approach can be employed, instead of creating a huge monolithic design, where all of the hardware and firmware is intertwined and tightly coupled. Sometimes, when the pin capacities of a single MCU are reached, it is an indication that the MCU is performing the functionality of several different subsystems. Often, if these subsystems are broken down and individually developed, they can be *dropped* into future products without modification, which can greatly decrease future projects' risks and schedule.

High-reliability systems

High-reliability systems will often include multiple cores or processors for their critical functionality. However, rather than using this extra processing power to run individual parallel operations, they are set up for some level of redundancy. There are different ways of achieving redundancy. One path to creating a redundant system is for the cores to run in lockstep with one another. The results of each processor are meticulously checked against one another to detect any discrepancies. If a problem is found, the core (or processor) is taken offline and reset, with a set of tests run to ensure it comes back up correctly—then, it is put back into service.

In systems like these, there can be environmental considerations, such as EMI from running motors, solenoid valves, or other actuators. Sometimes the source of the environmental noise is more extraordinary, such as solar radiation, which is often a concern for high-altitude and space-bound systems.

Now that we've explored the reasons why having multiple processors in a system can be useful, let's take a look at how to get all of these processors talking to one another.

Exploring inter-processor communication

Inter-processor communication was mentioned briefly in the context of distributed systems. Let's take a look at some of the considerations that go into choosing a suitable inter-processor bus.

Choosing the right communication medium

There are many considerations when choosing the communication medium used between processors, which we can break into a few different major categories.

The first is **timing**. In a real-time system, timing considerations are often some of the most important. If a message sent between nodes doesn't make it to its destination on time and intact, it can have serious consequences:

- **Latency**: How long will it take for a message to be sent and a response to be received? Having the ability to react quickly to communication between subsystems is often quite important.
- **Maximum jitter**: How much variability is there in the latency? Each system has its own requirements for how much variability is acceptable.
- **Error detection/reliability**: Does the communication medium provide a way of determining whether a message was received correctly and on time?
- **Throughput**: How much data can be pushed over the communication medium? For communication mediums that contain control data, throughput will often be measured in messages, rather than raw data (such as KB/sec or MB/sec). Often, maximum reliability and minimal latency will come at the cost of raw data transfer throughput—each message will contain additional overhead and handshaking.

The next category of considerations is **physical requirements**. Sometimes, physical requirements are quite important, other times they may hardly be a constraint. Here are some simple points to consider:

- **Noise immunity**: Does the communication channel need to run through an electrically noisy environment? What types of cabling are required for proper EMI shielding?
- **Number of nodes in the system**: How many nodes are required in the complete system? Most standards will have an upper bound on the number of connections due to electrical constraints.

- **Distance**: How long will the run need to be? Will it be a short, chip-to-chip run within the PCB or a long run between buildings? Distributed systems can have widely different meanings to different developers and industries.
- **Required peripherals**: How much extra circuitry is acceptable? What kinds/sizes of connectors can be tolerated?

Then, we have **development team/project constraints**. Each team and project is fairly unique, but there are some common topics that should be covered:

- **Complexity**: How much code is required to get the protocol up and running? Has the required external circuitry been proven to be functional? Does our team feel like the features provided by the solution are worth the development time required to implement it?
- **Existing familiarity**: Has anyone on the team used this communication scheme before and is that experience directly relevant to the current project/product? Do we need to learn something new that is a better fit, rather than using something we're already comfortable with but isn't actually the best solution?
- **Budget**: Does the communication scheme require any expensive components, such as exotic ICs, connectors, or proprietary stacks? Is it worth buying in aspects of the solution or contracting out some of the implementation?

As you can imagine from the long list of considerations, there is no *one-size-fits-all* communication mechanism that is an excellent fit for all applications. That's why we have so many to choose from.

For example, while an industrial Ethernet communication solution may provide excellent latency and noise performance, the fact that it requires specialized hardware will make it unsuitable for many applications where it is not an explicit requirement. On the flip side, a low-performance serial protocol such as RS-232 may be extremely easy to implement but have an unacceptably high amount of EMI and be susceptible to noise when used at high speeds. On the other hand, the complexity of a full TCP/IP stack might put off many would-be adopters, unless someone on the team already has familiarity with it and a driver stack is readily available for the target platform.

Communication standards

From the previous list of considerations, we can see that choosing a method for inter-processor communication isn't one size fits all. To help provide an idea of what's available, here are some examples of commonly used buses for MCU-based systems and some brief commentary on how they might be useful in a multi-processor system. This list is by no means exhaustive. Also, each standard has its own merits under different circumstances.

Controller area network

A **controller area network (CAN)** is the communication backbone for many subsystems in the automotive industry. The advantages of CAN are its robust physical layer, a prioritized messaging scheme, and multi-master bus arbitration. Many MCUs include dedicated CAN peripherals, which helps to ease the implementation. CAN is most naturally suited for shorter messages, since the data field of extended frames may only contain up to 8 bytes.

Ethernet

Nearly all medium- to high-performance MCUs have provisions for Ethernet, requiring an external PHY, magnetics, and a connector for the hardware implementation. The sticking point here is ensuring suitable networking protocol stacks are available. The advantage of this approach is a wide range of options for popular protocols that run on top of TCP and UDP, as well as readily available, inexpensive hardware that can be used to build out a full network if required.

Similar to Modbus, Ethernet will often be chosen as the externally facing interface, rather than an inter-processor bus. Depending on the system architecture and hardware availability, there might not be a reason that it couldn't be used for both.

Inter-integrated communication bus

Inter-integrated communication bus (I2C) is most often used for communicating with low-bandwidth peripherals, such as sensors and EEPROMs. Most often, an MCU will be configured as the I2C bus master with one or more slave I2Cs. However, many MCUs contain I2C controllers that can be used to implement either the master or slave side of I2C. There are many aspects of the I2C protocol that make it non-deterministic, such as the ability for slaves to hold the clock line until they are ready to receive more data (clock stretching) and multi-master arbitration.

Local interconnect network

Local interconnect network (**LIN**) is a commonly used automotive network subsystem for a maximum of 16 nodes when a full CAN is too complex or expensive to implement. The LIN physical layer is less fault-tolerant than CAN, but it is also more deterministic, since there can only be one bus master. STM32 USARTS will often have some helpful LIN-mode functionality built into the peripheral, but an external PHY IC is still required.

Modbus

Modbus is a protocol that historically ran on top of an RS-485 physical layer and is very popular in the industrial space as an externally facing protocol (although these days, the protocol is commonly found on top of TCP). Modbus is a fairly simple register-oriented protocol.

Serial peripheral interface

A **serial peripheral interface** (**SPI**) can also be very useful as an easy-to-implement, highly deterministic inter-processor communication medium, especially when the accuracy of a slave isn't high enough to achieve the tight tolerances required for high baud rates on an asynchronous serial port. All the same drawbacks for custom asynchronous protocols also exist for SPI-based custom protocols, with the additional constraint that slave devices will have hard real-time constraints imposed based on how quickly the master needs responses back from the slave(s).

Since the SPI clock is driven by the master, it is the only device that can initiate a transfer. For example, if a slave is required to have a response ready within 30 µS of receiving a command from the master and it takes the slave 31 S, the transfer is likely to be worthless. This can make SPI very attractive when tight determinism is required, but unnecessarily difficult to implement otherwise. Depending on the environment, the MCU's onboard SPI peripheral might need to be used with external differential transceivers to increase signal integrity.

USB as an inter-processor communication bus

Now that more medium- to high-performance MCUs include a USB host, it is becoming more viable as an inter-processor communication bus. Whether or not USB is viable in a given application hinges on the number of nodes and the availability of a full USB stack and developers that can harness it. While the USB virtual comm class used in this book wasn't deterministic since it used bulk endpoints, interrupt transfers can be used to achieve deterministic scheduling of transfers over USB, since they are polled by the host at a rate defined during enumeration. For example, on a high-speed USB link (which will often require an external PHY), this equates to messages up to 1 KB polled every 125 µS.

We've only scratched the surface of the possibilities for inter-processor communication in this section—there are many other options available, each with their own features, advantages, and disadvantages, depending on your project's requirements.

Now that we have a good understanding of what multi-core and multi-processor systems are, some common topologies, and some ways of communicating between the processors, let's take a step back and evaluate whether a multi-core or multi-processor design is necessary.

Choosing between multi-core and multi-processor systems

With more powerful MCUs and CPUs being announced every month, there is a virtually endless number of options to pick from. Multi-core MCUs are becoming more common. But the real question is—do you really need multiple cores or multiple processors in your design? Yes, they are readily available, but will it ultimately help or hurt the design in the long run?

When to use multi-core MCUs

There are several cases where multi-core MCUs are an excellent fit:

- When true parallel-processing is required and space is constrained
- When tightly coupled parallel threads of execution are required

If your design is space-constrained, requires true parallel processing, or communication speed between two parallel processes is extremely critical, a multi-core MCU may be the best option. If the application requires parallel processing from multiple cores and can't be implemented using other hardware already present on the MCU—for example, running multiple CPU-intensive algorithms in parallel—a multi-core MCU might be the best fit for the application.

However, it is important to be aware of some downsides and alternatives. A multi-core MCU will likely be more challenging to replace (both in finding a replacement and porting the code) than discrete MCUs. Does the application truly need parallel execution at the CPU level or is there simply a need to perform some operations (such as communication) in parallel? If there is parallel functionality required that can be implemented using dedicated peripheral hardware (for example, filling communication buffers using DMA connected to a hardware peripheral), implementing the *parallel* functionality could be achieved without a second core.

Some potential alternatives to multi-core MCUs are as follows:

- Offloading some processing to hardware peripherals
- Ensuring DMA is utilized as much as possible
- Multiple MCUs

When to use multi-processor systems

Multi-processor systems are useful in a wide variety of circumstances, such as the following:

- When subsystem reuse is possible
- When multiple teams are available to work on a large project in parallel
- When the device is large and physically dispersed
- When EMI considerations are paramount

However, while multi-processor systems are useful, they do have some potential drawbacks:

- Additional latency compared to having a single MCU.
- Real-time multi-processor communication can become complex and time-consuming to implement.
- Additional up-front planning is required to ensure proper subsystems are developed.

Summary

In this chapter, you were introduced to both multi-core and multi-processor systems and we covered some examples of each. You should now have an understanding of what the differences between them are and when designing a system using either approach is appropriate. Several examples of inter-processor communication schemes were also introduced, along with some highlights and advantages of each, as they relate to embedded real-time systems.

The great thing about multi-core and multi-processor topologies is that once you have a solid understanding of the building blocks for the concurrent system design (which we've covered), creating systems with more cores is just a matter of judiciously placing hardware where concurrent processing and abstraction will have the most impact.

In the next chapter, we'll be covering some of the problems you'll likely encounter during development and some potential solutions.

Questions

As we conclude, here is a list of questions for you to test your knowledge on this chapter's material. You will find the answers in the *Assessments* section of the appendix:

1. What is the difference between a multi-core architecture and a multi-processor architecture?
2. A mixture of operating systems and bare-metal programming can be used in an asymmetric multi-processing architecture.
   - True
   - False
3. When selecting an inter-processor communication bus, the bus with the highest available transfer rate should always be used.
   - True
   - False
4. Should multi-processor solutions be avoided because they add complexity to the architecture?

Further reading

- NXP AN11609—LPC5410x dual core usage: `https://www.nxp.com/docs/en/data-sheet/LPC5410X.pdf`
- Keil—USB concepts: `https://www.keil.com/pack/doc/mw/USB/html/_u_s_b__concepts.html`

Troubleshooting Tips and Next Steps

17

This chapter explores some of the most useful tips and tools for analyzing and troubleshooting an RTOS-based system. Periodically checking your system during development, as well as having a few standard steps to take when troubleshooting, can be a huge timesaver when evaluating a problematic system – things don't always go as planned! After we've covered some tips, we'll take a look at some of the next steps we can take to continue learning and sharpening our embedded programming skills.

In this chapter, we will cover the following topics:

- Useful tips
- Using assertions
- Next steps

Technical requirements

No hardware or software is required for this chapter.

Useful tips

Beginning development with an RTOS can be quite a shift if you've only used a *bare-metal* programming approach, especially if you're also shifting from 8-bit MCUs to a 32-bit MCU such as the STM32F7 we've been using in the examples throughout this book. Here are some tips that should help keep your project on track and help you work through issues when they come up.

Using tools to analyze threads

Being able to get a clear understanding of what all the threads in a system are doing is a huge help – for novices and experts alike. Tooling is especially helpful for this. Using a visualization tool such as SEGGER SystemView or Percepio Tracealyzer can be invaluable in understanding interactions between various tasks and interrupts in a system (see `Chapter 6`, *Debugging Tools for Real-Time Systems*, for details).

Having an RTOS-aware debugger is also a huge help since it allows us to stack the analysis of multiple tasks. This debugger can be part of your IDE or a standalone debugger such as SEGGER Ozone (see `Chapters 5`, *Selecting an IDE*, and `Chapter 6`, *Debugging Tools for Real-Time Systems*).

Keeping an eye on memory usage

Memory usage is a very important aspect to consider when using an RTOS. Unlike a super-loop with a single stack – which, along with the heap, would consume whatever RAM was *left over* – each FreeRTOS task's stack needs to be explicitly sized. In `Chapter 15`, *FreeRTOS Memory Management*, in the *Keeping an eye on stack space* section, we showed you how to observe the available stack space, as well as how to implement hooks if an overflow was detected.

If your application is using dynamic memory allocation, you should strongly consider enabling and implementing the failed MALLOC hooks provided by FreeRTOS. This was covered in `Chapter 15`, *FreeRTOS Memory Management*, in the *Keeping an eye on heap space* section as well.

Stack overflow checking

If you have a memory protection unit available, it is an excellent idea to make use of it since it will detect access violations such as stack overflows with better reliability than any of the software-based solutions (see `Chapter 15`, *FreeRTOS Memory Management*, the *Using a memory protection unit* section).

Another way of keeping an eye on the stack is to set up stack monitoring, which was also covered in `Chapter 15`, *FreeRTOS Memory Management*, in the *Keeping an eye on stack space* section.

A real-world example of debugging a system that has a stack overflow and checking memory is covered in the next section.

Fixing SystemView dropped data

In the examples we've looked at throughout this book, SystemView shows that we can stream data visualization by running code on the MCU to store events in a local buffer. The contents of the buffer are then transferred data via debug hardware to the PC for viewing. Sometimes, during high utilization, you'll see large red blocks in the trace, as shown in the following screenshot:

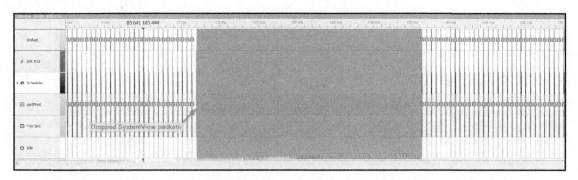

These blocks indicate that SystemView has detected dropped packets. The frequency of dropped packets can be decreased by doing any of the following:

- Increasing the size of the SystemView buffer on the MCU. SEGGER_SYSVIEW_Conf.h defines the buffer on line 132. It is important to note that since this buffer resides on the MCU, increasing the size of the buffer will decrease the memory available to other pieces of code.:

      #define SEGGER_SYSVIEW_RTT_BUFFER_SIZE

- Increasing the clock speed of the debugger under **Target Interface and Speed**. In some cases, a debugger that supports a faster clock will help (for example, a dedicated SEGGER J-Link or J-Trace).
- Decreasing the traffic to the debugger hardware while SystemView is running. To do this, you can, for example, close any live trace windows in open debug sessions (such as Ozone or STM32CubeIDE).

In the next section, we'll learn how to debug our system by using assertions.

Using assertions

Assertions are excellent tools for catching conditions that simply *shouldn't happen*. They provide us with a simple means to check assumptions. See the *Creating a task – checking the return value* section of `Chapter 7`, *The FreeRTOS Scheduler,* for an example of how to add simple assertions to prevent code from running when the system is in an unacceptable state.

A special FreeRTOS flavor of the assert construct is `configAssert`.

configAssert

`configAssert` is used throughout FreeRTOS as a way of guarding against an improperly configured system. Sometimes, it is triggered when a non-interrupt version of the API is called from inside an ISR. Often times, code inside an interrupt will attempt to call a FreeRTOS API, but its logical priority is higher than what the RTOS will allow.

Rather than allowing an application to run with undefined behavior, FreeRTOS will regularly test a set of assertions to ensure all prerequisites are met. On their own, these checks are helpful at preventing a system from careening completely out of control with no hope of figuring out what the problem is. Instead, the system is immediately halted when the invalid condition occurs. FreeRTOS also contains thorough documentation on the underlying reasons the assertion has failed (sometimes with links to web-based documentation).

> Don't ever *cover up* a `configAssert` by disabling it in any way. They are often the first notification that a serious configuration problem exists. Disabling the assertion will only compound the underlying issue, making it harder to find later.

Let's go through an example that shows what the normal symptoms of a system halted with `configAssert` might look like, as well as the steps that can be taken to diagnose and solve the underlying issue.

Debugging a hung system with configAssert()

When you first bring up the codebase and create some example code to introduce SystemView, several problems need to be worked through.

Here's our example:

After it was ensured that all of the code was syntactically correct and the LEDs were blinking, it's time to connect SystemView to the running application and get some timing diagrams. The first couple of times SystemView is connected, a few events are shown, but then the system goes unresponsive:

- The LEDs stopped blinking
- No additional events were showing up in SystemView, as shown in the following screenshot:

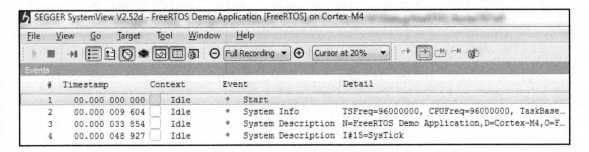

Let's diagnose and solve the underlying issue in a couple of steps.

Collecting the data

Sometimes, it is tempting to take guesses as to what might be happening or make assumptions about the system. Rather than doing either of these things, we'll simply connect our debugger to the system to see what the problem is.

Since SEGGER Ozone is exceptionally good at connecting to a running system without modifying its state, we're able to connect to the hung application without disrupting anything. This allows us to start debugging an application after it's crashed, even if it was previously *not* running through the debugger. This can come in very handy during product development since it allows us to run the system normally, without constantly starting it from the debugger. Let's learn how to do this:

1. Set up Ozone with the same code that is running on the target. Note that the development board must be connected via USB (see `Chapter 6`, *Debugging Tools for Real-Time Systems*, for details).

2. After that, select **Attach to Running Program**:

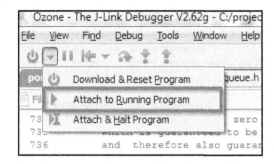

3. Upon attaching and pausing execution, we're greeted with the following screen and are immediately able to make some observations:

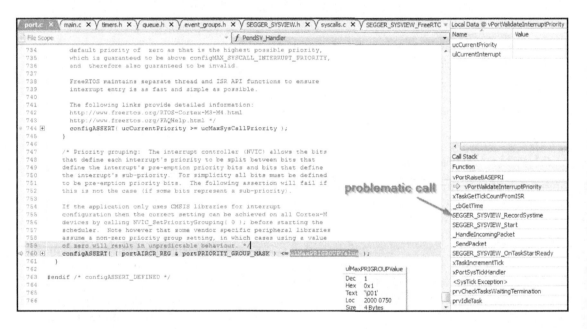

Notice the following:

- The LEDs have stopped blinking because we're spending all of our time in an infinite loop because of a failed assertion.
- By looking at the **Call Stack**, we can see that the offending function is `SEGGER_SYSVIEW_RecordSystime`, which is apparently making a call to a function called `_cbGetTime`, which in turn calls `xTaskGetTickCountFromISR`.

- Reading through the detailed comment above line 760, it sounds like there may be some misconfigured NVIC priority bits.
- The maximum acceptable value of `ulMaxPROGROUPValue` (which can be seen by hovering over the selected variable) is `1`.

Now that we know *which* assertion failed, it's time to figure out the root cause of *why* exactly it failed.

Digging deeper – SystemView data breakpoints

So far, we've determined where our processor is stuck, but we haven't uncovered anything to help us determine what needs to be changed to get the system operational again. Here are the steps we need to take to uncover the root cause of the issue:

1. Let's take a look at the assertion again. Here, our goal is to troubleshoot exactly why it is failing. Run the following command:

   ```
   configASSERT( ( portAIRCR_REG & portPRIORITY_GROUP_MASK ) <=
   ulMaxPRIGROUPValue );
   ```

2. Using SystemView's memory viewer, analyze the value of `portAIRCR_REG` in `port.c`:

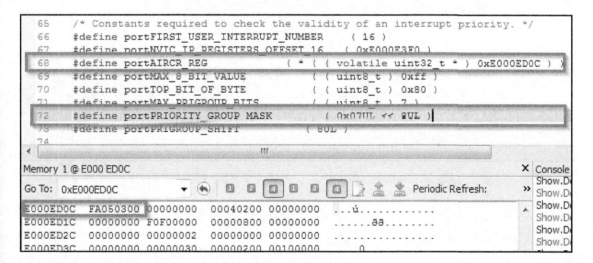

3. Since this is a hardcoded memory location, we can **Set Data Breakpoint**, which will pause execution each time the memory location is written. This can be a quick way to track down all of the ways a variable is accessed, without attempting to search through the code:

4. Upon restarting the MCU, the write breakpoint is immediately hit. Although the program counter is pointing to HAL_InitTick, the actual data write to the 0xE000ED0C address was done in the previous function, that is, HAL_NVIC_SetPriorityGrouping. This is exactly what we expect since the assert is related to interrupt priority groups:

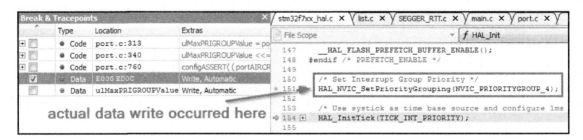

5. Some quick searching through the code for `NVIC_PRIORITYGROUP_4` reveals the following comment in `stm32f7xx_hal_cortex.c`:

```
*  @arg NVIC_PRIORITYGROUP_4: 4 bits for preemption priority
*                             0 bits for subpriority
```

Priority grouping: The interrupt controller (NVIC) allows the bits that define each interrupt's priority to be split between bits that define the interrupt's preemption priority bits, as well as the bits that define the interrupt's sub-priority. For simplicity, all bits must be defined to be preemption priority bits. The following assertion will fail if this is not the case (if some bits represent a sub-priority).

Based on this information, there should be 0 bits for the subpriority. So, why was the value of the priority bits in `portAIRCR_REG` non-zero?

From the *ARM® Cortex® -M7 Devices Generic User Guide*, we can see that to achieve 0 bits of subpriority, the value of the **AIRCR** register masked with **0x00000700** must read as 0 (it had a value of **3** when we looked at the value in memory):

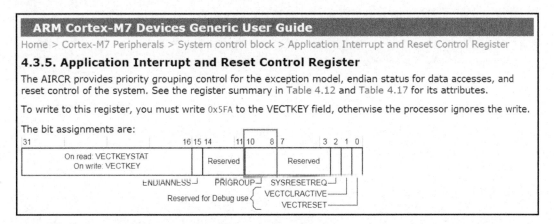

Here is the explanation for PRIGROUP in the same manual. Notice that PRIGROUP must be set to 0b000 for 0 subpriority bits:

Binary point

The PRIGROUP field indicates the position of the binary point that splits the PRI_*n* fields in the Interrupt Priority Registers into separate *group priority* and *subpriority* fields. Table 4.18 shows how the PRIGROUP value controls this split. Implementations having PRI_*n* fields of less than 8 bits treat the least-significant bits as zero.

Table 4.18. Priority grouping

| | Interrupt priority level value, PRI_*N*[7:0] | | | Number of | |
PRIGROUP	Binary point[a]	Group priority bits	Subpriority bits	Group priorities[b]	Subpriorities[b]
0b000[c]	bxxxxxxx.y	[7:1]	[0]	128	2
0b001[c]	bxxxxxx.yy	[7:2]	[1:0]	64	4
0b010[c]	bxxxxx.yyy	[7:3]	[2:0]	32	8
0b011[c]	bxxxx.yyyy	[7:4]	[3:0]	16	16
0b100	bxxx.yyyyy	[7:5]	[4:0]	8	32
0b101	bxx.yyyyyy	[7:6]	[5:0]	4	64
0b110	bx.yyyyyyy	[7]	[6:0]	2	128
0b111	b.yyyyyyyy	None	[7:0]	1	256

[a] PRI_*n*[7:0] field showing the binary point. x denotes a group priority field bit, and y denotes a subpriority field bit.

This certainly warrants further investigation... why was the value of PRIOGROUP 3 instead of 0? Let's take another look at that configAssert() line:

```
configASSERT( ( portAIRCR_REG & portPRIORITY_GROUP_MASK ) <=
ulMaxPRIGROUPValue );
```

Note the following definition of ulMaxPRIOGROUPValue in port.c. It is defined as *static,* which means it has a permanent home in memory:

```
#if( configASSERT_DEFINED == 1 )
  static uint8_t ucMaxSysCallPriority = 0;
    static uint32_t ulMaxPRIGROUPValue = 0;
```

- As expected, something was accessed by the `BaseType_t xPortStartScheduler( void )` function in `port.c`
- The curious part about the data access breakpoint is that it is hit when the program counter is inside `SEGGER_RTT.c`, which doesn't look right since `ulMaxPRIGROUPValue` is privately scoped to `xPortStartScheduler` in `port.c`
- Looking at the debugger – the problem is staring right at us:
  - The `ulMaxPRIGROUPValue` static variable is being stored in `0x2000 0750`.
  - The data write breakpoint was hit with the stack pointer at `0x200 0740`.
  - The stack has been overrun:

We've just uncovered a stack overflow. It manifested itself as a write into a static variable (which happened to trigger a `configAssert` in an unrelated part of the system). This type of wildly unexpected behavior is a common side effect of stack overflows.

Currently, the minimum values of each stack in `main.c` has been set to 128 words (1 word = 4 bytes), so increasing this to 256 words (1 KB) gives us plenty of headroom.

This example is fairly representative of what happens when functionality is added to a preexisting task that was working properly previously. If the new functionality requires more functions to be called (with each having local variables), those variables will consume stack space. In this example, this problem only showed up after adding the SEGGER print functionality to an existing task. Because there wasn't additional stack space available, the task overflowed its stack and corrupted the memory that was being used by another task.

The problem in this example would have likely been caught if we had the stack overflow hooks set up – it would have certainly been caught if the MPU port was being used.

Next steps

Now that you've been through this book and tinkered with each ready-to-run example – wait... you haven't run the examples yet?! Time to get started on that! They have been included because having hands-on experience will help drive these concepts home, providing you with both valuable practice and a base development environment you can use for your own projects.

So, assuming you've already run through the examples included, an excellent next step to gain an even more in-depth understanding of FreeRTOS is to read *Richard Barry's* book, *Mastering the FreeRTOS™ Real-Time Kernel*. This book focuses on how to apply the general knowledge that is required to get started with embedded systems and build a solid foundation for future development. Mastering FreeRTOS, however, is laser-focused on the specific details of FreeRTOS, with examples for each of the APIs. Having a hardware environment set up, a basic understanding of the fundamentals, and debug/visualization tooling at hand will help you get the most out of his book. After you have a system up and running, the code provided in *Mastering the FreeRTOS™ Real-Time Kernel* can be easily tested and experimented with using real hardware and a visual debugging system.

While we're on the subject of building solid foundations, you'll want to consider getting acquainted with test-driven development. As you start to create loosely coupled code, as we did in Chapter 12, *Tips on Creating Well-Abstracted Architecture*, and Chapter 13, *Creating Loose Coupling with Queues*, testing these subsystems is a natural next step. *James Grenning* has many resources available on his website (https://blog.wingman-sw.com), specifically for embedded C/C++. Other TDD resources specific to embedded C include *Matt Chernosky's* site (http://www.electronvector.com/) and the unique *Throw the Switch* (http://www.throwtheswitch.org/). A great all-around embedded resource that's been created from decades of hard-earned experience is *Jack Gannsle's* site, which you can access at http://www.ganssle.com/.

Summary

In this final chapter, we covered a few tips that will help smooth out some of the bumps in the road of your RTOS journey, as well as a few suggested next steps.

That's it, folks! I hope you've enjoyed this hands-on introduction to developing firmware for real-time embedded systems using FreeRTOS, STM32, and SEGGER tools. Now, it's time to get out there and start understanding systems, solving problems, and analyzing your solution! I'd love to hear about how you've applied what you've learned in this book – give me a shout on LinkedIn, Twitter, or GitHub! If you've really enjoyed this book and think others would also like it, consider leaving a review – they help spread the word!

Questions

As we conclude this book, here is a list of questions for you to test your knowledge regarding this chapter's material. You will find the answers in the *Assessments* section of the *Appendix*:

1. When your system crashes after you've added an interrupt or used a new RTOS primitive, what steps should you take?
2. Name one common cause of unexpected behavior (caused by firmware) when developing with an RTOS.
3. Since your system has no way of outputting data (no exposed serial port or communication interface), it will be impossible to debug.
   - True
   - False

Assessments

Chapter 1

1. No. A system with real-time requirements simply means that actions need to be deterministic. The timing requirements are determined by the needs of each system.
2. No. There are several different ways to achieve real-time performance.
3. No.
4. Any system that has a deterministic response to a given event can be considered as *real-time*.
5. Most industrial controls, closed-loop control systems, UAV flight controllers, **Anti-Lock Braking Systems (ABS)**, **Engine Control Units (ECUs)**, inkjet printers, test equipment (such as oscilloscopes and network analyzers), and so on.
6. An MCU-based RTOS's strong point is moderately complex systems.

Chapter 2

1. Both of the above options.
2. False.
3. Complex super loops tend to have a large amount of variability in how long it takes them to execute the loop. This can lead to poor determinism in the system, since there is no easy way to provide a means for higher-priority work to take precedence over everything else happening in the loop.
4. Interrupts and DMA can both be used to improve the response of super loops to external events. They allow hardware peripherals to be serviced without waiting to be polled during a super-loop cycle.
5. There is only one super loop being run in the system. It shares the system stack. Tasks, however, each receive their own dedicated stack. Each task receives a priority, unlike a superloop, which has no inherent concept of prioritization.
6. Prioritization.
7. A preemptive scheduler attempts to ensure that the task with the highest priority is always the one executing.

Chapter 3

1. Queues.
2. Yes.
3. Semaphore.
4. Networking stacks or anything where a maximum number of simultaneous users must be enforced.
5. Priority inheritance.
6. Mutex.
7. Priority inversion allows lower-priority tasks to take precedence over a higher-priority task. This is dangerous because it increases the chances of a high-priority task missing a deadline.

Chapter 4

1. Firmware programming, especially for MCUs, is extremely low-level, meaning it is very close to the hardware. There are often hardware-specific features that firmware engineers must be familiar with to get the best performance out of an MCU.
2. False.
3. Hardware peripherals.
4. Rapid prototyping, pre-existing hardware, community, consistent high-level APIs across different MCUs.
5. Evaluation boards often showcase a product's main differentiating qualities. They are also designed to be as complete as possible, providing easy access to all aspects of a device.
6. Sleep current, wake-up time, power efficiency (uA/MHz), the functionality of low-power modes, and power supply voltage.
7. To make it accessible for the widest number of readers – so make sure to get one and work through the exercises on some real hardware!

Chapter 5

1. False. The ideal IDE will reflect personal/organizational preferences. A particular IDE that fits well into one team or workflow may not be suitable somewhere else.

2. False. Many of the freely available IDEs are well suited for professional embedded system development.
3. False. Vendor-supplied IDEs will often vary widely in their quality. Be careful of getting too tightly bound to a vendor's IDE, especially if you prefer to use MCUs from other vendors.
4. False. At a minimum, we would expect software-generated code to be syntactically correct the first time. Beyond this, the code generation is only as good as the frontend supplying it, which tends to evolve more slowly than the underlying code bases (so you'll still need to write in customizations later on).
5. False. The IDE for this book was selected based on cost and only considered compatibility with STM32 devices.
6. Device selection, hardware bring-up, and middleware integration. *Why* it is useful in each of these areas is covered in the *Considering STMCube* section.

Chapter 6

1. False. In this chapter, the ST-Link on the Nucleo development board was re-flashed to provide the same functionality as a J-Link.
2. False. There are many ways to verify the timing requirements of a real-time system. Segger SystemView provides a means to measure response time, as does looking at system inputs and outputs via a traditional logic analyzer.
3. False. An RTOS-aware debugger provides the ability to view all of the stacks in the system. This is also an option with any Open GDB-based debugging using Eclipse, as mentioned in the previous chapter.
4. False. Each module that you write should be tested as thoroughly as possible to minimize any surprises and complex interactions when it is time to integrate the modules and perform a system-level test.
5. Unit testing. In unit testing, each individual module is tested as it is developed. Integration testing is testing to ensure multiple modules work as expected after they have been "integrated" with one another. System testing tests the complete system (typically after everything has been integrated). Black-box testing is simply a style of testing that assumes nothing about the system inside the "black box," and only compares outputs against the expected behavior given a set of inputs.
6. **Test-Driven Development (TDD)**.

Chapter 7

1. There are two options – `xTaskCreate()` and `xTaskCreateStatic()`.
2. True. `xTaskCreate()` may fail if the required memory is not available.
3. True. `vTaskStartScheduler()` may fail if the required memory for the IDLE task is not available.
4. False. The required RAM for each task is 64 bytes plus the task stack size. The exact stack size requirements are completely dependent on your code, not FreeRTOS.
5. False. Tasks can be removed by calling `vTaskDelete()`, provided a compatible heap is used (see `Chapter 15`, *FreeRTOS Memory Management*, for details).

Chapter 8

1. Synchronization; shared resource protection.
2. Priority inversion (visit the *Priority inversion (how not to use semaphores) section* for details)
3. **MUT**ual **EX**clusion, which refers to how access to a shared resource is controlled.
4. They limit priority inversion by ensuring high-priority tasks block as little as possible by automatically raising the priority of a low-priority task holding a mutex that the high priority task is waiting on.
5. False. Although easy to use, software timers have limitations including jitter and frequency.

Chapter 9

1. A queue can hold any data type, thanks to the underlying `void*` input parameter.
2. A task waiting to send data to a queue is placed into the blocked state (suspended if `portMAX_DELAY` was specified).

3. There were three considerations mentioned: data ownership of the underlying value, ensuring the correct data type is passed into the queue, and making sure the data stays intact (by not placing it onto a volatile stack).
4. False. Task notifications only store a single `uint32_t` and allow a single task with a known task handle to be unblocked. Queues are capable of storing any datatype and can be used across multiple arbitrary tasks.
5. False. Task notifications only store a single `uint32_t`.
6. Speed and RAM efficiency.

Chapter 10

1. Interrupt-driven drivers are more complex because there are at least three pieces of code involved (setup code, ISR code, and callback code). With a polled driver, all of this happens serially.
2. False. Only functions ending in `FromISR` may be called within an ISR.
3. False. Interrupts take precedence over the scheduler since the scheduler should be configured to run from the lowest priority interrupt.
4. DMA – it uses hardware to transfer data between peripherals and memory, without any CPU intervention.
5. Direct Memory Access.
6. Attempting to receive data at any point in time is very difficult to do well with a raw buffer. Raw buffers can also become a bit complex when receiving data of unknown length.

Chapter 11

1. False.
2. False. Timing trade-offs such as increased latency and lower determinism, along with less communication bandwidth, must also be taken into account before deciding a shared hardware peripheral is acceptable.
3. All of the above.
4. False. Stream buffers can be used by a single writer and a single reader. These writers and readers don't need to be the same task. If there are multiple writers or multiple readers, then a synchronization mechanism (such as a mutex) is required.
5. Mutexes.

Chapter 12

1. False. Abstractions are useful even in the smallest MCUs.
2. False. A method for implementing consistent interfaces was presented in this chapter.
3. Possible answers include the following:
   - Common components will be reused in other projects.
   - Portability to different hardware is desirable.
   - Code will be unit tested.
   - Teams will be working in parallel.
4. False. Review the *Avoiding the copy-paste-modify trap* section for more details.
5. False. When properly written, tasks can be excellent candidates for reuse across projects (see the *Reusing code containing tasks* section for more details).

Chapter 13

1. False. Queues create a definitive interface, which decouples components from one another.
2. False. Any datatype can be placed into a queue.
3. No, omitting the underlying formatting allows more flexibility for the producers of items to be queued. If the data isn't tied to a specific format, the format can be modified without affecting the queue or the consumer of data coming out of the queue.
4. Possible answers include the following:
   - A queued item's lifetime doesn't need to be taken into consideration since a copy of it is made.
   - The queued item's scope doesn't need to be taken into account if it is passed by value into the queue.
   - If an item is passed by reference, a clear understanding of who *owns* the item is necessary, as well as who is responsible for freeing the resources associated with it.
5. Possible answers include the following:
   - Latency introduced by deep queues
   - Non-deterministic behavior caused by requests sitting in a queue instead of being immediately executed (or rejected)
   - Memory constraints

Chapter 14

1. **CMSIS-RTOS** stands for **Cortex Microcontroller Software Interface Standard - Real-Time Operating System**. The CMSIS-RTOS specification was written by ARM, but there are many vendors that can elect to supply CMSIS-RTOS-compliant interfaces in their RTOSes.
2. Linux and Android.
3. False.
4. False.

Chapter 15

1. False.
2. False.
3. There are five implementations: `heap_1.c` through `heap_5.c`.
4. `vApplicationStackOverflowHook` and `vApplicationMallocFailedHook`.
5. **MPU** stands for **Memory Protection Unit**. It is used to guard against illegal memory access, especially as a way to partition tasks so they are only allowed access to their own memory space.

Chapter 16

1. *Multi-core* means multiple cores on the same IC while *multi-processor* means multiple processors (ICs) in the same design.
2. True. Asymmetric architectures don't require the various processing cores to be treated in the same way, so any combination of operating systems and bare-metal programming languages can be used (within the restrictions of the hardware).
3. False. There are many aspects to consider when selecting the *best* bus for a given application since each application will have its own set of unique circumstances and requirements.
4. The additional complexity needs to be weighed against the possibility of not performing the same work twice. When reusable subsystems are developed, they can create considerable cost savings under the right circumstances. They have little to no **nonrecurring engineering** (**NRE**) costs associated with them when re-used.

Chapter 17

1. You should do the following:
    1. Connect a debugger.
    2. Figure out where the program stopped.
    3. If it is a `configASSERT`, read the comments surrounding the assertion. If it fails before the scheduler starts, you've likely overflowed your FreeRTOS heap.

2. Any one of the following:
    - Task stack overflows
    - Misprioritized ISRs
    - Inadequate heap size

3. False. Debugging tools such as Segger SystemView exist, which provide both printf-style output as well as instrumentation for observing the code's behavior.

Other Books You May Enjoy

If you enjoyed this book, you may be interested in these other books by Packt:

Internet of Things Projects with ESP32
Agus Kurniawan

ISBN: 978-1-78995-687-0

- Understand how to build a sensor monitoring logger
- Create a weather station to sense temperature and humidity using ESP32
- Build your own W-iFi wardriving with ESP32. Use BLE to make interactions between ESP32 and Android
- Understand how to create connections to interact between ESP32 and mobile applications
- Learn how to interact between ESP32 boards and cloud servers
- Build an IoT Application-based ESP32 board

Internet of Things Programming Projects

Colin Dow

ISBN: 978-1-78913-480-3

- Install and set up a Raspberry Pi for IoT development
- Learn how to use a servo motor as an analog needle meter to read data
- Build a home security dashboard using an infrared motion detector
- Communicate with a web service that sends you a message when the doorbell rings
- Receive data and display it with an actuator connected to the Raspberry Pi
- Build an IoT robot car that is controlled through the internet

Leave a review - let other readers know what you think

Please share your thoughts on this book with others by leaving a review on the site that you bought it from. If you purchased the book from Amazon, please leave us an honest review on this book's Amazon page. This is vital so that other potential readers can see and use your unbiased opinion to make purchasing decisions, we can understand what our customers think about our products, and our authors can see your feedback on the title that they have worked with Packt to create. It will only take a few minutes of your time, but is valuable to other potential customers, our authors, and Packt. Thank you!

Index

F

field-programmable gate arrays (FPGAs) 15, 86
firm real-time systems 20
First In First Out (FIFO) 54
flexible code
  testing 338
free MCU vendor IDEs 106
Free Open Source Software (FOSS) 148
free
  replacing 409
FreeRTOS API
  selecting 386
  using, from interrupts 246, 247, 248
FreeRTOS application
  hardware initialization 155
  task functions, defining 155, 156, 157
FreeRTOS heap 395
FreeRTOS heap implementations
  comparing 405, 406, 407
FreeRTOS Labs distribution
  download link 382
FreeRTOS memory hooks
  implementing 410
FreeRTOS POSIX application
  creating 381, 382, 383, 384
FreeRTOS primitives
  dynamic allocation 398
  static allocation 398
FreeRTOS scheduler
  starting 159, 160
FreeRTOS task states
  about 168
  blocked state 169
  optimization 170
  optimization, for increasing performance 171
  optimization, for reducing CPU time 170
  optimizing, for minimizing power consumption
   171
  ready state 169
  running state 169
  suspended state 170
FreeRTOS task
  creating 157, 158
  return value, checking 158, 159
FreeRTOS, versus CMSIS-RTOS

considerations, during migration 368
  functions, cross-referencing 368
FreeRTOS-Labs
  download link 385
FreeRTOS
  about 22
  considerations, for increasing heap 175
  features 367
  reference link 23
  using, with POSIX 381
  versus CMSIS-RTOS 366
full queue send 55, 56
functions, FreeRTOS versus CMSIS-RTOS
  delay functions 369
  EventFlags 369
  kernel control and information 370
  memory pools 376
  message queues 371
  mutexes 372, 373
  semaphores 373
  thread control/information 375, 376
  thread flags 374
  timers 376

G

GCC 111
GCC for Cortex-M
  reference link 112
general-purpose operating system (GPOS) 419
generic RTOS APIs
  about 364
  advantages 365
  disadvantages 365, 366
GNU Debugger (GDB) 104
graphics processing units (GPUs) 418

H

hard real-time systems 20
Hardware Abstraction Layer (HAL) 119
hardware floating-point unit (FPU) 79
hardware peripherals, MCU
  audio support 83
  communication interfaces 80
  connectivity 78
  dedicated touch interfaces 82

Printed in Great Britain
by Amazon